Vivre en Suisse 1999-2000
Leben in der Schweiz 1999–2000

Population, Family, and Society
Population, Famille et Société

Volume 3

Edited by / Edité par
Michel Oris

PETER LANG
Bern • Berlin • Bruxelles • Frankfurt am Main • New York • Oxford • Wien

Erwin Zimmermann & Robin Tillmann
(éds/Hrsg.)

Vivre en Suisse 1999-2000
Leben in der Schweiz 1999–2000

Une année dans la vie des ménages et familles en Suisse

Ein Jahr im Leben der Schweizer Familien und Haushalte

PETER LANG
Bern • Berlin • Bruxelles • Frankfurt am Main • New York • Oxford • Wien

Information bibliographique publiée par «Die Deutsche Bibliothek»
«Die Deutsche Bibliothek» répertorie cette publication dans la «Deutsche Nationalbibliografie»; les données bibliographiques détaillées sont disponibles sur Internet sous ‹http://dnb.ddb.de›.

L'enquête *Vivre en Suisse* est un projet mené conjointement par le Fonds national suisse de la recherche scientifique, l'Office fédéral de la statistique et l'Université de Neuchâtel.

Die Befragung *Leben in der Schweiz* wird vom Schweizerischen Nationalfonds für wissenschaftliche Forschung, dem Bundesamt für Statistik und der Universität Neuenburg gemeinsam durchgeführt.

Illustrations de couverture:
Illustration en haut à gauche: © l'Express/David Marchon
Illustration en haut à droite: © Thomas Jaberg, Berne
Illustration en bas: © Getty Images

Réalisation de couverture: Thomas Jaberg, Peter Lang AG, Berne

ISSN 1660-6043
ISBN 3-03910-370-9

Hochfeldstrasse 32, Postfach 746, CH-3000 Berne 9
info@peterlang.com, www.peterlang.com, www.peterlang.net

Imprimé en Allemagne

Table des matières / Inhaltsverzeichnis

3. Pratiques et modes de vie / Lebensstile

4. Médias et politique / Medien und Politik

5. Qualité de vie et santé / Lebensqualität und Gesundheit

Appendix

Introduction

The *Swiss Household Panel* and the Nature of this Book

Robin Tillmann and Erwin Zimmermann[1]

Overview

The main aim of the *Swiss Household Panel* (SHP)[2] is to observe social change, in particular, the dynamics of how living conditions change over time for the population of Switzerland. During the period 1998–2003, the SHP was one of the structural projects undertaken by the SPP Zukunft Schweiz / Demain la Suisse with the following two main purposes (Budowski et al. 2001; Farago 1996; Höpflinger and Wyss 1997; Joye and Scherpenzeel 1997): 1) to ensure a solid database for social reporting about stability and changes in living arrangements and well-being in Switzerland to complement data collected by the Swiss Federal Statistical Office, and 2) to promote the opportunities for quantitative social science research, by making high quality data available to Swiss social scientists and to the international social science research community. The Swiss Household Panel is a joint project run by the Swiss National Science Foundation, the Swiss Federal Statistical Office and the University of Neuchâtel.

Since its inception in 1998, the *Living in Switzerland* survey of the Swiss Household Panel (SHP) has built up a unique longitudinal database in Switzerland. The SHP survey is conducted using computer-assisted telephone interviewing (CATI). In comparison with panels such as the SOEP in Germany and the BHPS in Britain which concentrate on socio-economic conditions, the SHP covers a broad range of topics and approaches in the social

1 The content of this introductory chapter is based on work and writings by all the members of the SHP-team. The authors wish to thank in alphabetical order: Denise Bloch, Monica Budowski, Alexis Gabadinho, Roberto Genesi, Nicolas Portmann, Jean-Hugues Ravel, Annette Scherpenzeel, Boris Wernli.

2 The website of the Swiss Household Panel is: www.swisspanel.ch

sciences. The questionnaires (household and individual) are designed to collect both *objective* data (resources, living conditions, life events, social position, participation, etc.) and *subjective* data (attitudes, perceptions, satisfaction with various life domains, etc.). The analysis of the SHP data enables a large variety of research questions to be covered and produces a wealth of results with potentially important policy implications:

a) *Evolving patterns in changing living conditions, quality of life and life satisfaction:* Who is progressively better or worse off, and why? What are the living conditions necessary for a good quality of life? Which objective and subjective factors most strongly determine life satisfaction?
b) *Family life and interaction with society at large:* What are the consequences of various forms of cohabitation? In terms of social support and solidarity? Which "services are produced and consumed" within the family unit, obtained from the outside or provided by external units (e. g. care for children and the elderly)?
c) *Labour market participation, work and life satisfaction:* What are the different forms of labour market participation (full-time vs. part-time employment, precarious and insecure employment, sub-employment vs. over-employment, under- and over-qualification, etc.) and their relationships with work and life satisfaction? How do people (especially women with small children) handle conflicting demands from the workplace and from home?
d) *Poverty and social exclusion:* What kind of living conditions are associated with poverty and social exclusion? What are the family or individual characteristics of the poor and the mechanisms which lead to poverty and lead out of it? Who remains poor despite policy measures of support? What are the complex relationships between poverty, social isolation and externally induced social exclusions?
e) *Gender, social, and economic participation:* How do life trajectories diverge depending on gender? Why do professional careers of men and women with similar educational resources still diverge?
f) *Social determinants of health:* How is the life course of individuals and families of widely different origins and social conditions related to health behaviour and outcomes? What are the consequences of worsening living conditions on health? What impact does ill-health have on living conditions, employment and quality of life later in time?

Evidence-based answers to these and other questions are highly valuable for developing and implementing new policies; through increased transparency they facilitate political decision-making.

The *sample* of the SHP is a stratified random sample of private households whose members represent the non-institutional population resident in Switzerland. For the first wave in 1999, slightly over 5,000 households and almost 8,000 persons have been successfully interviewed. To date, the five waves have been carried out successfully and the sixth wave will start with an up-dated sample in September 2004.

By the end of 2003, the *Living in Switzerland* research network had 260 registered members and about 160 researchers analysing data on a variety of topics: types of households and families, poverty, health, living conditions of elderly people, living conditions of first and second-generation immigrants, political participation, and life satisfaction, etc. The rapid growth in data use has been considerably aided by the NSF "SHP-Data Analysis Grant" administered by the SHP Scientific Board. The active data users belong to the following institutions: *Swiss universities* (56 %), *public administrations* (19 %), *private institutes* (15 %), *international academic institutions* (12 %).

Created as a "data generator", the database allows analyses in different disciplines using a large variety of conceptual approaches. At the outset the SHP survey was designed and operationalized so that national and international comparative analyses would be possible. SHP data is compatible with various databases generated by the *Swiss Federal Statistical Office* (SFSO), in particular the two largest periodic population surveys, the Swiss Labour Force Survey and the Swiss Health Survey. In May 2002 the *Swiss National Science Foundation* and the *Swiss Federal Statistical Office* finalized a strategic agreement called "LiS 2020 – Living in Switzerland 2020" (Zimmermann et al. 2002) dealing with the continued operation of the Swiss Household Panel after 2003 in conjunction with the EU-SILC *(European Statistics on Income and Living Conditions)*. Both institutions are equal partners in the collection of annual cross-sectional and panel data and share the funding. A cooperative project will begin in 2004 and hopefully trigger considerable synergies between the "statistical and academic communities". The agreement builds on and expands the already fruitful collaboration between Swiss social sciences and official statistics.

With regard to international collaboration, the SHP is a partner in the *Consortium of Household Panels for European Socio-Economic Research* (CHER). The CHER core data set on income, employment, living conditions and health contains information from the following countries: *Germany* (since 1984); *United Kingdom* (since 1991); *Denmark, Netherlands, France, Ireland, Italy, Greece, Spain* and *Portugal* (since 1994); *Austria* and *Finland* (since 1995); *Sweden* (since 1997); *Switzerland* (since 1999). The SHP also forwards its data to the LIS (Luxembourg Income Study). Both data sets enable international comparisons in the fields of labour-market participation and income from various sources both at the household and individual levels. Finally, starting in 2004, the SHP data will be comparable to the data from the *European Statistics of Income and Living Conditions* (EU-SILC) which is the continuation of the European Community Household Panel (ECHP). Its main purpose is to collect comparable cross-sectional and longitudinal data on living conditions and income, with particular emphasis on poverty and social exclusion, for each country and for the European Union as a whole.

The annual collection of panel data from a relatively large sample is a costly undertaking. The Swiss National Science Foundation's Priority Programme *SPP* – Zukunft Schweiz / Demain la Suisse has allocated considerable financial resources to the Swiss Household Panel since its inception in 1998. As the SPP has come to an end in December 2003, the Swiss National Science Foundation (SNF) is committed to further financing the SHP from 2004 onwards. This has been made possible by the creation of a new NSF section supporting lasting infrastructures in physics, medicine and the social sciences.

Various organisations located in Neuchâtel and in some way connected to its university are engaged in quantitative social science research. They are: the *Swiss Household Panel* (SHP), the *Swiss Information and Data Archive Service for the Social Sciences* (SIDOS) and the *Swiss Forum for Migration and Population Studies* (FSM) and the *Swiss Federal Statistical Office* (SFSO). For Switzerland, they represent a great potential for applied quantitative social science research. The University of Neuchâtel has committed itself to the creation of a centre of excellence, called the *Swiss Observatory of Social Change*, as an integrating platform for the already existing project oriented collaborations and scientific exchanges.

Social Change and Household Panels

Dynamic transformations on a multitude of levels constitute an important characteristic of modern societies (Leisering and Walker 1998; Suter and Pahud 2000; Therborn 1995). Demographic changes call for analyses (Fux et al. 1997), as well as various changes in the labour market (Flückiger 2000). The latter, in particular, are considered to impact on the well-being (material and psychological) of households and individuals (Paugam 2000), as well as on the informal production of services, such as child care or care of elderly (Bauer 1998). The proportion of women in the labour market is increasing, often entailing changes in the organization of domestic life (Buchmann et al. 2002). In Switzerland, data is available to describe the current social structure. Panel data allow for more: *panel data* are data collected about the same units at more than one point in time. They allow insight into dynamic transformations – social processes and changes over time (Berthoud and Gershuny 2000). Instead of simply taking a snapshot of people and households at any given point in time, interviewing the same households and their members annually enables changes to be observed for the same entities and the reconstruction of the nature and development of their actions, the examination of precedents, concurrent dynamics, and the consequences of alternative strategies.

Household panels provide insights into the population on three levels: (i) social change can be studied at a micro-level, (ii) on an intermediate level (the level linking the individual with society, i. e. the household level) and (iii) the level regarding the assessments of dynamics between the structural and the cultural dimension and behaviour over time. (i) *The first perspective* enables the observation of individual lives, relating them to living conditions, and decisions or reactions following life events. (ii) An intermediate level of analysis permits an understanding of the interrelationship between socio-structural and cultural aspects and individuals' resources, constraints, and strategic responses or deliberate choices. Household and family dynamics shed light on gender, generation relationships and their possible consequences. Household and family strategies and reactions may be studied, as in principle all the household members aged 14 and older are interviewed. This perspective leads to a better understanding of the link between individuals and society. Households (often equivalent to families) as units of analysis provide a rare opportunity to examine the "black box" of household dynamics, i.e. the constraints or privileges of unequal access to resources across time (e.g. division of labour in terms of paid and unpaid work, or caring responsibilities, unequal access to household resources such as time and money, life events, etc.). (iii) Finally, panel data offer the opportunity to go beyond the description of the status quo, by allowing us to assess the dynamics between the structural and the cultural dimension and behaviour over time. In many domains, change takes place slowly and gradually, even though it may not be immediately apparent. Furthermore, although the dynamics and/or patterns of the same social phenomenon may have changed, the phenomenon as such continues to exist. For example, although poverty may be present at a fairly constant rate over time, the mechanisms of entry and exit may have altered, or the population groups constituting the "poverty-prone" may have changed. Alternatively, the institution "family" may continue to exist but its meaning, internal organization or other factors may have varied. Snapshots from transversal surveys reveal a status quo and reveal over time net change or, alternatively, document stability. Gross changes, however, cannot be measured. In sum, household panels are considered to be tools for fine-tuning our conceptions and analyses of social dynamics. The dynamics (or social changes) at the macrosocial level do not directly belong to the field of observation covered by a panel survey. What panel surveys are intended to investigate, however, are the effects of changes at the macrosocial level on the living conditions of individuals and households, the manner in which these changes affect them and how they produce social change on a microsocial level.

While a repeated cross-sectional survey allows us to calculate *net transitions* between two dates (e.g. a drop in the proportion of the population receiving social benefits, or a rise in unemployment), *gross transitions* (e.g. the number of unemployed still without a job one year later) can only be estimated with panel or cohort data. Beyond the sheer estimation of gross transitions the analysis of panel data also helps to "understand" the observed transitions i.e. the circumstances (family events, a change in the activity status, events related to the state of health, etc.) causing movements in and out of a given state (e.g. the fact that an individual or a household is living below the poverty line). In other words, it is not only possible to study the change in numbers but also the flows between various states and to establish links of causal relationships between different factors and sequences of events. Last but not least, panel data also reveal the continuities, the stable features over time. Where a status quo can be defined, change as well as continuity can be examined. Indeed, despite profound structural changes that contemporary societies are currently undergoing, which are the consequence of economic globalization, uneven regional development around the world, and worldwide demographic changes in general, daily life is characterized more by stability than change. This is true as much for social structures, norms and values, as for individual and institutional behaviour. Daily life is enacted within a prevalent social order in time and place, characterized by a structural and cultural dimension that is lived, produced, reproduced, and altered by behaviour. These dimensions (the structural and cultural dimension, and that concerning behaviour) are found both on a macro and a micro level. Change may take place within any of the three dimensions and need not necessarily go hand in hand with changes in the other dimensions.

The *Swiss Household Panel* and other National Household Panels

Thus, the principal aim of the *Swiss Household Panel* (SHP) is to observe social change, in particular, the dynamics of changing *living conditions* in the population of Switzerland, which has been carried out in annual surveys since 1999.

The Swiss Household Panel was inspired by various international panel studies. However, it is not a blend of existing panels for two main reasons: the SHP (1) covers various domains of everyday life and not only one or two in depth and (2) attempts to define the dimensions necessary to continuously anticipate social change in Switzerland. This is done by means of a yearly panel survey based on an architecture, situating the types of questions to be chosen for the survey ("objective questions" such as questions about living conditions; "subjective questions", such as the evaluation of certain objective situations and behaviour as a reaction to them). The two types of questions are necessary to understand both the change of "objective" conditions and the importance given to them or the assessments made about them. Changes may occur regarding the subjective assessments or regarding the objective conditions, and they need not occur simultaneously. Thematic and methodological adaptations to the particularities of Switzerland were carried out and proved to be necessary.

The *household questionnaire* covers the following areas:

Composition of the household: containing basic information about all the members of the household, such as the age, sex, relations between the members of the household, nationality, level of education and occupational status;

Accommodation: containing "objective" elements, such as the type and size of the accommodation, home ownership or tenancy, the cost of and/or the subsidies received for housing, as well as "subjective" elements, such as satisfaction with the accommodation, evaluation of the state of the accommodation and assessment of perceived nuisances;

Standard of living: referring to a list of goods owned by the household or activities that its members can carry out, together with the reason (financial or otherwise) why goods are not owned or activities not carried out;

The household's financial situation: containing "objective" information such as the existence of financial difficulties (and the household's reactions to different situations), indebtedness and the reasons for it, the total household income, the amount of tax paid, and the social and private transfers, as well as "subjective" elements, such as satisfaction, an estimate of the minimum income the household considers necessary or an evaluation of how the household's financial situation has evolved;

The household and the family: collecting information on any external help available to the household for housework or child-care, the sharing of tasks, and decision-making within the household.

The *individual questionnaire* is administered to every household member aged 14 years or older; the interviews cover the following topics:

The household and the family: comprising "objective" elements, such as the existence of children living outside the household, the sharing of housework and child-care, as well as "subjective" elements, such as satisfaction with private life and with the sharing of the housework;

Health and "victimization": covering "objective" elements, such as general illness and health problems, visits to the doctor and hospitalization, long-term handicaps, threats or attacks endured, together with "subjective" elements such as the self-perceived state of health, the estimated evolution of the state of health, or satisfaction with one's own health;

Social origins: referring to information related to profession, professional position, educational level, and the nationality of both parents together with possible financial difficulties in the family of origin;

Education: covering the various levels of achieved education, education currently being pursued, fluency in foreign languages, and participation in on-the-job training;

Employment: considering four different aspects: firstly, the collection of information necessary to determine the status of the interviewee in the labour market, secondly, information covering the current main employment, thirdly, information on second jobs, and finally details about the last main job held; these modules also comprise "objective" elements, such as profession, status of the profession, the number of hours worked, work schedule, atypical work, as well as "subjective" elements such as satisfaction with various aspects of the job, the evaluation of promotion prospects or of personal qualifications;

Income: including information such as total personal income, total professional income, received social transfers, received private transfers, and other income, and "subjective" elements, such as satisfaction with the financial situation and an evaluation of changes concerning the personal financial situation;

Participation, integration, networks: taking into account "objective" elements, such as frequency of social contacts, non-remunerated work outside the home, participation in associations, membership of and participation in religious groups, and "subjective" elements such as the evaluation of potential practical help and emotional support (from the partner, family, friends, etc.);

Politics and values: referring to "objective" elements such as political participation, membership, party identification, political positioning; and "subjective" elements such as satisfaction with the political system, the evaluation of issues or even political values; a few indicators of gender attitudes are available; and finally

Leisure and media: comprising "objective" elements, such as leisure activities and the use of the media (e.g. Internet), as well as "subjective" elements, such as satisfaction with leisure and free time[3].

3 For a more detailed presentation, see Robin Tillmann, Erwin Zimmermann, Monica Budowski, Boris Wernli, Annette Scherpenzeel, and Alexis Gabadinho (2001). *«Vivre en Suisse». Panel suisse de ménages 1999-2003. Présentation du projet.* Actualités OFS. Neuchâtel: Office Fédéral de la Statistique (also available in German).

From the second wave on, the questionnaire also includes a "life events" module and an "occupational calendar" module (covering the 12 months prior to the interview). From the third wave onwards a module, containing both subjective and objective elements, about the situation of young people in school or studying was added. The income module was continuously improved and has become comparable with the SILC (European Statistics on Income and Living Conditions) for all questions that can be asked using the CATI data collection mode.

From the very start, the SHP planned to obtain, on a single occasion, additional information about the respondents' life course prior to their panel study involvement. A retrospective *biographical questionnaire* was developed for that purpose, asking about educational, working, and family history. This questionnaire was to be sent by mail. However, the main objective of a panel study is to obtain repeated measures and it therefore is crucial to keep the drop-out rate between interviewing waves as low as possible. It was feared that an extra mail questionnaire between two regular interview waves would burden the respondents and thus discourage some of them from further participation in the phone survey. In general, the drop-out rate of panels appears to be highest at the second wave of interviewing and attain a stable rate from the third wave onwards. Therefore, the biographical questionnaire was only sent after the second survey wave. A pre-test was carried out to estimate the effect of the mailing of the biographical questionnaire on the response rates in the subsequent panel wave. In addition, the effect of combining the questionnaire with a special incentive was evaluated (Scherpenzeel et al. 2002). As a result of the evaluation of the "experiment", namely that no particularly high drop-out rate (defined as more than 5 %) could be found, the final biographical self-administered questionnaire was sent after the third wave (2002) to all persons, 14 years and older who are eligible respondents of participating households and who had not been sent a biographical questionnaire after the second wave (2001) during the "experiment". The participation rate is 70 % for the "experiment" and slightly lower for the final survey.

The *sample* of the SHP is a stratified random sample of private households whose members represent the non-institutional population resident in Switzerland. The first wave of the SHP-survey data was collected in autumn 1999 through February 2000 (Table 1). These households and their members are to be re-interviewed annually for 10 to 15 years. Due to continuous loss of these original (longitudinal) sample members (deaths, hospitalization, migration, refusals) the SHP will refresh the sample every four years by injecting the number of "new" households required to obtain a starting base in 2004 of 5,000 households that includes the remaining number of households with longitudinal respondents.

Table 1: Participation in the "Living in Switzerland Survey" 1999–2003

Number of participating units	1999	2000	2001	2002	2003*
Participating households	5,074	4,532	4,314	3,690	3,150
Persons living in participating households	12,931	11,678	11,116	9,544	8,000
Persons over 14 years old eligible for individual interview	10,293	9,297	8,942	7,515	6,300
Interviewed persons	7,799	7,073	6,601	5,705	5,200
Proxy Interviews	2,638	2,381	2,174	1,987	1,800
Longitudinal respondents	–	6,335	5,425	4,480	3,900

* provisional figures
Source: Swiss Household Panel

The reference population for the Living in Switzerland survey is the population permanently resident in Switzerland. The sample which has been chosen is representative of the whole of Switzerland, without regional imbalances. It includes households of various nationalities provided that their members live on Swiss territory throughout the year. Seasonal workers, cross-border workers, and foreign tourists are not part of the permanent resident population and are therefore not taken into account in the sample (Table 2). Switzerland is divided into seven large statistical regions. The methodology section of the Swiss Federal Statistical Office drew a random sample in each of these on the basis of SWISSCOM's electronic telephone directory (TERCO) which covers over 98 % of all private households[4]. The households selected in this way are a proportionally stratified random sample of the various social groups in all regions of Switzerland. However, as the interviews are carried out in the

4 In 1999, only 2 % of households in Switzerland did not have a phone connection. In the absence of a reliable and accessible comprehensive register of Swiss households, the phone directory TERCO by Swisscom offers the best base for random sampling of households. Due to the considerable expansion of mobile phones, the situation is changing quickly. In 2000, an estimated 8 % of households do not have a registered phone connection.

three official national languages (German, French, and Italian), population groups which have recently migrated to Switzerland are likely to be under-represented.

Table 2: The resident population of Switzerland and SHP sample characteristics

Code	Regions of the national territory (cantons)	Population in 1999		SHP sample, 1999 (1st wave, number of eligible persons)		SHP sample, 1999 (1st wave, number of individual interviews)	
		#	in %	#	in %	#	in %
1	Lake Geneva region (VD, VS, GE)	1,295,000	18 %	1,797	17 %	1,366	17 %
2	Mittelland (BE, FR, SO, NE, JU)	1,656,000	23 %	2,622	25 %	2,001	26 %
3	North-west Switzerland (BS, BL, AG)	988,000	14 %	1,491	14 %	1,146	15 %
4	Zurich	1,199,000	17 %	1,680	16 %	1,254	16 %
5	Eastern Switzerland (GL, SH, AR, AI, SG, GR, TG)	1,042,000	15 %	1,406	14 %	1,012	13 %
6	Central Switzerland (LU, UR, SZ, OW, NW, ZG)	677,000	9 %	920	9 %	693	9 %
7	Ticino	308,000	4 %	453	4 %	327	4 %
	Totals	7,165,000	100 %	10,369	100 %	7,799	100 %

The *household* concept refers not only to households comprising individuals or groups of individuals but also collective households (e. g. homes or prisons) and non-profit organizations (NPO) such as charitable organizations, political parties, trade unions, religious communities. However, the Living in Switzerland survey includes *only private households*, collective households and NPOs are excluded. The Living in Switzerland survey has adopted a fairly broad definition of a "household" so that it does not automatically underestimate new types of cohabitation (in particular collective non-institutionalized ways of living) as compared with the classic concept of the "household/family". Consequently, the *SHP household definition* is based on five fundamental cumulative criteria: 1) sharing *at least one common dwelling room*; 2) *sharing certain expenses*; 3) taking *at least one meal together per week*; 4) *stability* (the household is considered a long-term arrangement); and 5) the individuals consider it to be their *main dwelling* (rather than a second home, work-related accommodation, etc.). In each household a "reference person" needs to be defined. In the Living in Switzerland survey the reference person is designated freely by the household itself. However, it is specified that this person should *know the household very well*. The reference person should also, as far as possible, be 1) an adult (age 18 or older), 2) a *longitudinal respondent* of the panel – an original sample member (OSM), and 3) the *same person* from one wave to the next. In the first wave, it is the reference person who answers the questions of the grid and the household questionnaire (in addition to the individual questionnaire).

The *method* of data collection is CATI (Computer Assisted Telephone Interviewing). This method was complemented by a written self-administrated biographical questionnaire that was carried out during the months of April to June in 2001 as an experiment to examine whether this written survey would have a negative impact on the CATI survey response rates. As this was not the case (Scherpenzeel et al. 2002), the written self-administrated biographical questionnaire was sent in 2002 to all the 2001 wave respondents that had not taken part in the "experiment". The written self-administrated biographical questionnaire will also therefore complement the CATI method periodically for the panel survey once in between four consecutive waves to obtain the same information from the "new" members of the panel as are available for the original sample members from 1999 in order to provide greater "depth" for longitudinal analyses of the data collected with the CATI method.

The data collection of the *first wave* was carried out from September 1999 to February 2000. Of the 14,174 addresses receiving an invitation to participate in the survey, telephone contacts were made with 12,084 households (85 %). At the household level, the net response rate was 64 %. To warrant reliable extrapolations for the whole resident population of Switzerland and a panel of about 4,000 households and 6,600 individuals for the second wave, it was necessary to obtain the participation of at least 5,000 households in the first wave. This goal was achieved, as the first wave yielded valid data for 5,074 households and 7,799 individuals. As the first wave was to furnish a wealth of "baseline information", the questionnaire was very detailed and rather long regarding the interview time. The household interviews lasted an average of 12 minutes and individual interviews an average of 55 minutes. In total, slightly fewer than 8,500 hours of telephone interviews were carried out. The data collection for the *second wave* started in September 2000 and ended in February 2001. Valid data was collected for 4,425 households and 7,073 individuals. The longitudinal sample (individuals interviewed in the first and second waves) comprises 6,335 individuals.[5] The data collection for the *third wave* was carried out from mid-September 2001 to the end of January 2002. With the exception of "final refusals", all the first wave households were contacted in early September 2001. 4,139 households and 6,601 persons were validly interviewed. The data collection for the *fourth wave* was carried out from mid-September 2002 to the end of January 2003. 3,587 households and 5,705 persons were validly interviewed. By the end of the fourth wave, the longitudinal sample comprised around 4,500 individuals. Table 3, below, displays interview participation figures for the years 1999–2002. Due to panel attrition (non-traceable departures, refusals, deaths, etc.), the number of households and individuals validly interviewed in wave 4 represent roughly 70 % of the corresponding numbers in 1999 (wave 1).

Table 3: Participation rates

	1999		2000		2001		2002	
	gross	net	gross	net	gross	net	gross	net
Individual response rate	76 %	85 %	76 %	84 %	74 %	88 %	76 %	89 %
Grid response rate	42 %	64 %	87 %	91 %	82 %	88 %	80 %	86 %

Source: Swiss Household Panel.
Remarks: The *gross* response rate is the ratio of the number of respective interviews completed to number of individuals or households who were contacted but did not participate for whatever reason. The first year, 1999, however, is an exception, as the gross individual response rate refers to the ratio of number of individuals interviewed to the number of all household members eligible to be interviewed. The *net response rate* is the ratio of the number of interviews completed to the number of individuals or household reached excluding those who did not participate for neutral reasons.

Given that in a panel survey it is important that the data obtained continue to be representative of the target population, it is most important to ensure that respondents continue to participate year-on-year, or more precisely said, that no systematic losses of participants occur. Given that the losses are most

5 These data are principally used in this book.

probably not random, a high and continued participation rate is the best solution to ensure representativity. Representativity of the sample is important not only for the examination of incidences of phenomena, but also for the analyses of changes in individual trajectories and circumstances and the identification of the reasons for them. Various means or strategies are possible to counteract attrition: (i) measures of encouragement for participation and panel maintenance strategies (information, utility, interest), and (ii) methodological analyses as to which strategies might be most conducive to best response rates. The Swiss Household Panel has from the beginning applied both these two strategies (Zimmermann and Budowski 2003).

For panel designs, *cross-sectional* and *longitudinal* weights need to be distinguished. The cross-sectional weights are to improve the *sample estimates* for the population from which the sample is drawn. The longitudinal weights aim at maintaining the first wave sample characteristics over time, despite losses of original sample members. *Cross-sectional weights* compensate for unequal selection probabilities *(design weights)* and response rates *(response weights)*, most public surveys assign weights to the response units (households and persons). Under certain conditions, weighting the data helps obtain approximately unbiased estimates of population parameters. The characteristics of a sample may still be improved by adjusting sample distributions to the distributions observed in the population *(post stratification weights)*. The *cross-sectional household weights* for the SHP-first wave data adjust for *design* and *non-response* biases (Cornali and Vonlanthen 2001). The household weights correct mainly the non-response of households composed of foreign nationals and elderly persons, a bias which is common in Swiss household surveys. Within the participating households *individual weights* are computed in order to adjust a) for *non-response* differences according to sex, age and nationality and b) for deviations from the structural characteristics of the resident population in Switzerland, mainly sex within age groups, nationality and geographic regions. *Statistics Canada* has been mandated to calculate the *cross-sectional* and *longitudinal weights* for waves 2 to 4 (Latouche and Naud 2001).

The data obtained was checked for its *validity* by comparison with existing data sources. The comparison with 1990 census data indicates that single-person households are somewhat underrepresented within the SHP. This tends to be the case in surveys in general as single persons are more difficult to reach at home (see Table 4).

Table 4: The SHP household structure in comparison with the census data 1990

Type of households	SHP-1999		SFSO-1990	
	#	%	#	%
Single-person households	1,355	26.7 %	920,330	32.2 %
Single parents	300	5.9 %	145,108	5.1 %
Couples without children	1,442	28.4 %	755,989	26.4 %
Couples with children	1,811	35.7 %	919,433	32.2 %
Other households	166	3.3 %	118,906	4.2 %
Total	5,074	100.0 %	2,859,766	100.0 %

The data from the first wave of the SHP is very similar to that obtained in other household surveys carried out periodically by the Swiss Federal Statistical Office (SFSO). For example, Table 5 compares the distribution of the population according to status within the labour market.

Table 5: Status in the labour market according to sex (percentages, weighted results)

Status in the Labour Force	Swiss Labour Force Survey 1999			ERC98 Living conditions			Living in Switzerland 1999		
	men	women	total	men	women	total	men	women	total
Working employed	74.4	55.5	64.7	76.4	56.7	66.2	74.4	55.1	64.4
Unemployed	3.7	2.6	3.1	1.9	2.3	2.1	1.4	2.3	1.9
Non-working	21.9	41.8	32.2	21.7	40.9	31.6	24.2	42.6	33.7

The Nature of this Book

This book is the result of collaboration between the members of the Swiss Household Panel and various authors from several institutions (see list of authors at the back of the book). Its purpose is to introduce the Swiss Household Panel, both to general readers and to potential users, and to demonstrate its usefulness for understanding change in Switzerland. The book gives a first picture of cross-year change in the late 1990s. It uses the available data from the Swiss Household Panel at the beginning of the project: including Wave 1 (collected between September 1999 and February 2000) and Wave 2 (started in September 2000 and completed in February 2001). One chapter uses the data from the biographical questionnaire. Each wave contains a large body of information about events, conditions and subjective assessments during this period. It does provide some knowledge about Swiss social trends that is unavailable elsewhere, albeit with all the necessary cautionary warnings associated with inferring change from only two waves of data.

The initial findings presented here will form the basis of more in-depth longitudinal research over the coming years.

This book contains five parts and thirteen chapters. The *first part* is concerned with *social stratification and resources.*

In *Chapter 1*, *Tillmann and Budowski* tackle the question of poverty in Switzerland. After an overview of the problems linked to definition, measurement, and poverty indicators, the authors define various approaches to explain the phenomenon (in terms of social stratification, cumulated disadvantages, and finally individualization). Two of their results can be mentioned in this introduction. First of all, the population consistently defined as poor increases slightly during the period of observation; in addition, the flows into and out of poverty are not negligible. Thus, for example, a significant proportion of people considered poor in 1999 are no longer poor one year later (approx. 44 %). In addition, the authors consider that none of the three approaches chosen covers by itself all observations. However, the results tend to show that the social stratification approach is the best predictor of a situation of persistent poverty.

In *Chapter 2*, *Falter and Flückiger* cover a closely related topic: low wages and the working poor. The study shows the characteristics of individuals who have a low salary or who live in a precarious situation. After a description of their methodology, the authors analyse the extent of the phenomenon, the likelihood of belonging to the underprivileged categories, as well as the transitions towards the status of low salaries or working poor. The observation tends to confirm the extent of the phenomenon (the authors obtain, for example, a proportion of working poor higher than 6 % of the working population in 1999 and in 2000). In general, this chapter shows that professional income is not the only factor to determine the likelihood of belonging to the working poor. It can be seen in particular that the family structure is a major risk factor.

In the *third Chapter* by *Joye and Bergman*, professional careers are examined on the basis of a biographical analysis. The core of the analysis comprises the construction of a typical career profile. The authors define three major types: the first (39 % of respondents) relates to full-time professional activity and provides a conception of life centering around paid work; the second (45 %) also shows a major insertion in professional life, but in this case on a part-time basis after an initial period of working full-time; the third type (16 %) corresponds to a career characterized by a return to the domestic sphere after an initial phase devoted to paid work. The authors establish in particular that, although it is possible to distinguish some intra-generational social mobility within careers, it is not particularly pronounced. Furthermore, such intra-generational advancement appears to be stronger for older generations. This means that the potential for upward mobility within a career trajectory decreases for younger cohorts.

The essays in the *second part* of this book are about *working, family and social life*.

In *Chapter 4, Widmer and Levy* look at *the professional and domestic involvement according to the position in the life cycle*. Family living evolves through stages which considerably influence the involvement of family members in the spheres of professional and domestic activities. Considering the various stages of the family life cycle introduces a longitudinal perspective and overcomes the more traditional static perceptions of families. According to the presence and the ages of the children in the household, six phases of family life are distinguished: (1) young couples in the pre-children stage, (2) families with children of pre-school age, (3) families with school age children, (4) families with children out of school, (5) couples whose children have already left home, and (6) couples without children (women older than 36 years). Within the

2,884 family households interviewed twice, in 1999 and 2000, 7 % have switched from one stage to another during this one-year period. Looking more closely at the transitions it appears that these changes are quite significant: a) 12 per cent of young couples (stage 1) have moved into stage 2 with children of pre-school age; b) 14 percent of families with pre-school children in 1999 have at least one child in school by the year 2000; c) 10 per cent evolve from school-age children to the out-of-school stage; and d) in 6 per cent of the families with out-of-school children, the children have left home, moving consequently from stage 5 to stage 6. Relating the phases of family life to the amount of domestic work, it appears that the number of weekly hours of housework is considerably higher for women with children but quite constant for men across the various family life stages. For women the passage from the pre-children to the pre-school children stage adds about five hours of domestic work per week. The contrary can be observed for the labour force participation of women, for which the birth of a child causes a reduction from 80 to 20 percent. In brief, while young couples without children share quite equally the amount of housework and are both professionally active, the birth of the first child changes radically the situation for both members of the couple.

Chapter 5, written by *Baumgartner and Fux* is closely related to the previous chapter but focuses more specifically on *the differences between men and women with regard to their participation in the labour force.* During the last few decades, women's labour force participation has increased. Nevertheless, aggregate data indicate only marginal corresponding behavioural change for fathers, in particular no increased involvement in household chores. In addition, the individual-level data analysed in the present essay indicate that the labour force participation of men is barely influenced by the composition of the family; only very few fathers work part-time. The wish to reduce the amount of working hours, frequently expressed by fathers, does not materialize; on the contrary, fathers tend to increase their workload after the birth of their first child. Traditional work patterns appear to be well-established; fathers adapt their labour force participation only very marginally to the changing needs of family life.

In *Chapter 6*, titled *Social Relationships and Social Support*, *Suter, Iglesias and Oegerli* investigate the social relationships by which individuals are connected with their fellow human beings and with their social environment. The majority of the Swiss population have a broad social network. Despite phenomena such as individualization, plurality of life styles, larger numbers of one-person households and increasing divorce rates, over 90 per cent have a partner or family and enjoy good relationships with relatives and friends. These networks of both primary and secondary relationships contribute to "good" social support, though family life and friendship are of greatest importance. The relevance of these networks for social support is, however, quite different for men and women. Partnership in the couple plays for men a far greater role than for women, especially in the realm of emotional support. While men have, in general, a broader network, women have more intensive contacts and enjoy greater social emotional and practical support within their everyday social environment. In addition, social support promotes well-being and health. In particular, during times of personal and social stress, social support considerably alleviates their potentially negative impacts on health. While social networks and social support hardly changed from 1999 to 2000, changes at the individual level are quite notable. As these changes remain unexplained by changes in living conditions and the occurrence of network-relevant life events, most of these apparent changes are likely to be due to the random and situational variability of response behaviour.

The *third part* of this book is devoted to *lifestyles and practices*.

In *Chapter 7, Wanner and Gabadinho* analyse *the situation of families and any mobility observed* (formation of couple, births, separation of couple) in terms of certain socio-economic characteristics. The authors underline the limitations of their study on account in particular of the small number of family transitions during the period under observation. But despite this they present some interesting results. Thus family mobility characterises more than one in ten private households; in addition we can underline the relative inability to predict family events over time, in particular those with a negative connotation (separation or divorce, accident or illness, death).

In *Chapter 8, Modetta, Gazareth and Branger* examine *cultural and leisure activities*. The authors determine in particular different dimensions of leisure activities. Their cross-sectional analysis shows a very heterogeneous situation in terms of cultural activities: the differences according to age groups are striking, but there are also differences according to the level of education and the amount of household income. The longitudinal analysis of the major changes to have occurred in leisure activities between the two waves of the survey – which takes account of social positioning and life cycle elements (gender, age, nationality, domicile, family situation, main activity, socio-professional position, and health) – shows that age plays a decisive role. The authors observe a very strong proclivity for change among the youngest and great stability among the oldest participants. These results are closely linked to various family and professional elements that appear as important and that characterise different stages of the life cycle.

In *Chapter 9, Becci and Bovay* examine religious attitudes and practices. The authors find that religion nowadays is both a private matter and a public one. And it is in this perspective that they carry out their empirical analyses of the data from the Swiss Household Panel. They examine both religious practice and membership, discussion and tolerance. However, their longitudinal analysis concentrates on changes in the frequency of attendance of religious services. In particular, the authors highlight two distinct yet associated phenomena: firstly, we can observe that a society whose level of education increases sees its average practice of collective activity drop; secondly those who have a high level of practice (the elderly, those with less education in particular) tend to reduce their practice more than others. This appears to be a sort of general social or cultural phenomenon, relatively independent of specific biographical factors. All in all, the authors consider that we can observe an evolution marked by a reduction in institutional religion (collective practice) in favour of individual choices (prayer and discussion).

The *fourth part* of this book is devoted to the domains of the *media and politics*.

In *Chapter 10, Molo-Bettelini, Wernli and Alippi* analyse the *uses and impacts of the Internet*. In comparison with the other countries of the European Union, Internet use in Switzerland is among the highest. By the end of the year 2000, the Internet is used by 47 per cent of the Swiss population aged 14 years and over (57 % among men and 37 % among women). Internet use is most common among professionally active young men with a high educational level. On average, little less than four hours is dedicated weekly to its use. The vast majority of Internet users look for "specific information" (96 %), enjoy it for "entertainment" (64 %), read "newspapers or magazines" (50 %), make "financial transactions" (32 %), and last but not least "send and receive electronic mail" (92 %). Highly educated and professionally active persons make practical use of the Internet, while less educated and professionally inactive persons use it for entertainment purposes. Internet use is rapidly expanding. It has almost doubled over the one-year period under investigation (27 % in 1999 and 47 % in 2000). The profile of new users (women, increased average age, lower education) indicates the diffusion of the Internet to all strata of society. More detailed analyses also show how users move over time from a recreational to a more utilitarian use of the Internet.

Chapter 11, authored by *Wernli* looks at *changes in political attitudes and behaviour over the one-year period 1999–2000*. The political landscape of Switzerland has undergone a profound evolution over the past few decades. Party identification has declined from 63 % in 1971 to 37 % in 1999 and the traditionally strong centrist parties have weakened in favour of both the left and the right of the political spectrum. Net changes in political attitudes and behaviour between 1999 and 2000, though statistically significant, are rather small and most likely due to the panel selection process: longitudinal participants tend to be politically more alert and more satisfied with the Swiss political institutions. There is nevertheless a indication of a small shift towards the political left and a slight decrease in the proportion of persons favourable to the adhesion of Switzerland to the European Union. Considering the changes at the individual level, overall stability prevails as evidenced by high inter-wave correlations ($r \geq .70$). More such changes are observed in the respondents' attitudes towards their own political influence and activism. Indicators of changes in living conditions such as household finances, only slightly explain the individual changes in political attitudes over the one-year period. In contrast, changes in partisan orientation appear to be a consequence of corresponding changes of the individuals' political orientation, particularly as related to the parties' positions towards the European Union.

The *fifth part* of this book covers changes in *quality of live and health* in the Swiss population.

Chapter 12 by *Scherpenzeel* concentrates on one-year changes in *life satisfaction*. Satisfaction with life is often used as an indicator of quality of living or "subjective well-being". The thought that satisfaction is changeable, that you could make people happier if you knew the necessary conditions, stimulated research into the causal mechanisms of satisfaction. In this study the predictions of the most common causal theories with regard to changes in life satisfaction are formulated. The dynamic model used to test these predictions is a structural equation model describing changes in satisfaction through time, effects of changes in living conditions, comparative evaluations, and the effect of a stable component. The same model is tested several times, within different domains. Sociological theories of invariant societal position would predict no change in satisfaction or in living conditions over time. This prediction was proven wrong, because in all domains change was found. The psychological trait theory of satisfaction was proven partially true, because on the one hand the effects of the stable component were significant but on the other hand changes in living conditions did affect satisfaction. The latter finding also disproved the comparative theories of satisfaction. At the same time these theories proved partially true because comparisons with the past did contribute to the explanation of satisfaction. Finally, sociological theories of changeable satisfaction or "social engineering" were confirmed by finding satisfaction to be highly related to living conditions. The conclusion of the model tests is that trait theory, comparison theory, and sociological change theory all three explain a significant part of satisfaction. We therefore propose the "Composite model", which defines satisfaction as a composition of living conditions, comparison with standards and stable traits.

In *Chapter 13*, *Zimmermann and Burton-Jeangros* analyse changes in *health* over a one-year period. Switzerland currently enjoys the highest life expectancy at birth of all European countries. The overall illness prevalence has remained stable over the last two decades. It is shown that this apparently constant net 'stock of ill people' masks changes in health at the individual level: 15 to 20 per cent of the respondents report changes in their health between the two interviews which took place roughly one year apart. By demonstrating the impact of social characteristics such as *gender*, *education* and *ethnicity*, the analyses of longitudinal data confirm the already well-known connection between a person's position within the social structure and health. However, it goes further then typical studies of health inequalities by highlighting how social determinants also affect health evaluations and changes over time, even when prior health and health threatening life events are taken into account. In terms of future health policies, the results suggest that health promotion should target the reduction of social inequalities in the long term, or at least try to prevent a widening of the gap between the bottom and the top of Swiss society.

Bibliography

Bauer, Tobias (1998). The impact of family structure on time use and potential wage in Switzerland. *International Journal of Manpower* 19 (17): 507–519.

Berthoud, Richard and Jonathan Gershuny (2000). *Seven Years in the Lives of British Families. Evidence on the dynamics of social change from the British Household Panel Survey.* Bristol: The Policy Press.

Buchmann, Marlis, Irene Kriesi, Andrea Pfeifer, and Stefan Sacchi (2002). *Halb drinnen – halb draussen. Analysen zur Arbeitsmarktintegration von Frauen in der Schweiz.* Zürich: Rüegger.

Budowski, Monica, Robin Tillmann, Erwin Zimmermann, Boris Wernli, Annette Scherpenzeel, and Alexis Gabadinho (2001). The Swiss Household Panel 1999–2003: Data for research on micro-social change. *ZUMA-Nachrichten* 50 (49).

Cornali, Anne and Christian Vonlanthen (2001). *Description de la pondération de l'échantillon du panel suisse de ménages.* Working Paper 4_01. Neuchâtel: Swiss Household Panel (SHP).

Farago, Peter (1996). *Gesellschaftliche Dauerbeobachtung im SPP "Zukunft Schweiz/Demain la Suisse".* Working Paper 1/96. Bern: Swiss Priority Programme "Switzerland Towards the Future", Swiss National Science Foundation.

Flückiger, Yves (2000). Les conséquences économiques et sociales des mutations actuelles de l'emploi. Pp. 52–71, in: Christian Suter and Claude Pahud (Eds.), *Rapport social 2000.* Zürich: Seismo.

Fux, Beat, Andi Bösch, Priska Gisler, and Doris Baumgartner (1997). *Bevölkerung – und eine Prise Politik. Die schweizerische Migrations-, Familien- und Alterspolitik im Fadenkreuz von Einstellungen und Bewertungen.* Zürich: Seismo.

Höpflinger, François and Kurt Wyss (1997). *Konzeption einer periodischen Sozialberichterstattung aus sozialwissenschaftlicher Sicht.* Working Paper 3/97. Zürich: SPP "Zukunft Schweiz". Schweizerischer Nationalfonds zur Förderung der wissenschaftlichen Forschung.

Joye, Dominique and Annette Scherpenzeel (1997). *Observation à long terme : Projet de panel.* Working Paper 2/97. Berne: Programme Prioritaire "Demain la Suisse". Fonds national suisse de la recherche scientifique.

Latouche, Michel and Jean-François Naud (2001). *Swiss Household Panel. Wave 2. Weighting. General Description.* Working Paper 7_01. Neuchâtel: Swiss Household Panel (SHP).

Leisering, Lutz and Robert Walker (1998). *The Dynamics of Modern Society.* Briston: The Policy Press.

Paugam, Serge (2000). *Le salarié de la précarité. Les nouvelles formes de l'intégration professionnelle.* Paris: Presses Universitaires de France.

Scherpenzeel, Annette, Erwin Zimmermann, Monica Budowski, Robin Tillmann, Boris Wernli, and Alexis Gabadinho (2002). *Experimental pre-test of the biographical questionnaire.* Working Paper 5_02. Neuchâtel: Swiss Household Panel (SHP).

Suter, Christian and Claude Pahud (2000). *Rapport social 2000.* Zürich: Seismo.

Therborn, Göran (1995). *European Modernity and Beyond. The Trajectory of European Societies, 1945–2000.* London, Thousand Oaks, New Delhi: Sage Publications.

Tillmann, Robin, Erwin Zimmermann, Monica Budowski, Boris Wernli, Annette Scherpenzeel, and Alexis Gabadinho (2001). *"Vivre en Suisse". Panel suisse de ménages 1999-2003. Présentation du projet.* Actualités OFS 20. Neuchâtel: Office Fédéral de la Statistique.

Zimmermann, Erwin and Monica Budowski (2004). The Swiss Household Panel Survey: A Multidimensional Database for Monitoring Social Change, in: Isabelle Renschler and Dominique Joye, (eds.), *Observation of Social Change: Structures and Turbulences.* Neuchâtel: SIDOS.

Zimmermann, Erwin and Monica Budowski, with the collaboration of Robin Tillmann, Ruedi Epple, and Beat Schmid (2002). *Leben in der Schweiz 2020; Ein Joint Venture Projekt.* Working Paper 1_02. Neuenburg: Schweizerischer Nationalfonds für wissenschaftliche Forschung, Bern, Bundesamt für Statistik, Neuenburg.

1. Stratification sociale et répartition des ressources
Soziale Schichtung und Ressourcenverteilung

La pauvreté en Suisse*

Robin TILLMANN** et Monica BUDOWSKI***

Introduction

D'un point de vue macro-économique, le produit intérieur brut par habitant de la Suisse est un des plus élevés du monde. Au niveau micro-économique de même, le niveau de vie et le bien-être matériel des individus et des ménages sont en moyenne élevés. Cependant, malgré cette richesse générale, les inégalités de revenus – mesurées par exemple par le coefficient de Gini – sont parmi les plus fortes des pays développés (Osberg et Xu, 1997). Ainsi, la pauvreté reste un problème majeur (Fluder et al., 1999), bien que les pauvres en Suisse se trouvent moins défavorisés que les pauvres dans d'autres pays (Osberg et Xu, 1997; Smeeding et Rainwater, 2001).

La première étude sur la pauvreté à l'échelle nationale, menée en 1992, estimait que le pourcentage de la population résidante que l'on pouvait alors qualifier de pauvre se situait, suivant différents seuils de revenus, entre 5,6 et 10,3 % (Leu et al., 1997). C'est dire qu'entre 400 000 et 700 000 personnes environ vivaient dans la pauvreté en Suisse. Selon cette même étude, on constatait que, parmi les divers groupes de la population, les étrangers, les indépendants, les hommes seuls, les femmes divorcées et les personnes élevant seules leurs enfants étaient plus souvent touchés par la pauvreté que la moyenne. Depuis lors, d'autres études – menées sur la base d'enquêtes également représentatives

* Cette contribution fait partie de l'ouvrage collectif *Vivre en Suisse 1999-2000* (Erwin Zimmermann et Robin Tillmann (éds), Editions Peter Lang, Berne (2004)). Les analyses et résultats se basent sur les deux premières vagues de l'enquête longitudinale Vivre en Suisse réalisée auprès de 6 335 personnes interviewées en 1999 et 2000. La collecte des données, effectuée par M. I. S. Trend sous la responsabilité du Panel suisse de ménages de l'Université de Neuchâtel, a été financée par le PP Demain la Suisse du Fonds national suisse de la recherche scientifique (Subsides No. 5004-53205 / 5004-57894 / 5004-67304). Des informations complémentaires peuvent être obtenues sur le site www.swisspanel.ch

** Panel suisse de ménages, Université de Neuchâtel et Office fédéral de la statistique

*** Panel suisse de ménages, Université de Neuchâtel

de l'ensemble de la population résidant en Suisse – ont permis de renouveler suivant différentes méthodes les estimations relatives à l'ampleur de la pauvreté en Suisse et de définir les groupes les plus sensibles à ce phénomène (voir les travaux récents de Streuli et Bauer, 2001; Branger et al., 2002; Budowski et al., 2002).

Les travaux mentionnés précédemment présentent principalement des analyses transversales. Or, de nombreuses recherches récentes, basées sur l'analyse de données de panels, ont mis en évidence l'importance de la dynamique de la pauvreté (par exemple Whelan et al., 2000). De fait, même les auteurs les plus prudents admettent qu'il existe d'une année à l'autre un nombre important d'entrées-sorties de pauvreté. En vérité, il est désormais reconnu que la pauvreté doit être étudiée selon une approche longitudinale. En effet, alors que les études transversales laissent penser que les pauvres forment un groupe stable et homogène, les approches longitudinales montrent que certaines personnes connaissent certes de longues périodes de pauvreté, mais qu'il existe également un fort taux de rotation parmi les personnes pauvres. Récemment, des études de type dynamique ont été réalisées en Suisse. Elles ne portent toutefois que sur des sous-populations: soit sur la population active occupée (Streuli et Bauer, 2001; Müller, 2002), soit sur les mères seules (Budowski et Suter, 2002). Malgré des méthodologies différentes, ces études convergent au moins sur deux points. D'une part, elles révèlent l'existence, en Suisse aussi, d'une alternance fréquente des périodes de pauvreté et de non-pauvreté. D'autre part, elles reconnaissent l'importance des qualifications et de l'emploi comme moyens de sortie de la pauvreté; même si cela ne constitue pas toujours une condition suffisante comme en témoigne le phénomène des «working poor».

Dans ce chapitre, nous commençons à exploiter le potentiel, certes encore limité, d'une enquête panel en étudiant les transitions en matière de pauvreté entre la vague 1 (1999) et la vague 2 (2000) du Panel suisse de ménages. Nous procédons en trois temps principaux. Après un bref rappel des différentes approches possibles de la pauvreté, nous présentons la définition opérationnelle et les indicateurs longitudinaux auxquels nous avons recours. Enfin, nous exposons les résultats de l'analyse dynamique de la pauvreté durant la période d'observation. L'analyse mentionnée est menée en fonction d'une tentative de mise à l'épreuve empirique de trois schèmes d'interprétation de la pauvreté: en termes de stratification sociale, de cumul de désavantages et d'individualisation.

Concepts et définitions de la pauvreté

Fondamentalement, la définition de la pauvreté dépend de la conception que l'on se donne des besoins humains. Ces derniers ne se réduisent pas à des besoins biologiques. En outre, ils sont historiquement et socialement définis. C'est dire que les besoins humains peuvent (doivent) être compris comme à la fois biologiques (ce qui se traduit en termes d'alimentation et de logement, par exemple) et sociaux (soit entre autres en termes de participation sociale, de loisirs ou de culture). Ceci dit, tous ces besoins ne doivent pas nécessairement être inclus dans la définition de la pauvreté. En effet, à ce niveau, vouloir introduire presque toutes les dimensions de la souffrance et des désavantages sociaux – à l'instar de la définition du Programme des Nations Unies pour le développement[1] par exemple – débouche sur une (relative) confusion entre l'état de pauvreté d'une part, et ses causes et ses effets d'autre part. En conséquence, il s'agit de classer les besoins humains en deux catégories distinctes: (1) ceux dont la satisfaction dépend en priorité de conditions économiques et (2) ceux dont la satisfaction dépend principalement de conditions non-économiques. Dès lors, il est possible d'avancer que, si la définition de la pauvreté doit désigner un objet suffisamment précis, il faut alors la lier aux seuls besoins dont la satisfaction dépend de conditions économiques structurellement déterminées.

Ceci posé, la littérature exhibe de nombreuses manières de définir et de mesurer la pauvreté.[2] A titre d'illustration, on relèvera que Spicker (Gordon et Spicker, 1999, pp. 150 et suivantes) repère onze familles de définitions de la pauvreté, chacune pouvant comprendre plusieurs branches. Boltvinik (1999),

1 Cette définition est la suivante: «La pauvreté a plusieurs visages et représente plus qu'un bas revenu. Elle renvoie à une mauvaise santé, à des lacunes de connaissance et de communication, à l'incapacité d'exercer ses droits humains et politiques et au manque de dignité, de confiance et de respect de soi» (PNUD, 1997; traduction propre).

2 La plupart des approches de la pauvreté reposent sur un concept dichotomique de celle-ci impliquant que l'on peut faire une distinction claire et tranchée entre pauvre et non-pauvre. Or, une telle distinction n'est pas très réaliste. En effet, quelle que soit la définition retenue, il y a un continuum entre les situations et en conséquence toute coupure a quelque chose d'arbitraire. Il n'en demeure pas moins qu'il est nécessaire de se donner un ordre de grandeur de la population concernée. Dès lors, afin de réduire l'arbitraire tout en maintenant la possibilité d'évaluer l'ampleur du phénomène, un certain nombre d'auteurs proposent des démarches qui visent à traduire les transitions graduelles de la pauvreté à la non-pauvreté.

quant à lui, présente environ une vingtaine d'approches méthodologiques différentes de la pauvreté, en les regroupant en quelques grands types: méthodes non-normatives, méthodes directes et multidimensionnelles, méthodes indirectes et unidimensionnelles, enfin un groupe de méthodes combinant certains éléments des approches précédemment mentionnées. Ce n'est pas le lieu d'en faire une recension détaillée; nous nous contentons de mentionner brièvement certains clivages qui traversent le champ des définitions de la pauvreté, afin de situer l'approche utilisée ici.

La première opposition retenue est celle des définitions objectives et subjectives. Grosso modo, les définitions objectives de la pauvreté utilisent une ou plusieurs informations objectives (revenus, biens disponibles, activités pratiquées) sur la population enquêtée pour évaluer la pauvreté. Au contraire, les définitions subjectives de la pauvreté ont recours aux opinions exprimées par la population elle-même. La définition que nous utilisons dans ce chapitre est clairement de type objectif, excluant la perception que peuvent avoir les personnes de l'aisance dans laquelle elles vivent ou de l'écart qui peut exister entre le revenu minimal qui leur permettrait de «joindre les deux bouts» et leur revenu réel.

Un deuxième clivage oppose les définitions absolues et relatives de la pauvreté. Les définitions absolues partent de l'idée que la pauvreté est une situation où le niveau de vie des personnes est inférieur à un seuil déterminé traditionnellement en fonction d'un panier de produits de première nécessité qui reste constant en toutes circonstances et en tous lieux. A l'opposé, les définitions relatives se donnent des seuils de pauvreté qui dépendent de la société et de la période considérées. De fait, ce clivage n'en est peut-être pas vraiment un. En effet, on a progressivement admis que la définition des besoins minimaux était conventionnelle et se référait malgré tout au mode de vie de la société et de l'époque observées. Dès lors, cette opposition semble plutôt se réduire à la question du degré de relativité que l'on veut bien admettre. En tous les cas, l'approche utilisée ici est strictement relative.

La troisième opposition est celle des approches directes et indirectes de la pauvreté. Les définitions directes évaluent la pauvreté en observant la situation réelle (en termes de conditions de vie ou de consommation) de la population concernée, alors que les définitions indirectes considérent les ressources (les revenus essentiellement) comme déterminantes pour l'estimation de la pauvreté. Ce clivage a fait l'objet de nombreux débats. Ringen, le premier, a opéré cette distinction entre approches directes et indirectes. Dans le même temps, il relevait d'une part que les études de pauvreté combinaient (trop) souvent une définition directe et une mesure indirecte de celle-ci, et estimait par la même nécessaire l'établissement d'une correspondance entre définition et mesure (de préférence directes) de la pauvreté d'autre part. Non sans contradiction, Ringen affirme également que la pauvreté peut être mesurée en utilisant à la fois des informations sur les ressources et sur les modes de vie (Gordon et Spicker, 1999, pp. 39-42). Quoi qu'il en soit, la méthode défendue ici – qui ne tranche pas entre les approches directes et indirectes – est de celles qui, à la suite des travaux de Townsend (1979), identifient la population pauvre à celle ayant à la fois de faibles ressources et faisant l'expérience de privation en termes de conditions de vie. En ce qui concerne les pays industrialisés, ce type de démarche est généralement considéré comme scientifique (Gordon et Spicker, 1999, p. 116).[3]

Le dernier clivage, en partie contenu dans la distinction précédente, oppose les approches unidimensionnelles et multidimensionnelles. On a pu montrer (Budowski et Tillmann, 2002) que la majorité des études de pauvreté s'appuient finalement sur une définition de celle-ci en termes d'exclusion des modes de vie communs (acceptables) dans une société donnée. Cette position impliquant en particulier assez clairement une définition multidimensionnelle de la pauvreté. Or, malgré cela, la plupart des mêmes travaux ont recours à une mesure unidimensionnelle du phénomène (le plus souvent en termes de revenu). Afin de réduire le hiatus fréquent entre définition et mesure, l'approche présentée dans ce chapitre s'inscrit dans les démarches de type multidimensionnel.

En somme, l'approche de la pauvreté adoptée ici est de nature objective, relative, mixte (directe et indirecte) et donc aussi multidimensionnelle. Elle est de la famille des définitions de «pauvreté consistante». Ce dernier terme correspondant à la situation de personnes qui, à la fois, ont un revenu inférieur à une certaine fraction du revenu moyen et connaissent une privation en termes de conditions de vie (de biens et d'activités jugés essentiels). Dans ce cadre, s'il fallait poser une définition de la pauvreté, elle serait la suivante: des personnes vivent dans des situations de pauvreté si leur revenu est insuffisant et

3 On peut également avancer des arguments strictement empiriques en faveur de ce type d'approche. De fait, en raison notamment d'erreurs de mesures, se baser sur la seule pauvreté monétaire ou la seule pauvreté d'existence (conditions de vie), quand on travaille sur des fichiers d'enquête, semble risqué (Lollivier et Verger, 1997).

que de plus elles n'accèdent pas aux conditions de vie généralement considérées comme acceptables dans la société dont elles sont membres.

Ces quelques précisions en termes de concepts et de définitions faites, venons en très brièvement à différents types d'interprétation de la pauvreté (pour un aperçu: Layte et Whelan, 2002). Au cours de ces dernières années, deux perspectives interprétatives de la pauvreté – celle du cumul des désavantages et celle de l'individualisation – ont émergé; toutes deux peuvent être considérées comme s'inscrivant en faux vis-à-vis des traditions d'analyse en termes de classes sociales. Cette dernière perspective pose que, peu ou prou, la position sociale d'un individu est ce qui donne la meilleure prévision de ses conditions de vie, de ses pratiques et de ses représentations (tout en admettant l'existence d'autres facteurs pouvant compliquer l'effet propre de celle-ci). Dans cette perspective, les situations de pauvreté devraient être associées aux positions dominées de l'espace social. L'analyse en termes de cumul de désavantages prend une autre direction. En effet, elle définit un clivage principal au sein de la société entre une large majorité intégrée et une minorité victime d'exclusion. Cette perspective propose donc un modèle simple et dichotomique de la structure sociale (inclus, exclus).[4] La minorité ainsi définie est censée être constituée de groupes cumulant les désavantages et les transmettant de génération en génération. Dans ce cadre, la pauvreté est donc conçue comme étant de nature plutôt permanente. A l'opposé, l'hypothèse de l'individualisation de la pauvreté – apparue en partie en réaction à l'approche précédemment mentionnée – considère ce phénomène comme relativement transitoire, associé à des événements particuliers et à des étapes du cycle de vie. Par conséquent, il serait aussi assez indépendant des clivages sociaux traditionnels.

Nous procéderons par la suite à une première évaluation (fortement limitée par le peu de recul historique autorisé actuellement par les données utilisées) des ces différentes interprétations.

4 Au moins dans ses versions «vulgaires» ou «vulgarisées».

Mesures, indicateurs et hypothèses

Nous considérons donc comme pauvres les ménages et les personnes qui présentent deux signes d'indigence, soit ceux qui cumulent une pauvreté monétaire et une pauvreté d'existence. Dès lors, plusieurs étapes sont nécessaires pour identifier la population pauvre suivant cette approche.

Dans un premier temps, nous devons définir un seuil de pauvreté monétaire comme une fraction du revenu moyen ou médian de l'ensemble de la population. Cette première démarche est basée sur le revenu net (annuel) global du ménage, comprenant les revenus d'activités rémunérées, ceux de transferts d'institutions publiques ou privées, les revenus provenant de personnes privées et enfin d'autres revenus résiduels réguliers, après déduction des cotisations sociales, mais avant impôts, et rapporté au nombre d'unités de consommation.[5] En effet, pour passer du revenu global du ménage à son niveau de vie, afin de tenir compte des différents types de ménages, on divise ce revenu par la «taille-équivalente» du ménage à l'aide d'une échelle d'équivalence. On a recours ici aux unités de consommation telles qu'elles sont utilisées dans les études internationales récentes (échelle de l'OCDE modifiée), soit 1 pour le premier adulte, 0,5 pour les autres adultes et 0,3 pour les enfants (15 ans et moins). Suivant différents seuils qu'il est possible d'adopter (50 ou 60 % de la moyenne ou de la médiane), le tableau 1 montre les proportions diverses d'individus vivant dans les ménages qui peuvent être définis comme pauvres au sens de la pauvreté «monétaire» en 1999 et 2000.[6]

5 Le revenu utilisé est un revenu sans aucune imputation ni redressement de sous-estimation.

6 Les chiffres mentionnés dans le texte et les tableaux se basent sur *l'échantillon longitudinal du panel (soit les ménages/personnes de 14 ans et plus qui ont été interrogés en 1ère et en 2e vagues)*. Ils peuvent en conséquence différer de chiffres issus d'analyses portant sur les échantillons transversaux (de 1ère et/ou de 2e vague).

Tableau 1: Taux de pauvreté monétaire selon différents seuils

Définition	1999	2000
50 % du revenu moyen	12,9	12,8
60 % du revenu moyen	22,2	22,3
50 % du revenu médian	7,2	6,4
60 % du revenu médian	15,5	15,0

Panel suisse de ménages, échantillon longitudinal, pondération transversale individu, n non pondéré: 1999 = 5186; 2000 = 5469.

Comme on le sait, la proportion de personnes pauvres varie sensiblement en fonction de la méthode retenue. Ainsi, l'observation permet de voir que – selon la définition dont on tient compte – le taux de pauvreté monétaire oscille entre 6 et 22 % environ de la population considérée. On peut relever que de manière générale les différents taux s'avèrent stables entre 1999 et 2000. Suivant l'actuelle définition d'Eurostat (Office statistique des Communautés européennes), nous adoptons désormais le seuil de 60 % du revenu médian. Cette définition isole environ 15 % de personnes pauvres en 1999 et 2000.[7]

Limitations méthodologiques

Le Panel suisse de ménages fournit une variété de données au sujet de la pauvreté, incluant des indicateurs de pauvreté monétaire, en termes de conditions de vie ou encore de pauvreté subjective. Il constitue donc une bonne base de données pour l'étude de la pauvreté. Toutefois, il connaît des limitations non négligeables. Il faut en mentionner trois. La première relève du type d'enquête auquel appartient le panel, à savoir que la grande pauvreté (sans-domicile, individus hébergés en institution) échappe par définition à une enquête menée auprès des ménages ordinaires. La deuxième limitation provient des modalités de collecte des données. Certaines informations relatives aux revenus du ménage, aux problèmes financiers rencontrés, aux biens disponibles et aux activités du ménage, etc., sont collectées auprès d'une unique personne de «référence». En conséquence, on est amené à

7 Cette dernière proportion est très proche de celle de 14,6 % obtenue sur la base de l'Enquête sur les revenus et la consommation 1998 de l'Office fédéral de la statistique, voir Branger et al. (2002).

admettre que les réponses de cette personne représentent correctement la situation de l'ensemble du ménage et ne sont pas biaisées par ses caractéristiques propres. La troisième correspond aux implications de la remarque qui précède. Dans le panel, comme dans la plupart des enquêtes, le ménage reste à certains égards une sorte de boîte noire. Ceci implique de le considérer comme une unité homogène et à ignorer la répartition des ressources au sein de celui-ci. On est donc dans l'obligation de supposer un égal accès de tous les membres du ménage aux ressources de celui-ci (en l'occurence nous devons notamment admettre que tous les membres d'un ménage pauvre sont pauvres). Or les recherches, allant au-delà du ménage considéré comme une boîte noire, montrent qu'en réalité les ressources au sein des ménages ne sont pas distribuées de manière égale.

Dans un deuxième temps, il s'agit d'opter pour une mesure d'évaluation directe de la pauvreté. Traditionnellement, deux démarches peuvent être suivies à cet égard: d'une part, s'appuyer sur les dépenses de consommation; d'autre part, avoir recours à un indice de privation basé sur une série d'éléments censés traduire les modes de vie acceptables dans une société donnée. On considère généralement que la deuxième méthode, soit l'évaluation directe de la privation de certains biens jugés nécessaires ou de l'accès à certains services ou activités, est la plus adéquate (Gordon et Spicker, 1999). Nous utilisons donc une méthode de ce type, désormais nommée approche de la pauvreté par les conditions de vie (ou pauvreté d'existence).

Le questionnaire du panel permet de partir d'une liste de 13 éléments appartenant au champ des conditions de vie ici considéré. Plus précisément, certains éléments relèvent de biens à disposition du ménage, nommément: télévision couleur, voiture privée, logement avec jardin ou terrasse, lave-vaiselle, lave-linge à usage exclusif, ordinateur privé et résidence secondaire. D'autres éléments correspondent à des activités ou capacités des ménages, à savoir: visite chez le dentiste en cas de nécessité, au moins 1 semaine de vacances par an hors du domicile, épargner au moins 100 francs par mois, recevoir des amis pour un repas au moins 1 fois par mois, repas au restaurant au moins 1 fois par mois, épargne dans un 3ᵉ pilier. Ceci dit, notre démarche vise à repérer les ménages et les individus dont le mode de vie ne correspond pas à un minimum acceptable dans notre société. En conséquence, et à partir de ce qui précède, il s'agit tout d'abord de définir les éléments qui peuvent être retenus comme signes de privation, puis de déterminer les ménages qui sont dans l'obligation de s'en priver par manque de ressources financières. Concernant le premier point, deux méthodes de sélection ont été généralement utilisées. La première option est de ne retenir comme signes de privation que les manques relatifs aux pratiques diffusées dans la majorité de la population. Cette démarche tient donc compte d'un standard objectif (voir Townsend, 1979) défini par un «contrôle par la fréquence», un élément minoritaire ne pouvant faire partie du mode de vie commun à la population. La seconde option consiste à ne tenir compte que des manques considérés comme défavorables par une large majorité de la population (voir Mack et Lansley, 1985). Il s'agit dans ce cas d'un standard social donnant lieu à un «contrôle par le consensus», un élément répandu pouvant ne pas être perçu positivement ou simplement ne pas être généralement accepté comme faisant partie d'un minimum social devant être garanti. Les données du panel nous amènent à appliquer la première méthode (contrôle par la fréquence). Pratiquement, cela signifie que les biens possédés ou les activités pratiquées par 50 % ou plus de la population constituent une majorité «démocratique» et sont dès lors supposés représenter le mode de vie commun pour notre investigation. L'indicateur de pauvreté en termes de conditions de vie est donc basé sur une sélection des 13 éléments considérés à l'origine et communs à 50 % ou plus de la population. De facto, seule la possession d'une résidence secondaire est ainsi exclue de la construction de cet indicateur. Ce dernier est de forme dichotomique: les ménages qui doivent se passer pour des raisons financières de deux éléments ou plus sont considérés pauvres en termes de conditions de vie, ceux qui ne sont privés pour les mêmes raisons que d'un élément ou d'aucun ne le sont pas.[8] Le tableau 2 montre globalement la proportion d'individus vivant dans les ménages touchés par une privation en termes de conditions de vie en 1999 et 2000.

8 Comme tout seuil, celui retenu de deux éléments de privation revêt quelque arbitraire. Ce choix peut toutefois être argumenté, notamment: (1) au sein des ménages connaissant la privation, la moyenne pondérée des éléments manquants est d'un peu plus de 2 (le seuil correspond donc à la notion de mode de vie commun) et (2) techniquement, choisir un seuil supérieur (3 éléments) réduit les observations et rend les analyses presque impossibles.

Tableau 2: Proportion d'individus victimes de privation pour des raisons financières

Eléments manquants	1999		2000	
	En %	En % cumulés	En %	En % cumulés
0	70,7	70,7	69,2	69,2
1	14,7	85,4	14,0	83,2
2	6,5	91,9	7,4	90,6
3	3,4	95,2	4,1	94,8
4	2,2	97,4	2,3	97,0
5	1,3	98,7	1,4	98,4
6	0,6	99,3	0,7	99,2
7+	0,7	100	0,8	100
Total	100		100	

Panel suisse de ménages, échantillon longitudinal, pondération transversale individu, n non pondéré: 1999 = 6335; 2000 = 6327.

Environ 70 % des personnes (70,7 % en 1999 et 69,2 % en 2000) ne subissent strictement aucune privation en termes de conditions de vie pour des raisons financières. Le reste de la population connaît au moins une privation de cet ordre. Toutefois, si l'on applique la définition choisie de la pauvreté d'existence (deux privations ou plus pour des raisons financières), on isole alors 14,7 % (en 1999) et 16,7 % (pour 2000) d'individus faisant l'expérience de ce type d'indigence.

Finalement, dans un troisième temps, nous pouvons croiser les deux dimensions prises en compte – pauvreté monétaire et pauvreté en termes de conditions de vie – afin de définir les sous-populations pertinentes. Dès lors, il est possible de scinder la population en quatre groupes. Le premier est constitué des ménages exhibant les deux signes d'indigence retenus, c'est-à-dire les ménages qui sont à la fois pauvres en termes monétaires (en dessous du seuil de 60 % du revenu médian) et en termes de conditions de vie (soit qui sont privés pour des raisons financières de deux éléments ou plus). Ce groupe représente la population pauvre à strictement parler selon la définition donnée plus haut de la pauvreté consistante. Le deuxième groupe que nous distinguons est formé par les ménages qui ne sont pauvres qu'en termes monétaires. Ce sont les ménages que l'on tiendrait pour pauvres si l'on ne considérait que la seule mesure indirecte de la pauvreté par les ressources financières. A l'inverse, le troisième groupe considéré correspond aux ménages faisant uniquement l'expérience d'une pauvreté en termes de conditions de vie. Il s'agit donc ici de ménages que l'on définirait pauvres si l'on ne tenait compte que d'une mesure directe de la pauvreté. Ces deux derniers groupes ne sont donc pas véritablement pauvres selon la définition que nous utilisons dans ce chapitre. Enfin, le dernier groupe de ménages est constitué de ceux qui ne manifestent aucun signe d'indigence. Le tableau 3 permet d'observer la proportion d'individus vivant dans les ménages répartis dans les quatre groupes ainsi définis en 1999 et 2000.

Tableau 3: Distribution des individus dans les sous-groupes définis

Groupes de la population	1999	2000
Pauvreté consistante	6,1	6,6
«Pauvreté» d'existence	9,4	8,4
«Pauvreté» monétaire	9,6	10,8
Non pauvreté	75,0	74,2
Total	100	100

Panel suisse de ménages, échantillon longitudinal, pondération transversale individu; n non pondéré: 1999 = 5186; 2000 = 5468.

Dès lors et brièvement, l'analyse montre qu'environ trois quarts de la population échappe à toutes formes de pauvreté. On relèvera de plus que l'indicateur de «pauvreté» monétaire augmente d'environ 1 point entre 1999 et 2000; alors que celui de «pauvreté» d'existence baisse d'un point durant le même temps. Quant à elle, la population définie comme pauvre de manière consistante est en légère augmentation durant la (brève) période d'observation, passant de 6,1 % à 6,6 %. Une fois encore, seul ce dernier groupe est désormais considéré pauvre dans notre perspective.

Les différentes étapes précédentes effectuées, nous pouvons en arriver à l'objet principal de notre travail: la dynamique de la pauvreté. Le panel suisse de ménages permet la construction d'indicateurs longitudinaux de pauvreté. De manière générale, ces indicateurs peuvent être classés en trois catégories: les indicateurs d'incidence de la pauvreté, ceux de persistance de celle-ci, enfin les indicateurs de flux d'entrée-sortie de pauvreté (Zoyem, 2002). L'indicateur d'incidence de la pauvreté utilisé ici est défini par le risque pour un individu de connaître au moins une fois la pauvreté sur la période d'observation. Ce risque est estimé par la proportion d'individus qui ont été pauvres au moins une fois entre 1999 et 2000. La persistance de la pauvreté peut s'apprécier en fonction du nombre d'années passées dans cet état. Habituellement, on considère qu'un ménage ou un individu est pauvre de façon persistante lorsqu'il a été pauvre pendant un certain nombre d'années au cours de la période observée. Compte tenu du peu de recul historique des données actuelles du panel, l'indicateur de persistance de la pauvreté utilisé est défini par le risque pour un individu de faire l'expérience de la pauvreté durant toute la période d'observation. Ce risque est donc estimé par la proportion d'individus pauvres en 1999 et en 2000. Ces deux premières approches de la dynamique de la pauvreté sont synthétisées par le recours à une classification longitudinale des individus en trois catégories: (1) pauvres persistants (pauvres en 1999 et en 2000), (2) pauvres occasionnels (pauvres en 1999 ou en 2000) et (3) non pauvres durant toute la période d'observation. Enfin, les flux d'entrée-sortie de pauvreté permettent également d'observer la pauvreté de façon longitudinale. Le flux de sortie de pauvreté est mesuré par la proportion des individus pauvres en 1999 et qui ne le sont plus en 2000. Inversement, le flux d'entrée en pauvreté est mesuré par la proportion d'individus non pauvres en 1999 qui le deviennent en 2000.

Avant de passer à la présentation des principaux résultats des analyses, il faut encore revenir sur les différentes interprétations possibles du phénomène de la pauvreté. Plus précisément, sur la manière de les mettre à l'épreuve des données collectées par le panel. Pour rendre compte de la dynamique de la pauvreté, plusieurs éléments peuvent donc être retenus et privilégiés. En général, la littérature identifie plusieurs catégories de facteurs explicatifs (au niveau micro): (1) des facteurs usuels de catégorisation de l'individu (tels que l'âge, le sexe, le niveau d'éducation, le statut matrimonial, le type de ménage, etc.); (2) des facteurs qui correspondent à la trajectoire passée de l'individu (notamment l'expérience et la durée d'éventuels épisodes de pauvreté antérieurs) et (3) des facteurs relatifs à la survenance d'événements liés à l'emploi ou d'événements familiaux. Grosso modo, nous retenons des catégories de facteurs assez similaires, les sélectionnant toutefois en fonction des types d'interprétation indiqués précédemment, soit: en termes de stratification sociale, de cumul de désavantages et d'individualisation.

Dans une optique de stratification sociale, il suffit ici de poser que l'état de pauvreté (comme sa dynamique) est prioritairement lié à la position sociale de l'individu. C'est dire que le risque de pauvreté doit être d'autant plus fort que la position de l'individu est basse et/ou éloignée du marché du travail considéré comme centre hiérarchisé d'allocation des ressources. Dans ce cadre, nous retenons deux variables d'analyse. Il faut préciser rapidement que la plupart des indicateurs de position sociale se basent avant tout sur la profession exercée. En conséquence, ces indicateurs ne permettent en principe de classer que les personnes en emploi (actives occupées). Plusieurs options se présentent toutefois si l'on veut pouvoir tenir compte de l'ensemble de la population.[9] Nous procédons ainsi: en ce qui concerne les personnes actives occupées, nous les classons en fonction du schéma de classe de Goldthorpe; les personnes «non actives» sont quant à elles classées suivant leur situation actuelle propre. En somme, l'indicateur de position sociale utilisé est un mixte d'un indicateur de position sociale à proprement parler et d'un indicateur de statut d'activité, visant à attribuer un statut social à tous les individus (et non aux seuls actifs occupés). Dans un premier temps, les individus sont donc distribués dans les catégories suivantes (qui peuvent être regroupées): cadres supérieurs, cadres inférieurs, employés, indépendants avec employés, indépendants sans employés, contremaîtres, ouvriers qualifiés, ouvriers semi et non qualifiés, ouvriers agricoles, agriculteurs exploitants, chômeurs, personnes en formation, personnes au foyer, retraités. Toutefois, en raison des effectifs réduits, nous avons empiriquement recours à une version agrégée de l'indicateur de position sociale. Ainsi, le schéma de Goldthorpe se réduit par recodage à un indicateur à cinq positions: travailleurs en col-blanc, petite bourgeoisie, travailleurs de l'agriculture, travailleurs qualifiés, travailleurs non qualifiés.[10] La deuxième variable d'analyse retenue est le niveau de formation de l'individu (facteur pouvant à certains égards être considéré comme une variable intermédiaire entre l'origine sociale et la position sociale atteinte) en trois niveaux: primaire, secondaire, tertiaire.

L'interprétation en termes de cumul de désavantages admet notamment un processus d'exclusion sociale dans le sens d'une séquence temporelle du parcours de vie où les désavantages rencontrés persistent et débouchent sur la pauvreté. Schématiquement, il y aurait donc une séquence causale allant de la famille d'origine au statut de pauvreté, en passant par la formation, l'emploi

9 Les personnes «non actives» peuvent ainsi éventuellement être classées en fonction de leur dernière profession, de la profession de leur conjoint ou de leur situation actuelle.

10 La terminologie originale est la suivante: White-collar workers, Petty bourgeoisie, Farm workers, Skilled workers, Non-skilled workers.

et le chômage. Compte tenu des données disponibles, il nous est impossible de reconstituer rigoureusement une telle séquence. On peut toutefois sélectionner des informations traduisant en quelque sorte des moments du processus complet. Comme auparavant, souhaitant faire porter nos analyses sur l'ensemble de la population (et non sur la seule population en emploi), nous optons pour une définition restrictive du cumul. Dès lors, nous avons calculé un index à partir d'une série de variables appartenant à trois blocs: (1) origine sociale (soit expérience de problèmes d'argent dans la famille d'origine, niveau de formation des parents, position sociale des parents), (2) niveau de formation et (3) statut sur le marché du travail. En fonction des points attribués aux valeurs de ces différentes variables, l'index oscille entre un maximum de 16 (indiquant un minimum de désavantages) et un minimum de 3 points (indiquant un maximum de désavantages). Après avoir testé plusieurs seuils, nous avons retenu celui de 10 points pour opérer une dichotomisation de la population en inclus et exclus traduisant le modèle simplifié de la structure sociale de l'interprétation en termes de cumul de désavantages. Sous cette dernière perspective, une fois encore, l'état de pauvreté doit persister dans le temps d'une part, et l'on doit pouvoir identifier une sous-population exposée à un taux de pauvreté particulièrement élevé d'autre part.

La thèse de l'individualisation avance de manière générale que les comportements individuels sont de moins en moins influencés par les normes et valeurs traditionnelles, de même que par les identités collectives ou l'appartenance à une catégorie sociale. Plus spécifiquement, le risque de pauvreté, lié aux transformations de l'emploi et à la précarisation, est censé se «démocratiser» dans le sens où il frapperait des groupes autrefois protégés, tels que les cadres par exemple. Trois hypothèses au moins peuvent être formées dans le cadre de ce type d'interprétation: (1) les inégalités face au risque de pauvreté entre les différentes classes et les différents niveaux de formation doivent décliner avec le temps, (2) le risque de pauvreté est déterminé par des facteurs relevant du parcours de vie plus que par les facteurs de stratification sociale et (3) les périodes de pauvreté sont relativement courtes. Seules les deux dernières hypothèses peuvent être abordées par le biais des données du panel. Les facteurs mentionnés relevant du parcours de vie doivent être spécifiés en termes d'événements. Nous distinguons les événements d'emploi et les événements familiaux. Les premiers seront définis à partir de la variable statut sur le marché du travail (accès à l'emploi; perte d'emploi: chômage ou inactivité). Les seconds à partir de variables relatives aux types de ménages et à l'état civil.

Résultats et discussion

Une remarque préalable nous semble nécessaire avant d'en venir aux résultats des analyses, afin d'en alléger la présentation. Dans les sciences sociales, toute assertion est indissociable d'un contexte particulier d'observation. C'est dire qu'en principe la validité (éventuelle) d'une proposition n'est nullement universelle mais seulement «locale». En toute rigueur, il faudrait donc toujours au moins rappeler – lors de la présentation et de la discussion des résultats – le lieu (la société suisse) et la période (la fin des années nonante) concernés par l'analyse. Par souci de forme, nous ne le ferons pas dans ce qui suit, mais il s'agit de garder en mémoire ce bref rappel. En outre, compte tenu du peu de recul historique des données disponibles actuellement, les résultats présentés devraient s'entendre presque toujours «en première analyse» ou «en première approximation». Ceci dit, les résultats de l'analyse longitudinale sont présentés en deux moments principaux. Dans un premier temps, nous nous penchons sur l'incidence et la persistance de la pauvreté durant la période d'observation, en insistant sur la synthèse de ces deux approches constituée par une classification longitudinale des individus. Dans un second temps, nous étudions les flux d'entrée-sortie de pauvreté. Volontairement, les analyses se concentrent sur la mise à l'épreuve (provisoire) des différents types interprétatifs mentionnés, et non pas sur l'ensemble des variables généralement utilisées en matière de pauvreté.

L'incidence de la pauvreté est mesurée par la proportion d'individus qui ont été pauvres au moins une fois entre 1999 et 2000. Cette proportion est d'environ 11 % de l'ensemble de la population. C'est dire que sur la période d'observation un individu sur dix a fait l'expérience d'une période de pauvreté (consistante). Nous n'analysons pas plus avant ce phénomène dans la mesure où nous estimons qu'aucun des trois modèles d'interprétation de la pauvreté (en termes de stratification, d'exclusion ou d'individualisation) ne formule nécessairement une hypothèse quant à l'ampleur de la pauvreté en soi. Quant à elle, la persistance de la pauvreté est donnée par la proportion d'individus pauvres en 1999 et en 2000. Celle-ci correspond à 3,5 % de la population dans son ensemble. On peut admettre ici que l'interprétation en termes de stratification sociale ne fait en principe aucune hypothèse au sujet de la durée des situations de pauvreté. Ce n'est pas le cas des deux autres interprétations dont on tient compte dans ce chapitre. Ainsi, la lecture en termes d'exclusion sociale (cumul de désavantages) pose clairement que l'état de pauvreté doit persister dans le temps. Au contraire, la thèse de l'individualisation implique que les périodes de pauvreté sont relativement brèves. Or, si l'on met en parallèle l'incidence de la pauvreté (soit l'ensemble des individus touchés par la pauvreté durant la période d'observation) et la persistance de celle-ci (à savoir l'ensemble des individus pauvres durant toute la période considérée), on constate que ces derniers ne constituent qu'une minorité (environ un tiers) des individus faisant l'expérience de la pauvreté. A ce premier stade de l'analyse, l'interprétation en termes d'individualisation semble donc rendre mieux compte du phénomène que celle dite de l'exclusion sociale. On peut dès lors faire un pas supplémentaire dans la description et la compréhension de la dynamique de la pauvreté. En effet, à partir de là, il est possible de classer les individus en trois catégories: (1) les pauvres persistants (soit pauvres en 1999 et en 2000), (2) les pauvres occasionnels (c'est-à-dire pauvres en 1999 ou en 2000) et (3) les non pauvres durant toute la période d'observation. Le tableau 4 présente à titre indicatif la distribution des individus selon la classification longitudinale utilisée.

Tableau 4: Distribution des individus dans la classification longitudinale de la pauvreté

Groupes de la population	En %	En effectifs (non pondérés)
Pauvres persistants	3,5	146
Pauvres occasionnels	10,9	452
Non pauvres	85,6	4202
Total	100	4800

Panel suisse de ménages, échantillon longitudinal, pondération longitudinale individu

Dans ce qui suit, l'analyse porte sur le risque (probabilité) d'appartenance au groupe des *pauvres persistants*. Dans ce cadre, il faut tout d'abord spécifier les hypothèses des différents types d'interprétation. Dans une perspective de stratification sociale, ce risque doit croître de manière linéaire au fur et à mesure que l'on descend la hiérarchie sociale, mesurée par l'indicateur choisi de position sociale (au moins pour les catégories homogènes et clairement hiérarchisables). La même logique s'applique aux différents niveaux de formation, à savoir que le risque d'appartenir au groupe des pauvres persistants doit être d'autant plus élevé que le niveau de formation est bas. L'approche en termes d'exclusion sociale implique que le risque considéré est fonction d'un cumul d'éléments de désavantage. La sous-population définie par un tel cumul doit en conséquence être exposée à un risque de pauvreté persistante particulièrement élevé. Enfin, on a vu que la thèse de l'individualisation débouche notamment sur l'affirmation que le risque de pauvreté est déterminé par des facteurs relevant du parcours de vie. En l'occurrence, il s'agit de traduire pratiquement la notion de parcours de vie en événements fragilisants. Dès lors, et à ce stade de l'analyse, nous retenons un événement relatif à l'emploi (cessation d'activité: chômage ou inactivité) et deux événements familiaux (cessation d'une relation de couple: séparation ou divorce et veuvage; survenance de la nécessité d'assumer seul(e) son ou ses enfants: famille monoparentale). Dans cette approche, les événements mentionnés doivent augmenter de manière significative le risque d'appartenance à la catégorie des pauvres persistants.[11]

Le risque d'appartenance au groupe des pauvres persistants (et l'évaluation en première analyse de la validité des trois types d'interprétation de la pauvreté) est examiné à l'aide d'un modèle logistique de régression. Les tableaux 5 à 7 présentent les résultats des analyses.

En ce qui concerne la thèse de la stratification sociale, le tableau 5 montre en somme que l'indicateur de position sociale et le niveau de formation contribuent à la probabilité d'appartenir au groupe des pauvres persistants. On peut relever en outre que l'indicateur de position sociale s'avère un meilleur prédicteur (d'appartenance au groupe des pauvres persistants) que l'indicateur du niveau de formation (Wald). L'indicateur de position sociale n'étant pas toujours clairement hiérarchisé, on relèvera simplement que les travailleurs de l'agriculture et les retraités encourent un risque d'appartenance au groupe des pauvres persistants particulièrement élevé. Enfin, les résultats relatifs au niveau de formation (considéré également comme un indicateur de stratification et strictement hiérarchique quant à lui) confirment l'hypothèse selon laquelle le risque de pauvreté persistante est d'autant plus fort que le niveau d'éducation est bas (Exp(B)).

11 A ce niveau, les événements dont nous parlons ne sont pas rigoureusement parlant des événements dont la survenance est bien définie. De facto, nous les induisons de variables d'état (exemple: si la variable d'état civil indique divorcé, c'est bien que l'événement divorce a eu lieu indépendamment de sa datation précise).

Tableau 5: Appartenance au groupe des pauvres persistants: approche en termes de stratification sociale: régression logistique

Stratification sociale	Sig.	Wald	Exp(B)
Position sociale:	***	105,33	
Travailleurs en col-blanc			
Petite bourgeoisie	*		2,73
Travailleurs de l'agriculture	*		12,56
Travailleurs qualifiés	(*)		2,03
Travailleurs non qualifiés	*		2,29
Chômeurs	(*)		2,82
En formation	(*)		2,05
Au foyer	***		3,97
Retraités	***		9,07
Niveau de formation:	***	19,59	
Degré obligatoire	***		3,34
Degré secondaire II	(*)		1,91
Degré tertiaire			
Nagelkerke R Square[12]	,125		
n (non pondéré)	4768		

Panel suisse de ménages, échantillon longitudinal, pondération longitudinale individu.
Degrés de signification: n. s. = non significatif; (*) = p < 0,1; * = p < 0,05; ** = p < 0,01; *** = p < 0,001
Remarques: groupes inclus dans l'analyse: pauvres persistants/pauvres occasionnels & non pauvres. Catégorie de référence en italique. Le modèle présenté dans le tableau ne tient compte d'aucune variable de contrôle. Le modèle a toutefois aussi été calculé en contrôlant les variables suivantes: sexe, âge dichotomisé (25-54 ans versus autres classes d'âge), nationalité dichotomisée (Suisse, étranger).

Le tableau 6 montre que les personnes caractérisées par un cumul de désavantages (les dénommés exclus) connaissent une probabilité trois fois plus élevée d'appartenir au groupe des pauvres persistants que les personnes en situation d'inclusion (entendue comme absence relative de désavantages). Cette observation ne confirme toutefois que partiellement la thèse de l'exclusion, au moins si l'on admet que cette dernière doit poser que la population victime d'un cumul

12 Le Nagelkerke R Square oscille entre 0 et 1 et indique la part de la «variance» de la variable dépendante expliquée par le modèle de régression.

Tableau 6: Appartenance au groupe des pauvres persistants: approche en termes de cumul des désavantages: régression logistique

Cumul des désavantages	Sig.	Wald	Exp(B)
Modèle dichotomique de la structure sociale:			
Inclus			
Exclus	***	48,28	3,17
Nagelkerke R Square	,04		
n (non pondéré)	4773		

Panel suisse de ménages, échantillon longitudinal, pondération longitudinale individu.
Degrés de signification: n. s. = non significatif; (*) = $p<0,1$; * = $p<0,05$; ** = $p<0,01$; *** = $p<0,001$
Remarques: groupes inclus dans l'analyse: pauvres persistants/pauvres occasionnels & non pauvres. Catégorie de référence en italique. Le modèle présenté dans le tableau ne tient compte d'aucune variable de contrôle. Le modèle a toutefois aussi été calculé en contrôlant les variables suivantes: sexe, âge dichotomisé (25-54 ans versus autres classes d'âge), nationalité dichotomisée (Suisse, étranger).

de désavantages doit encourir un risque particulièrement élevé de pauvreté persistante.

Les résultats relatifs aux variables censées illustrer l'approche en termes d'individualisation sont présentés dans le tableau 7. Il en ressort que le statut sur le marché de l'emploi (actifs occupés comparés aux chômeurs, aux personnes au foyer et en formation et enfin aux retraités) contribue le plus fortement à la probabilité de se trouver en situation de pauvreté persistante. Plus précisément, le risque considéré est d'autant plus fort que l'éloignement du marché de l'emploi est important; en termes du moins d'éloignement en principe provisoire (chômeurs, personnes au foyer ou en formation) ou définitif (retraités). L'état civil et le type de ménage jouent un moindre rôle. Globalement, le modèle d'individualisation a un pouvoir de prévision de la pauvreté persistante moindre que les modèles de stratification et d'exclusion.

On peut en venir maintenant à la seconde phase de l'analyse, à savoir celle des entrées-sorties de pauvreté. Dès lors, nous en revenons tout d'abord à l'opposition binaire entre la population pauvre de manière consistante (pauvres en termes monétaires et du point de vue des conditions de vie) et le reste de la population (définie alors comme non pauvre dans son ensemble). A ce niveau, les flux d'entrées-sorties de pauvreté se montent à presque 11 %. On relèvera

Tableau 7: Appartenance au groupe des pauvres persistants: approche en termes d'individualisation: régression logistique

Individualisation	Sig.	Wald	Exp(B)
Statut sur le marché de l'emploi:	***	54,96	
En emploi			
Au chômage, au foyer & en formation	**		2,05
Retraité	***		5,75
Statut d'état civil:	*	8,60	
Mariage			
Célibat	*		0,54
Veuvage	n. s.		0,50
Séparation & Divorce	n. s.		1,18
Types de ménage:	n. s.	7,00	
Couples sans enfant			
Couples avec enfant(s) dépendant(s)	*		1,67
Personnes seules de 64 ans et moins	n. s.		1,23
Personnes seules de 65 ans et plus	n. s.		1,60
Famille monoparentale	n. s.		1,98
Autre situation	(*)		2,39
Nagelkerke R Square	,09		
n (non pondéré)	4780		

Panel suisse de ménages, échantillon longitudinal, pondération longitudinale individu.
Degrés de signification: n. s. = non significatif; (*) = p < 0,1; * = p < 0,05; ** = p < 0,01; *** = p < 0,001
Remarques: groupes inclus dans l'analyse: pauvres persistants/pauvres occasionnels & non pauvres. Catégorie de référence en italique. Le modèle présenté dans le tableau ne tient compte d'aucune variable de contrôle. Le modèle a toutefois aussi été calculé en contrôlant les variables suivantes: sexe, âge dichotomisé (25-54 ans versus autres classes d'âge), nationalité dichotomisée (Suisse, étranger).

simplement que les personnes non pauvres en 1999 ne tombent que peu souvent dans l'état de pauvreté (4,5 %); au contraire, une proportion importante des personnes pauvres en 1999 ne le sont plus une année après (44 % environ).[13] La probabilité de sortir de l'état de pauvreté semble donc élevée. Toutefois, le

13 Résultats non présentés dans un tableau.

recours aux quatre catégories définies au tableau 3 (pauvreté consistante, pauvreté monétaire, pauvreté d'existence et non pauvreté), qui traduisent mieux la gradation des situations, permet de nuancer cette observation. Ainsi, le tableau 8 permet entre autres de constater qu'uniquement 11 % des pauvres «consistants» en 1999 se retrouvent en situation de non pauvreté en 2000, les autres «sortants» de cette catégorie n'accèdent en fait qu'aux catégories relativement vulnérables de la pauvreté monétaire et d'existence; alors que plus de la moitié de cette population reste en situation de pauvreté consistante.

Tableau 8: Flux d'entrées-sorties de pauvreté entre 1999 et 2000, % horizontaux

Groupes de la population	Non pauvreté	Pauvreté monétaire	Pauvreté d'existence	Pauvreté consistante
Non pauvreté	89,0	6,4	3,8	0,9
Pauvreté monétaire	36,4	49,1	4,1	10,4
Pauvreté d'existence	38,0	5,7	35,7	20,7
Pauvreté consistante	11,3	16,5	20,4	51,8

Panel suisse de ménages, échantillon longitudinal, pondération longitudinale individu, n non pondéré = 4800. Exemple de lecture: 89 % des personnes en situation de non pauvreté en 1999 restent dans cette catégorie une année après, 6,4 % sont devenus pauvres en termes monétaires, 3,8 % le sont en termes de pauvreté d'existence, enfin 0,9 % d'entre elles sont tombées dans la pauvreté consistante.

Cette brève analyse descriptive présentée, il est possible de préciser les différentes hypothèses que l'on peut formuler en fonction des trois approches sous revue. Dans le cadre de la stratification sociale, on admettra que le risque de tomber en situation de pauvreté est d'autant plus élevé que la position sociale est basse ou le niveau de formation faible. Inversement, la probabilité de sortir de l'état de pauvreté doit dans cette perspective être d'autant plus forte que la position sociale est élevée ou le niveau de formation supérieur. En ce qui concerne la thèse de l'exclusion sociale, on peut estimer que les personnes caractérisées par un cumul de désavantages doivent faire l'expérience d'un risque de chuter dans la pauvreté particulièrement élevé. Au contraire, les mêmes individus doivent connaître une probabilité faible de sortir de l'état de pauvreté. On admet ici que l'approche en termes d'individualisation se doit de poser les hypothèses suivantes. L'entrée en pauvreté doit être associée aux événements suivants: cessation d'activité (chômage ou inactivité), cessation d'une relation de couple (séparation, divorce ou veuvage), survenance de la nécessité d'assumer seul(e) son ou ses enfants (famille monoparentale). Quant à elle, la sortie de l'état de pauvreté doit être liée aux événements (contraires) suivants: prise d'emploi, mariage, mise en couple. Malheureusement, les analyses exploratoires effectuées ont montré qu'en l'état les données disponibles ne permettent pas de mettre à l'épreuve ces hypothèses (notamment en raison de la faiblesse des effectifs concernés). Dès lors, seule l'étude des relations entre une modification de statut sur les indicateurs retenus pour illustrer les différentes approches (mobilité au sein des indicateurs de stratification, de cumul ou d'individualisation) et la probabilité de connaître un mouvement d'entrée-sortie de pauvreté a été possible. En première approximation, les analyses menées permettent malgré tout trois observations à cet égard: (1) les changements de position sociale sont liés aux flux d'entrée-sortie de pauvreté, mais la relation est faible et ne correspond pas toujours aux attentes; (2) de même, une relation existe, mais très faible, entre ces flux et une modification du statut inclus-exclus; en particulier, l'entrée en pauvreté semble liée au cumul de (nouveaux) désavantages; (3) la relation la plus forte observée est celle entre les flux d'entrée-sortie de pauvreté et une modification de statut sur le marché de l'emploi (emploi, chômage, inactivité); en raison des effectifs réduits, les événements familiaux ne peuvent être analysés. On peut en outre tirer de ces analyses exploratoires qu'une forte proportion des flux d'entrée-sortie de pauvreté n'est pas associée à des modifications de position sociale ou à des événements de vie.[14]

En somme, on peut provisoirement porter à la discussion les points suivants. Tout d'abord, aucune des trois approches (en termes de stratification, d'exclusion et d'individualisation) ne rend compte en elle-même de l'ensemble des observations. On peut évidemment en conclure au moins deux choses: soit que nous avons simplifié à l'excès ces approches, les rendant ainsi inaptes à refléter précisément les phénomènes sous revue, soit que ces derniers sont –

14 Ce déficit d'explication est probablement partiellement lié à une question de méthode. En effet, les caractéristiques étudiées relèvent de l'individu, tandis que la définition de la pauvreté se fait au niveau du ménage. Dès lors, une personne dont les caractéristiques restent constantes peut passer sous le seuil de pauvreté en raison d'une modification des caractéristiques d'autres personnes vivant dans le ménage.

indépendamment des indicateurs utilisés pour traduire les différentes thèses en présence – en soi peu susceptibles d'être expliqués par une seule et unique approche. Ensuite, on peut avancer que les résultats tendent à privilégier l'approche en termes de stratification sociale. Ainsi, la position sociale semble le meilleur prédicteur des situations de pauvreté. Toutefois, l'indicateur de position sociale utilisé ici est en vérité un mixte d'un indicateur de position sociale à proprement parler et d'un indicateur de statut d'activité; en conséquence, il n'est pas clairement hiérarchisable. Il s'ensuit qu'une face de la thèse de l'approche en termes de stratification (grosso modo, que le risque de pauvreté doit être d'autant plus fort que la position de l'individu est basse) ne peut pas véritablement être mise à l'épreuve. Il s'agirait donc, de manière beaucoup plus générale, de disposer d'un indicateur capable de classer de manière clairement hiérarchique l'ensemble de la population (et non pas seulement les personnes en emploi) et tenant compte de l'ensemble des dimensions de la stratification telles que le genre ou l'âge par exemple.

Bibliographie

Boltvinik, Julio (1999): *Poverty Measurement Methods – An Overview* (SEPED Series on Poverty Reduction) UNDP/Poverty [www.undp.org/poverty/publications/pov_red/].

Branger, Katja, Pascale Gazareth, Caterina Modetta, Paul Röthlisberger, Beat Schmid, Jacqueline Schön-Bühlmann et Robin Tillmann (2002): *Revenu et bien-être. Niveau de vie et désavantages sociaux en Suisse.* Neuchâtel: Office fédéral de la statistique.

Budowski, Monica and Christian Suter (2002): Living Arrangement and the Dynamics of Poverty: Lone Parenting in the Life Courses of Mothers. *Revue suisse de sociologie* 28 (2): 319-338.

Budowski, Monica et Robin Tillmann (2002): Pauvreté et exclusion: définition et usage des concepts, éléments de reformulation et premiers résultats pour la Suisse. *Observation du changement social et monitoring politique*, Neuchâtel: Office fédéral de la statistique, 329-362.

Budowski, Monica, Robin Tillmann and Max Bergman (2002): Poverty, Stratification and Gender in Switzerland. *Revue suisse de sociologie* 28 (2): 297-317.

Fluder, Robert, Marion Nolde, Tom Priester et Antonin Wagner, eds (1999): *Comprendre la pauvreté, pour mieux la combattre.* Neuchâtel: Office fédéral de la statistique.

Gordon, David and Paul Spicker, eds (1999): *The International Glossary on Poverty.* New York, London: Zed Books.

Layte, Richard and Christopher T. Whelan (2002): Cumulative Disadvantage or Individualisation? A comparative analysis of poverty risk and incidence. *European Societies* 4 (2): 209-233.

Leu, Robert E., Stefan Burri und Tom Priester (1997): *Lebensqualität und Armut in der Schweiz*. Bern: Haupt.
Lollivier, Stéfan et Daniel Verger (1997): Pauvreté d'existence, monétaire ou subjective sont distinctes. *Economie et statistique* (308-309-310): 113-142.
Mack, Joanna and Stewart Lansley (1985): *Poor Britain*. Londres: Allen et Unwin.
Müller, Georg P. (2002): Explaining Poverty: On the Structural Constraints of Income Mobility. *Social Indicators Research* 59 (3): 301-319.
Osberg, Lars and Kuan Xu (1997): International Comparisons of Poverty Intensity: Index Decomposition and Bootstrap Inference. *Luxembourg Income Study Working Paper*, 165.
Pahl, Jan (1989): *Money and Marriage*. Basingstoke: Macmillan.
PNUD (1997): *Informe sobre el desarrollo humano*. Edited by Programa de las Naciones Unidas para el Desarrollo. Madrid: Mundi-Prensa.
Smeeding, Timothy M. and Lee Rainwater (2001): Nations: Real Incomes at the Top, the Bottom, and the Middle. *Luxembourg Income Study Working Paper*, 266.
Streuli, Elisa et Tobias Bauer (2001): *Les «working poor» en Suisse. Etude de la problématique, de l'ampleur du phénomène, et de ses causes*, info: social 5: 01. Neuchâtel: Office fédéral de la statistique.
Townsend, Peter (1979): *Poverty in the United Kingdom*. London: Penguin.
Whelan, Christopher T., Richard Layte, Bertrand Maître and Brian Nolan (2000): Poverty Dynamics. An analysis of the 1994 and 1995 waves of the European Community Household Panel Survey. *European Societies* 2 (4): 505-531.
Zoyem, Jean-Paul (2002): *La dynamique des bas revenus: une analyse des entrées-sorties de pauvreté*. Document de travail. Paris: Institut National de la Statistique et des Etudes Economiques.

«Bas salaires» et «working poor» en Suisse*

Jean-Marc Falter et Yves Flückiger

1. Introduction

Depuis une dizaine d'années, de nombreuses études ont essayé d'expliquer l'augmentation de l'inégalité des salaires et l'accroissement de la catégorie des «working poor» observés dans la plupart des pays occidentaux. Plusieurs explications ont été suggérées. Certaines ont mis l'accent sur le rôle des changements technologiques qui impliquent une demande croissante de main-d'œuvre qualifiée. D'autres travaux ont insisté sur l'impact de la globalisation et, en particulier, de l'ouverture croissante aux échanges commerciaux et financiers internationaux, dont la conséquence vraisemblable est la diminution relative de la demande de main-d'œuvre non qualifiée. Une troisième approche a mis en exergue le rôle exercé par les migrations internationales qui auraient eu pour effet de faire pression sur les «bas salaires». Finalement, certains chercheurs se sont attachés à montrer l'importance de changements d'ordre plutôt institutionnels, qu'il s'agisse d'une baisse du taux de syndicalisation ou des variations du taux de salaire minimum, modifications qui, elles non plus, n'ont pas joué en faveur des individus se trouvant dans la partie inférieure de l'échelle des salaires.

Peu de travaux ont cependant été consacrés à une analyse des caractéristiques des individus qui ont un bas salaire ou qui vivent en situation de

* Cette contribution fait partie de l'ouvrage collectif *Vivre en Suisse 1999-2000* (Erwin Zimmermann et Robin Tillmann (éds), Editions Peter Lang, Berne (2004)). Les analyses et résultats se basent sur les deux premières vagues de l'enquête longitudinale Vivre en Suisse réalisée auprès de 6 335 personnes interviewées en 1999 et 2000. La collecte des données, effectuée par M. I. S. Trend sous la responsabilité du Panel suisse de ménages de l'Université de Neuchâtel, a été financée par le PP Demain la Suisse du Fonds national suisse de la recherche scientifique (Subsides No. 5004-53205 / 5004-57894 / 5004-67304). Des informations complémentaires peuvent être obtenues sur le site www.swisspanel.ch

précarité[1]. Les études portant spécifiquement sur le cas des «working poor» en Suisse sont encore plus rares. On peut citer Deutsch, Flückiger et Silber (1999) ainsi Streuli et Bauer (2001) qui font usage des données de l'enquête suisse sur la population active (ESPA). Ces études ont adopté des approches distinctes: la première étude considère les «working poor» comme un sous-groupe des «bas salaires» alors que Streuli et Bauer distinguent très nettement les deux populations en utilisant les informations liées au revenu de l'ensemble du ménage. Cette seconde approche porte spécifiquement sur la pauvreté alors que la démarche de Deutsch et al. se concentre plutôt sur les personnes situées tout au bas de l'échelle salariale[2]. Il faut constater que chacune de ces études aboutissent à des conclusions similaires, à savoir que la précarité a augmenté lors des années 1990.

Le premier but de notre étude est d'essayer d'obtenir des informations sur la population des «bas salaires» et des «working poor» en Suisse à l'aide des données du Panel suisse des ménages (PSM). Pour ce faire, nous appliquerons des techniques empruntées à l'analyse de la pauvreté. Le second objectif de notre recherche est de déterminer le degré de persistance d'une situation de «working poor» ou de bas salaire et les facteurs de précarité touchant les ménages. Pour ce faire, nous utiliserons les deux premières vagues du PSM afin de déterminer quelles sont les caractéristiques (âge, sexe, éducation, etc...) susceptibles d'influencer la probabilité de tomber dans la catégorie des «working poor» ou des «bas salaires» entre 1999 et 2000.

Cet article est divisé en deux parties principales. La première porte principalement sur des aspects techniques. Dans un premier temps, nous définirons précisément les concepts de «bas salaire» et de «working poor». Ce volet méthodologique sera encore complété par une brève présentation des outils statistiques utilisés dans le cadre de notre étude et nous justifierons le

1 Pour la Suisse, les travaux de Buhmann (1991), Farago et Füglistaler (1992), Füglistaler (1992), Hainard et al. (1990), Leu et al. (1997), Leu and Burri (1999), Mäder et al. (1991), Perruchoud-Massy (1992), Rossi et Sartoris (1991), Toppi et Marazzi (1991) ainsi que Ulrich et Binder (1992) fournissent des informations intéressantes sur ce sujet. Malheureusement, elles restent la plupart du temps limitées à un seul canton ou basées sur des données partielles.

2 Comme il est explicité dans la section méthodologique de ce document, il est possible qu'une personne appartienne au groupe des «bas salaires» sans être pauvre ou, inversement, soit pauvre alors qu'elle n'appartienne pas au groupe des «bas salaires».

choix et la construction des variables utilisées, en soulignant les implications potentielles de nos décisions sur les résultats obtenus. La deuxième partie sera quant à elle consacrée entièrement à l'analyse des données issues du PSM pour déterminer tout d'abord l'importance de la population défavorisée en Suisse et pour examiner ensuite les facteurs qui influencent la probabilité de vivre dans une situation précaire en raison d'un salaire particulièrement bas ou à cause d'un revenu insuffisant pour échapper à la pauvreté.

2. «Bas salaires» et «working poor»: définitions

Les notions de bas salaire ou de «working poor» sont éminemment subjectives. Ceci signifie, et c'est particulièrement vrai dans le cas des «working poor», que les définitions attachées à ces phénomènes diffèrent selon les auteurs et leur sensibilité. Avant d'aller plus en avant dans cette section méthodologique, il est bon de rappeler ce qui distingue les «bas salaires» des «working poor». Concernant le premier groupe, il s'agit exclusivement d'individus situés au bas de la distribution des salaires ou des revenus professionnels. Dans ce cas, on ne tient aucunement compte d'éventuels revenus annexes (revenus de la propriété, du conjoint, du capital ou de la fortune) qui pourraient affecter la situation de l'individu. Ceci signifie qu'un individu se trouvant en situation de bas salaire n'est pas forcément dans une situation économique défavorable. Par contre, le groupe des «working poor» est constitué d'individus qui travaillent mais dont le revenu professionnel n'est pas suffisant pour permettre à leur ménage d'échapper à la pauvreté. Dans cette optique, la pauvreté est définie par le biais du seuil de revenu par adulte à partir duquel les besoins de base ne peuvent plus être satisfaits. Ainsi, une personne dont le revenu professionnel est assez élevé pour éviter de figurer dans la catégorie des «bas salaires», peut très bien être comptabilisée comme «working poor» si elle vit dans un ménage considéré comme pauvre.

Dans cette étude, nous définirons les «bas salaires» (ou bas revenus) comme les personnes dont le revenu professionnel net (en terme annuel) est inférieur à la moitié de la médiane de la population de référence. Cette définition est couramment utilisée dans ce type de recherche. Une mesure alternative pourrait être basée sur des valeurs arbitraires pertinentes dans le cadre d'un débat de politique économique. Par exemple, en 2001, les milieux syndicaux ont revendiqué un salaire mensuel minimal de 3000.– francs. A n'en point douter, ce montant correspond à la perception de ce que peut-être un bas salaire pour les syndicats. Cependant, afin de ne pas surcharger notre exposé, nous nous limiterons à une seule définition des «bas salaires».

La notion de «working poor» fait appel quant à elle à des méthodes liées aux mesures de la pauvreté. Suite aux travaux de Sen (1973), de nombreuses études se sont attachées à définir des indices de pauvreté. Ces recherches ont en général distingué deux étapes dans la définition d'un indice de pauvreté. Dans un premier temps, il est nécessaire de fixer un seuil de pauvreté tel que les personnes dont le revenu est inférieur à ce seuil sont considérées comme pauvres. La détermination d'un tel seuil peut être basée sur une approche dite «absolue», auquel cas on fixe généralement un panier de consommation minimale, souvent lié à des considérations alimentaires, tel que les individus qui n'ont pas la possibilité d'obtenir ce panier sont considérés comme pauvres. Il existe également une approche dite «relative» où le seuil de pauvreté est défini comme étant égal à un certain pourcentage du revenu ou de la consommation moyenne ou médiane des individus (Sen, 1983). Le terme «relatif» indique évidemment que, selon cette approche, on peut être pauvre même si on a suffisamment à manger car on est toujours démuni par rapport à quelqu'un. Notons que lorsque les données utilisées pour déterminer le seuil de pauvreté se rapportent au revenu ou à la consommation des ménages, on utilisera généralement ce que l'on appelle des «échelles d'équivalences» qui permettent de comparer des ménages de taille différente et, par conséquent, des individus appartenant à des ménages qui ne comprennent pas le même nombre de personnes. En divisant les ressources totales du ménage par l'échelle d'équivalence propre à sa taille, il est possible ensuite de confronter le montant de son revenu équivalent (ou de sa consommation équivalente) au seuil de pauvreté préalablement défini.

Différentes approches peuvent être employées pour mesurer ces échelles d'équivalence. La première que l'on peut envisager consiste à diviser tout simplement les ressources totales du ménage par le nombre d'individus qui le constitue. Cependant, pareille méthode fait abstraction des économies d'échelles réalisées au sein d'un ménage composé de plusieurs membres. Elle contribuerait à sous-estimer le bien-être des familles nombreuses par rapport à leur niveau de vie réel. Il faut dès lors avoir recours à des échelles d'équivalence plus complexes. Dans le cadre de cet article, nous avons choisi d'utiliser celle de l'OCDE qui a l'avantage d'être reconnue de manière plus ou moins universelle. Elle peut s'écrire à l'aide de la formule suivante:

$$EQ_{OCDE} = 1 + (nbr\_adulte - 1) \times 0{,}7 + nbr\_enfant \times 0{,}5$$

où «nbr_adulte» symbolise le nombre d'adultes et «nbr_enfant» le nombre d'enfants vivant dans le ménage. Dans ce cas particulier, un adulte est défini comme une personne âgée de plus de 14 ans[3].

La seconde étape de ce calcul d'un indice de pauvreté est ce que l'on appelle communément le stade de l'agrégation. Il s'agit ici, une fois que l'on a été capable de faire la distinction entre les individus considérés comme «pauvres» et ceux qui ne le sont pas, de dériver un indice synthétique qui donnera une indication sur l'importance du phénomène de pauvreté. La solution la plus simple est évidemment de compter le nombre d'individus «pauvres» et de comparer ce nombre avec la population totale de façon à estimer la proportion de pauvres dans la population. Un tel indicateur s'appelle le *«headcount ratio»* [4].

Le seuil de pauvreté choisi pour notre étude est basé sur les directives de la Conférence suisse des institutions d'action sociale (CSIAS) qui servent à établir les montants accordés par l'aide sociale au niveau suisse. Le minimum vital établit par la CSIAS pour un ménage d'une seule personne se monte à 2 100 francs par mois[5]. Si le revenu d'un ménage, après déduction des impôts, se situe en dessous du seuil de pauvreté, le ménage en question est pauvre. Un individu sera considéré comme pauvre si il fait partie d'un ménage dont le revenu se situe en-dessous du seuil de pauvreté.

3 Le choix d'une échelle d'équivalence est complexe vu la multiplicité des choix qui s'offrent aux chercheurs. Une solution alternative aurait consisté à estimer par nos propres moyens une échelle d'équivalence pour la Suisse à l'aide des données existante en Suisse (Enquête sur les revenus et la consommation des ménages, OFS). Néanmoins, chaque approche contient des jugements de valeur, ce qui implique qu'aucune méthode n'est clairement préférable.

4 Il existe également des indicateurs plus complexes où le niveau de pauvreté est agrégé sous la forme d'indice prenant en compte, entre autres choses, l'écart entre le revenu observé et le seuil de pauvreté. Sen (1976) a proposé un tel indice mais de nombreuses autres suggestions ont été faites dans ce sens et l'indice qui est aujourd'hui probablement le plus populaire est l'indice dit FGT suggéré à l'origine par Foster, Greer et Thorbecke (1984).

5 Le minimum vital s'obtient en additionnant les besoins de bases (nourriture, habillement, éducation), le loyer et les assurance-maladies.

3. «Bas salaires» et «working poor» en 1999 et 2000

Nous reportons dans le tableau 1, les taux de travailleurs appartenant à la catégorie des «bas salaires» et des «working poor» en 1999 et 2000. L'échantillon est constitué d'actifs âgés de 20 à 60 ans. Il est bon de rappeler qu'un individu appartenant à la catégorie des «bas salaires» n'est pas forcément pauvre. Ceci se vérifie dans notre base de données. Ainsi, seulement 13,25 % des «bas salaires» appartiennent aux «working poor» en 2000 (10,14 % en 1999). Par contre, 42,94 % des «working poor» en 2000 appartiennent aux «bas salaires» (41,18 % en 1999)[6]. Ainsi les «bas salaires» ne semblent expliquer que partiellement le phénomène des «working poor». Comme notre définition des «bas salaires» se réfère au revenu professionnel brut sans distinction de temps de travail, il est patent que ce dernier élément est un facteur important des «bas salaires». Ainsi, aussi bien en 1999 qu'en 2000, plus de 40 % des individus à temps partiel appartiennent à la catégorie des «bas salaires» contre seulement 3 % des personnes à plein temps.

Cette différence entre temps partiel et temps plein explique très largement l'importante proportion de «bas salaires» parmi les femmes. Il en est de même pour le taux de «bas salaires» selon la taille du ménage. Plus le ménage est grand, plus la proportion de bas salaire est importante. Enfin, il peut paraître surprenant que le taux de bas salaire soit plus important parmi les Suisses que parmi les étrangers. A nouveau, ce résultat ne reflète pas la situation économique des intéressés étant donné que le temps partiel est une forme d'emploi plus fréquente parmi les résidents suisses qu'au sein des résidents étrangers[7]. Il est intéressant de constater que les résultats ne sont guère différents selon l'année. On peut cependant noter que le taux de bas salaire parmi les indépendants varie fortement entre 1999 et 2000 ce qui illustre la forte variabilité des revenus découlant de cette forme de travail.

Dans le tableau 1, nous reportons également le taux de «working poor». Nous pouvons constater que la population des «bas salaires» et celle des «working poor» ne sont pas identiques. Ceci provient essentiellement de notre définition des «bas salaires» qui met principalement l'accent sur le taux d'occupation. Ainsi, on observe aucune différence (à un niveau statistiquement significatif[8]) entre hommes et femmes en ce qui concerne les «working poor».

6 Streuli et Bauer trouvent que 67 % des «working poor» ont un bas salaire.

7 Le lecteur intéressé peut se référer à Falter et al. (2000).

Par contre, on constate désormais que la situation des étrangers est moins favorable que celle des Suisses. Selon le tableau 1, le principal déterminant d'une situation de «working poor» est la taille du ménage. Les ressources du ménage doivent être partagées entre un plus grand nombre d'individus, souvent des enfants non-actifs, ce qui augmente la probabilité d'être un «working poor». Il est bon de rappeler que les résultats concernant la taille du ménage dépendent de manière cruciale du choix de l'échelle d'équivalence.

Dans une seconde phase, nous nous concentrons sur les individus travaillant à plein-temps (tableau 2). A nouveau, on constate que le taux de bas salaires est plus important parmi les femmes que parmi les hommes. Ceci découle probablement des discriminations salariales que subissent les femmes sur le marché du travail suisse mais aussi des différences de niveau d'éducation qui existent aujourd'hui encore entre les femmes et les hommes, pour ne citer que les deux facteurs explicatifs les plus importants. En effet, le groupe formé d'individus ne disposant que d'une formation élémentaire est le seul dont la proportion de bas salaire est supérieur à la moyenne en 1999.

Dans le tableau 2, nous reportons également les taux de «working poor» parmi les actifs à plein-temps. Une fois encore, on constate qu'une situation de bas salaire n'implique pas forcément une situation de pauvreté (et vice-versa). Ainsi, le taux de «working poor» est inférieur parmi les femmes que parmi les hommes. Cependant, le lecteur doit être attentif au fait que l'on se concentre sur les actifs à plein-temps, donc on ne peut conclure au vu de ces chiffres que la situation des femmes, en général, est meilleure que celle des hommes. De manière peu surprenante, la taille du ménage demeure un des facteurs les plus important concernant la propension à être «working poor». Ainsi, environ 20 % des personnes appartenant à un ménage de 5 personnes ou plus sont considérées comme «working poor». A l'opposé, moins de 2 % des personnes seules se trouvent dans pareille situation. Les différences selon le niveau de formation achevée sont également très marquées. La situation de «working poor» est extrêmement marginale pour celle et ceux qui ont pu accomplir une formation universitaire. Ceci contraste fortement avec le taux relativement élevé (environ 15 %) de «working poor» parmi les personnes avec une formation élémentaire. Enfin, on constate que le taux de «working poor» des étrangers est cette fois-ci largement supérieur à celui des Suisses.

8 Les tests statistiques ne sont pas reportés dans ce document.

Tableau 1: Taux de «bas salaires» et «working poor» selon les caractéristiques

Caractéristiques analysées	1999		2000	
	Bas salaires	Working poor	Bas salaires	Working poor
Population active occupée[a]	16,07	6,31	16,77	7,18
Canton				
Suisse alémanique	17,24	6,50	17,88	5,92
Suisse romande	13,65	5,05	14,63	8,49
Tessin				
Taille du ménage				
1 personne	5,91	4,14	5,17	3,63
2 personnes	12,09	1,81	11,68	3,21
3 personnes	22,80	7,04	23,51	7,15
4 personnes	21,90	7,71	20,76	8,95
5 personnes ou plus	23,75	18,84	27,84	18,59
Age				
moins de 25 ans	33,49	4,15	32,10	10,52
25-34 ans	12,65	6,28	16,40	6,78
35-44 ans	16,56	6,63	15,70	7,94
45-54 ans	13,37	5,78	14,72	6,17
55 ans ou plus	21,48	7,69	17,68	6,72
Sexe				
Hommes	4,12	5,96	3,46	7,27
Femmes	31,83	6,78	33,80	7,06
Nationalité				
Etrangers	12,36	7,16	14,89	9,97
Suisses	16,83	6,11	17,27	6,45
Formation achevée				
Formation élémentaire	31,97	14,68	33,63	14,56
Ecole secondaire professionnelle	16,69	6,56	15,33	7,22
Ecole secondaire générale	21,80	6,36	24,33	8,10
Ecole supérieure professionnelle	6,06	3,55	7,70	4,09
Formation universitaire	8,46	1,92	8,15	1,46
Temps de travail				
Plein temps	3,07	5,35	2,83	6,17
Temps partiel	41,43	8,16	44,71	8,91
Type d'activité				
Indépendant	25,99	11,01	16,63	7,05
Salarié	14,74	5,68	16,83	7,22

Sources: PSM 1999-2000. Notes: a) population âgée de 20 à 60 ans. Moyenne pondérée. Taille des échantillons: 2189 observations en 1999, 2526 observations en 2000. Ecart-types disponible auprès des auteurs. Seuils de bas-salaire: 24 948.– francs en 1999, 26 000.– francs en 2000.

Tableau 2: Taux de «bas salaires» et de «working poor» parmi les actifs à plein-temps

	1999		2000	
Caractéristiques analysées	Bas salaires	Working poor	Bas salaires	Working poor
Canton				
Suisse alémanique	2,65	5,41	2,26	4,62
Suisse romande	3,75	4,32	4,56	6,95
Taille du ménage				
1 personne	1,99	1,49	2,82	1,12
2 personnes	3,70	1,23	2,52	1,63
3 personnes	6,64	7,12	7,28	8,60
4 personnes	2,50	7,25	2,13	9,10
5 personnes ou plus	3,43	20,91	4,53	18,75
Age				
moins de 25 ans	20,82	4,57	22,29	11,25
25-34 ans	2,38	6,15	2,05	4,60
35-44 ans	2,55	5,51	1,41	7,53
45-54 ans	1,92	5,24	1,31	5,66
55 ans ou plus	0,56	3,24	1,14	4,83
Sexe				
Hommes	2,06	5,98	1,72	6,99
Femmes	6,30	3,39	6,32	3,62
Nationalité				
Etrangers	2,16	8,20	2,78	9,98
Suisses	3,34	4,54	2,85	5,02
Formation achevée				
Formation élémentaire	12,63	14,79	9,43	15,85
Ecole secondaire professionnelle	2,21	5,60	1,71	5,73
Ecole secondaire générale	2,58	7,18	5,06	8,19
Ecole supérieure professionnelle	0,85	2,76	1,02	3,91
Formation universitaire	2,49	0,49	2,62	0,47

Sources: PSM 1999-2000. Notes: a) population âgée de 20 à 60 ans. Moyenne pondérée. Taille des échantillons: 1382 observations en 1999, 1596 observations en 2000. Ecart-types disponible auprès des auteurs. Seuils de bas-salaire: 24 948.– francs en 1999, 26 000.– francs en 2000.

4. Analyse multivariée de la probabilité d'appartenir à la population des «bas salaires» ou des «working poor» en 1999 et 2000

Comme nous l'avons indiqué précédemment, une telle analyse permet de savoir si une variable donnée a un effet sur la probabilité d'appartenir à la population des «bas salaires» ou des travailleurs paupérisés, toutes choses égales par ailleurs, c'est-à-dire de déterminer l'impact spécifique de cette variable lorsque les autres variables restent constantes. Nous avons étudié d'abord séparément les résultats pour chaque vague du PSM pour les années 1999 et 2000 respectivement. Ils sont présentés dans la première section consacrée à l'analyse statique. Puis, dans un second temps, nous avons examiné les variables susceptibles d'expliquer la transition vers un statut de bas salaire ou de «working poor» entre 1999 et 2000.

a) Analyse statique

Dans le cas de notre analyse multivariée, la variable expliquée est susceptible de prendre deux valeurs: 1 lorsque l'individu considéré appartient à la population étudiée, celle des personnes caractérisées par un bas salaire ou par une appartenance aux «working poor» et 0 lorsque l'individu en question ne fait pas partie de la population analysée. C'est pour cette raison que nous faisons appel au modèle logit.

Le tableau 3 se concentre sur la probabilité d'appartenir aux «bas salaires». Pour comprendre le contenu des tableaux présentés dans cette section, il n'est pas inutile de mentionner que les variables prises en référence pour évaluer l'impact des caractéristiques mentionnées sont respectivement les cantons latins, les hommes, les étrangers, les salariés, les célibataires et les personnes dont la formation s'est achevée à la fin de leur scolarité obligatoire. La colonne «O/R» (odds ratio) s'interprète aisément dans le cas de variables binaires. Par exemple, un coefficient égal à 2,89 pour les travailleurs indépendants signifie que ces derniers ont une probabilité 2,89 fois supérieure à celle des employés de se trouver en situation de bas salaire.

On constate tout d'abord que le facteur le plus important est le travail à temps partiel. En effet, une personne travaillant à temps partiel à environ 15 fois plus de chance d'appartenir aux «bas salaires» qu'une personne à plein-temps en 2000. Ceci n'est guère étonnant connaissant notre définition des «bas salaires». Il est intéressant de noter que le coefficient attaché au sexe féminin n'est pas statistiquement différent de zéro, ce qui signifie que les femmes n'ont pas une plus grande probabilité d'appartenir aux «bas salaires». Le fait que l'on observe plus de femmes parmi les «bas salaires» provient largement des caractéristiques de leur travail, en particulier du fait que le temps partiel soit prédominant parmi les femmes ou en raison de la séparation très traditionnelle des tâches à l'intérieur du ménage. A ce sujet, on peut noter que l'effet du mariage diffère selon le genre. En effet, une femme mariée à une plus forte probabilité de se trouver dans la catégorie des «bas salaires», alors que le mariage produit un effet exactement inverse pour les hommes. Ce tableau met également en évidence que l'effet de l'âge n'est pas linéaire. Ce facteur permet dans un premier temps de réduire la probabilité d'appartenir à la population démunie, influence qui s'estompe cependant progressivement pour s'inverser au-delà d'un certain âge ainsi qu'en témoigne le signe positif associé à la variable *«âge au carré»*. Il permet également de compléter des observations faites sur la base de statistiques plus descriptives. Ainsi, il apparaît que l'origine ne constitue pas un facteur nécessairement discriminant sur la probabilité de faire partie de la population des «bas salaires». Cela signifie donc que si le pourcentage d'étrangers au sein de la population défavorisée est particulièrement élevé, ce résultat provient avant tout du niveau de formation atteint par ce groupe démographique qui est relativement défavorable compte tenu de l'impact exercé par cette variable sur la probabilité d'appartenir à la population des «bas salaires».

Le tableau 4 répète le même exercice, la variable dépendante étant désormais la probabilité d'appartenir aux travailleurs paupérisés. Les résultats obtenus partagent quelques similitudes avec ceux reportés dans le tableau 3. C'est le cas pour le niveau d'éducation qui est un facteur important réduisant la probabilité des individus à se trouver en situation de «bas salaires» ou de travailleurs paupérisés. Dans le même temps, on observe que les travailleurs indépendants et ceux à temps partiel ont une plus forte probabilité de se trouver dans une situation défavorable. Enfin, le nombre de personnes dans le ménage augmente considérablement la probabilité d'appartenir à la catégorie des «working poor»[9]. Ceci peut s'expliquer de deux manières: premièrement, la présence d'enfants dans le ménage peut réduire les perspectives de carrière des femmes, réduisant

9 En estimant des effets marginaux, nous constatons que le nombre de personne dans le ménage est le facteur le plus important conditionnant la probabilité d'appartenir aux «working poor».

Tableau 3: Analyse logit: probabilité d'appartenir aux «bas salaires»

	1999			2000		
	Coeff.	Stat-t	O/R*	Coeff.	Stat-t	O/R*
Constante	3,728	3,60	–	4,247	4,04	–
Taille du ménage			–			
Nombre de personnes dans le ménage	0,488	7,97	–	0,452	7,38	–
Age						
Age de l'individu	–0,391	–6,71	–	–0,427	–7,41	–
Carré de l'âge de l'individu	0,005	6,37	–	0,005	6,89	–
Région linguistique						
Canton suisse allemand	0,221	1,29	1,25	0,103	0,65	1,10
Genre						
Sexe féminin	–0,009	–0,03	0,99	0,164	0,54	1,18
Nationalité						
Suisse	0,255	1,03	1,29	0,058	0,22	1,06
Type d'emploi						
Travailleur indépendant	1,061	4,32	2,89	0,592	3,38	1,81
Temps partiel	2,384	10,35	10,85	2,746	11,42	15,59
Etat civil						
Marié	–1,285	–3,29	0,28	–1,284	–3,13	0,27
Femme mariée	2,227	5,47	9,27	2,345	5,49	10,43
Formation achevée						
Ecole secondaire professionnelle	–0,980	–4,50	0,37	–0,697	–3,47	0,50
Ecole secondaire générale	–1,045	–3,88	0,35	–0,775	–3,10	0,46
Ecole supérieure professionnelle	–1,629	–5,06	0,20	–1,176	–4,07	0,31
Formation universitaire	–1,814	–5,29	0,16	–1,630	–5,26	0,20

Note: population âgée de 20 à 60 ans; les écart-types sous-jacent à la statistique t sont robustes (méthode Huber/White), corrigés pour les observations non-indépendantes au niveau du ménage. Taille des échantillons: 2189 observations en 1999, 2526 observations en 2000.

Tableau 4: Analyse logit: probabilité d'appartenir aux travailleurs paupérisés

	1999			2000		
	Coeff.	Stat-t	O/R*	Coeff.	Stat-t	O/R*
Constante	–2,261	–1,68	–	–2,633	–1,88	–
Taille du ménage			–			
Nombre de personnes dans le ménage	0,552	6,32	–	0,513	5,92	–
Age						
Age de l'individu	–0,089	–1,16	–	–0,046	–0,63	–
Carré de l'âge de l'individu	0,001	1,15	–	0,000	0,60	–
Région linguistique						
Canton suisse allemand	–0,065	–0,30	0,94	–0,614	–2,99	0,54
Genre						
Sexe féminin	0,440	1,01	1,55	0,406	1,11	1,50
Nationalité						
Suisse	–0,044	–0,15	0,96	–0,255	–0,95	0,77
Type d'emploi						
Travailleur indépendant	0,785	3,10	2,19	0,363	1,69	1,43
Temps partiel	0,647	2,66	1,91	0,946	3,86	2,57
Etat civil						
Marié	0,360	0,81	1,43	0,273	0,72	1,31
Femme mariée	–1,047	–2,23	0,35	–1,398	–3,22	0,25
Formation achevée						
Ecole secondaire professionnelle	–0,927	–3,62	0,40	–0,472	–1,94	0,62
Ecole secondaire générale	–1,252	–3,30	0,29	–0,785	–2,37	0,45
Ecole supérieure professionnelle	–1,600	–4,24	0,20	–1,054	–3,08	0,35
Formation universitaire	–2,299	–4,89	0,10	–2,543	–4,65	0,08

Note: population âgée de 20 à 60 ans; les écart-types sous-jacent à la statistique t sont robustes (méthode Huber/White), corrigés pour les observations non-indépendantes au niveau du ménage. Taille des échantillons: 2189 observations en 1999, 2526 observations en 2000.

le revenu de ces personnes. D'autre part, le revenu du ménage est réparti sur un plus grand nombre de personnes, réduisant la part obtenue par chaque individu, toutes choses étant égales par ailleurs. Les résultats obtenus lors des estimations de la probabilité d'appartenir aux «bas salaires» et de la probabilité d'appartenir aux travailleurs paupérisés semblent démontrer que les deux effets agissent simultanément.

Si les tableaux 3 et 4 partagent de nombreuses similitudes, démontrant que le phénomène de «bas salaires» et de travailleurs paupérisés sont étroitement liés, il faut néanmoins relever d'importantes différences. C'est le cas en ce qui concerne le rôle de l'état civil. Ainsi, les femmes mariées ont une plus faible probabilité que les hommes ou les femmes célibataires d'appartenir à la catégorie des «working poor». Ceci amène un nouvel éclairage sur les coefficients attachés à la variable femme mariée du tableau 3. Ces résultats semblent être dus à l'allocation interne du ménage, les femmes amenant un salaire d'appoint permettant aux ménages d'échapper à la pauvreté.

Comme nous l'avons déjà mentionné, nos résultats dépendent directement du taux d'activité des individus. De plus, le taux d'activité n'est pas parfaitement exogène dans nos estimations car, dans la plupart des cas, il a été choisi par les individus[10]. Etant donné que ces choix d'activité se basent, entre autres choses, sur des considérations de revenu, nos résultats deviennent difficiles à interpréter. C'est pourquoi, nous avons également estimé la probabilité d'appartenir aux «bas salaires» et aux travailleurs paupérisés en nous concentrant sur les individus à plein-temps. A des fins de brièveté, nous reportons uniquement les résultats pour l'an 2000. Plusieurs d'entre eux méritent notre attention.

Premièrement, la variable «nombre de personnes dans le ménage» augmente toujours la probabilité d'appartenir aux «bas salaires». Ceci semble indiquer que les enfants pénalisent ceux ou celles qui en ont la charge. En effet, des enfants en bas âge peuvent impliquer des arrêts dans la carrière des individus. De plus, les entreprises ont souvent tendance à réduire leurs investissements en capital humain en faveur des femmes susceptibles d'avoir des enfants. Ce phénomène peut également expliquer la plus forte probabilité des femmes mariées à appartenir aux «bas salaires». En effet, ces dernières ont dix fois plus de chance d'appartenir à cette catégorie que les hommes ou les femmes

10 Selon Falter et al. (2000), seulement 10 % des femmes à temps partiel et 15 % des hommes à temps partiel désirent travailler à plein temps.

Tableau 5: Analyse logit: probabilité d'appartenir aux «bas salaires» ou aux travailleurs paupérisés en 2000 (plein-temps)

	Bas salaires			Working poor		
	Coeff.	Stat-t	O/R*	Coeff.	Stat-t	O/R*
Constante	7,686	3,18	–	–3,360	–1,81	–
Taille du ménage			–			
Nombre de personnes dans le ménage	0,327	3,32	–	0,694	6,22	–
Age						
Age de l'individu	–0,545	–4,39	–	–0,015	–0,17	–
Carré de l'âge de l'individu	0,006	4,08	–	0,000	0,20	–
Région linguistique						
Canton suisse allemand	–0,749	–2,14	0,47	–0,728	–2,62	0,48
Genre						
Sexe féminin	0,362	0,94	1,43	–0,029	–0,06	0,97
Nationalité						
Suisse	0,082	0,16	1,08	–0,534	–1,63	0,59
Type d'emploi						
Travailleur indépendant	0,857	2,47	2,36	0,433	1,62	1,54
Etat civil						
Marié	–1,996	–2,96	0,14	–0,058	–0,14	0,94
Femme mariée	2,393	2,93	10,95	–0,487	–0,66	0,61
Formation achevée						
Ecole secondaire professionnelle	–1,674	–4,04	0,19	–0,608	–1,77	0,54
Ecole secondaire générale	–1,109	–1,98	0,33	–0,679	–1,35	0,51
Ecole supérieure professionnelle	–1,488	–2,20	0,22	–1,096	–2,52	0,33
Formation universitaire	–0,853	–1,44	0,43	–3,312	–3,18	0,04

Note: population âgée de 20 à 60 ans; les écart-types sous-jacent à la statistique t sont robustes (méthode Huber/White), corrigés pour les observations non-indépendantes au niveau du ménage. Taille de l'échantillon: 1596 observations.

célibataires. Sinon, on peut constater que la partition linguistique semble avoir son importance lorsque l'on se concentre sur les travailleurs à plein-temps. Ainsi, les personnes habitant dans un canton alémanique ont une plus faible probabilité de se trouver parmi les «bas salaires» ou les travailleurs paupérisés. Finalement, on peut noter que les indépendants ont une plus forte probabilité de se trouver dans une situation défavorable. Ce résultat est conforme avec ceux de Falter (2002) qui a mis en évidence, à l'aide de l'Enquête suisse sur la population active (ESPA), que les indépendants ont une plus forte probabilité de se trouver dans le bas et dans le haut de la distribution des revenus.

b) Transitions: analyse de la vulnérabilité face à la précarité

Dans cette section, nous nous intéressons aux transitions vers le statut de «bas salaire» ou vers celui de «working poor». Avant d'aller plus en avant dans cette analyse, il est bon de préciser les limites et inconvénients de ce genre d'analyse. Nous avons défini nos variables de «bas salaires» ou de travailleurs paupérisés à l'aide d'un seuil de revenu en-dessous duquel un individu est considéré comme appartenant à la catégorie défavorisée. Cette approche binaire ne distingue pas l'individu qui se situe à un niveau relativement proche de ce seuil de celui qui s'en trouve relativement éloigné. De plus, de par et d'autre de ce seuil de revenu, les individus qui s'en trouvent proches jouissent d'un niveau de bien-être très similaire mais ils vont être catégorisés différemment. Quand on se concentre sur les évolutions d'une année sur l'autre, les individus qui ont la plus forte probabilité de changer de statut (par exemple de devenir un travailleur paupérisé) sont ceux qui avaient initialement un niveau de revenu proche du seuil établi. Lorsque l'on sait que les variables de revenu sont souvent sujettes à des erreurs de mesures, il a fort à parier que nombre des transitions observées ne reflètent pas nécessairement des changements dans la situation économique des individus ou des ménages.

Dans un premier temps, il nous a semblé intéressant d'analyser les matrices de transitions (tableaux 6 et 7) entre les différents statuts de 1999 à 2000. On constate ainsi que 13,19 % de l'échantillon fait partie de la catégorie des bas-salaires aussi bien en 1999 qu'en 2000. On remarque également que la majorité (73,78 %) des bas-salaires en 1999 demeure dans le même statut en 2000. Il semble donc que la situation de bas-salaire soit durable. Par ailleurs, on constate que le taux de transition vers le statut de bas-salaire est relativement faible (2,59 %). Plus faible en tous les cas que le pourcentage de personnes qui parviennent à quitter le statut de bas salaire en 2000 après y avoir séjourné en 1999. Toutefois, on peut noter que pour les deux années sur lesquelles porte notre analyse, 20 % des individus se trouvent dans le statut de bas-salaire soit en 1999 soit en 2000.

Tableau 6: Matrice de transitions des bas-salaires de 1999 à 2000

	2000	
1999	Bas-salaires	Autres travailleurs
Bas-salaires		
% de l'échantillon	13,19 %	4,69 %
% de la ligne	73,78 %	26,22 %
Autres travailleurs		
% de l'échantillon	2,13 %	80,00 %
% de la ligne	2,59 %	97,42 %

Notes: 2570 observations; les différences entre ce tableau et le tableau s'explique par l'attrition entre les deux vagues du panel.

Le statut de «working poor» est moins répandu étant donné qu'il ne touche que 10,98 % de notre échantillon sur l'ensemble des deux années considérées. Il semble également que ce statut soit plus temporaire, étant donné que seulement 45,95 % des «working poor» en 1999 le sont encore en 2000. Toutefois, cette affirmation doit être prise avec prudence car le risque d'erreur susceptible d'entacher la mesure du revenu du ménage étant sans doute plus élevé que celui qui grève la saisie des revenus individuels. De ce fait, la plus grande variabilité de la population des «working poor» reflète également une moindre fiabilité des données relatives à ce groupe particulier de travailleurs.

Tableau 7: Matrice de transitions des «working poor» 1999-2000

	2000	
1999	Working poor	Autres travailleurs
Working poor		
% de l'échantillon	3,54 %	4,17 %
% de la ligne	45,95 %	54,05 %
Autres travailleurs		
% de l'échantillon	3,27 %	89,02 %
% de la ligne	3,54 %	96,46 %

Notes: 2192 observations; les différences entre ce tableau et le tableau s'explique par l'attrition entre les deux vagues du panel.

Une étude des transitions observées dans les tableaux 6 et 7 revient en fait à estimer les facteurs de vulnérabilité de la population face aux risques de tomber dans la précarité et d'y rester ensuite durablement en ayant peu de chance d'en sortir. Dans la suite de cette section, nous avons donc utilisé une analyse multivariée de la probabilité de transiter vers le statut de «bas salaire» et de «working poor». Malheureusement, analyser les transitions de sortie depuis les statuts de «bas salaire» ou de «working poor» n'est pas possible en raison du nombre trop faible d'observations disponibles.

Les résultats de l'analyse logit des transitions sont reportés dans le tableau 8. La variable dépendante prend la valeur de 1 si on observe une transition vers le statut de bas salaire («working poor») et de 0 si l'individu n'appartient pas à la catégorie des «bas salaires» («working poor») en 1999 et 2000. Les variables indépendantes se réfèrent à l'année 1999. On fait explicitement l'hypothèse que c'est la situation initiale qui a une influence sur la situation finale des individus. Cette hypothèse est discutable, mais elle est cohérente avec une approche mettant l'accent sur la vulnérabilité des individus.

Les résultats sont assez décevants étant donné que peu de coefficients s'avèrent significatifs statistiquement au seuil de 5 % (statistique-t supérieure ou égale à 1,96). Dans le cas des transitions vers les «bas salaires», seules les variables de temps partiel et celle intitulée «femme mariée» produisent des coefficients statistiquement différents de zéro au seuil susmentionné. On peut noter que le coefficient attaché au travail indépendant est statistiquement significatif au seuil de 10 % (statistique-t supérieure ou égale à 1,65). Il est intéressant de noter qu'aucun groupe ne semble particulièrement prémuni contre une éventuelle transition vers la catégorie des «bas salaires».

Le deuxième jeu de résultats reportés dans les trois dernières colonnes du tableau 8 concerne la probabilité de devenir «working poor». On note tout d'abord que le nombre de variables significativement différentes de zéro au seuil de 5 ou 10 % est nettement plus grand que dans pour l'estimation de la probabilité de devenir un bas salaire. On peut relever ainsi certains facteurs qui semblent réduire la vulnérabilité des individus. Par exemple, vivre dans un canton suisse allemand, être une femme mariée ou être détenteur d'une formation universitaire réduit significativement la probabilité de devenir «working poor». A l'inverse, les travailleurs indépendants ont une plus forte probabilité de devenir «working poor» ce qui illustre la volatilité des revenus découlant de cette forme de travail.

Tableau 8: Analyse logit: transitions vers les «bas salaires» ou les travailleurs paupérisés 1999-2000

	Bas salaires			Working poor		
	Coeff.	Stat-t	O/R*	Coeff.	Stat-t	O/R*
Constante	–3,173	–0,89	–	–5,051	–1,85	–
Taille du ménage						
Nombre de personnes dans le ménage	0,097	0,51	–	0,340	1,98	–
Age						
Age de l'individu	–0,130	–0,79	–	0,052	0,35	–
Carré de l'âge de l'individu	0,002	0,80	–	–0,000	–0,35	–
Région linguistique						
Canton suisse allemand	–0,176	–0,48	0,84	–0,971	–2,80	0,38
Genre						
Sexe féminin	0,093	0,14	1,09	1,053	1,58	2,87
Nationalité						
Suisse	–0,239	–0,42	0,79	–0,093	–0,22	0,91
Type d'emploi						
Travailleur indépendant	0,910	1,66	2,48	0,843	2,29	2,32
Temps partiel	1,720	3,53	5,58	0,629	1,76	1,88
Etat civil						
Marié	–0,782	–0,85	0,46	0,457	0,60	1,58
Femme mariée	1,94	1,96	6,96	–1,656	–2,27	0,19
Formation achevée						
Ecole secondaire professionnelle	1,029	1,40	2,79	–0,297	–0,63	0,74
Ecole secondaire générale	0,732	0,86	2,08	–1,607	1,92	0,20
Ecole supérieure professionnelle	–0,300	–0,30	0,74	–0,689	–1,38	0,50
Formation universitaire	0,128	0,15	1,13	–1,354	–2,17	0,26

Note: population âgée de 20 à 60 ans; les écart-types sous-jacents à la statistique-t sont robustes (méthode Huber/White), corrigés pour les observations non-indépendantes au niveau du ménage. Taille de l'échantillon: 1596 observations.

5. Conclusions

Le phénomène des travailleurs paupérisés a bénéficié d'une attention croissante au cours de la dernière décennie. En effet, il peut paraître choquant que même en Suisse, l'activité lucrative ne protège pas de la pauvreté. Notre étude, utilisant les données du Panel suisse des ménages, confirme l'importance de ce problème. En effet, nous avons obtenu un taux de «working poor» supérieur à 6 % de la population active occupée aussi bien en 1999 qu'en 2000. Nous avons étudié en parallèle le phénomène des «bas salaires», afin de dégager les similitudes et les différences entre ces deux phénomènes. Force est de constater que les «bas salaires» n'expliquent que partiellement le phénomène des «working poor». Ainsi, environ 40 % des «working poor» ont un «bas salaire». Il faut noter que l'appartenance aux bas salaires dépend grandement du taux d'occupation qui est souvent choisi. L'instauration d'un salaire horaire minimum n'aurait donc pas nécessairement un impact important sur le niveau de «working poor».

Il ressort en effet de notre étude que le revenu professionnel n'est pas le seul facteur déterminant la probabilité d'appartenir aux travailleurs paupérisés. On constate notamment que la structure familiale est un facteur particulièrement prépondérant. En effet, la présence d'enfants réduit le temps de travail des membres du ménage, particulièrement des femmes, et obèrent les possibilités de carrière en raison des interruptions de la vie professionnelle qu'ils induisent. En outre, plus le ménage est grand, plus la part de revenu par tête sera faible, toutes choses étant égales par ailleurs.

Le phénomène des «working poor» ne peut être ramené à un seul facteur. Notre étude indique que ce problème relève aussi bien de la politique familiale que de la politique du marché du travail. Des efforts de formation seraient également particulièrement bienvenus pour lutter contre ce problème. En effet, les personnes avec un faible niveau de formation sont les plus exposées au risque de pauvreté.

Bibliographie

Buhmann, B. I. (1991), *Wohlstand und Armut in der Schweiz,* Verlag Rüegger, Chur, Zürich, 2e édition.

Deutsch, J., Y. Flückiger et J. Silber (1999), *La population des «bas salaires» et des «working poor» en Suisse,* OFS, Neuchâtel.

Falter, J.-M., G. Ferro Luzzi et Y. Flückiger (2000), *Le travail à temps partiel: caractéristiques et développement prévisible,* FNRS, Programme prioritaire «Demain la Suisse».

Falter, J.-M. (2002), *Occupational Choice: Empirical Studies on Self-Employment in Switzerland,* Thèse de doctorat, Université de Genève.

Farago, P. (1992), *Armut im Kanton Zürich,* Institut für Praxisorientierte Sozialforschung, Zürich.

Farago, P. und P. Füglistaler (1992), *Armut verhindern: Die Zürcher Armutstudien: Ergebnisse und sozialpolitische Vorschläge,* Fürsorgedirektion des Kantons Zürich, Zürich.

Foster, J. E., J. Greer and E. Torbecke (1984), *«A Class of Decomposable Poverty Measures»,* Econometrica, 52(3): 761-766.

Füglistaler, P. (1992), *Armut und Einkommensschwäche im Kanton Zürich,* Hochschule Sankt-Gallen für Wirtschafts- und Sozialwissenschaften. Forschungsinstitut für Arbeit und Arbeitsrecht, St. Gallen.

Hainard, F., M. Nolde, G. Memminger et M. Micheloni (1990), *Avons-nous des pauvres? Enquête sur la précarité et la pauvreté dans le canton de Neuchâtel,* Cahiers de l'ISSP, volume 12. EDES, Neuchâtel: Université de Neuchâtel, Institut de sociologie et de science politique.

Leu, R. E., S. Burri und T. Priester (1997), *Lebensqualität und Armut in der Schweiz,* Verlag P. Haupt, Bern, Stuttgart, Wien.

Leu, R. E. and S. Burri (1999), *Poverty in Switzerland,* Swiss Journal of Economics and Statistics, vol. 135, no. 3, pp. 303-328.

Mäder, U., F. Biedermann, B. Fischer und H. Schmassmann (1991), *Armut im Kanton Basel-Stadt,* Social Strategies Publ. Basel.

Perruchoud-Massy, M.-F. (1992), Existence et intensité de la pauvreté dans les cantons du Tessin, Neuchâtel et Valais, *Cahiers médico-sociaux,* 36: 243-251.

Rossi, M. e E. Sartoris (1991), *Mimimi vitali e scale di equivalenza,* Documento di lavoro 91.03, Istituto di Ricerche Economiche, Bellinzona.

Sen, A. K. (1973), *On Economic Inequality,* Clarendon Press, Oxford.

Sen, A. K. (1983), *Poor, Relatively Speaking,* Oxford Economic Papers, 35(2): 153-169.

Streuli, E. et T. Bauer (1999), *Les working-poor en Suisse,* OFS, Neuchâtel.

Toppi, S. e C. Marazzi (1991), *La povertà in Svizzera: Sintesi delle ricerche sul fenomeno della povertà,* Dipartimento delle opere sociali, Bellinzona.

Ulrich, W. und J. Binder (1992), *Armut im Kanton Bern: Bericht über die kantonale Armutsstudie,* Gesundheits- und Fürsorgedirektion des Kantons Bern, Bern.

Carrières professionnelles: une analyse biographique*

Dominique Joye et Manfred Max Bergman

1. Introduction

De très nombreux travaux ont été consacrés à la mobilité sociale intergénérationnelle, c'est-à-dire la différence de position entre la position sociale que le répondant occupe, mesurée en fonction de sa profession, et celle que son père occupait. Les travaux consacrés aux parcours professionnels sont par contre beaucoup plus rares. Pour la Suisse, on peut mentionner les tentatives réalisées par Levy et al. (1997). Pourquoi cet état de fait?

La raison essentielle réside dans le manque de données longitudinales: la plupart des enquêtes ne sont réalisées qu'à un moment donné et posent du coup un problème lorsque l'on s'intéresse, comme ici, à un processus: comment en est-on arrivé à la place que l'on occupe?

Des données de panel sont à priori l'instrument idéal pour apprécier les changements en suivant les événements survenant aux mêmes individus. Le panel suisse des ménages (PSM), par exemple, permet de suivre un tel processus dans la mesure où il enregistre, année après année, la situation professionnelle et familiale ainsi que les éventuels changements. Malheureusement, celui-ci est encore jeune et seulement trois vagues sont disponibles pour une telle analyse. Ses concepteurs ont toutefois eu l'idée de demander aux répondants de remplir un «questionnaire biographique» qui permet de retracer les différentes étapes du parcours de vie, y compris de la carrière professionnelle. Ce sont les données que nous utiliserons ici.

* Cette contribution fait partie de l'ouvrage collectif *Vivre en Suisse 1999-2000* (Erwin Zimmermann et Robin Tillmann (éds), Editions Peter Lang, Berne (2004)). Les analyses et résultats se basent sur les deux premières vagues de l'enquête longitudinale Vivre en Suisse réalisée auprès de 6 335 personnes interviewées en 1999 et 2000. La collecte des données, effectuée par M. I. S. Trend sous la responsabilité du Panel suisse de ménages de l'Université de Neuchâtel, a été financée par le PP Demain la Suisse du Fonds national suisse de la recherche scientifique (Subsides No. 5004-53205 / 5004-57894 / 5004-67304). Des informations complémentaires peuvent être obtenues sur le site www.swisspanel.ch

L'analyse sera menée en fonction de 3 variables explicatives de base: sexe, âge et formation. La raison en est fort simple: le genre détermine souvent des rapports fort différents au marché du travail et donc à l'insertion sociale; l'âge renvoie à des cohortes, c'est-à-dire à des classes d'âge qui, chacune, peuvent avoir connu un destin particulier (Chauvel 1998). La formation enfin renvoie à une indication sur les ressources sociales dont les répondants peuvent disposer.

Mais auparavant, un petit excursus méthodologique.

2. Qui répond?

A priori, un échantillonnage aléatoire bien conçu, et celui du panel est bien conçu, remplit une condition essentielle: une probabilité connue d'inclusion dans l'échantillon.[1] Ceci dit, dans la pratique, la situation est bien plus compliquée. En outre, les difficultés peuvent s'additionner suivant les modes d'enquêtes, en particulier dans le cas qui nous intéresse ici: un questionnaire écrit, demandant de reconstituer sa biographie, et distribué après trois vagues régulières du panel. Quelles sont les causes de possibles difficultés? Sans être exhaustifs, on peut mentionner les points suivants qui, d'une manière ou d'une autre, peuvent influencer la «probabilité de répondre» et donc introduire un biais:

1. tout le monde n'a pas répondu à la première vague de 1999: même si un taux de réponse de plus de 60 % est excellent en Suisse, même si des contrôles de validité ont amené à comparer population de référence et échantillon de répondant sans constater d'effets notoires, un biais est toujours susceptible d'intervenir, peut-être précisément lié au phénomène étudié;
2. toutes les personnes d'un ménage n'ont pas nécessairement répondu, en particulier, à l'intérieur d'un ménage donné, certaines personnes sont soit

1 Une probabilité égale d'inclusion que l'on retrouve souvent dans les enquêtes auprès des ménages, est une commodité mais en aucun cas une nécessité. D'ailleurs, si la base d'échantillonnage est une liste de ménages et que l'on souhaite interroger des individus, une correction est à faire pour éviter que les individus faisant partie de petits ménages soient proportionnellement trop présents dans l'échantillon au moment de faire une inférence à l'ensemble de la population.

plus difficiles à atteindre, soit plus difficile à convaincre: ceci est source de biais si un tel mécanisme n'est pas aléatoire;

3. les refus et pertes au fur et à mesure des vagues ne sont pas nécessairement non plus aléatoires: qu'il s'agisse de personnes à plus forte mobilité spatiale par exemple ou de répondants peu intéressés par ce type d'exercice;
4. répondre à un questionnaire biographique supplémentaire comme celui utilisé ici peut être une contrainte supplémentaire qui décourage encore plus des répondants faiblement motivé par ce type d'enquête;
5. la difficulté de ce questionnaire dépend de l'expérience passée: une personne âgée aura beaucoup plus d'événements à relater qu'un jeune, ce qui peut aussi induire un côté décourageant;
6. en outre, il s'agit d'un questionnaire écrit, ce qui veut dire que des répondants peu lettrés auront d'autant moins de chances de répondre!

En fait, et heureusement, les distorsions n'apparaissent pas aussi importante que ce à quoi l'on aurait pu s'attendre après cette liste de difficultés potentielles. Certes, la probabilité de répondre a été un peu plus élevée pour les femmes que pour les hommes (55,5 % plutôt que 51 %), plus grande aussi pour les répondants «d'âge moyen» (22 % plutôt que 19,5 % pour les 30-39 ans alors que la différence va en sens inverse pour les 20-29 ans). Le biais le plus important, quoique encore limité, renvoie à la formation: comme il sied à un questionnaire écrit, les formations moyennes et longues assurent un meilleur taux de réponse.

Tableau 1: Caractéristiques des répondants au questionnaire supplémentaire

Niveau de formation	Répondant au questionnaire	Non-répondant au questionnaire
Obligatoire	28,2 %	33,1 %
Apprentissage	51,9 %	48,1 %
Maturité, technicum	18,6 %	13,9 %
Universités, HES	15,2 %	10,3 %
	100 %	100 %
(n)	(4607)	(3928)

Note: vague 1 et 2 croisée avec les répondants au biographique.

Dans l'ensemble c'est donc conforme à ce que l'on pouvait attendre: une sur-représentation, mais relativement faible, des formations les plus longues. Ceci dit, l'analyse des réponses et des étapes du parcours de vie devient possible. Commençons précisément par la formation.

3. La formation

La formation tient une bonne place dans le vie de nos répondants. En moyenne, après un parcours obligatoire jusqu'à 15 ans révolus, les hommes ajoutent 4,5 années de formation et les femmes 3,4. En moyenne aussi la durée de formation post obligatoire s'allonge: moins de 3 ans pour les plus de 60 ans, plus de 4 pour les moins de 40 ans.

Le plus intéressant est sans doute de décomposer ce résultat par génération et par genre car un des enjeux est de savoir si l'écart entre hommes et femmes s'accroît ou diminue. Pour les générations nées après la deuxième guerre mondiale, la durée de formation n'a que peu augmenté pour les hommes alors que la moyenne d'ensemble a bel et bien augmenté: la raison est que les femmes rejoignent aujourd'hui les modes de faire masculin alors que la durée de formation post-obligatoire masculine était près de deux fois plus grande pour les générations les plus âgées.[2]

Notons que même si la Suisse a échappé à la deuxième guerre mondiale, les répondants nés entre 1930 et 1940, de même d'ailleurs dans une certaine mesure que la génération précédente, ont connu une formation relativement plus courte, et ce aussi bien pour les hommes que pour les femmes.

2 En fait, il y a un gain surtout à travers l'université et le bac, c'est-à-dire des formations longues, empruntées de plus en plus souvent par des femmes. Pour l'école obligatoire, il y a encore un léger avantage pour les hommes, qui sont suscpetibles de faire des postformations. Pour les apprentissages, il y a tendance à une différence d'une année au début de l'histoire des générations, différence qui tend elle aussi à disparaître.

Graphique 1: années de formation par âge et génération

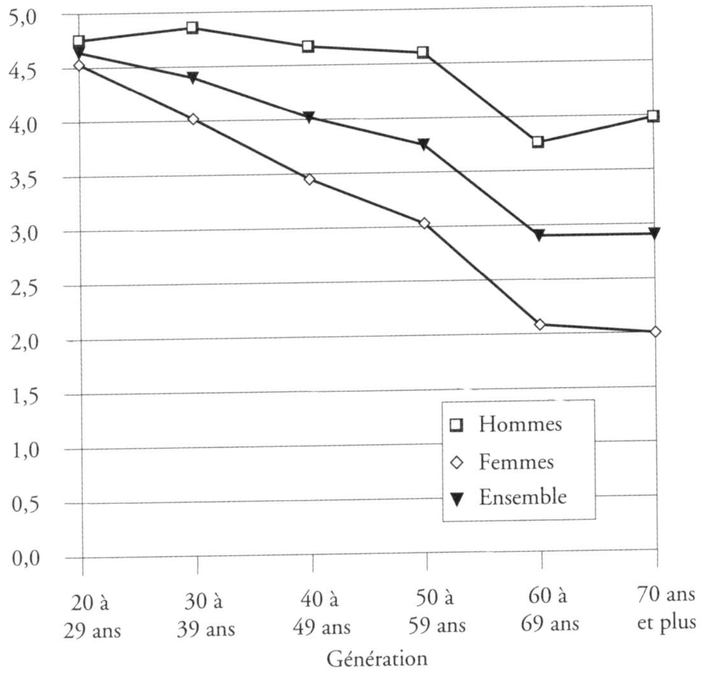

4. Le nombre d'emplois

Le nombre d'emplois que l'on a occupé est bien sûr une donnée de base dès lors que l'on s'intéresse aux parcours professionnels.[3] Dans les graphiques qui suivent, il faut souligner que 850 personnes ont été exclues de l'analyse parce qu'elles n'ont pas répondu aux questions sur les parcours professionnels. Ce chiffre peut paraître important mais dans plus de la moitié des cas (472 pour être précis), il s'agit de répondants âgés de moins de 20 ans qui effectivement n'ont pu encore participer au marché du travail. Et si la limite est mise à 30 ans,

3 Notons que la question même d'une occupation professionnelle peut parfois être interprétée différemment par les répondants. Par exemple, l'apprentissage était certes mentionné comme formation mais parfois aussi comme emploi. Par mesure d'homogénéité nous avons décidé de le compter uniquement comme formation.

Graphique 2: Moyenne du nombre d'emploi par genre et génération

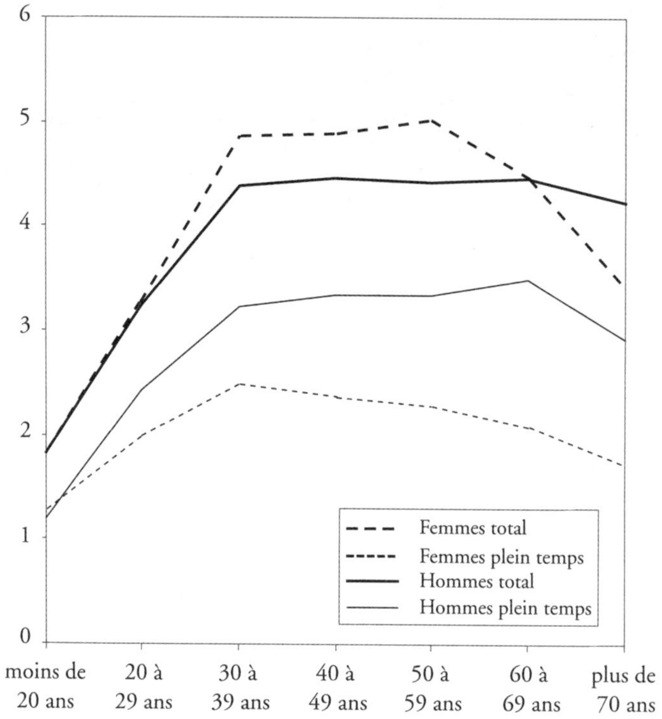

il n'est que 35 hommes et 85 femmes qui n'ont jamais eu d'emploi… ou bien ont esquivé la question.

Le graphique 2 met en exergue deux résultats très intéressants si l'on s'intéresse au total des emplois occupés.

1. D'abord le nombre d'emploi occupé s'accroît très vite pour rester ensuite quasiment constant. Ceci peut s'expliquer aussi bien par une forte mobilité professionnelle pour les plus jeunes et une stabilisation professionnelle pour les plus âgés que par une augmentation de la mobilité professionnelle pour les classes d'âge les plus jeunes.
2. Les femmes ont un nombre supérieur d'emploi. Cela peut s'expliquer par une insertion plus complexe dans le monde du travail, marquée par des interruptions et des reprises. Cette différence est toujours vraie, quel que soit le niveau de formation.

Pour les emplois à plein temps,[4] la différence change bien sûr et les hommes ont un nombre d'emploi nettement plus grand. Il faut souligner que la différence entre les genres s'accroît fortement avec les générations.

5. L'entrée dans la vie active

L'entrée dans la vie active est aussi susceptible d'avoir changée avec les années. A priori on peut postuler que l'allongement des études doit avoir retardé cette entrée.

L'examen de ce graphique montre que ce résultat est vrai mais que l'effet n'est peut être pas aussi fort que ce à quoi l'on aurait pu s'attendre. Ainsi, pour les plus jeunes génération, 20 % avait déjà un travail à 18 ans alors que c'était le cas de 30 % pour les plus âgés. Et même pour les études plus longues: près des trois quarts avaient un emploi à 22 ans et ceci est vrai pour les plus jeunes comme pour les plus âgés.

Et comment cela se différencie-t-il suivant les formation et le genre? L'analyse est ici délicate puisque toutes ces variables sont inter-reliées: par exemple on a vu que la durée de formation est plus longue pour les hommes que pour les femmes, en tous cas pour les générations les plus âgées. Pour simplifier, mentionnons néanmoins qu'un peu plus de femmes que d'hommes travaillent à 20 ans après une formation obligatoire ou un apprentissage, ce qui laisse supposer un complément de formation pour ces derniers ou des formations un peu plus longues. En outre ceci ne semble guère avoir changé suivant les générations. Pour les formations universitaires, il ne semble par contre pas y avoir de différences systématiques suivant les genres, même en changeant l'âge d'entrée au marché du travail.

Le moment de l'entrée sur le marché du travail semble donc assez peu différencié suivant les genres. On sait pourtant que les choses sont fortement susceptibles de changer après. D'où l'idée de s'intéresser à l'ensemble de la carrière professionnelle.

4 La définition d'un emploi à plein temps ou à temps partiel peut toujours être objet de débats. En l'occurrence, nous suivons le questionnaire du PSM qui proposait a) temps plein (occupation à 90-100 %); b) temps partiel (occupation à 50-89 %) et c) moins de 50 %.

Graphique 3: Proportion de répondants ayant un emploi aux âges de 16, 18, 20, 22, 24 et 26 ans respectivement

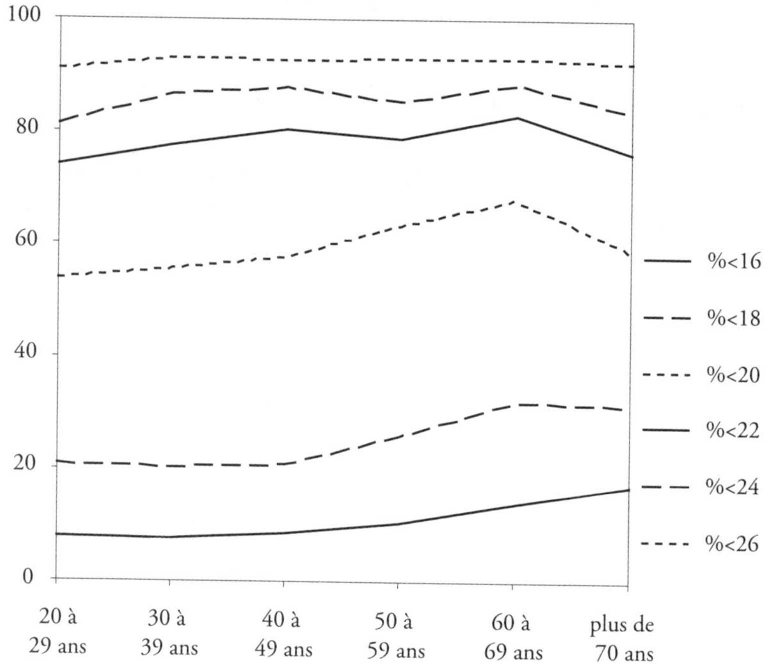

6. Des profils de carrière?[5]

A partir de là, il est tentant de construire une typologie des profils de carrière. Les ingrédients sont là, et faciles à conceptualiser: chaque année, un répondant peut être en formation, homme ou femme au foyer, empêché de participer au marché du travail pour cause de maladie ou de chômage, travaillant sur ce marché à plein temps ou à temps partiel, être déjà à la retraite, voire encore se trouver dans une autre situation, peu ou mal définie.[6]

5 L'analyse sur le plein temps ne change quasiment pas ces résultats ce qui veut dire aussi que le premier emploi est souvent à plein temps, les aménagements se produisant plus tard dans la carrière.

6 Ce type d'analyse n'est cependant pas facile, et ce beaucoup plus pour des raisons conceptuelles et logiques que statistiques. Certes il est facile de ne pas tenir compte d'un individu

A priori, on pourrait bien sûr s'imaginer des modèles et attribuer chaque individu à un tel «profil idéal» en fonction de son propre parcours de vie. Indépendamment des difficultés propres à une telle démarche, la tendance peut être grande de «forcer» l'attribution de profils atypiques dans un moule dominant. Dans ce sens, une typologie empirique, plus inductive, laisse davantage de places à ce type de découverte.

Une telle typologie pose une double difficulté: comment calculer une distance entre deux situations une année donnée et comment traiter des parcours qui peuvent se reproduire avec des décalages ou des inversions? La première question peut être résolue en établissant une matrice de coûts décrivant le passage d'un état à l'autre, partant par exemple de l'idée qu'il est moins coûteux pour un individu de passer d'un emploi à temps partiel à un emploi à plein temps que de stopper toute activité rémunérée pour se consacrer uniquement au foyer familial.[7]

La deuxième se résout à l'aide d'une technique particulière pour l'analyse de séquences: «l'optimal matching». L'idée de cette technique, initialement pensée pour décrire les séquences d'ADN, est de compter les transformations nécessaires pour passer d'une séquence à l'autre (Abbott and Hrycak 1990).

Sur cette matrice de distance, une analyse typologique peut être effectuée, regroupant petit à petit tous les cas jusqu'à ne conserver que quelques groupes significatifs.[8]

---

qui a complètement omis de répondre à une partie du questionnaire. Mais, par exemple, comment traiter les individus pour qui un événement ne s'est pas encore produit? Nous avons considéré ici les seuls individus de plus de 30 ans pour être sûr qu'une partie au moins de ce parcours ait été réalisée.
Comment traiter aussi les questionnaires qui «omettent» une période ou oublient d'en définir la caractéristique? Autre exemple, l'apprentissage doit-il être considéré comme emploi ou formation alors même qu'il peut être effectué dans un contexte scolaire ou professionnel. Dans ce dernier cas nous l'avons systématiquement considéré comme période de formation mais dans d'autres cas, une catégorie «indéfinie» a dû être conservée.

7 En l'occurrence, nous avons repris la matrice présentée dans Widmer, Eric, René Levy, Alexandre Pollien, Raphaël Hammer, and Jacques-Antoine Gauthier. 2003. «Between Standardisation, Individualisation and Gendering: An Analysis of Personal Life Courses in Switzerland» *Swiss Journal of Sociology* 29: 35-65.

8 Utilisation de l'analyse typologique hiérarchique qui ne remet jamais en cause les regroupements antérieurs. Méthode de Ward en SPSS.

Cette séquence de techniques est relativement bien établie aujourd'hui[9] même si, comme toute approche en analyse des données, elle pose des difficultés qui lui sont propres.[10] Mais elle a aussi été utilisée récemment sur un jeu de données proche (Widmer et al. 2003) et la mise en perspective de ces deux analyses n'est sans doute pas sans intérêt.

Une analyse simplifiée permet de dégager trois grands types.

Le premier modèle (39 %) est celui de l'activité professionnelle à plein temps: si l'on excepte la catégorie «au foyer» qui réapparaît pour les répondants les plus âgés et qui est lié au regroupement fort des types, ce modèle renvoie à une conception de la vie où le travail rémunéré est au centre.

Graphique 4: Parcours de type 1: «plein temps»

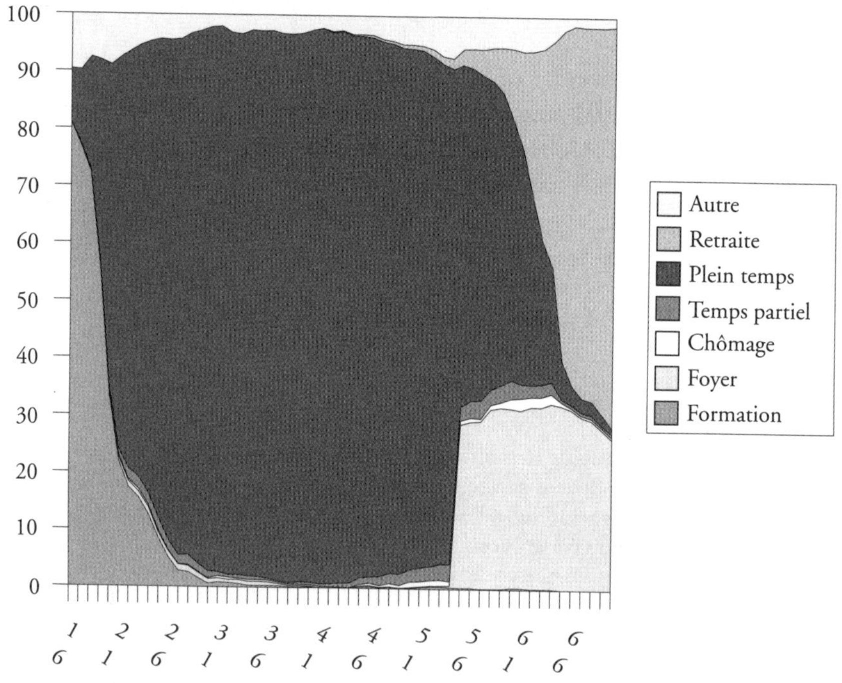

9 Utilisation par exemple du programme TDA. Cf. notamment Blossfeld, Peter, and Görz Rohwer. 1995. *Techniques of Event History Modelling: New approaches in Causal Analysis.* Hillsdale: Lawrence Erlbaum.

10 L'essentiel est bien sûr ici la question de la détermination du nombre de types à retenir pour l'interprétation.

Le deuxième modèle (45 % des répondants classés) montre lui aussi une insertion forte dans le monde professionnel, mais plutôt sous l'angle du temps partiel, après une première période à plein temps.

Graphique 5: Parcours de type 2: «temps partiel»

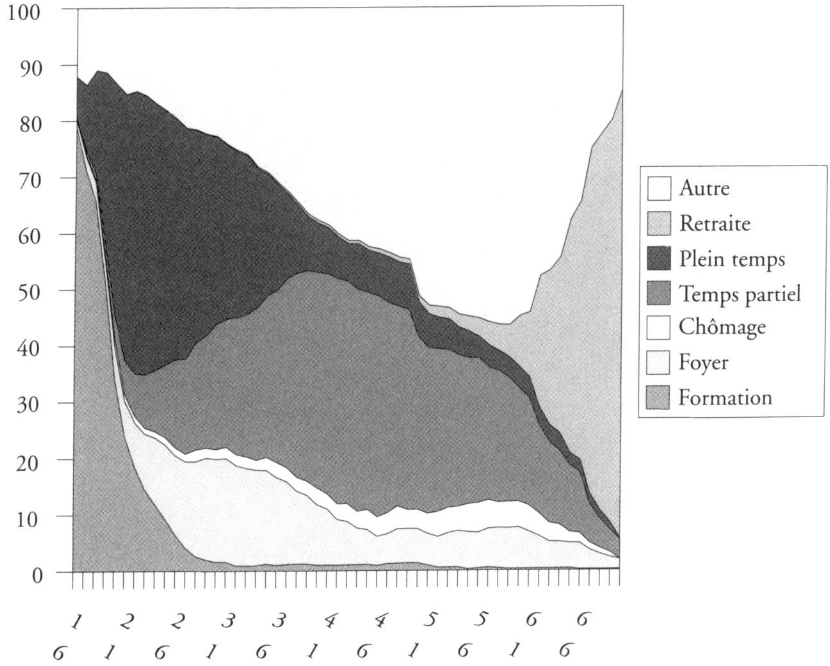

Le troisième (16 %) peut aussi se décrire suivant une forme canonique: après une phase initiale consacrée au travail, il y a un repli sur la sphère domestique.

Graphique 6: Parcours de type 3: «au foyer»

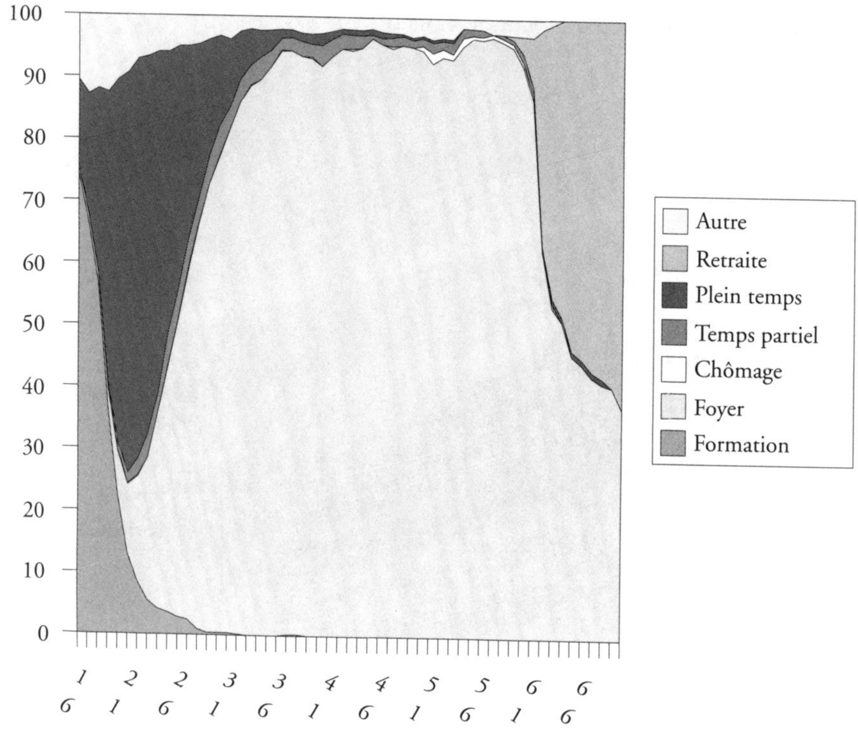

Ces trois profils peuvent se décrire suivant les variables retenues dans l'ensemble de l'analyse: genre, formation et âge.

Tableau 2: Profil de carrière suivant le genre

	Plein temps	Temps partiel	Au foyer	
Hommes	66,8 %	32,6 %	0,6 %	100 % 1555
Femmes	13,8	56,7	29,5	1761
Total	38,6 %	45,4 %	16,0 %	

Autrement dit, les hommes ne choisissent qu'exceptionnellement le modèle «au foyer» et investissent au contraire plutôt des modèles où le plein temps est la règle. Ce résultat n'a rien d'extraordinaire en soi, si ce n'est peut-être la force de la relation.

Tableau 3: Profils de carrière suivant la formation

2	Plein temps	Temps partiel	Au foyer	
Obligatoire	25,6	46,7	27,7	100 %
Apprentissage	38,0	44,4	17,6	100 %
Maturité	46,1	42,3	11,6	100 %
Uni, HES	44,5	48,8	6,7	100 %

Tout en sachant qu'il y a une certaine corrélation entre formation et genre, il est quand même frappant de voir que plus la formation est longue et exigeante, plus la probabilité est grande de la voir rentabilisée en gardant un contact étroit avec le marché du travail.

Tableau 4: Profils de carrière suivant les générations

	Plein temps	Temps partiel	Au foyer	
Moins de 39 ans	18,7	63,9	17,4	100 %
40 à 49	46,0	37,8	16,2	100 %
50 à 59	47,8	40,4	11,8	100 %
60 à 69	50,8	32,6	16,6	100 %
70 ans et plus	42,9	36,7	20,4	100 %

Dans ce dernier cas, il est difficile de voir un effet qui laisserait supposer un changement de modèle. Autrement dit, ce découpage, simplifié à l'extrême, garderait une garnde part de sa pertinence.[11]

11 En fait, l'intérêt de l'analyse, n'est probablement pas tant dans les cas extrêmes que dans les cas intermédiaires qu'est capable de dégager la typologie. La première solution que nous avons retenue dégageait huit types. L'espace qui nous est attribué ici nous interdit cependant ce type de développement.

7. Et la mobilité?

La mesure de la mobilité professionnelle est complexe. Dans le cas particulier, elle l'est d'autant plus que nous avons une seule indication: la profession occupée. En d'autres termes, nous n'avons aucune indication de la position hiérarchique. Cela est d'autant plus crucial à considérer qu'une bonne partie des promotions se font à l'intérieur d'une profession donnée, dont l'intitulé peut rester alors même que les responsabilités changent.[12]

La profession a été recodée suivant l'échelle CAMSIS (Bergman and Joye 2001), (Bergman et al. 2002) qui attribue à chaque individu une note décrivant sa position sociale, sur une échelle comprise entre 0 et 100.

Tableau 5: Moyenne des échelles CAMSIS suivant l'âge et la génération

Age Génération	Entre 20 et 30 ans	Entre 30 et 40 ans	Entre 40 et 50 ans	Entre 50 et 60 ans	Plus de 60 ans
Nés après 1970	51,77				
Nés entre 1960 et 1970	51,84	52,66			
Nés entre 1950 et 1960	53,12	53,08	52,75		
Nés entre 1940 et 1950	53,03	54,47	54,26	54,61	
Nés entre 1930 et 1940	50,04	51,91	52,77	52,86	52,49
Nés avant 1930	49,92	52,64	53,73	54,66	54,10
Total	52,01	53,02	53,31	54,00	53,07

Les différences sont faibles en valeur absolue mais néanmoins significatives par le sens de leur variation et la manière dont elles se disposent.

Ce tableau peut se lire dans deux sens.

- A un âge donné, peut-on détecter une différence suivant les générations? A priori, on pourrait voir que la position sociale entre vingt et trente ans était légèrement meilleur dans les années soixante-dix que dans les années cinquante ou aujourd'hui. Cet effet se retrouve, quoique moins fortement, en s'interrogeant sur la position sociale entre trente et quarante ans.

12 En outre, la profession a été déclarée spontanément par l'enquêté. La précision de cette déclaration peut donc varier suivant son idiosyncrasie et la manière dont il interprète les consignes. Le résultat est donc moins fortement standardisé que si c'est un enquêteur expérimenté qui conduit l'entretien.

- Peut-on voir une mobilité ascendante à l'intérieur de la carrière professionnelle? Dans ce cas, la lecture se fait, pour chaque génération, en suivant les lignes du tableau. On s'aperçoit alors, que cet outil de mesure permet effectivement de distinguer une progression sociale à l'intérieur des carrières mais que celle-ci reste faible. En outre, elle semble plus forte pour les générations les plus âgées que pour les plus jeunes. Autrement dit encore le potentiel de mobilité ascendante à l'intérieur d'une carrière serait en train de diminuer.

Il serait utile de poursuivre l'analyse en croisant parcours de vie, genre, formation et position sociale, et ce suivant les différentes générations que nous avons distinguées. En même temps, une extrême prudence s'impose car un tel modèle d'analyse amène nos données à leur limite et c'est donc volontairement que nous ne reproduisons pas ici les tableaux détaillées. En simplifiant, deux résultats méritent néanmoins d'être mentionnés:

- La moyenne des positions sociales, telles que mesurée par l'échelle Camsis, augmente plus fortement dans les carrières où le plein-temps domine que dans celles où il s'agit du temps partiel.
- A l'inverse les carrières caractérisées par les «temps partiels» se situent un peu plus haut selon l'échelle Camsis, en tous cas au début de la vie active. Ceci s'explique aussi par le fait que ces parcours, majoritairement féminins, voient du coup leur score Camsis valorisé.[13]

8. Conclusion

Le schéma d'analyse que nous avons suivi ici est volontairement resté très descriptif: il s'agissait de faire un portrait simple des parcours d'emploi en Suisse. Ceci dit, un certain nombre de conclusions apparaissent avec force.

Il faut d'abord souligner que des indicateurs très simples permettent effectivement de suivre les changements que différentes générations ont connus

13 Ceci peut se comprendre en se souvenant des bases de la construction de Camsis: la proximité entre professions à l'intérieur des couples. Or, traditionnellement, les femmes choisissent un partenaire dont le statut est égal ou supérieur au leur tandis que les hommes se retrouvent le plus souvent dans la configuration inverse. Dès lors, une profession occupée par une femme sera plus valorisée que la même occupée par un homme.

dans leur rapport au travail. Dans ce sens, l'analyse des parcours de vie introduit bien une dimension supplémentaire à l'étude des positions sociales. Nous espérons que cet article, qui se situe dans une perspective ouverte par l'article de (Widmer et al. 2003), mette correctement en exergue l'intérêt de ce type d'analyse.

La dimension de genre est également très discriminante. Certes, les différences changent en fonction du temps, certes un investissement important dans la formation tend à être valorisé dans le monde du travail; les parcours de vie montrent toutefois des différences extrêmement marquées suivant les genres.

Enfin, les résultats par rapport à la mobilité sociale méritent aussi d'être soulignés. Certes les différences ne sont pas extrêmes mais elles montrent en tous cas que l'hypothèse d'une croissance linéaire du statut n'est plus vrai pour les générations les plus jeunes. En termes de «destin des générations» et des attentes qui peuvent se créer au cours d'une carrière professionnelle, un tel résultat n'est sans doute pas sans conséquences sociales.

9. Références

Abbott, Andrew, and Alexandra Hrycak. 1990. «Measuring Resemblance in Sequence Data: An Optimal Matching Analysis of Musicians' Careers.» *American Journal of Sociology* 96: 144-185.

Bergman, Manfred Max, and Dominique Joye. 2001. «Comparing Social Stratifications Schemas: CAMSIS, CSP-CH, Goldthorpe, ISCO-88, Treiman, and Wright.» *Cambridge Studies in Social Research* 9: 1-37.

Bergman, Manfred Max, Paul Lambert, Kenneth Prandy, and Dominique Joye. 2002. «Theorization, Construction and Validation of a Social Stratification Scale: Cambridge Social Interaction and Stratification Scale (CAMSIS) for Switzerland.» *Swiss Journal of Sociology* 28: 7-25.

Blossfeld, Peter, and Görz Rohwer. 1995. *Techniques of Event History Modelling: New approaches in Causal Analysis.* Hillsdale: Lawrence Erlbaum.

Chauvel, Louis. 1998. *Le destin des générations. Structure sociale et cohortes en France au XXe siècle.* Paris: PUF.

Levy, Rene, Dominique Joye, Olivier Guye, and Vincent Kaufmann. 1997. *Tous égaux? De la stratification aux représentations.* Zurich: Seismo.

Widmer, Eric, René Levy, Alexandre Pollien, Raphaël Hammer, and Jacques-Antoine Gauthier. 2003. «Between Standardisation, Individualisation and Gendering: An Analysis of Personal Life Courses in Switzerland.» *Swiss Journal of Sociology* 29: 35-65.

2. Vie familiale, professionnelle et sociale
Familie, Arbeit und soziale Beziehungen

L'Implication dans les champs domestique et professionnel selon les phases de la vie familiale*

Eric Widmer, René Levy et Jacques-Antoine Gauthier

Une critique souvent faite aux recherches sociologiques portant sur la famille concerne leur *statisme*. En raison de recherches qui n'incluent le plus souvent – pour des raisons de commodité et de contrôle des variables – qu'un âge de la vie, on a pu confondre une famille avec son mode de fonctionnement tel que saisi lors d'une observation unique, sans tenir compte du fait qu'au cours de son existence ce groupe se structure différemment, en raison notamment de l'âge des enfants. Ces changements structurels, associés au parcours de vie, ont des conséquences pour le mode de fonctionnement familial qui ont souvent été ignorées.

L'attention de la recherche à ce problème a été alimentée par deux sources. D'une part, la démographie sociale a mis en évidence le fait que les ressources familiales – en particulier le revenu familial disponible par membre – varient au long du parcours de vie, composant ainsi une structure d'opportunités spécifique à chaque âge (cf. par exemple, Lansing et Kish, 1957; Glick, 1947; 1955; 1977). D'autre part, la perspective du «développement familial» inspirée de la psychologie du développement (Havighurst, 1948), étudie les tâches prioritaires que toute famille, un peu à l'instar des individus, doit affronter, à divers moments de son existence, pour garantir sa pérennité et son adaptation au contexte environnant. Ainsi en va-t-il par exemple de l'établissement des

* Cette contribution fait partie de l'ouvrage collectif *Vivre en Suisse 1999-2000* (Erwin Zimmermann et Robin Tillmann (éds), Editions Peter Lang, Berne (2004)). Les analyses et résultats se basent sur les deux premières vagues de l'enquête longitudinale Vivre en Suisse réalisée auprès de 6 335 personnes interviewées en 1999 et 2000. La collecte des données, effectuée par M. I. S. Trend sous la responsabilité du Panel suisse de ménages de l'Université de Neuchâtel, a été financée par le PP Demain la Suisse du Fonds national suisse de la recherche scientifique (Subsides No. 5004-53205 / 5004-57894 / 5004-67304). Des informations complémentaires peuvent être obtenues sur le site www.swisspanel.ch

rôles conjugaux et parentaux et de la transition vers le *«empty nest*[1]*»*. Elle a également montré comment les genres de communication et de partage, ou encore le niveau de conflit, pouvaient dépendre de la complexité des rôles (conjugaux, parentaux, fraternels, etc.) en présence (cf. Aldous, 1996, pour une synthèse).

Or nombre d'études ont révélé que cette dynamique structurelle et fonctionnelle des couples est scandée par la sexuation des processus sociaux (qu'il s'agisse de la famille ou d'autres sphères de la vie sociale). A chaque changement important de l'organisation de la famille – l'entrée en couple et la formation du ménage, le mariage, la première naissance, la scolarisation du premier enfant, la sortie du premier enfant du système scolaire, le départ des enfants du ménage parental, la retraite des conjoints de la vie professionnelle – cette sexuation intervient, mettant en jeu une dialectique entre tâches familiales et contraintes institutionnelles (acquis de socialisation, exigences des professions, rythmes et coutumes des établissement scolaires, etc.). Les parcours de vie des deux conjoints entrent ainsi en résonance – c'est-à-dire s'influencent réciproquement – en réponse aux contraintes associées à chaque phase familiale, et cela quelle que soit l'autonomie acquise par les conjoints dans la constitution et la gestion du groupe familial (Berger et Kellner, 1988). C'est le principe des «vies liées» (Elder, 1974) qui trouve ici une application.

Le Panel suisse des ménages, par la richesse de ses indicateurs consacrés à la famille et à l'activité professionnelle, et par sa périodicité annuelle, permet de rendre compte, dans le cas helvétique, de la manière dont des changements structurels de la famille, associés au parcours de vie, affectent son fonctionnement interne. Par leur dimension longitudinale, ces données permettent de dépasser certaines des limites associées aux recherches synchroniques portant sur la famille. Nous commencerons par présenter brièvement la logique de constitution des phases familiales, dont nous décrirons ensuite l'importance statistique. Puis, nous estimerons leurs effets sur le fonctionnement conjugal, en nous centrant sur la répartition du travail domestique et de l'activité professionnelle dans le couple. Les résultats seront mis en perspective, à la lumière de l'hypothèse des statuts-maîtres sexués (Krüger et Levy, 2000 et 2001, Widmer, Kellerhals et Levy, 2003).

1 Littéralement «nid vide», période qui suit le départ du dernier enfant du domicile parental.

Les phases de la vie familiale dans les perspectives métastatique et longitudinale

Si nombre d'études portant sur la famille pèchent par leur statisme, la notion de phase de la vie familiale a permis d'introduire une perspective longitudinale dans des analyses de données synchroniques (pour la Suisse, Held et Levy 1974, Levy 1977, Levy et al. 1997, Widmer, Kellerhals et Levy, 2003), démarche à la fois problématique et fertile que nous avons appelée «métastatique». Sa valeur heuristique réside, en l'absence de données longitudinales, dans la possibilité de produire des résultats que l'on peut interpréter dans le sens diachronique. Pour résumé, il s'agit de classer les couples dans des phases de leur biographie familiale différentes et de considérer les associations entre ces phases et des aspects centraux du fonctionnement familial en partant d'une observation unique, non répétée dans le temps. La typologie que nous avons utilisée antérieurement (Widmer, Kellerhals et Levy, 2003; Krüger et Levy, 2001; Levy et al., 1997) tient compte de la présence d'enfants dans le ménage ou la famille, et de leur âge. Elle distingue six modalités: les couples sans enfants mais qui sont assez jeunes pour en avoir à l'avenir[2], que l'on a dénommé «couples pré-enfants», les familles avec enfants en âge pré-scolaire[3], avec enfants d'âge scolaire, avec enfants d'âge post-scolaire, les couples dont les enfants ont quitté le ménage, et les couples sans enfants[4], qui ne sont pas dans une phase spécifique des parcours familiaux standards. La figure 1 explicite la logique de construction des phases de la vie familiale.

Dans d'autres publications (Levy et al., 1997; Widmer, Kellerhals et Levy, 2003), nous avons analysé l'effet de l'inscription dans une phase du parcours de vie familial sur le fonctionnement conjugal dans cette perspective «métastatique». L'effet des phases était fort, notamment sur la division du travail domestique et sur le taux d'activité professionnelle des femmes. Les modèles de régulation souples et relativement égalitaires dans la répartition des rôles fonctionnels et relationnels fléchissent considérablement dans la phase pré-scolaire pour ne jamais retrouver la même représentativité statistique que dans la phase

2 Cette limite a été fixée à l'âge de 36 ans pour la femme, sur la base de l'enquête sur les couples en Suisse (Widmer, Kellerhals et Levy, 2003).

3 Pour les couples avec plusieurs enfants, c'est l'âge du plus jeune qui a été pris en compte.

4 Les couples sans enfants se distinguent des couples pré-enfants par l'âge de la femme, de plus de 36 ans dans leur cas.

Figure 1: Construction de la variable des phases familiales

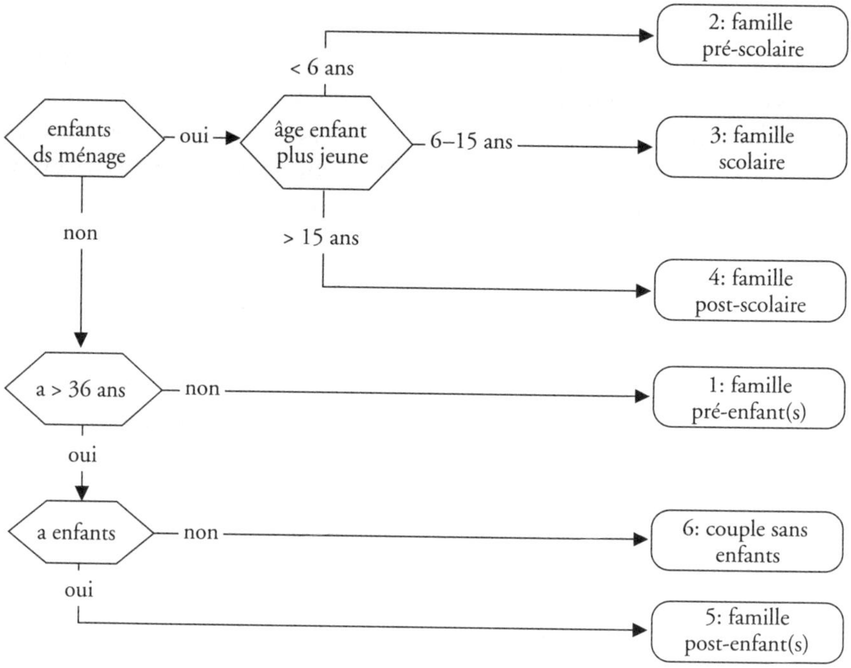

pré-enfant, même dans la phase post-enfant. Ces résultats suggéraient alors que l'arrivée du premier enfant coïncide avec la mise en place de styles d'interactions conjugales très sexués et relativement peu sensibles aux transitions ultérieures.

Cette perspective «métastatique» reste cependant quelque peu spéculative car il n'est pas possible de «créer» des informations «datées», donc temporalisées, quand elles ne le sont pas au départ. Les couples n'étant pas réinterviewés, les différences entre phases ne peuvent pas avec une entière certitude être attribuées à des effets de transition: un effet de cohorte peut toujours être postulé. Les données du Panel suisse des ménages apportent de ces points de vue un complément précieux puisqu'elles permettent une exploration longitudinale de cette même problématique. Pour les analyses qui suivent, nous nous limitons aux 2884[5] ménages du Panel ayant inclu le même couple (marié ou

5 Les données ont été pondérées au niveau des ménages, de manière à conserver la représentativité de l'échantillon pour l'année 2000.

concubin), avec ou sans enfants, tant en 1999 qu'en 2000[6]. Non seulement nous pourrons, en utilisant les deux premières vagues du Panel, cerner l'effet des phases, mais également, ce que les données métastatiques ne permettaient pas de faire (Widmer, Kellerhals et Levy, 2003), saisir l'effet des transitions entre les phases[7].

Combien de couples interviewés dans le Panel appartiennent-ils alors à l'une ou l'autre de ces phases, et combien ont-ils été, entre 1999 et 2000, en transition entre elles? [8] Les couples se répartissent assez uniformément entre les quatre phases retenues: 9 % des couples sont dans la phase pré-enfant, 20 % dans la phase pré-scolaire, 21 % dans la phase scolaire, 15 % dans la phase post-scolaire et 26 % dans la phase post-enfant, les différences tenant à la longueur différente des phases. Cette répartition reproduit presque exactement celle que nous avait révélée notre enquête sur les couples résidant en Suisse, dont les conjoints étaient âgés de 20 à 70 ans (Widmer, Kellerhals et Levy, 2003).

Sur l'ensemble, 7 % des couples ont passé dans une nouvelle phase entre 1999 et 2000. On peut donc estimer qu'un couple sur quinze connaît un changement majeur dans son parcours durant chaque année civile, ce qui est loin d'être négligeable. Si l'on rapporte les couples en transition non pas au total mais à leur phase d'origine, on constate que 12 % des familles pré-enfants en 1999 sont devenues pré-scolaires en 2000; 14 % des familles pré-scolaires sont passées à la phase scolaire en 2000; 10 % sont passées de la phase scolaire à la phase post-scolaire et 6 % de la phase post-scolaire à la phase post-enfants. Les cas où l'ordre des phases n'est pas respecté sont extrêmement rares. En effet, seuls 1,5 % des couples du sous-échantillon ont, durant l'année considérée, soit sauté une ou plusieurs étapes, soit sont revenus à une étape antérieure. Le

6 Cela représente environ 60 % des 5074 ménages constituant la base du Panel en 1999, parmi lesquels 30 % sont des ménages d'une seule personne. Le 10 % restant concerne des ménages dans lesquels une mise en couple ou une séparation a eu lieu ou pour lesquels les données sont incomplètes.

7 Il en découle que ces analyses partagent certaines des limites des études antérieures: elles ne considèrent pas, en particulier, les phases familiales associées au divorce et au remariage, qui produisent des effets de remise en cycle (Aldous, 1996) particulièrement intéressants mais complexes à cerner et qui seront l'objet d'analyses ultérieures.

8 Les effectifs des catégories de personnes ayant vécu une transition entre 1999 et 2000 sont parfois assez faibles, ce qui invite à une certaine prudence lors de l'interprétation de certains résultats.

Figure 2: Transitions et phases de la vie familiale (en %). Situation lors de la deuxième vague (N = 2884 ménages)

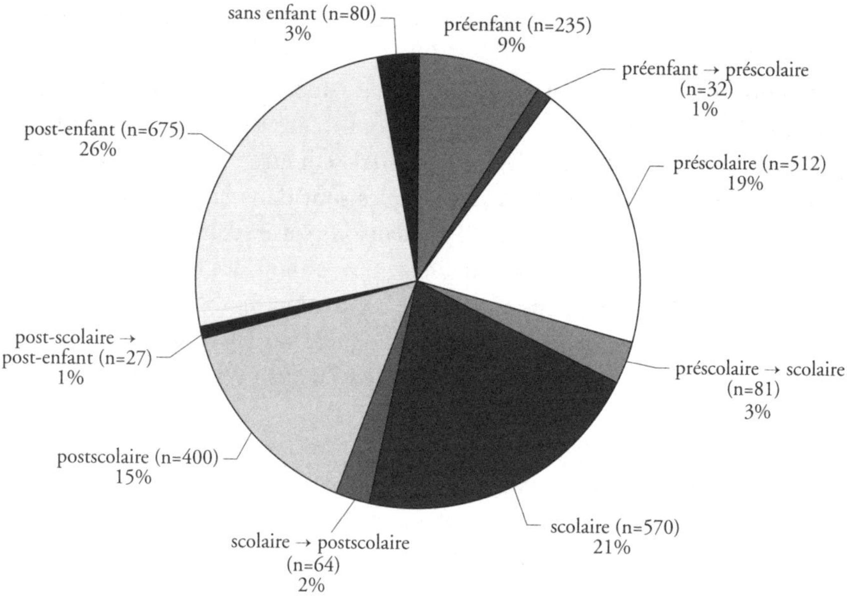

parcours de vie familial des couples «intacts[9]», avec ou sans enfants est donc bien décrit par cette catégorisation relativement linéaire.

Phases de la vie familiale et insertion dans le champ familial

Les phases de la vie familiale font-elles une différence quant à l'organisation des tâches domestiques au sein de la famille? Une première manière de voir les chose est de considérer le nombre d'heures de travail domestique effectuées par l'homme et la femme en fonction de la phase de la vie familiale[10].

9 C'est-à-dire ceux n'ayant pas été rompus par un divorce ou un veuvage entre les deux années d'observation.

10 L'intitulé de la question est le suivant: «Combien d'heures en moyenne consacrez-vous au travail domestique (laver, cuisiner, nettoyer) une semaine ordinaire? (Sans compter la prise en charge des enfants).»

Figure 3: Nombre d'heures de travail domestique hebdomadaires, selon la phase de la vie familiale et le sexe. Situation lors de la deuxième vague (N = 2884 ménages)

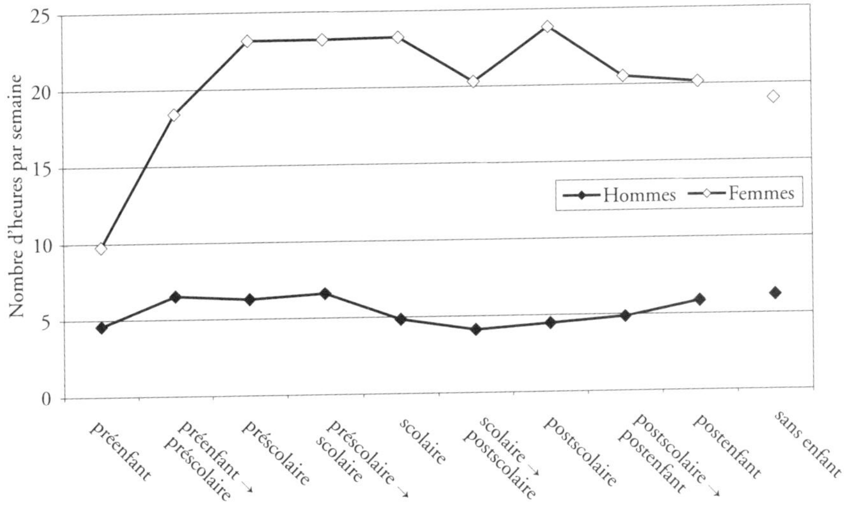

Partant d'une situation d'amblée inégalitaire dans la phase pré-enfant (où la femme en fait déjà deux fois plus que l'homme), la transition à la parentalité est accompagnée d'un renforcement considérable du modèle sexué de division des tâches domestiques. Les phases pré-scolaire, scolaire et post-scolaire sont effet caractérisées par une implication quatre fois plus importante de la femme que de l'homme dans les tâches domestiques. C'est seulement dans la transition à la phase post-enfants, quand les enfants quittent le domicile parental, que la tendance s'inverse, la division du travail domestique restant tout de même, dans ce dernier cas, très fortement inégalitaire.

Une autre manière de voir les choses est de considérer l'apport relatif au travail domestique des deux conjoints en fonction de la phase familiale, c'est-à-dire, la proportion des tâches faite par l'un et par l'autre. On peut alors comparer les différentes transitions du point de vue du nombre d'heures de travail domestique en moins ou en plus qu'elle implique pour l'homme et la femme. On ne considère, dans la figure suivante, que les couples ayant été en

Figure 4: Variation du nombre d'heures de travail domestique hebdomadaires consécutive à chaque transition d'une phase familiale à une autre, selon le sexe. Comparaison entre la première et la deuxième vague (N = 2884 ménages)

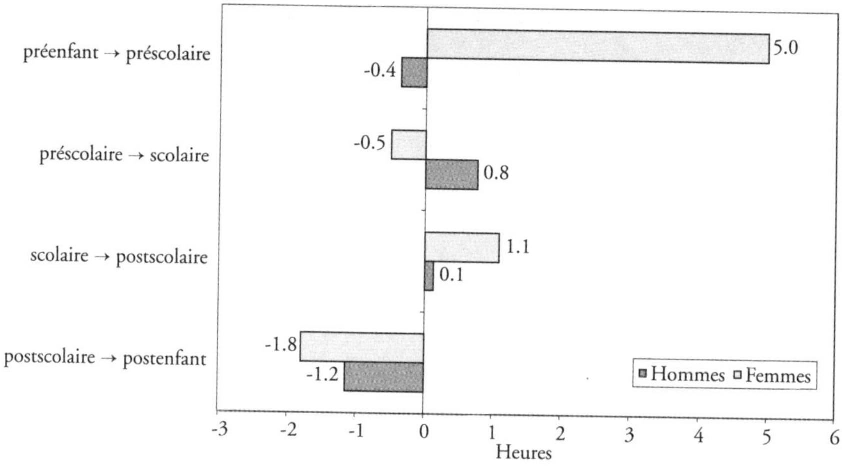

transition entre deux phases durant la période d'observation, de manière à bien saisir l'effet desdites transitions[11].

La transition de la phase pré-enfant à la phase pré-scolaire est accompagnée d'une augmentation de cinq heures, en moyenne du travail domestique féminin, contre une diminution d'une demi-heure du travail domestique masculin. Les deux transitions suivantes sont accompagnées d'ajustements modestes. Ce n'est que lorsque les enfants quittent le domicile parental, qu'une diminution certes secondaire mais significative (une heure par semaine) a lieu. La venue du premier enfant s'accompagne donc d'une transformation assez radicale de la division du travail domestique, également perceptible si l'on considère

11 La figure 3 présente les données de la deuxième vague seulement et compare le nombre d'heures de travail domestique hebdomadaire réalisé en moyenne par les conjoints dans chaque phase (différence entre les moyennes), alors que la figure 4 calcule pour chaque individu ayant vécu une transition la différence du nombre d'heures de travail domestiques hebdomadaires entre la première et la deuxième vague (moyenne des différences).

Figure 5: Proportion du travail domestique fait par la femme (en pourcentage du nombre d'heures de travail domestique fait par le couple). Situation lors de la deuxième vague (N = 2884 ménages)

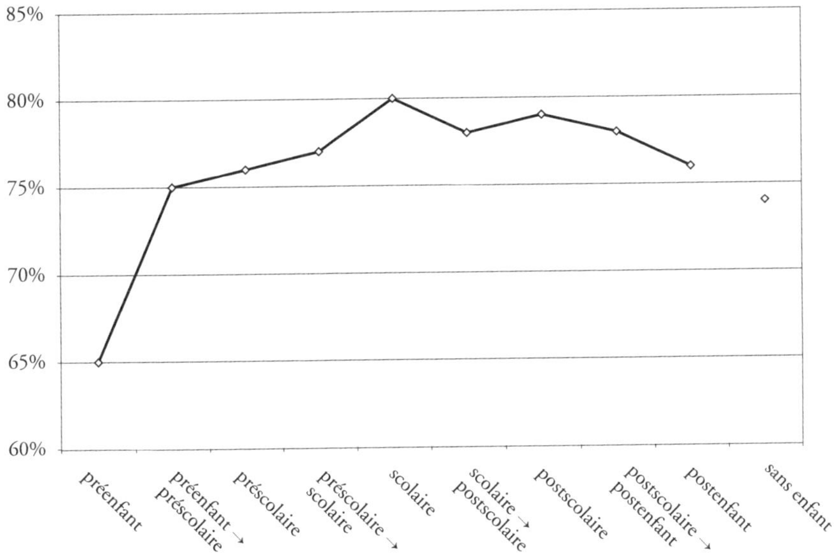

la proportion de travail domestique incombant à la femme, par rapport au volume de travail domestique total assumé par le couple.

La transition de la phase pré-enfant à la phase enfant pré-scolaire est décisive quant à la mise en place du modèle sexué de division du travail domestique. Alors que la phase pré-enfant voit les hommes s'investir pour en moyenne un tiers du travail domestique à faire, les autres phases les voient réduire substantiellement leurs contributions. Dans les familles avec enfants en âge scolaire, 80 % du temps de travail domestique est fait par les femmes. Les phases de la vie familiale font donc une réelle différence pour la division du travail dans le couple. La transition de la phase pré-enfant à la phase pré-scolaire, en particulier, crée des modes d'organisation familiale beaucoup plus sexués. Les modèles mis en place à cette occasion ont une forte résistance et l'affaiblissement des contraintes associées aux enfants (dans les phases post-scolaires et post-enfants) ne permet pas un hypothétique retour en arrière, vers des modèles plus égalitaires, moins différenciés.

Les variations dans la sphère professionnelle et leur impact sur les variations dans la sphère domestique

Les variations de l'implication des hommes et des femmes dans la sphère domestique selon la phase de la vie familiale considérée trouvent-elles leur pendant dans des variations de l'implication des conjoints dans la sphère professionnelle? Le graphique suivant présente les taux moyens d'activité professionnelle des hommes et des femmes (où un emploi à plein-temps correspond à 100 %). Dans les couples pré-enfants, c'est le modèle de la double participation professionnelle à plein temps qui domine très nettement, avec une différence minime entre les taux d'activité de l'homme et de la femme. Avec l'arrivée du premier enfant, le taux d'activité féminin moyen baisse considérablement dans l'année de transition pour se stabiliser ensuite, dans les familles pré-scolaires à environ 20 %. Le taux d'activité féminin augmente ensuite quelque peu mais ne dépasse jamais la limite des 40 %.

Il n'existe rien de tel pour les hommes. Jusqu'à la phase post-scolaire, en effet, leur taux d'activité professionnelle est très proche du 100 %. La transition de la phase pré-enfant à la phase pré-scolaire ne s'accompagne pas, contrairement à ce qui se passe pour les femmes, d'une diminution drastique de leur taux d'activité. Finalement, la participation professionnelle des hommes varie uniquement en fonction de leur âge «institutionnel» – fin de la formation et mise à la retraite –, alors que celle des femmes est très directement fonction des phases de la vie familiale[12].

On fait le même constat si l'on considère la part du revenu conjugal apporté par l'homme et la femme. A nouveau, la transition de la phase pré-enfant à la phase pré-scolaire génère un profond changement dans les contributions comparées des deux conjoints.

Alors que les femmes dans la phase pré-enfant contribuent pour près de la moitié du revenu du couple, ce taux décline dans la transition à la parentalité pour se stabiliser, dans les couples ayant eu des enfants, au quart du revenu conjugal. Dans les faits, la timide augmentation de leur contribution relative

12 Il faut rappeler ici que la perspective métastatique ne permet pas de mesurer d'éventuels effets de cohorte. On ne peut pas exclure qu'une partie au moins des variations observées est attribuable à des modèles culturels du fonctionnement conjugal propres à des périodes historiques particulières. Les effets à long terme de l'accroissement de la participation des femmes au marché du travail ne sont pas non plus visibles ici.

Figure 6: Taux d'activité professionnelle selon la phase de la vie familiale et le sexe. Situation lors de la deuxième vague (N = 2884 ménages)

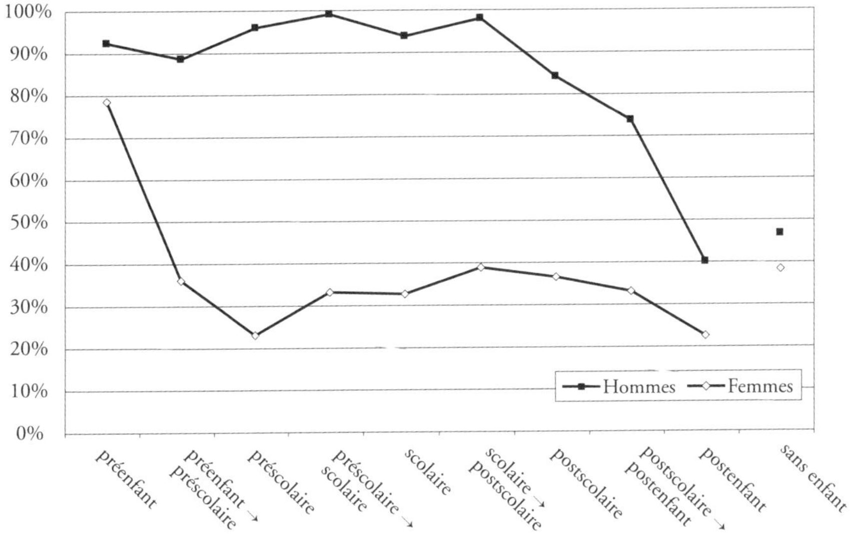

Figure 7: Proportion du revenu conjugal amené par la femme (en pourcentage du revenu conjugal total). Situation lors de la deuxième vague (N = 2884 ménages)

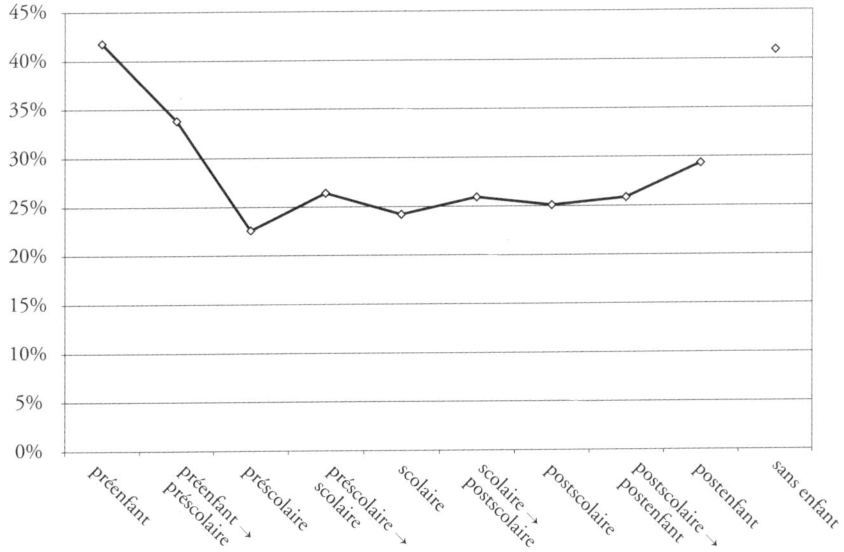

dans la phase post-enfant est due tant à la hausse de leur contribution absolue, qu'à une diminution de la contribution absolue de l'homme, conséquence de situations de retraite professionnelle qui deviennent fréquentes dans cette phase. C'est dire que l'homme, par son investissement dominant dans la sphère professionnel emmagasine dès les premières années de vie commune un avantage sur lequel il ne sera jamais possible de revenir dans la suite du parcours de vie familial.

Conclusion

Les données longitudinales du Panel illustrent l'effet des transitions entre les phases de la vie familiale sur la division du travail dans le couple. La transition de la phase pré-enfant à la phase pré-scolaire s'accompagne pour les couples d'une transformation en profondeur du mode de coopération. Alors que les couples dans la phase pré-enfant présentent une division du travail domestique très égalitaire, associée à une insertion comparable dans le champs professionnel, produisant des revenus personnels, sinon identiques du moins très proches, entre partenaires, la transition à la parentalité repose presque exclusivement sur la femme. Celle-ci voit ses heures de travail domestique considérablement augmenter, alors que le nombre de tâches dont elle est principalement responsable s'accroît très significativement. Rien de tel pour l'homme, dont la trajectoire est très peu sensible à cette transition et qui reste entièrement centré sur l'activité professionnelle. Ce modèle n'est alors remis en cause, marginalement, qu'avec le départ des enfants.

Comment expliquer cet effet des transitions entre les phases de la vie familiale, sur la division du travail familial? On peut faire référence à l'hypothèse des statuts-maîtres sexués (Krüger et Levy, 2001; Widmer, Kellerhals et Levy, 2003) pour comprendre la persistance de ces inégalités de genre structurant à la fois, et de manière complémentaire, les champs professionnel et familial. Cette hypothèse avance qu'il y a, pour chacun des sexes, un domaine d'activité dominant ou privilégié auquel les autres domaines sont subordonnés, le caractère dominant d'un domaine d'activité tenant au fait que sa logique et ses exigences prédominent par rapport à celles des autres champs d'insertion d'un acteur. Par conséquent, les personnes ne développent leurs activités dans des domaines non dominants que dans la mesure où les exigences du domaine dominant le permettent. Ainsi, actuellement en Suisse, le champ professionnel est le domaine d'activité dominant des hommes, alors que le champ familial reste celui des femmes. En ce sens, la prépondérance d'un domaine pour un sexe n'est pas synonyme de son exclusion de l'autre domaine; elle implique seulement que les investissements faits par les individus dans leur champ d'activité secondaire soient contingents des disponibilités que leurs laissent leurs investissements dans leur champ d'activité principal ou «dominant». Dans ce sens, l'hypothèse des statuts-maîtres sexués couvre un éventail de situations plus large que la notion «classique» de ségrégation sexuelle des fonctions familiales. Les statuts-maîtres sexués et complémentaires définissent donc les champs d'activité (en l'occurrence la famille et l'activité professionnelle) dont chaque sexe est considéré comme prioritairement responsable.

Sur quelles assises se fondent alors les statuts-maîtres? Il est légitime de postuler qu'ils trouvent leur origine non seulement dans les valeurs et les normes auxquelles les conjoints adhèrent ou dans des intérêts individuels à propos desquels ils négocieraient un accord, mais aussi dans des régulations institutionnelles qui poussent les couples à rentrer dans un modèle que nombre de processus extra-familiaux présupposent dans leur fonctionnement ordinaire (écoles, commerces, administrations, services publics etc.). Les «suppositions de normalité» sous-jacentes au fonctionnement institutionnel participeraient ainsi à une forme de *doing gender* qui ne serait pas d'un ordre purement interactionnel, interindividuel, mais également, et peut-être surtout, institutionnel. Une analyse approfondie des données du Panel devrait amener des éclaircissements sur ce point. En tous les cas, la dimension longitudinale du Panel confirme clairement le caractère décisif du parcours de vie pour la bonne compréhension des processus de régulation conjugale des champs familiaux et professionnels.

Références

Aldous, Joan (1996), *Family Careers: Rethinking the Developmental Perspective*, Thousand Oaks Calif., Sage Publications.

Berger, Peter L. et Kellner, Hansfried (1988), Le mariage et la construction de la réalité, *Dialogue*, 6-23. (Trad. (1964) de «Marriage and the construction of reality», *Diogenes*, 46, 1-32.)

Elder, Glen H. Jr. (1974), *Children of the Great Depression: Social Change in Life Experience*, Chicago, IL: University of Chicago Press. (1999, reissued as 25th Anniversary Edition, Boulder, CO: Westview Press.)

Glick, Paul C. (1947), The family cycle, *American Sociological Review*, 12, 164-174.
Glick Paul C. (1955), The life cycle of the family, *Journal of Marriage and the Family*, 17, 3-9.
Glick, Paul C. (1977), Updating the family cycle, *Journal of Marriage and the Family*, 39 (1), 5-13.
Havighurst, Robert J. (1948), *Developmental Tasks and Education*, Chicago, Chicago University Press.
Held, Thomas et Levy, René (1975), *Femme, famille et société*, Vevey, Delta.
Lansing, John B. et Kish, Leslie (1957), Family life cycle as an independent variable, *American Sociological Review*, 22, 512-519.
Krüger, Helga et Levy, René (2001), Linking Life Courses, Work, and the Family: Theorizing a not so Visible Nexus between Women and Men, *Canadian Journal of Sociology/Cahiers canadiens de sociologie*, 26, 2, 145-166.
Krüger, Helga et Levy, René (2000), Masterstatus, Familie und Geschlecht. Vergessene Verknüpfungslogiken zwischen Institutionen des Lebenslaufs, *Berliner Journal für Soziologie*, 10(3), 379-401.
Levy, René (1977), *Der Lebenslauf als Statusbiographie*, Stuttgart, Enke.
Levy, René, Joye, Dominique, Guye, Olivier et Kaufmann, Vincent (1997), *Tous égaux? De la stratification aux représentations*, Zürich, Seismo.
Widmer, Eric, Kellerhals, Jean et Levy, René (2003), *Couples contemporain: Cohésion, régulation et conflits. Une enquête sociologique*, Zürich, Seismo.

Und sie bewegen sich doch nicht: die Männer

Zur geschlechtsspezifischen Verteilung der Erwerbsarbeit in Familien*

A. Doris BAUMGARTNER und Beat FUX

Einleitung

Es gehört zweifellos zum sozialwissenschaftlichen Basiswissen, dass sich mit dem Auseinanderbrechen des ‚ganzen Hauses' einerseits der Bereich des ausserhäuslichen Produktions- und Erwerbssystems sowie andererseits das innerhäusliche System der Familie im Sinne eines Reproduktions- und Konsumsystems ausdifferenzierten. Wurde die Familienorientierung der Frau zunächst und noch bis in die 50er und 60er Jahre des zwanzigsten Jahrhunderts gemeinhin positiv gewürdigt, im Sinne einer vermehrten Teilhabe breiter Mittelschichten am wirtschaftlichen Aufschwung der Nachkriegszeit, so wechselte ungefähr ab Mitte der 1960er Jahre die Perspektive. Der Umstand, dass die Zuteilung der Rollen von Mann und Frau in der Regel nach dem zugeschriebenen Kriterium Geschlecht erfolgt und dem Paar meist wenig Spielraum für Aushandlungsprozesse lässt, wird mit Fug als undemokratisch und frauendiskriminierend wahrgenommen. Angesichts der Allgemeingültigkeit von Normen wie Partnerschaftlichkeit, Gleichberechtigung oder Chancengleichheit ist es daher nicht weiter verwunderlich, dass im Verlauf der vergangenen drei Dekaden nicht nur ein Bewusstseins-

* Der vorliegende Beitrag findet sich im Sammelband *Leben in der Schweiz 1999–2000* (Erwin Zimmermann & Robin Tillmann (hrsg.), Verlag Peter Lang, Bern (2004)). Die Auswertungen und Ergebnisse stammen aus den ersten zwei Wellen der Längsschnittsbefragung Leben in der Schweiz, worin 6 335 Personen in den Jahren 1999 und 2000 befragt wurden. Als Mandat des Schweizer Haushalt-Panel der Universität Neuchâtel wurde die Datenerhebung von M. I. S. Trend durchgeführt und vom SPP Zukunft Schweiz des Schweizerischen Nationalfonds für wissenschaftliche Forschung finanziert (Gesuche Nr. 5004-53205 / 5004-57894 / 5004-67304). Weitere Information finden sich auf der Webseite www.swisspanel.ch.

wandel einsetzte, sondern dass sich auch das Erwerbsverhalten, insbesondere jenes der Frauen verändert hat. Dennoch kommen Frauen und Männern unterschiedliche Rollen in Haushalt und Familie einerseits und in der ausserhäuslichen Erwerbstätigkeit andererseits zu. Für Männer sind Familie und Arbeitsmarkt nach dem UND-Prinzip organisiert. Für Frauen hat die Arbeitsmarktbeteiligung den Status eines Zusatzprogramms oder Lückenfüllers und ist strukturell weniger festgelegt. Denn die Institution Familie setzt für die Frau, definiert als Familienerhalterin, inhaltlich und zeitlich andere Normen und Verfügbarkeitsansprüche. Arbeit in der Familie bedeutet intern erbrachte Versorgung, was Frauen bei gleichzeitiger Partizipation am Erwerbssystem sowohl in normative als auch in zeitliche Zwickmühlen bringen muss. Der ‚normale' Biographieverlauf der Frau fördert zudem die ideale männliche Lebenslaufgestaltung, während umgekehrt die männliche Biographiegestaltung die weibliche einschränkt bzw. als qualitativ andere fordert (Born et al. 1996, 27).

Zwar hat die Erwerbspartizipation der Mütter in den letzten Jahrzehnten markant zugenommen, gleichzeitig blieben die Männer aber mehrheitlich vollerwerbstätig, unabhängig von ihren familialen Verpflichtungen und beteiligen sich nur in bescheidenem Ausmass an Haushalt und Familie (vgl. Bauer / Strub 2002 und Widmer / Levy / Gauthier, in diesem Band). Dennoch gibt es auch die Alltagserfahrung, wonach es einem vorkommt, als ob immer mehr Männer auch werktags mit dem Kinderwagen unterwegs sind. Handelt es sich hierbei um ein Problem der selektiven Wahrnehmung oder könnte sich tatsächlich ein leiser Wandel andeuten? Und kündigt sich darin, dass sich im alltäglichen Handlungszusammenhang auch Männer bemerkbar machen, die sich an der Kinderbetreuung beteiligen, gar ein Bewusstseinswandel an, der sich inskünftig auch in den Massendaten zum Erwerbsverhalten niederschlagen wird?

In diesem Beitrag wird deshalb das Erwerbspensum von Vätern und Müttern vor dem Hintergrund von familialen Verpflichtungen erörtert, während die Arbeitsleistung von Frauen und Männern im Haushalt im Zentrum des vorangehenden Beitrags von Widmer, Levy und Gauthier ist. Ausserdem sollen die möglichen feinen Veränderungen im Erwerbsausmass, die sich innerhalb eines Jahres ergeben, analysiert werden.

Mit den Daten des Schweizerischen Haushaltpanels lässt sich der Erwerbsumfang von Frauen und Männern ziemlich genau erfassen. Dabei interessiert weniger das Erwerbsverhalten der Gesamtheit aller Männer und Frauen, sondern vor allem dasjenige aller Personen mit Kindern. Denn in früheren Studien hat sich wiederholt gezeigt, dass es die Kinder sind, welche das Erwerbsausmass der Mütter bestimmen (Blossfeld / Hakim 1997; Lauterbach 1994; Schulze Buschoff 1998), während sie den Erwerbsumfang der Väter kaum berühren. Zwischen Männern und kinderlosen Frauen nehmen die Unterschiede im Erwerbsumfang zwischen den Generationen dagegen stark ab, und das Erwerbsverhalten gleicht sich zwischen den Geschlechtern an. Wenn Anpassungsleistungen von Männern vollbracht werden, dann sollten sie sich am ehesten bei Familien mit Kindern im Vorschulalter abzeichnen, während Frauen ihre Erwerbstätigkeit generell am Grad der Abhängigkeit ihrer Kinder ausrichten. Aufgrund dieser Hypothese werden bestimmte Familienkonstellationen besonders betrachtet. Zum zweiten wird der Zusammenhang zwischen Erwerbsumfang und Familiensituation beleuchtet.

Da wir davon ausgehen, dass sich Senkungen des Erwerbsumfangs am ehesten bei der effektiven und der Normal-Stundenzahl erkennen lassen, sollen drittens Vollzeitstellen im Hinblick auf ihre Normalstundenzahl näher analysiert werden. Schliesslich soll die Stabilität bzw. der Wandel einzelner Arrangements anhand von Kohortenunterschieden erfasst werden. In einem letzten Analyseschritt werden die Arbeitsteilungsmodelle in ihrer Gesamtheit dargestellt bevor wir ein abschliessendes Fazit ziehen.

Erwerbstätigkeit von Vätern und Müttern

Wie erwartet zeichnen sich deutliche Geschlechterunterschiede beim Erwerbspensum ab. Während sechs von sieben Vätern vollerwerbstätig sind, ist ziemlich genau eine von sieben Müttern in Vollzeit tätig. Von dem Sechstel Väter, der nicht Vollzeit arbeitet, ist der überwiegende Teil entweder überhaupt nicht erwerbstätig (1999: 5.1 %) oder aber beinahe voll erwerbstätig (1999: 3.5 %). Geringe Arbeitspensen sind bei den Vätern äusserst selten. Das Erwerbspensum der Frauen verteilt sich dagegen gleichmässiger über sämtliche Arbeitspensen, wobei Frauen besonders häufig eine Teilzeitstelle bis zu etwa einem halben Pensum annehmen. Etwa ein Drittel aller Mütter (einbezogen sind Frauen der Jahrgänge 1945–1984 mit Kind) sind als Familienfrauen tätig, ohne gleichzeitig Erwerbsarbeit auszuüben.

Abbildung 1: Das Erwerbspensum (kategorisiert) von Müttern und Vätern 1999 und 2000, in %

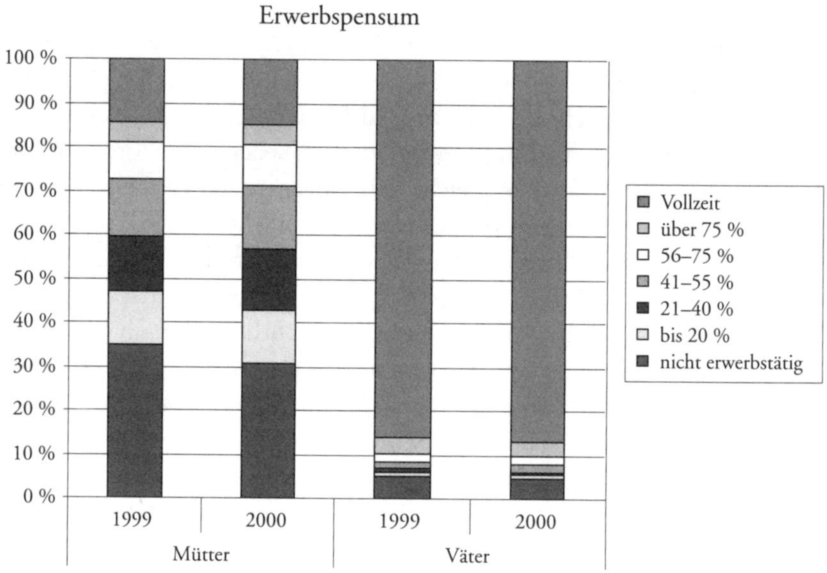

1999: N = 2506; 2000: N = 2522

Longitudinales Individualfile mit longitudinalem Personengewicht unter Beibehaltung der Stichprobengrösse (weip00ls)

Nun interessiert insbesondere, ob sich die Erwerbspensen nach familialer Situation unterscheiden. Wir differenzieren die Familienkonstellation nach dem Alter des jüngsten Kindes[1]. Ob jeweils ein Paar zusammen mit Kind(ern) die Familie bildet oder ein Elternteil allein die Kinder erzieht, wird aus methodischen Gründen nicht unterschieden. Wir wissen jedoch, dass der Erwerbsumfang der allein erziehenden Mütter grösser ist (vgl. Baumgartner 2002, Buchmann et al. 2002).

1 Kleinkinder sind Kinder bis zu zwei Jahren. Drei- bis sechsjährige Kinder sind Vorschulkinder. Das Alter zwischen sieben und fünfzehn Jahren bezeichnet das Schulalter. Ältere Kinder haben die obligatorische Schulzeit in der Regel hinter sich (16 und älter).

Abbildungen 2 und 3: Erwerbsumfang der Mütter (Abb. 2) und Väter (Abb. 3) nach familialer Situation, 1999, in %

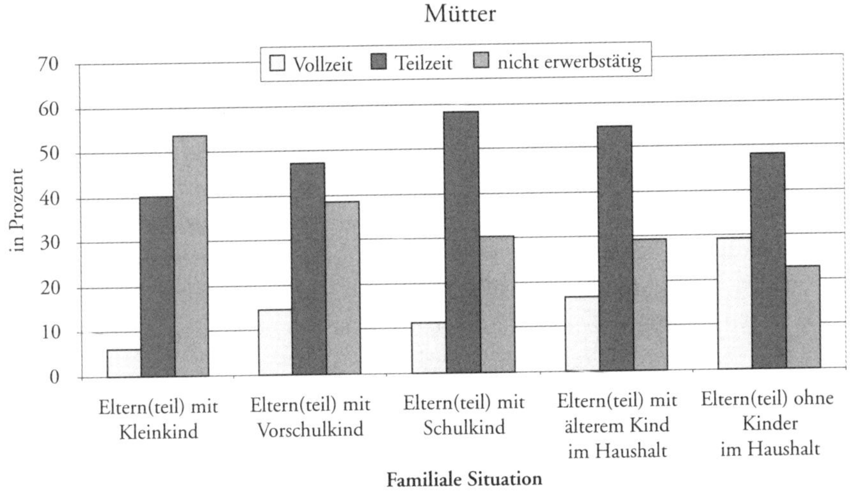

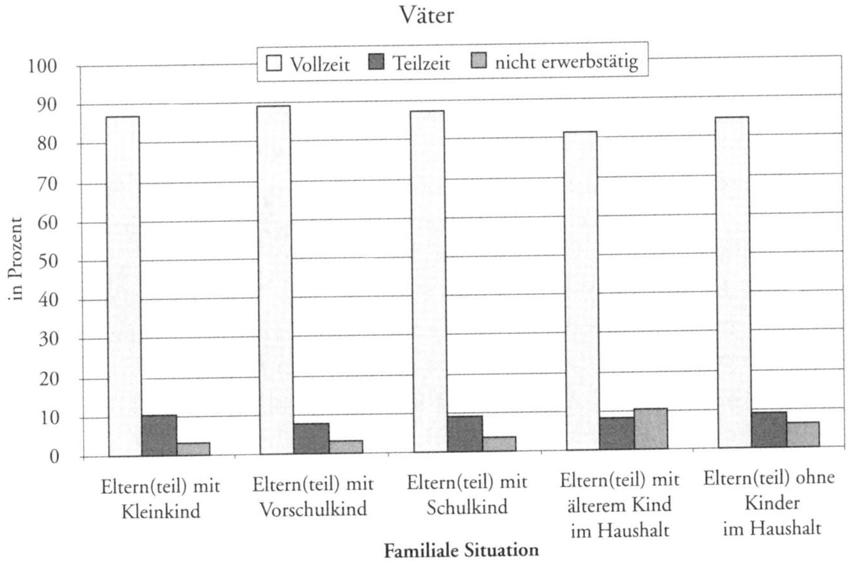

Abb. 2: N = 1338; Abb. 3: N = 1168

Longitudinales Individualfile mit longitudinalem Personengewicht unter Beibehaltung der Stichprobengrösse (weip00ls)

Bei den Frauen zeigen sich deutliche Zusammenhänge zwischen dem Erwerbspensum und der Familienkonstellation. Während Teilzeitarbeit mit dem Alter des Kindes leicht zunimmt, konzentriert sich die Nicht-Erwerbstätigkeit vor allem auf Frauen mit Kleinkindern und geht ca. um die Hälfte zurück, bis die Kinder den elterlichen Haushalt verlassen haben. Umgekehrt nimmt die Vollzeitarbeit mit steigendem Alter der Kinder zu.

Bei den Männern ist der Zusammenhang zwischen dem Erwerbspensum und der familialen Situation gering. Der Anteil Vollzeit Erwerbstätiger bleibt beinahe über alle Familienphasen hinweg konstant. Ebenso verändert sich der Anteil der Teilzeitbeschäftigten nicht gravierend. Einzig der Anteil Nicht-Erwerbstätiger variiert. Er nimmt zu, wenn die Kinder älter sind. Die Gründe dafür lassen sich daher kaum in der Familiensituation finden. Dem soll im nächsten Abschnitt nachgegangen werden.

Gründe für ein reduziertes Arbeitspensum bzw. für Nicht-Erwerbstätigkeit

Tatsächlich ist kaum ein Mann wegen Familienpflichten nicht erwerbstätig. Meist sind es Arbeitslosigkeit, gesundheitliche Beeinträchtigungen oder Ausbildungen, welche Männer davon abhalten, einer Erwerbstätigkeit nachzugehen. Nicht-erwerbstätige Frauen geben dagegen zu vier Fünfteln an, dass sie keine Stelle suchten, weil sie für Haus und Kinder sorgten. Nur vereinzelt sind andere Gründe für das Fernbleiben vom Arbeitsmarkt verantwortlich, welche jedoch kaum einheitlich sind.

Ebenso begründen drei Viertel aller Frauen ihre Teilzeitarbeit mit familiären Pflichten. Bei den wenigen Männern, die in Teilzeit arbeiten (8.7 %), tun dies immerhin fast zwei Fünftel aus familiären Gründen. Die anderen nennen diverse Gründe, machen daneben eine Ausbildung oder können aus gesundheitlichen Gründen keine Vollzeitstelle annehmen (vgl. Delsen 1995, Van Emmerick / Hermkens 1999).

Männer wie Frauen sind am ehesten teilzeitlich tätig, wenn sie ein Kleinkind zuhause haben. Fast alle Frauen (94.3 %) geben diese Begründung an, immerhin drei Viertel aller Männer bleiben in dieser Familiensituation wegen der Kinder zuhause. Mit steigendem Alter der Kinder verblasst dieser Grund. Sobald die Kinder die Schule verlassen haben, entfällt die Begründung für Männer weitestgehend.

Abbildung 4: Teilzeitbeschäftigung aus familiären Gründen nach Geschlecht, 1999, in %

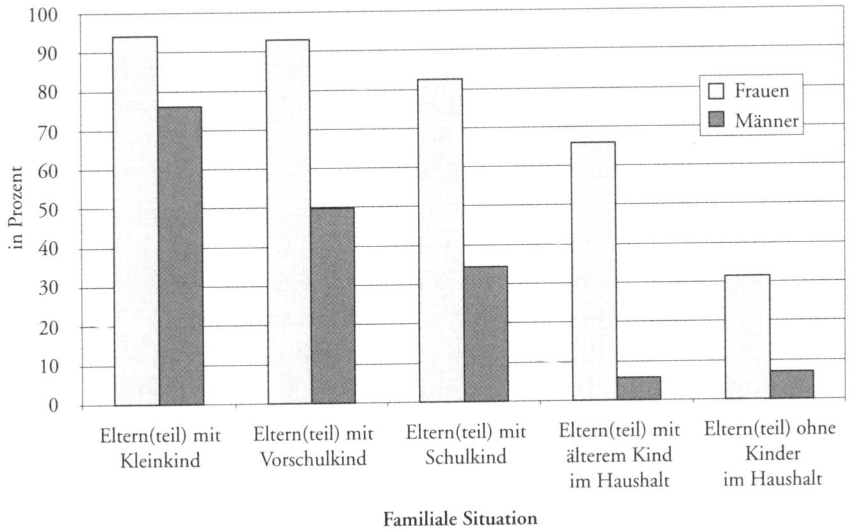

Frauen: N = 754, Männer: N = 40

Longitudinales Individualfile mit longitudinalem Personengewicht unter Beibehaltung der Stichprobengrösse (weip00ls)

Für Frauen bildet die Familie zweifellos den Hauptgrund, nicht erwerbstätig zu sein oder teilzeitlich beschäftigt zu sein, hinter den alle anderen Motive zurücktreten. Dagegen ist Nicht-Erwerbstätigkeit bei Männern kaum von der Familienkonstellation abhängig, wodurch sich auch der höhere Anteil nicht erwerbstätiger Männer, die keine Kinder mehr im Haushalt haben, erklärt. Einzig Teilzeitarbeit kann in eingeschränktem Mass auch für Väter familienbegründet sein. Daraus entsteht das Paradox, dass zwar die Hälfte aller erwerbstätigen Männer weniger arbeiten möchte, gegenüber einem Drittel aller erwerbstätigen Frauen, dass aber die meisten Väter Vollzeit erwerbstätig sind und diejenigen, welche ihre Arbeitszeit reduzieren, die Zeit eher selten für die Familie einsetzen.

Zeitsuche durch geringes Normalstundenzahlbudget

Formell reduzieren offensichtlich nur wenige Väter ihre Erwerbsarbeit. Ausserdem geht aus dem vorangehenden Kapitel hervor, dass die Beteiligung der Männer an Haushalts- und Kinderbetreuungsarbeiten ebenfalls bescheiden ist. Sollten sich Väter trotzdem vermehrt ihrem Nachwuchs zuwenden, bleibt noch die Möglichkeit, dass sie zwar Vollzeitstellen bekleiden, dass diese aber eine verhältnismässig tiefe Normalstundenzahl aufweisen, die durch die effektiv geleisteten Stunden auch nicht wesentlich überschritten wird. Besonders bei hoher Arbeitsplatzautonomie könnte auf diese Weise etwas Zeit resultieren, die mit den Kindern verbracht wird. Da zudem die Beteiligung an der Familien- und Haushaltarbeit und das Erwerbspensum keiner 1 : 1 Relation entsprechen muss, sondern eine gewisse Variabilität aufweist, wird der genaue Erwerbsumfang einer Vollzeitstelle resp. von erhöhten Teilzeitpensen ab 75 Prozent näher studiert.

Ein erster Überblick über die Erwerbsstundenzahlen von Männern ohne Kinder und Männern mit Kindern (derselben Kohorten) im Haushaltpanel fällt allerdings ernüchternd aus, indem Väter rund 1.5 Stunden mehr arbeiten (45.3 Stunden) als kinderlose Männer (43.8 Stunden) bei einem Medianwert von 42 Stunden. Die effektiv geleistete Stundenzahl der Referenzwoche fällt sogar noch höher aus mit einem noch grösseren Unterschied zwischen Vätern und kinderlosen Männern[2]. Nun deckt sich dies mit den statistischen Angaben der Volkszählung 1990 (vgl. Lüscher et al. 1996) und den SAKE-Daten für das Jahr 2000 (Bauer / Strub 2002). Da wir aber nach jüngsten Veränderungen fragen, differenzieren wir die Angaben der Väter wiederum nach Familiensituation und vergleichen sie mit den Müttern, die ebenfalls mindestens zu 75 Prozent erwerbstätig sind (N = 1388).

Es stellt sich heraus, dass insgesamt keine gesicherten Unterschiede zwischen den verschiedenen Familienphasen auszumachen sind. Hingegen bleiben die Geschlechterunterschiede weiterhin hoch signifikant. Frauen, welche mindestens zu 75 Prozent erwerbstätig sind, arbeiten im Mittel knapp 37 Stunden, Männer im Schnitt über 7 Stunden mehr. Nur ein Teil dieser Differenz dürfte auf das Konto unterschiedlicher Berufszusammensetzung mit

2 Diese Werte werden nicht eigens in einer Tabelle dargestellt. Sie beziehen sich auf 1456 Männer (1999) der Kohorten 1945–1984; Eta: .084**.

branchenspezifischen Arbeitszeiten zwischen Männern und Frauen zurückgehen. Es gibt demnach selbst unter den vollzeitig Erwerbstätigen markante Unterschiede zwischen den Geschlechtern.

Stabilität oder Wandel der Erwerbsarbeit von Vätern und Müttern?

Betrachtet man Erwerbsquote und -umfang der 25–55-Jährigen über längere Zeit hinweg, kann festgestellt werden, dass bei den Männern wenig Wandel sichtbar wird, sieht man vom erhöhten Anteil in Ausbildung stehender im dritten Lebensjahrzehnt ab (vgl. SAKE 2003). Bei den Frauen sind jedoch relativ starke Veränderungstendenzen festzustellen (Baumgartner 2003a; SAKE 2003), die sich folgendermassen zusammenfassen lassen. Der Unterschied zwischen kinderlosen Frauen und Frauen mit Kindern ist geringer geworden, weil immer mehr Frauen über längere Zeit hinweg auch mit Kindern erwerbstätig sind. Zwar steigt noch immer rund die Hälfte aller Frauen bei der Geburt des ersten Kindes temporär aus dem Erwerbsleben aus, die Unterbrechungsdauer verkürzt sich aber stark von Kohorte zu Kohorte. Entsprechend nehmen Familienfrauen, die dauerhaft nicht erwerbstätig sind, und Frauen mit langen Unterbrechungsdauern ab. Aufgrund des generell gestiegenen Bildungsstandes der Frauen und der Tendenz mit gutem Bildungsrucksack, wenn überhaupt, dann nur kurzfristig familienbedingt dem Arbeitsmarkt den Rücken zuzukehren, erhöht sich die Erwerbsquote zusätzlich. Im Unterschied zu kinderlosen Frauen ist aber die überwiegende Zahl der Mütter in Teilzeit beschäftigt und zumindest die älteren Generationen kehren auch kaum mehr zur Vollzeittätigkeit zurück. Vollzeiterwerbstätigkeit wird in der Regel nur nach einem Bruch in der familialen Lebensform (meist wegen Scheidung) oder bei starken Karriereambitionen angestrebt (Baumgartner 2002; 2003a).

Das Studium des Wandels von Normen und Verhaltensmustern erfordert die kontinuierliche Beobachtung von individuellen Erwerbsverläufen. Mit den Daten der ersten beiden Wellen des SHP lässt sich daher kaum mehr als der Ist-Zustand dokumentieren. Erst in einigen Jahren wird sich weisen, ob sich die festgestellten Veränderungen zwischen 1999 und 2000 kohärent in eine längerfristige Entwicklungslogik einpassen lassen. Beobachtete Verschiebungen zwischen den beiden Zeitpunkten müssen daher vorsichtig interpretiert werden, weil sie zufällig sein können oder Teil von Schwankungen, die durch unberücksichtigte Faktoren und Stichprobenfehler zustande kommen. So bleibt ungewiss, ob der leichte Rückgang der vollzeitlich tätigen Väter mit Vorschulkindern[3] konstant bleibt. Andererseits passt die beobachtete Zunahme der Frauenerwerbstätigkeit bei Klein- und Vorschulkindern[4] zwischen 1999 und 2000 in die Entwicklung, welche die Volkszählung 2000 von der Erwerbsbevölkerung zeichnet. Hier wird festgestellt, dass die Zunahme der Erwerbsbevölkerung zwischen 1990 und 2000 hauptsächlich auf die Erwerbsbeteiligung der Mütter zurückzuführen ist, die heute grösstenteils weiterhin auch während der aktiven Familienphase tätig sind (SAKE 2003). So stieg insbesondere die Erwerbsquote der Frauen zwischen 25 und 45 Jahren mit mindestens einem Kind unter 7 Jahren von 39.6 Prozent (1990) auf 62.2 Prozent (2000). Demgegenüber verblassen konjunkturelle Veränderungen.

Mit dem SHP lassen sich jedoch Veränderungen im Lebenslauf bestimmen, indem Veränderungen innerhalb eines Jahres nach Geburtskohorte dargestellt werden können.

Mit Ausnahme der Kohorte 1965–69 sind im Jahr 2000 mehr Väter erwerbstätig sowie mehr Väter vollerwerbstätig als 1999. Dies drückt sich auch in leicht gestiegenen Stundenzahlen pro Woche im Jahr 2000 aus. Ausser bei der Kohorte 1970–74 weisen alle Werte in dieselbe Richtung. Gleichzeitig hat auch die Teilzeitarbeit mit einem höheren Pensum (mehr als 40 %) bei den mittleren Kohorten, die häufig noch Vorschulkinder haben, leicht zugenommen. Bei den jüngsten Geburtsjahrgängen ist der Anteil der in Teilzeit beschäftigten Väter allerdings sehr gering, vermutlich weil in Familien mit Kleinkindern öfters die Frauen ihre Erwerbstätigkeit für kürzere Zeit vollständig unterbrechen.

Insgesamt zeigen sich zwar Tendenzen in Richtung mehr Teilzeitarbeit mit höheren Stundenzahlen und generell mehr Erwerbstätigkeit über alle Kohorten hinweg, aber die Verschiebungen zwischen 1999 und 2000 bleiben insbesondere bei den Männern marginal[5]. Von einem sehr hohen Niveau an

3 Er reduziert sich von 89.1 Prozent im Jahr 1999 auf 87.7 Prozent im Jahr 2000.

4 1999 sind 40 Prozent der Mütter mit Kleinkind teilzeitlich erwerbstätig, im Jahr 2000 sind es 51 Prozent (vgl. Abbildung 1).

5 Die relativ deutlichen Veränderungen bei den Frauen gegenüber den Männern können hingegen kaum konjunkturell erklärt werden. Zwar ging die Arbeitslosenquote in diesem Zeitraum weiter zurück und die Zahl der offenen Stellen stieg, aber dies erklärt die markanten Unterschiede im Erwerbsverhalten zwischen den Geschlechtern nicht.

Abbildung 5: Erwerbsstatus und Normalstundenzahl bei Vollzeiterwerbstätigkeit nach Geschlecht, 2000, in % resp. in Stunden

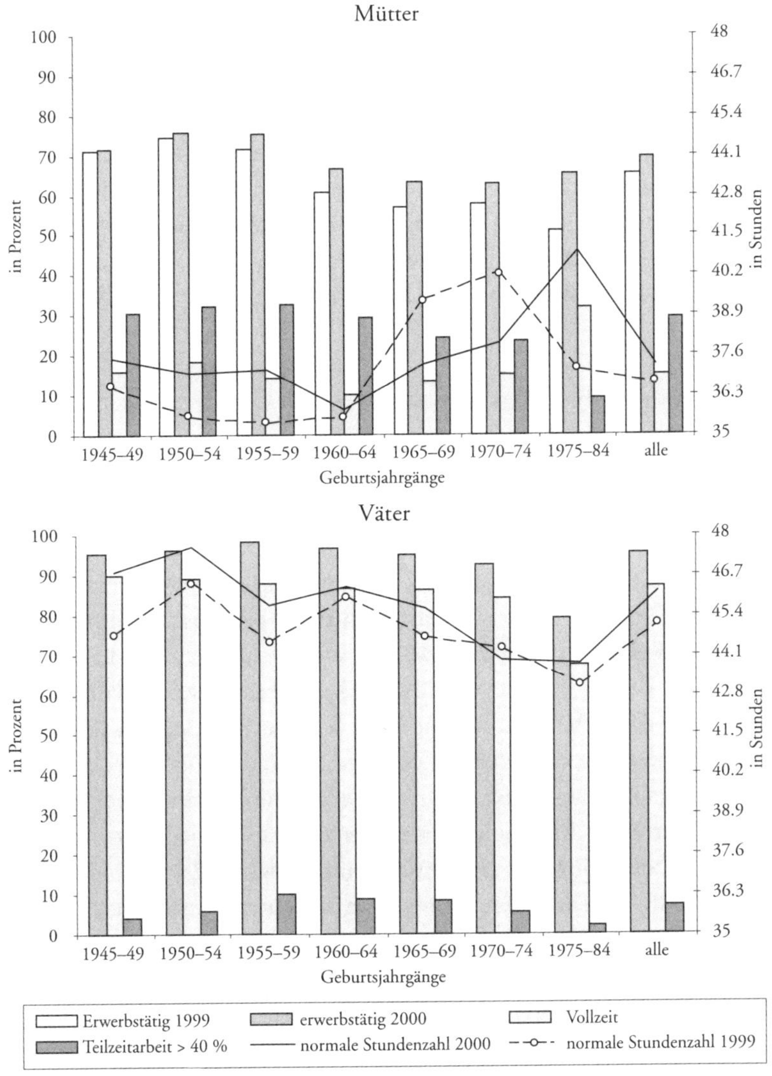

	Mütter	Väter
Erwerbstätigkeit:	N = 1373	N = 1187
Vollzeit Erwerbstätige	N = 363	N = 1028

Longitudinales Individualfile mit longitudinalem Personengewicht unter Beibehaltung der Stichprobengrösse (weip00ls)

Erwerbsstunden aus, erhöhen Väter fast aller Kohorten die Stundenzahl, was sicher nicht der besseren Verteilung der Pflichten in Haushalt und Familie dient. Auf der anderen Seite nähern sich ältere und junge Mütter mit zusätzlichen Erwerbsstunden und einer 4 %igen Steigerung der Erwerbsquote leicht dem Erwerbsverhalten der Väter an. Anpassungsleistungen werden somit auch beim Erwerbspensum vor allem von Frauen erbracht. Mit Kleinkindern (häufig in den jüngeren Geburtskohorten anzutreffen) ist die Erwerbsbeteiligung geringer. Andererseits steigt die Stundenzahl nur leicht an zwischen 1999 und 2000. Männer steigern hingegen ihr Erwerbspensum zwischen 1999 und 2000 sogar markant, so dass es mit einer gleichberechtigten Teilnahme an Aufgaben im Haushalt weiterhin hapern dürfte.

Rollenverteilung bei Paaren

Zum Abschluss des Beitrags wechseln wir den Blickwinkel vom Individuum weg hin zum Haushalt und fragen nach den wichtigsten Erwerbsmustern zwischen Partnern. Die Erwerbsmuster beschränken sich im wesentlichen auf drei Hauptmuster und eine Restkategorie, in der vereinzelte Muster zusammengefasst werden. Die drei Hauptmuster bezeichnen wir als das „egalitäre Erwerbsmodell", wo beide Partner in Vollzeit tätig sind, als das „duale Muster", wo in der Regel der Mann vollzeitig erwerbstätig ist und die Frau die Familienarbeit übernimmt und das „Vollzeit-Teilzeit-Modell". Dieses Modell konkurriert mit dem dualen Modell, während das egalitäre Erwerbsmodell bei Paaren mit Kindern in jeder Lebensphase relativ unbedeutend ist. Bei Kindern bis zum Schulalter dominiert das duale Modell der traditionellen inner- und ausserhäuslichen Arbeitsteilung. Mit dem Schuleintritt des jüngsten Kindes gewinnt jedoch das Vollzeit-Teilzeit-Modell stark an Bedeutung. Es bleibt auch in späteren Lebensphasen, wenn die Kinder ausgeflogen sind, das häufigste und wird nur leicht dadurch konkurrenziert, dass beide Partner voll erwerbstätig sind. In den meisten Familienphasen nimmt das Vollzeit-Teilzeit-Modell ausserdem zwischen 1999 und 2000 zu, während die Zwei-Verdiener-Haushalte nur bei kleinen Kindern zunehmen, bei älteren Kinder – sogar wenn diese den elterlichen Haushalt bereits verlassen haben – jedoch leicht zurückgehen.

Nach Kohorten unterteilt verbreitet sich das Vollzeit-Teilzeit-Modell ebenfalls bei allen Geburtsjahrgängen mit Ausnahme der jüngsten, die mit kleinen Kindern dem dualen Modell klar den Vorzug geben. Es ist abzusehen, dass

Abbildung 6: Erwerbsmuster nach Familienphase, 2000, in %

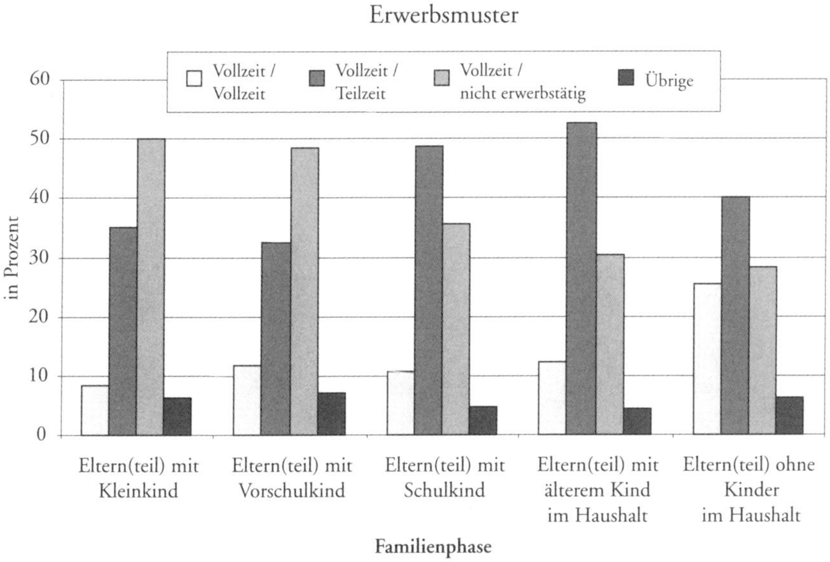

N Familienphase			
mit Kleinkind	N = 420	mit Vorschulkind	N = 424
mit Schulkind	N = 610	mit älterem Kind	N = 380
ohne Kinder im Haushalt	N = 205		

Longitudinales Individualfile mit longitudinalem Personengewicht unter Beibehaltung der Stichprobengrösse (weip00ls)

dieses Erwerbsmodell nur solange von Bedeutung bleibt, als kleine Kinder zu versorgen sind.

Bei den ältesten Kohorten, deren Kinder grösstenteils nicht mehr im elterlichen Haushalt leben resp. bereits erwachsen sind, kommt neben dem Trend zu mehr Erwerbstätigkeit auch ein Generationenmoment zum Tragen. Diese Jahrgänge (1945–54) sind selbst noch so sozialisiert worden, dass Frauen nach der Heirat entweder dauerhaft zuhause bleiben oder aber höchstens einen Zuverdienst zum Haushalteinkommen beisteuern. Dies drückt sich in einem relativ hohen Anteil Familienfrauen und einem verhältnismässig geringen Anteil von zwei Vollverdienern in diesen Kohorten aus.

Generell ist aber die steigende Teilzeitarbeit in Verbindung mit einer Vollzeitarbeit des Partners nicht auf ein Zuverdienermodell zu beschränken (Quack

Abbildung 7: Erwerbsmuster nach Geburtsjahrgängen, 2000 und 1999 (als Punkte), in %

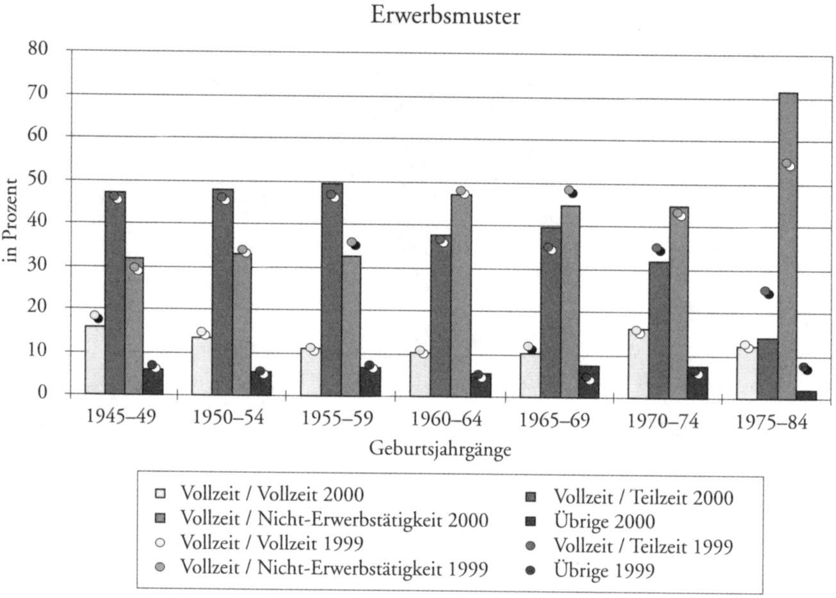

N für Geburtsjahrgänge (2000):

1945–49	N = 342	1950–54	N = 325	1955–59	N = 367	1960–64	N = 437
1965–69	N = 145	1970–74	N = 145	1975–84	N = 49		

Longitudinales Individualfile mit longitudinalem Personengewicht unter Beibehaltung der Stichprobengrösse (weip00ls)

1993). Wir haben andernorts (Baumgartner 2003b) dargelegt, dass sich hinter Teilzeitarbeit unterschiedliche Modelle verbergen. Neben der Teilzeitarbeit als Übergangstätigkeit oder als Anpassungsstrategie zur Vereinbarung von Beruf und Familie nimmt kontinuierliche, qualifizierte Teilzeitarbeit zu, die dauerhaft und ohne Orientierung an einer Vollzeitbeschäftigung ausgeübt wird. Dieser Typ von Teilzeitarbeit ermöglicht in der Regel finanzielle Unabhängigkeit und ist nicht komplementär zur männlichen Erwerbsarbeit zu verstehen. Mit dem Haushaltpanel ist es leider nicht möglich, die beschriebene Typologie einzuführen, jedoch gibt es Indizien, die in dieselbe Richtung weisen. Zum einen nimmt die Erwerbstätigkeit der Frauen zu, zweitens wächst der Anteil Teilzeitarbeit mit höherem Pensum und drittens hat das traditionelle duale Modell nur mehr in der Familienphase mit Kleinkindern seinen Platz.

Zum Schluss unserer Ausführungen fassen wir die verschiedenen Einflussfaktoren in einem multivariaten Modell zusammen. Das Modell[6] bestätigt im wesentlichen die bereits erläuterten bivariaten Zusammenhänge, fügt aber zusätzliche Faktoren ein. Wichtig für die Wahl des Erwerbsmusters sind neben der familialen Situation das Bildungsverhalten der Eltern. Vor allem zählt ihre Weiterbildung. Besonders Frauen, welche vor kurzem an Weiterbildungen teilgenommen haben, sind viel eher teil- oder vollzeitlich erwerbstätig. Dieser Einfluss verstärkt sich noch zwischen 1999 und 2000. Aber auch generell ein höheres Bildungsniveau der Mütter erhöht die Wahrscheinlichkeit der Erwerbstätigkeit beider Partner leicht. Daneben wirkt sich das partnerschaftliche Verhältnis bei der Kindererziehung und -betreuung aus. Tatsächlich wird das egalitäre Erwerbsmodell eher bevorzugt, wenn sich der Partner ebenfalls aktiv an der Kinderbetreuung beteiligt. Eine aktive Mithilfe im Haushalt beeinflusst aber nicht das Vollzeit-Teilzeit-Modell. Der Kohortenzugehörigkeit kommt kein zusätzlicher Erklärungsgehalt im Modell zu, so dass sie aus der Analyse ausgeschlossen wird. Wie erwartet neigen überdies Ausländerinnen eher zur Erwerbstätigkeit und besonders zur Vollzeiterwerbstätigkeit. Unterschiede zwischen den verschiedenen kulturellen Räumen in der Schweiz finden sich nur bezüglich des Vollzeit-Teilzeitmodells, welches sich verbreiteter in der Deutschschweiz findet.

6 Durchgeführt wurde ein multinomiales logistisches Modell mit den Hauptfaktoren Haushaltsform und Hilfe im Haushalt, Bildungsvariablen und den Kontextvariablen Nationalität, Sprachregion und Kohorte.

Tabelle 1: Das Erwerbsmuster, multinomiale logistische Regression mit Referenzkategorie duales Modell (Vollzeit / keine Erwerbstätigkeit)

	Vollzeit / Vollzeit		Vollzeit / Teilzeit	
	1999	2000	1999	2000
	Exp(B)	Exp(B)	Exp(B)	Exp(B)
Konstante	***	***	***	***
Eltern(teil) ohne Kind im Haushalt	Ref. kat.	Ref. kat.	Ref. kat.	Ref. kat.
Eltern(teil) mit Kleinkind	.107***	.155***	.829	.798
Eltern(teil) mit Vorschulkind	.135***	.174***	.958	.789
Eltern(teil) mit Schulkind	.288***	.287***	1.780***	1.533***
Eltern(teil) mit älterem Kind	.470***	.420***	2.044***	1.904***
keine Hilfe im Haushalt	Ref. kat.		Ref. kat.	
Partner hilft im Haushalt	1.513*		.911	
Schweizer	Ref. kat.	Ref. kat.	Ref. kat.	Ref. kat.
Ausländer	2.822***	3.398***	1.859***	1.901***
Südschweiz	Ref. kat.	Ref. kat.	Ref. kat.	Ref. kat.
Westschweiz	1.262	1.228	1.748*	1.679*
Deutschschweiz	1.291	1.251	2.401***	2.170***
Vater*Bildung		.981		1.040
Mutter*Bildung		1.118***		1.114***
Mutter ohne Weiterbildung	Ref. kat.	Ref. kat.	Ref. kat.	Ref. kat.
Vater mit Weiterbildung	1.286	2.023*	1.670***	1.752*
Mutter mit Weiterbildung	2.815***	3.343***	2.836***	3.546***
Vater ohne Weiterbildung	.940	1.403	1.021	1.303
Modell χ^2	550.323	566.695		
Freiheitsgrad	22	24		
Pseudo R^2	.18	.18		

Exp(B): standardisierter Effektkoeffizient
1999: N = 642; 2000: N = 706; Longitudinales Individualfile
* $p < 0.05$
** $p < 0.01$
*** $p < 0.001$

Fazit

Trotz individuellen Anstrengungen bleiben klare Differenzen im Erwerbsumfang zwischen Müttern und Vätern bestehen. Männer richten ihre Erwerbstätigkeit nur selten an der Familie aus. Wenn sie die Erwerbstätigkeit unterbrechen oder reduzieren, geschieht dies häufig aus anderen Gründen. Die wenigen, die Teilzeitarbeit aus familiären Gründen leisten, lassen sich kaum als Vorreiter verstehen, weil sie spätestens mit dem Schulalter der Kinder zurück zur Vollzeit wechseln, ohne dass sich ihre Erwerbsorientierung änderte. Und obschon Männer in professionalisierten Berufsbereichen ähnliche Chancen zur Teilzeitarbeit bezüglich Zugänglichkeit, Verbreitung und Entlöhnung haben wie die ebenbürtig ausgebildeten Frauen, nutzen sie diese Möglichkeiten offensichtlich sehr viel weniger als Frauen.

Die Frauenerwerbstätigkeit steht jedoch in einem längeren konstanten Trend zu mehr Erwerbstätigkeit unter Müttern und zu einer Erhöhung des teilzeitlichen Pensums, ohne deswegen in grösserem Umfang auf Vollzeiterwerbstätigkeit zurückzugreifen. Dennoch korrespondiert die Müttererwerbstätigkeit immer mit der familialen Situation und verhält sich komplementär dazu. Der Erwerbsumfang wird dem Alter der Kinder angepasst. Es findet demnach eine langsame, aber sehr einseitige Anpassung der Frauen an die Männer statt, die sich kaum von der Stelle bewegen.

Männer hingegen steigern die Stundenzahl eher noch, wenn Kinder zum Haushalt gehören. Zwischen ihrem Erwerbsengagement und der Familienphase besteht weitestgehend kein Zusammenhang. Bezüglich interner Arbeitsteilung im Haushalt und externer Arbeitsteilung herrscht jedoch für sie absolute Kongruenz. Wer voll erwerbstätig ist, kümmert sich sehr wenig um Aufgaben im Haushalt oder in der Familie.

Paare leben deshalb bevorzugt – sobald das Alter der Kinder es erlaubt – ein Vollzeit-Teilzeit-Modell, wobei die Rollenverteilung zwischen den Geschlechtern klar geregelt ist. Vollzeit tätige Frauen mit teilzeitlich beschäftigten Partnern sind äusserst selten. Soweit die Generationen bis heute überblickt werden können, behalten sie dieses Modell auch bei, wenn die Kinder längst ausgezogen sind. Dennoch müsste eigentlich zwischen verschiedenen Formen von Teilzeitarbeit differenziert werden, um den sinnhaften Gehalt der Rollenverteilung besser zu erfassen. Dann würde vielleicht auch stärker ein Wandel sichtbar. Mit dem vorliegenden Datenmaterial können wir nicht umhin, festzuhalten, dass ein Wandel sowohl in der internen wie in der externen Arbeitsteilung zwischen

Partnern – sollte er überhaupt stattfinden – so marginal ist, dass er statistisch nicht erfassbar ist. Auch mögliche informelle Verschiebungen von Zeitressourcen durch den Arbeitsrhythmus oder indem Männer Stellen mit kürzeren Normalarbeitsstunden einnehmen würden, werden nicht wahrgenommen, stattdessen besteht sogar in der eingeschränkten Gruppe der Vollzeiterwerbstätigen ein markanter Geschlechterunterschied bezüglich der Erwerbsstundenzahl.

Wir haben in diesem Beitrag danach geforscht, ob es zur alltäglichen Erfahrung, wonach hierzulande vermehrt Männer anzutreffen sind, die den Kinderwagen herumchauffieren oder ihren Nachwuchs auf den Spielplätzen betreuen, ein strukturelles Äquivalent gibt. Fündig geworden sind wir nicht. Gesetzt den Fall, es handle sich bei dieser Alltagsbeobachtung nicht bloss um eine selektive Wahrnehmung, wäre zu hoffen, dass sich wenigstens an den Rändern der Gesellschaft eine Avantgarde entwickelt, welche durchaus selbstbewusst Nachfrage zu schaffen versucht für Verhaltensmuster, ohne welche die Ziele von Chancengleichheit und Gleichstellung der Geschlechter nicht einzulösen sein dürften.

Literaturverzeichnis

Bauer, Tobias, Strub, Silvia (2002) *Wie ist die Arbeit zwischen den Geschlechtern verteilt? Eine Untersuchung zur Aufteilung von unbezahlter Arbeit in Fmilien in der Schweiz und im internationalen Vergleich*, Bern: Eidg. Büro für die Gleichstellung.

Baumgartner, A. Doris (2002) *Zwischen Karriere und Sackgasse. Formen diskontinuierlicher Frauenerwerbsverläufe unter besonderer Berücksichtigung der Bildungsressourcen*, Schlussbericht an den Schweizerischen Nationalfonds, Zürich: (mimeo).

Baumgartner, A. Doris (2003a) *Erwerbsverläufe von Frauen mit Kindern*, Synthesis 2, Bern/ Aarau.

Baumgartner, A. Doris (2003b) Teilzeitarbeit – Auf dem Weg zu einem neuen Normalarbeitsverhältnis?, *Schweizer Zeitschrift für Soziologie*, 29, 1.

Blossfeld, Hans-Peter, Hakim, Catherine (1997) *Between Equalization and Marginalization. Women Working Part-Time in Europe and the United States of America*, Oxford: Oxford University Press.

Born, Claudia, Krüger, Helga (Hrsg.) (2001) *Individualisierung und Verflechtung. Geschlecht und Generation im deutschen Lebenslaufregime*, Weinheim und München: Juventa.

Born, Claudia, Krüger, Helga, Lorenz-Meyer, Dagmar (Hrsg.) (1996) *Der unentdeckte Wandel: Annäherungen an das Verhältnis von Struktur und Norm im weiblichen Lebenslauf*, Berlin: Edition Sigma.

Buchmann, Marlis, Kriesi, Irene, Pfeifer, Andrea, Sacchi, Stefan (2002) *halb drinnen – halb draussen. Analysen zur Arbeitsmarktintegration von Frauen in der Schweiz*, Chur / Zürich: Rüegger.

Delsen, Lei (1998) When do Men Work Part-time?, in: Jacqueline O'Reilly, Fagan, Colette (Hrsg.) *Part-time Prospects: an International Comparison of Part-time Work in Europe, North America and the Pacific Rim*, London, New York: Routledge, 57–76.

Lauterbach, Wolfgang (1994) *Berufsverläufe von Frauen. Erwerbstätigkeit, Unterbrechung und Wiedereintritt*, Frankfurt a. M.: Campus.

Lüscher, Kurt, Thierbach, Rüdiger, Coenen-Huther, Josette, Goy, Marie-Françoise (1996) *Haushalte und Familien: die Vielfalt der Lebensformen*, Bern: Bundesamt für Statistik.

Quack, Sigrid (1993) *Dynamik der Teilzeitarbeit. Implikationen für die soziale Sicherung von Frauen*, Berlin: edition sigma.

SAKE (2003) Pressemitteilung: Deutliche Zunahme der Erwerbsbevölkerung. Eidgenössische Volkszählung 2000, *SAKE-News* 7/03.

Schulze Buschoff, Karin, Rückert, Jana (1998) *Teilzeitbeschäftigte in Europa. Arbeitsbedingungen, Familienkontext, Motive und subjektive Bewertungen*, Berlin: Wissenschaftszentrum Berlin für Sozialforschung.

Van Emmerick, Hetty, Hermkens, Piet (1999) *When are Men going to Work Less,* 4th European Conference of Sociology of the European Sociological Association, Amsterdam: (mimeo).

Annex

Tabelle 1A: Das Erwerbspensum von Müttern und Vätern

	Mütter		Väter	
	1999	2000	1999	2000
nicht erwerbstätig	35.1	30.8	5.1	4.6
bis 20 %	12.0	12.2	0.9	0.8
21–40 %	12.6	13.9	0.9	0.5
41–55 %	12.7	14.2	1.5	1.9
56–75 %	8.7	9.3	2.0	1.9
über 75 %	4.6	5.0	3.5	3.5
Vollzeit	14.3	14.8	86.2	86.9
	100.0	100.0	100.0	100.0
N	1338	1349	1168	1173

Tabelle 2A: Erwerbsumfang der Mütter nach familialer Situation in %

	Vollzeit		Teilzeit		nicht erwerbst.		N	
familiale Situation:	1999	2000	1999	2000	1999	2000	1999	2000
Eltern(teil) mit Kleinkind	6.2	6.0	40.1	50.7	53.8	43.3	260	233
Eltern(teil) mit Vorschulkind	14.5	12.2	47.1	45.3	38.4	42.5	242	254
Eltern(teil) mit Schulkind	11.3	12.8	58.2	62.1	30.5	25.1	390	398
Eltern(teil) mit älterem Kind im Haushalt	16.5	20.1	54.4	57.9	29.1	21.9	261	288
Eltern(teil) ohne Kinder im Haushalt	29.2	25.6	48.2	50.0	22.7	24.4	185	176

Tabelle 3A: Erwerbsumfang der Väter nach familialer Situation in %

	Vollzeit		Teilzeit		nicht erwerbst.		N	
familiale Situation	1999	2000	1999	2000	1999	2000	1999	2000
Eltern(teil) mit Kleinkind	86.9	87.6	10.2	8.3	3.0	8.3	237	226
Eltern(teil) mit Vorschulkind	89.1	87.7	7.8	10.9	3.2	10.9	220	219
Eltern(teil) mit Schulkind	87.5	87.5	8.8	8.7	3.7	8.7	327	345
Eltern(teil) mit älterem Kind im Haushalt	81.7	83.5	8.0	7.0	10.3	7.0	213	242
Eltern(teil) ohne Kinder im Haushalt	84.8	88.7	8.9	6.3	6.4	6.3	171	141

Tabelle 4A: Teilzeitbeschäftigung aus familiären Gründen nach Geschlecht, 1999, in %

Teilzeit beschäftigte	Frauen	N	Männer	N
Eltern(teil) mit Kleinkind	94.3	105	76.0	25
Eltern(teil) mit Vorschulkind	93.0	114	50.0	18
Eltern(teil) mit Schulkind	82.4	227	34.5	29
Eltern(teil) mit älterem Kind im Haushalt	66.0	141	5.9	17
Eltern(teil) ohne Kinder im Haushalt	31.5	89	7.1	14

Tabelle 5A: Erwerbsstatus und Normalstundenzahl bei Vollzeiterwerbstätigkeit nach Geschlecht, 2000, in % resp. in Stunden

Frauen	Erwerbstätig 1999	Erwerbstätig 2000	Vollzeit 2000	Teilzeit >40 %, 2000	Normalstunden, 2000	Normalstunden, 1999
1945–49	71.1	71.5	16.1	30.4	37.5	36.6
1950–54	74.5	75.9	18.6	32.3	37.0	35.6
1955–59	71.4	75.2	14.1	32.5	37.1	35.4
1960–64	60.7	66.5	9.9	29.2	35.8	35.6
1965–69	57.1	63.2	13.4	24.1	37.3	39.4
1970–74	57.6	62.6	15.2	23.3	38.0	40.3
1975–84	51.2	65.1	31.8	9.1	41.0	37.1
alle	65.3	69.4	14.9	28.4	37.3	36.7
N	886	942	200	384	363	313

Männer	Erwerbstätig 1999	Erwerbstätig 2000	Vollzeit 2000	Teilzeit >40 %, 2000	Normalstunden, 2000	Normalstunden, 1999
1945–49	95.7	95.2	90.0	4.3	46.8	44.8
1950–54	95.1	96.1	89.3	5.8	47.6	46.5
1955–59	97.8	98.2	87.7	10.0	45.7	44.5
1960–64	95.9	96.7	86.6	8.6	46.3	46.0
1965–69	97.8	95.0	86.3	8.2	45.6	44.7
1970–74	87.0	92.6	84.1	4.3	43.9	44.3
1975–84	75.0	79.1	67.4	2.2	43.8	43.1
alle	95.1	95.5	87.1	7.3	46.2	45.1
N	1116	1120	1020	85	1028	968

Tabelle 6A: Erwerbsmuster nach Familienphase 2000 in %

	Vollzeit / Vollzeit	Vollzeit / Teilzeit	Vollzeit / Nicht Erwerbstätig	Übrige	N
Eltern(teil) mit Kleinkind	8.3	35.2	50.0	6.4	420
Eltern(teil) mit Vorschulkind	11.8	32.5	48.6	7.1	424
Eltern(teil) mit Schulkind	10.8	48.7	35.7	4.8	610
Eltern(teil) mit älterem Kind im Haushalt	12.4	52.6	30.5	4.5	380
Eltern(teil) ohne Kinder im Haushalt	25.4	40.0	28.3	6.3	205
Gesamt	12.3	42.4	39.6	5.7	2039

Tabelle 7A: Erwerbsmuster nach Geburtsjahrgängen, 2000 und 1999, in %

Jahr 2000	Vollzeit / Vollzeit	Vollzeit / Teilzeit	Vollzeit / Nicht-Erwerbstätig	Übrige
1945–49	15.5	47.1	31.6	5.8
1950–54	13.5	48.0	32.9	5.5
1955–59	10.9	49.6	32.7	6.8
1960–64	10.1	37.7	46.9	5.3
1965–69	10.3	39.8	44.8	5.0
1970–74	15.9	31.7	44.8	7.6
1975–84	12.2	14.3	71.4	2.0

Jahr 1999	Vollzeit / Vollzeit	Vollzeit / Teilzeit	Vollzeit / Nicht-Erwerbstätig	Übrige
1945–49	18.1	45.7	29.4	6.8
1950–54	14.7	45.9	33.9	5.4
1955–59	10.8	46.8	35.5	7.0
1960–64	10.7	36.4	47.8	5.0
1965–69	11.9	34.9	48.4	4.9
1970–74	15.6	34.8	43.3	6.4
1975–84	12.5	25.0	55.0	7.5

Soziale Beziehungen und soziale Unterstützung*

Christian SUTER, Katia IGLESIAS und Thomas OEGERLI

Einleitung und Fragestellung

Jeder Mensch ist von Geburt an eingebunden in mehr oder weniger dauerhafte soziale Beziehungen. So gehen Kinder und Erwachsene in ihrem alltäglichen Leben und Handeln soziale Beziehungen ein, halten bestehende soziale Netzwerke aufrecht, schaffen neue soziale Kontakte oder brechen alte Beziehungen ab. Insbesondere Kinder sind angewiesen auf die Zuwendung von Erwachsenen – sowohl in emotionaler wie in alltagspraktischer Hinsicht. Jugendliche schliessen sich in ihrer Freizeit zu Gruppen und Cliquen zusammen, die für ihre Selbstidentität oft wichtiger sind als die Familie. Aber auch erwachsene Menschen sind auf Sozialbeziehungen angewiesen: erst über seine sozialen Beziehungen ist der Mensch mit seinen Mitmenschen und seiner sozialen Umwelt verbunden. Diese sozialen Netzwerke bilden sich durch wiederholte soziale Kontakte und Interaktionen zwischen zwei oder mehreren Personen. Die Dynamik sozialer Beziehungen ergibt sich dabei häufig nicht willentlich, sondern als Folge unbeabsichtigter Wirkungen individuellen Handelns.

Die meisten Menschen sind gleichzeitig in mehrere soziale Netze eingebunden: Partnerschaft und Familie, Verwandtschaft, Freundeskreis, Vertrauenspersonen, Arbeits- und Berufskollegen, Nachbarschaft, Vereins- und Freizeitbekanntschaften. Dabei unterscheiden sich die verschiedenen sozialen Beziehungsnetze hinsichtlich ihrer Intensität und ihren Funktionen. Beispiele

* Der vorliegende Beitrag findet sich im Sammelband *Leben in der Schweiz 1999–2000* (Erwin Zimmermann & Robin Tillmann (hrsg.), Verlag Peter Lang, Bern (2004)). Die Auswertungen und Ergebnisse stammen aus den ersten zwei Wellen der Längsschnittsbefragung Leben in der Schweiz, worin 6 335 Personen in den Jahren 1999 und 2000 befragt wurden. Als Mandat des Schweizer Haushalt-Panel der Universität Neuchâtel wurde die Datenerhebung von M. I. S. Trend durchgeführt und vom SPP Zukunft Schweiz des Schweizerischen Nationalfonds für wissenschaftliche Forschung finanziert (Gesuche Nr. 5004-53205 / 5004-57894 / 5004-67304). Weitere Information finden sich auf der Webseite www.swisspanel.ch.

dafür sind enge und langandauernde Freundschaften, emotionale Liebes- und Partnerbeziehungen, enge aber auf vergleichsweise kurze Lebensabschnitte konzentrierte Cliquenbeziehungen, alltäglich und lebenslange Beziehungen zwischen Geschwistern, zwischen Eltern und Kindern oder zwischen Grosseltern und Enkelkindern, flüchtige Kontakte zu entfernten Verwandten und Zufallsbekanntschaften oder regelmässige aber weitgehend instrumentell gestaltete Beziehungen zu Arbeits- und Berufskollegen.

Aus diesen Gründen ist es sinnvoll die intensiven Alltagsbeziehungen, die zwischen den engsten Bezugspersonen bestehen, von den weniger regelmässigen Kontakten zu unterscheiden. Familie und Partnerschaft sowie nichtfamiliale Formen des Zusammenlebens zählen zu den intensivsten und regelmässigsten Alltagsbeziehungen – sie werden deshalb häufig als das „primäre" soziale Netz bezeichnet. Demgegenüber werden soziale Netze, die weniger regelmässige und intensive Kontakte beinhalten wie Verwandtschaft, Nachbarschaft, Freundes- und Kollegenkreis, als das „sekundäre" Netz bezeichnet (Meyer und Suter, 1993).

Der vorliegende Beitrag beschäftigt sich genauer mit diesen sozialen Beziehungsnetzen. Dabei stehen drei Fragen im Vordergrund: *Erstens* wird danach gefragt, wie die sozialen Beziehungen und Netze der Menschen in der Schweiz gestaltet sind, d. h. wie breit die soziale Vernetzung ist, wie gross die Anzahl der Beziehungspersonen in den verschiedenen Teilnetzen ist, wie intensiv der Kontakt gepflegt wird und welche Veränderungen zwischen den zwei Erhebungszeitpunkten (1999 und 2000) sichtbar sind. *Zweitens* untersuchen wir, ob und in welchem Ausmass sich der Einzelne durch die Beziehungen in seinem sozialen Umfeld emotional und praktisch unterstützt fühlt. Dabei interessieren auch allfällige Unterschiede zwischen Frauen und Männer, zwischen jungen und älteren Menschen oder zwischen Grosstädtern und Dorfbewohnern. *Drittens* fragen wir nach den Wirkungen und Konsequenzen sozialer Beziehungen und sozialer Unterstützung. Wirkt sich eine gute soziale Unterstützung und Vernetzung auch positiv auf die Lebensqualität, die Gesundheit und auf das persönliche Wohlbefinden aus?

Soziale Beziehungen und soziale Netze als persönliche und gesellschaftliche Ressourcen

In der Wissenschaft wird v. a. den Ressourcenaspekt sozialer Netze thematisiert. Soziale Beziehungen schliessen nämlich nicht nur eine gegenseitige Kommunikation ein, sondern beinhalten häufig auch den Austausch von wertvollen Gütern oder den Zugang zu einflussreichen Positionen. Bei diesen Ressourcen kann es sich um Arbeitsplätze, vorteilhafte Konsummöglichkeiten, wichtige Informationen u. ä. handeln. Soziale Beziehungen eröffnen und begrenzen dadurch Handlungschancen und Wahlmöglichkeiten. Der Ressourcenaspekt sozialer Beziehungen wird sowohl auf individueller wie auf gesamtgesellschaftlicher Ebene thematisiert. So wird anhand der Sozialbeziehung zwischen den einzelnen Mitgliedern auf den sozialen Zusammenhalt und die Integrationskraft von sozialen Gruppen, Organisationen oder von ganzen Gesellschaften geschlossen.

Schon der arabische Historiker und Philosoph Ibn Khaldoun (1332–1406) erklärte die politische Vorherrschaft bestimmter Stämme und Staaten im arabischen und nordafrikanischen Raum mit der Stärke ihres gesellschaftlichen Gemeinsinns und Zusammengehörigkeitsgefühls. Dieses resultiere, so Ibn Khaldoun (1934), letztlich aus den gemeinsamen Verwandtschafts- und Blutbeziehungen oder vergleichbaren engen sozialen Bindungen. Dieser ressourcentheoretische Grundgedanke findet sich auch in den Netzwerk-, Kommunitarismus- und Sozialkapitalansätzen, die in den 1980er und 1990er Jahre entstanden (Bourdieu, 1983, Coleman, 1988, Etzioni, 1993, Putnam, 1995, Lin, 1999, OECD, 2001). Auch hier werden soziale Netze in erster Linie als instrumentelle Ressourcen verstanden, aus denen sich Sozialkapital oder gegenseitige gemeinschaftliche Unterstützung gewinnen lassen. Allerdings ist der Sozialkapitalansatz insofern umfassender, als er nicht nur persönliche soziale Netze, sondern auch das zivilgesellschaftliche Engagement und das Vertrauen in gesellschaftliche und politische Institutionen mitberücksichtigt.

Auf individueller Ebene zeigt sich diese instrumentelle Bedeutung sozialer Beziehungen beispielsweise im Zugang zu und im Erwerb von Berufs-, Karriere- und Statuspositionen. Der Sachverhalt, dass nicht alle Gesellschaftsmitglieder ihre sozialen Beziehungen in gleichem Masse instrumentell nutzen können und dass der auf sozialen Beziehungen basierende Zugang zu Statuspositionen häufig in Widerspruch zu universalistischen und leistungsbezogenen Zugangkriterien steht, wird insbesondere in der Ungleichheitsforschung betont (Lin, 1999). Der Ressourcenaspekt sozialer Beziehung ist auch ein wichtiges Thema in der Gesundheits- und Stressforschung, wobei insbesondere die Bedeutung sozialer Unterstützung für die Bewältigung von bestimmten Lebenssituationen und kritischen Lebensereignissen untersucht wird (Meyer und Suter, 1993).

In der Netzwerkanalyse wird zwischen drei verschiedenen Aspekten sozialer Beziehungen und sozialer Netze unterschieden, die auch in der vorliegenden Studie näher untersucht werden sollen (vgl. dazu Cohen und Syme, 1985, Meyer und Suter, 1993, Due et al., 1999).

Eine *erste Gruppe* von Merkmalen bezieht sich auf *formale* oder *strukturelle* Aspekte sozialer Beziehungen. Darunter ist das Vorhandensein verschiedener Beziehungsformen bzw. Netzwerktypen (Partnerschaft, Freundschaft etc.), die Grösse und der Umfang sozialer Netze, die Häufigkeit, Dauer und Intensität der sozialen Kontakte sowie die Diversität und Reziprozität der Beziehungen zu verstehen.

Eine *zweite Gruppe* von Merkmalen bezieht sich auf *qualitative* und *inhaltliche* Aspekte sozialer Beziehungen. Dazu gehört insbesondere der oben geschilderte Ressourcen- und Unterstützungsaspekt, der häufig als eigentliche Funktion sozialer Netzwerke betrachtet wird (Antonucci, 1990, Meyer und Suter, 1993). Soziale Unterstützung kann dabei in unterschiedlichen Formen geleistet und empfangen werden. Zwei wichtige Formen sind emotionale Unterstützung – also emotionale Zuwendung, Wertschätzung, Verständnis, Zugehörigkeitsgefühl – und instrumentelle oder praktische Unterstützung – also alltagsorganisatorische Unterstützung, finanzielle Hilfe, Informationen, Hilfeleistungen zur Erreichung konkreter Ziele. Granovetter (1973, 1983) hat Beziehungen, die einen hohen Gehalt an emotionaler Unterstützung aufweisen als „strong ties“ bezeichnet und sie den weniger intensiven, ausschliesslich instrumentell orientierten „weak ties“ gegenübergestellt. Tatsächlich lassen sich die verschiedenen Netzwerktypen eher den „strong ties“ (z. B. die sozialen Beziehungen des primären Netzes wie Partnerschaft und Familie aber auch enge Freunde oder sogenannte Vertrauenspersonen) oder den „weak ties“ zuordnen (z. B. ehemalige Arbeits-, Klassen- oder Studienkollegen).

Aus bisherigen Studien ist bekannt, dass die einzelnen sozialen Beziehungsnetze unterschiedliche Formen sozialer Unterstützung bereitstellen (Wellman und Wortley, 1990). Darüber hinaus variieren Unterstützungsformen und soziale Vernetzung zwischen den verschiedenen Bevölkerungsgruppen. Neben alters-, geschlechter-, einkommens- und schichtspezifischen Differenzen (Sprecher und Felmlee, 1992, Andress et al., 1995, Due et al., 1999, Ibarra, 1997) wurden auch Unterschiede zwischen ländlichen und urbanen Kontexten gefunden (Schilling und Wahl, 2002).

Im Rahmen der Sozialkapitalansätze fanden verschiedene empirische Studien enge positive Zusammenhänge zwischen Indikatoren der sozialen Vernetzung und Gesundheitsindikatoren (selbsteingeschätzter Gesundheitszustand, Lebenserwartung, Mortalität; z. B. Kawachi et al. 1997, 1999). Insbesondere die gesundheitssoziologisch orientierte Netzwerkforschung hat jedoch darauf hingewiesen, dass soziale Beziehungen nicht nur unterstützend und gesundheitsfördernd, sondern auch belastend wirken können (Lin und Ensel, 1989, Thoist, 1995). Quelle solcher Netzbelastungen sind Meinungsverschiedenheiten, Streit und Konflikte, Sorgen um enge Beziehungspersonen, (übermässige) Ansprüche von Personen aus den verschiedenen sozialen Teilnetzen, aber auch der Verlust sozialer Beziehungen durch Tod, Wegzug oder Trennung. Diese Belastungseffekte weisen auf den *dritten wichtigen Aspekt* der Netzwerkforschung hin: die *Wirkungen* sozialer Vernetzung – und zwar positiver wie negativer Art – auf andere zentrale Lebensbereiche wie beispielsweise die Gesundheit oder das subjektive Wohlbefinden. In verschiedenen Untersuchungen wurden die Gesundheitseffekte von sozialer Unterstützung und sozialer Belastungen analysiert. Dabei zeigte sich einerseits, dass soziale Belastungen die Gesundheit beeinträchtigen. Andererseits scheinen soziale Beziehungen und soziale Unterstützung die Gesundheit positiv zu beeinflussen, wobei sowohl direkte wie interaktive Effekte vorkommen können. Von einem interaktiven oder vermittelnden Effekt wird dann gesprochen, wenn soziale Unterstützung nur bei hoher (nicht aber bei niedriger) sozialer Belastung einen positiven Gesundheitseffekt aufweist.

In den nachfolgenden Abschnitten sollen die oben angesprochenen drei grundlegenden Aspekte sozialer Beziehungen und sozialer Netze für die Schweizer Haushalte und Familie genauer untersucht werden. Dabei soll auch der Fragen nachgegangen werden, wie stark sich diese Merkmale zwischen den zwei betrachteten Erhebungszeitpunkten (1999 und 2000) gewandelt haben. Aus Platzgründen können jedoch nicht alle Analysen in graphischer oder tabellarischer Form dargestellt werden.

Formale und strukturelle Aspekte soziale Vernetzung

Das Schweizer Haushalt-Panel enthält verschiedene Angaben zu formalen und strukturellen Aspekte sozialer Beziehungen. So wurden die Befragten gebeten, Angaben zum Vorhandensein und zur Intensität (Häufigkeit) sozialer Beziehungen in sechs verschiedenen Teilnetzen zu machen: Partnerschaft und Zusammenleben mit anderen Personen (Erwachsene oder Kinder), Kinder (ausserhalb des eigenen Haushalt), Verwandtschaft, Nachbarschaft, Freunde und Arbeits- und Freizeitkollegen.[1] Wir haben weiter oben auf die grosse Bedeutung des sogenannten „primären" Netzes hingewiesen. Für die vorliegende Studie verstehen wir unter dem primären Netz die Partnerschaft (mit oder ohne gemeinsamem Zusammenleben) sowie das Zusammenleben mit Kindern und/oder anderen Erwachsenen. Bei den Netzwerken Verwandtschaft, Freundeskreis, Arbeits- und Freizeitkollegen, Nachbarschaft werden nur jene Beziehungen berücksichtigt, bei denen die Befragten angeben, dass sie ein gutes und enges Verhältnis zu den jeweiligen Beziehungspersonen haben.

In einem *ersten Schritt* betrachten wir das Vorhandensein von sechs verschiedenen sozialen Teilnetze: Primäres Netz (Partnerschaft und Zusammenleben mit anderen Erwachsene oder Kindern), Kinder (ausserhalb des eigenen Haushaltes), Verwandtschaft, Nachbarschaft, Freunde sowie Arbeits- und Freizeitkollegen. Dabei zeigt sich, dass in beiden betrachteten Jahren (1999, 2000) nur ein verschwindend kleiner Teil der Bevölkerung keine oder eine sehr schlechte soziale Vernetzung aufweist. So geht aus Abbildung 1 hervor, dass lediglich 1 % der Befragten über keines oder höchstens eines der genannten Teilnetze verfügt. Hingegen geben drei Viertel der Befragten vier oder mehr Teilnetze an.

1 Die Fragen zum Vorhandensein und zur Grösse sozialer Netzte lauteten: „Zu wie vielen Verwandten (Nachbarn, Kollegen etc.) haben Sie eine gute und enge Beziehung?" Die Fragen zur Intensität sozialer Beziehungen lauteten: „Und wie häufig haben Sie mit diesen Verwandten (Nachbarn, Kollegen etc) Kontakt?"

Abbildung 1: Anzahl vorhandener Teilnetzen (0–6); 1999/2000 (in %)

	1999	2000
Keines oder eines von sechs Teilnetze vorhanden	1.3 %	1.4 %
Zwei von sechs Teilnetzen vorhanden	5.6 %	6.8 %
Drei von sechs Teilnetzen vorhanden	16.4 %	17.5 %
Vier von sechs Teilnetzen vorhanden	31.3 %	32.5 %
Fünf von sechs Teilnetzen vorhanden	34.4 %	31.8 %
Alle sechs Teilnetzen vorhanden	11.0 %	10.0 %

Anmerkungen: Es wurden die folgenden sechs Teilnetze berücksichtigt: Partnerschaft und Zusammenleben mit anderen Personen (Erwachsene oder Kinder), Kinder (ausserhalb des eigenen Haushalt), Verwandtschaft, Nachbarschaft, Freunde, Arbeits- und Freizeitkollegen.
Stichprobe und Gewichtung: Schweizer Haushalt-Panel, Längsschnittstichprobe 1999–2000, Personen-Querschnittsgewichtung; Stichprobengrösse: N = 5921 (1999) bzw. N = 5642 (2000).

Betrachtet man die verschiedenen Teilnetze etwas genauer, zeigen sich beträchtliche Unterschiede in ihrer quantitativen Bedeutung. Dies lässt sich Abbildung 2 entnehmen, in der die Prozentanteile der Befragten dargestellt sind, die in ein bestimmtes soziales Teilnetz eingebunden sind. Über soziale Beziehungen innerhalb ihres primären Netzes, d.h. innerhalb der Partnerschaft sowie der familialen oder nicht familialen Formen das Zusammenleben, verfügen im Jahr 1999 84 % und im Jahr 2000 88 % der Befragten. Ähnlich hoch liegen die Anteile bei Verwandten und Freunden. So geben 1999 lediglich 6 % an, keinen Kontakt zu Verwandten zu pflegen (2000: 14 %). Auch der Freundeskreis findet sich bei fast allen Befragten: nur 9 % haben 1999 keine engen Freunde (2000: 14 %). Dagegen weist ein Drittel der Befragten keinen Kontakt zu Nachbarn oder Arbeits- und Freizeitkollegen auf. Letzteres ist v.a. dadurch zu erklären, dass nicht alle Befragten berufstätig sind (z.B. Hausfrauen, Rentner). Die relativ geringe quantitative Bedeutung des Teilnetzes der erwachsenen, ausserhalb des eigenen Haushalts wohnhaften Kindern erklärt sich hauptsächlich dadurch, dass dieses Sozialnetz erst ab einem bestimmten Alter (d.h. ab ca. 40 Jahre) und beim Vorhandensein von Kindern vorkommen kann. Berücksichtigt man nur diejenigen Personen, bei denen dieses Teilnetz theoretisch auch vorhanden sein kann, zeigt sich, dass Kontakte zu erwachsenen Kindern die Regel sind: Nur 3 % der Befragten mit Kindern, die nicht mehr im eigenen Haushalt wohnhaft sind, geben an, keinen Kontakt zu ihren Kindern zu pflegen.

Abbildung 2: Vorhandensein von sechs sozialen Teilnetzen; 1999/2000 (in %)

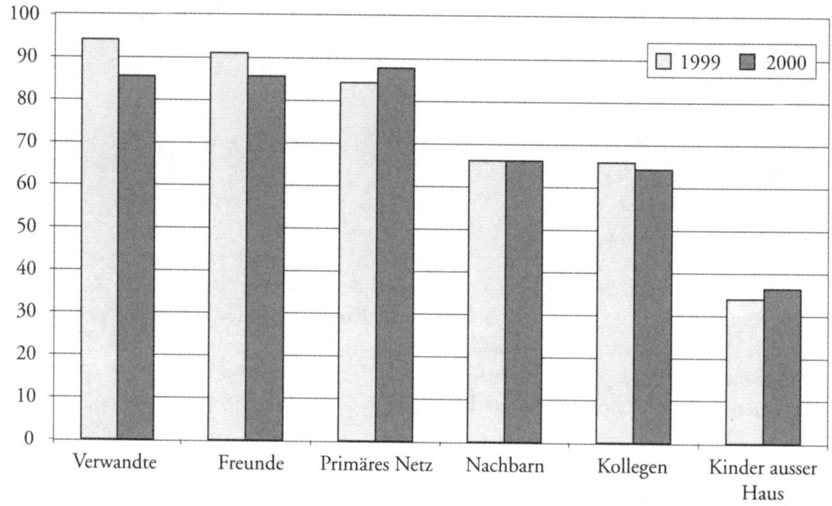

Anmerkungen: Es wurden die folgenden sechs Teilnetze berücksichtigt (in Klammern Stichprobengrösse): Verwandtschaft (1999: N = 5819; 2000: N = 5899), Freunde (1999: N = 5833; 2000: N = 5884), Primäres Netz: Partnerschaft und Zusammenleben mit anderen Personen (Erwachsene oder Kinder) (1999: N = 5921; 2000: N = 5942), Nachbarschaft (1999: N = 5887; 2000: N = 5846), Arbeits- und Freizeitkollegen (1999: N = 5921; 2000: N = 5942), Kinder (ausserhalb des eigenen Haushalt) (1999: N = 5916; 2000: N = 5939).
Stichprobe und Gewichtung: Schweizer Haushalt-Panel, Längsschnittstichprobe 1999–2000, Personen-Querschnittsgewichtung.

Aus den Abbildung 1 und 2 geht hervor, dass sich zwischen 1999 und 2000 die quantitative Bedeutung der sechs verschiedenen Teilnetze kaum verändert hat. Allerdings handelt es sich bei diesen Angaben um aggregierte Daten, hinter denen sich vermutlich Veränderungen auf individuellem Niveau verbergen. So wäre denkbar, dass zwar in beiden Jahren die Anzahl der Befragten mit einem bestimmten Teilnetz identisch ist, dass es sich dabei aber nicht um dieselben Personen handelt. Um solche Veränderungen auf individuellem Niveau zu prüfen, haben wir das Antwortmuster zwischen 1999 und 2000 für alle Befragten untersucht. Für jedes Teilnetz unterscheiden wir vier mögliche Varianten: 1) das entsprechende Teilnetz ist sowohl 1999 und 2000 vorhanden, 2) das entsprechende Teilnetz ist in keinem der beiden Jahre vorhanden, 3) das entsprechende Teilnetz ist 1999 vorhanden, aber nicht 2000, 4) das entsprechende Teilnetz ist 2000 vorhanden, aber nicht 1999.

Abbildung 3: Individuelle Veränderungen im Vorhandensein der verschiedenen Teilnetze zwischen 1999 und 2000 (in %)

Vorhandersein des Teilnetze 1999	2000	Primäres Netz	Kinder ausser-halb	Ver-wandte	Freunde	Nach-barn	Kollegen
Nicht vorhanden	Nicht vorhanden	11 %	60 %	3 %	5 %	20 %	18 %
Nicht vorhanden	Vorhanden	3 %	5 %	3 %	5 %	14 %	18 %
Vorhanden	Nicht vorhanden	1 %	3 %	12 %	9 %	14 %	19 %
Vorhanden	Vorhanden	85 %	32 %	82 %	81 %	53 %	46 %
Chi-Quadrat		4009.5	4010	308.2	681.1	851.4	272.9
Irrtumswahrscheinlichkeit				$p < .001$			

Anmerkungen: Es wurden die folgenden sechs Teilnetze berücksichtigt: Verwandtschaft, Freunde, Primäres Netz: Partnerschaft und Zusammenleben mit anderen Personen (Erwachsene oder Kinder), Nachbarschaft, Arbeits- und Freizeitkollegen, Kinder (ausserhalb des eigenen Haushaltes).
Stichprobe und Gewichtung: Schweizer Haushalt-Panel, Längsschnittstichprobe 1999–2000, Personen-Längsschnittgewichtung, N = 5900.

Die in Abbildung 3 aufgeführten Ergebnisse zeigen, dass die verschiedenen Teilnetze unterschiedlich stabil sind. Erwartungsgemäss sind das primäre Netz und die Beziehungen zu erwachsenen Kindern sehr stabil. Lediglich bei 4 % der Befragten (beim primären Netz) bzw. 8 % (erwachsene Kinder ausser Haus) gab es eine Veränderung in die eine oder andere Richtung. Etwas mehr Veränderungen – nämlich je 15 % – werden beim Sozialnetz der Verwandtschaft und des Freundeskreises angegeben. Die grössten Veränderungen finden in den Sozialnetzen der Nachbarschaft (28 %) und der Kollegen statt (37 %).

Inwieweit lassen sich diese individuellen Veränderungen interpretieren und erklären? Insbesondere bei den weniger engen Beziehungen (z. B. Nachbarschaft) dürften neben einer Fehlerkomponente auch nichtüberprüfbare individuelle Faktoren eine Rolle spielen. Darüber hinaus sind eine Reihe von Gründen denkbar, die zu einer Veränderung der jeweiligen Netze führen können – beim primären Netz z. B. des Ende einer Zweierbeziehung durch Trennung oder Tod, bei den Arbeitskollegen Eintritt in oder Austritt aus dem Arbeitsmarkt oder ein Stellenwechsel, bei der Nachbarschaft ein Wechsel des Wohnorts.

Eine systematische Überprüfung der individuellen Netzveränderungen mit Hilfe solchen Ereignisfaktoren ergab jedoch kaum interpretierbare Ergebnisse

(Methode: multinomiale logistische Regression). So liess sich für die Veränderungen im sozialen Teilnetz der Nachbarschaft kein einziger statistisch signifikanter Faktor finden, während sich beim Kollegenkreis lediglich der Faktor „Änderung des Beschäftigungsgrades" als statistisch signifikant erwies. Einzig für das primäre Netz der Partnerschaft gelang es, ein statistisch signifikantes Gesamtmodell zu schätzen. Dabei zeigten zwei Ereignisfaktoren einen bedeutsamen Zusammenhang, nämlich die Beendigung einer Beziehung und die Veränderung der Haushaltsform, wobei letzteres wohl eher die Folge der zu erklärenden Netzveränderung darstellt als deren Ursache. Einer der Gründe für den geringen Erklärungsgehalt dieser Modelle bilden die zu geringen Fallzahlen bei den Ereignisfaktoren (wie Trennungen, Umzug, Stellenwechsel etc. in den vergangenen 12 Monaten). Erschwerend kommt hinzu, dass mehrere Variablen einen beträchtlichen Anteil an fehlenden Angabe aufweisen. Dies führt dazu, dass ein grosser Teil der Zellen in den entsprechenden Mehrfeldertabellen keine oder sehr niedrige Frequenzen aufweist.

Ein *zweiter formaler Aspekt* der sozialen Vernetzung betrifft die Grösse und der Umfang der einzelnen Teilnetze. Dieser Aspekt ist insbesondere beim sekundären Netz von Bedeutung. Grösse und Umfang eines sozialen Teilnetzes lässt sich durch die Zahl der Beziehungspersonen, mit denen ein regelmässiger Kontakt gepflegt wird, bestimmen.

Aus Abbildung 4 lässt sich entnehmen, dass die Verwandtschaft das zahlenmässig grösste soziale Teilnetz bildet: Über 40 % der Befragten geben im Jahr 1999 an, mit zehn oder mehr Verwandten eine gute und enge Beziehung zu pflegen und immerhin 19 % nennen 6–9 Verwandte (2000: 31 % bzw. 22 %). Obgleich alle anderen Netze deutlich kleiner sind, ist auch dort der Anteil der Befragten mit sehr umfangreichen Beziehungen erstaunlich gross: So weisen über 27 % zehn oder mehr gute Arbeitskollegen auf (2000: 25 %), 23 % zehn oder mehr enge Freunde (2000: 17 %); sowie 12 % zehn oder mehr Nachbarn, zu denen ein gutes Verhältnis gepflegt wird (2000: 10 %). Allerdings müssen die Angaben zu dieser überwiegend guten und engen Vernetzung insofern mit Vorsicht interpretieren werden, als sich dahinter auch Verzerrungen aufgrund der Erwünschbarkeit der gemachten Antworten (d. h. einer grossen Zahl guter und enger Beziehungen) verbergen können.

Eine detailliertere Untersuchung zeigt, dass die Grösse des externen Netzes nur geringfügig mit anderen sozialstrukturellen Merkmalen in Zusammenhang steht. Der wichtigste Einfluss geht dabei vom Geschlecht aus: Männer weisen ein deutlich grösseres soziales Netz auf als Frauen. Erwartungsgemäss

Abbildung 4: Grösse und Umfang der Teilnetze: Anzahl von Verwandten, Freunden, Nachbarn und Arbeitskollegen zu denen man eine gute und enge Beziehung hat 1999/2000 (in %)

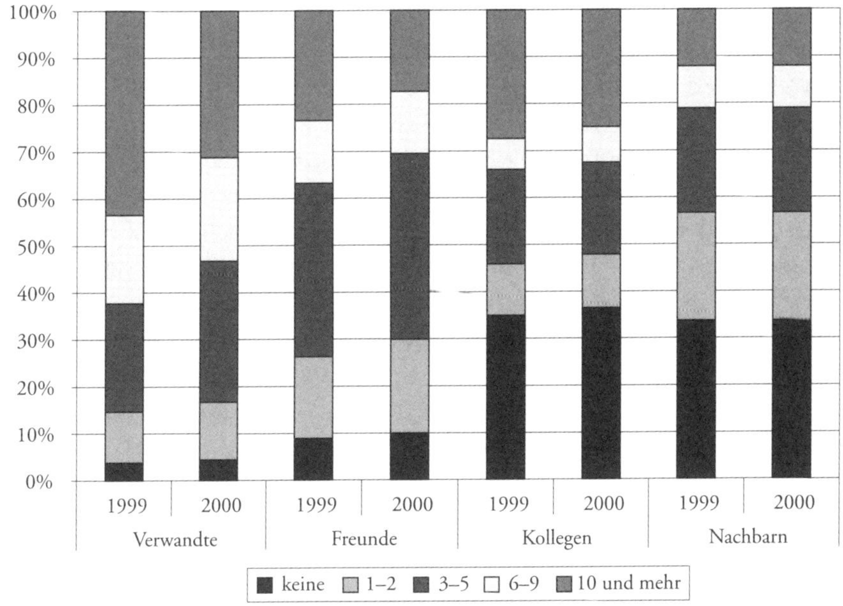

Anmerkungen: Grösse des sekundären Netzes: Anzahl von Verwandten, Freunden, Nachbarn und Arbeits- und Freizeitkollegen, zu denen man eine gute und enge Beziehung hat.
Stichprobe und Gewichtung: Schweizer Haushalt-Panel, Längsschnittstichprobe 1999–2000, Personen-Querschnittsgewichtung; Stichprobengrösse: Verwandte (1999: N = 5814, 2000: N = 5887), Nachbarn (1999: N = 5887, 2000: N = 5846), Freunde (1999: N = 5833, 2000: N = 5884), Kollegen (1999: N = 5771, 2000: N = 5817).

betreffen diese Unterschiede in erster Linie das Teilnetz der Arbeits- und Freizeitkollegen. Dies lässt sich einerseits mit der höheren Erwerbsquote der Männer erklären. Andererseits bestätigen diese Unterschiede auch die Befunde aus der Genderforschung, wonach Männer ein breiteres Netz von instrumentell mobilisierbaren „weak ties“ aufbauen. Während bei den zwei Teilnetzen der Freunden und Verwandten keine Geschlechterunterschiede vorliegen, geben die Männer jedoch auch ein grösseres Netz von guten Nachbarschaftskontakten an, wenngleich hier die Unterschiede weniger ausgeprägt sind als bei den Berufskollegen. Wie die Berufs- und Freizeitkollegen gehören Nachbarschaftskontakten eher zu den „weak ties" bei denen v. a. die instrumentelle und weniger die emotionale Bedeutung im Vordergrund steht. Allerdings könnten diese Geschlechterdifferenzen auch dadurch zustande kommen, dass Frauen und Männer unterschiedliche Vorstellungen darüber haben, was unter einer „guten und engen Beziehung" zu verstehen ist.[2]

Wenn wir die Veränderungen im Zeitverlauf betrachten, deutet Abbildung 4 auf vergleichsweise grosse Unterschiede zwischen den zwei Erhebungszeitpunkten 1999 und 2000 hin. Dabei scheint sich Grösse und Umfang aller vier Teilnetzen verringert zu haben. Am deutlichsten ist dies bei der Verwandtschaft der Fall, wo sich der Anteil der Befragten mit 10 und mehr Verwandten, zu denen man ein gutes Verhältnis pflegt, von 43 % auf 31 % verringerte. Tatsächlich ergibt eine Analyse der Angaben auf individueller Ebene grosse Fluktuationen. So antworten lediglich 30 % der Befragten, die im Jahre 1999 angaben, zu keinen einzigen Verwandten ein gutes Verhältnis zu pflegen, auch ein Jahr später auf dieselbe Weise. Beim Teilnetz der Freunde beträgt der entsprechende Anteil 46 %, bei den Kollegen 51 % und bei den Nachbarn 58 %. Ähnliches gilt bei der entgegengesetzten Extremkategorie: So geben lediglich 31 % der Befragten, die 1999 zu 10 und mehr Nachbarn ein gutes Verhältnis pflegten ein Jahr später dieselbe Antwort (Freunde: 40 %, Kollegen: 41 %, Verwandte: 48 %). Hinzu kommt, dass ein beträchtlicher Teil der Befragten sehr grosse „Bewertungssprünge" aufweist. So geben 15 % der Befragten, die 1999 mit keinen Verwandten ein gutes Verhältnis pflegten, ein Jahr später 10 oder mehr gute Verwandte an, bei 12 % sind es ein Jahr später anstelle von keinen Verwandten 6–9 und bei 20 % 3–5. Bei den anderen Teilnetzen sind die Veränderungen ähnlich, wenngleich weniger drastisch.

2 Eine hier aus Platzgründen nicht präsentierte multiple Regressionsschätzung für beide Jahre (1999, 2000) ergab, dass neben dem Geschlecht eine Reihe von weiteren Faktoren einen – allerdings deutlich geringeren – Zusammenhang mit dem Umfang der sozialen Vernetzung aufweisen (abhängige Variable: Anzahl von Verwandten, Freunden, Nachbarn und Arbeits- und Freizeitkollegen, zu denen man eine gute und enge Beziehung hat). Dazu gehört die soziale Schicht (kleineres Netz bei Befragten mit niedriger Schulbildung und hoher Deprivation), das primäre Netz (Befragte ohne Partner/Partnerin und ohne Kindern weisen ein kleineres Netz auf), die verfügbare Zeit (grösseres Netz bei mehr verfügbarer Freizeit) und die Religion (kleineres Netz bei Konfessionslosen). Keine Rolle spielt hingegen das Alter – so ist zwar die Anzahl der verschiedenen Teilnetze bei den älteren Befragten (über 65jährige) geringer, nicht aber die Anzahl der Personen, mit denen ein regelmässiger Kontakt gepflegt wird.

Die Grösse der sozialen Netze, d. h. die Zahl der engen Beziehungspersonen, sollte sich im Verlaufe von 12 Monaten eigentlich nicht in diesem Ausmass verändern – dies gilt insbesondere für die institutionalisierteren Beziehungsformen wie die Verwandtschaft. Eine Erklärung für die grosse Instabilität der Angaben könnte darin bestehen, dass nach der Zahl von Verwandten, Nachbarn und Kollegen mit „gutem" Kontakt bzw. nach „engen" Freunden gefragt wurde. Offensichtlich eröffnet diese subjektive Bewertung einen sehr grossen Bewertungsspielraum. Hinzu kommt, dass die Antworten aufgrund der sozialen Wünschbarkeit (von vielen guten Kontakten) verzerrt sein dürften. Entsprechend problematisch ist die Genauigkeit (oder Reliabilität) der Angaben zur exakten Grösse der sozialen Teilnetze einzustufen.

Ein *dritter und letzter formaler Aspekt* sozialer Netze betrifft die Dichte oder die Intensität sozialer Beziehungen. In der Erhebung des Schweizer Haushalt-Panels wurde danach gefragt, wie häufig Kontakte in ausgewählten sozialen Teilnetzen stattfinden. Die Ergebnisse zur Beziehungsintensität finden sich in Abbildung 5. Bei der Interpretation dieser Angaben ist zu beachten, dass nur für jene Teilnetze, in denen überhaupt Beziehungspersonen vorhanden waren, nach der Häufigkeit der Kontakte gefragt wurde. Erwartungsgemäss sind die Beziehungen innerhalb der Kernfamilie am intensivsten: So sehen die meisten Eltern, nämlich gegen 90 %, ihre Kinder, die nicht mehr zu Hause wohnen mindestens einmal pro Woche; davon weisen 15 % gar einen täglichen Kontakt auf und gegen 45 % geben an, ihre Kinder mehrmals wöchentlich zu sehen. Ähnlich intensiv wird auch die Nachbarschaft gepflegt, wenn eine Beziehung vorhanden ist: Gegen 85 % der Befragten geben an, mindestens einmal wöchentlich Kontakt zu pflegen, davon über 10 % täglich und ca. 45 % mehrmals wöchentlich. Etwas weniger intensiv sind Freundschafts- und Verwandtschaftsbeziehungen gestaltet: Bei den Freundesbeziehungen haben ca. 70 % und bei der Verwandtschaft ca. 65 % mindestens einmal pro Woche Kontakt, davon 5 % täglich und 35 % (Freunde) bzw. 25 % (Verwandte) mehrmals wöchentlich.

Wie bei der Grösse des sekundären Netzes weist auch die Intensität der sozialen Kontakte nur sehr geringe Zusammenhänge mit sozialstrukturellen Faktoren auf.[3] Auffallend ist jedoch, dass dort, wo Zusammenhänge sichtbar

3 Die folgenden Ausführungen basieren auf einer aus Platzgründen hier nicht dargestellten multiplen linearen Regressionsschätzung der Gesamtintensität der Kontakte des sekundären Netzes für die Jahre 1999 und 2000 (abhängige Variable: Anzahl der Kontakte in den vergangenen vier Wochen zu Kindern, die ausserhalb des eigenen Haushalts wohnen sowie zu Verwandten, Freunden und Nachbarn, zu denen eine gute und enge Beziehung besteht).

Abbildung 5: Intensität der Kontakte in vier Teilnetzen: Verwandtschaft, Freundschaft, Nachbarschaft, Kinder ausserhalb des eigenen Haushalts, 1999/2000 (in %)

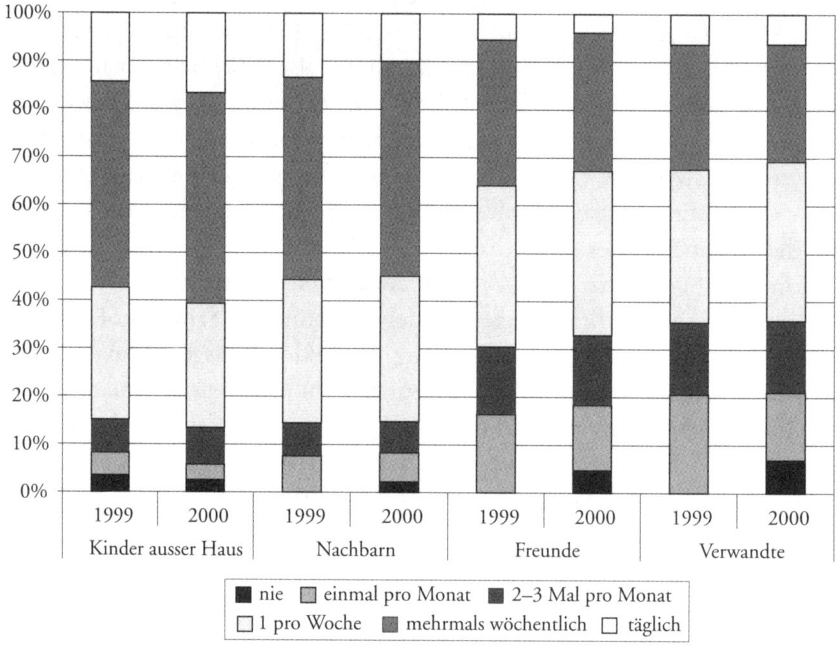

Anmerkungen: Intensität der Kontakte: Anzahl der Kontakte zu Kindern, die ausserhalb des eigenen Haushalts wohnen sowie zu Verwandten, Freunden und Nachbarn zu denen eine gute und enge Beziehung besteht.
Stichprobe und Gewichtung: Schweizer Haushalt-Panel, Längsschnittstichprobe 1999–2000, Personen-Querschnittsgewichtung; Stichprobengrösse: Kinder ausserhalb des eigenen Haushalts (1999: N = 2066, 2000: N = 2222), Verwandte (1999: N = 5355, 2000: N = 5418), Nachbarn (1999: N = 3857, 2000: N = 3940), Freunde (1999: N = 5244, 2000: N = 5286).

sind, die Beziehungen für Grösse und Intensität unterschiedlich verlaufen: So zeigen sich wie bei der Grösse des sekundären Netzes (vgl. oben) auch bei der Intensität der sozialen Beziehungen geschlechterspezfische Unterschiede – doch weisen diesbezüglich die Frauen intensivere Kontakte auf als die Männer. Ähnliches lässt sich bezüglich sozialer Schicht (geringere Intensität der Kontakte bei Befragten mit einem höheren Bildungsabschluss) und dem primären Netz feststellen (geringere Intensität bei Vorhandensein einer Partnerschaft).

Offensichtlich besteht zwischen der Grösse des sekundären Netzes und der Intensität der gepflegten Kontakte ein inverses Verhältnis. Allerdings könnte dafür auch die unterschiedlichen Fehlerkomponenten (soziale Erwünschbarkeit, Reliabilität) der beiden Indikatoren verantwortlich sein.

Die Angaben aus Abbildung 5 scheinen darauf hinzudeuten, dass die Kontaktintensität zwischen 1999 und 2000 relativ stabil geblieben ist. Betrachtet man jedoch die Veränderungen auf individueller Ebene, ergeben sich beträchtliche Fluktuation. So gibt lediglich eine Minderheit der Befragten keine Veränderungen in der Intensität ihrer Beziehungen an (35 % bei den Verwandten, 39 % bei den Nachbarn und den Freunden, 49 % bei den Kindern ausser Haus). Im Unterschied zu den Angaben zur Grösse der Teilnetze, handelt es sich bei der Mehrzahl dieser Veränderungen jedoch um Bewegungen zwischen angrenzenden Kategorien (z. B. von einmal pro Woche zu mehrmals wöchentlich). Mit anderen Worten: Grosse Intensitätssprünge sind relativ selten. Dies deutet darauf hin, dass Angaben zur Intensität der Kontakte verlässlicher sind als jene zur Grösse der sozialen Teilnetze.

Soziale Netze und soziale Unterstützung

Wie eingangs dargestellt, sind soziale Beziehungen und soziale Netzwerke deshalb von grosser Bedeutung, weil sie die Grundlage für instrumentelle, alltagspraktische und emotionale Unterstützung durch die Mitmenschen darstellen. Die formalen Aspekte sozialer Beziehungen – das Vorhandensein verschiedener sozialer Teilnetze, Grösse und Umfang der sozialen Netze sowie die Dichte und Intensität der Beziehungen – sollten gemäss dieser Perspektive in einem engen Zusammenhang mit dem Ausmass der sozialen Unterstützung stehen. Gemäss der ressourcentheoretischen Grundhypothese erwarten wir, dass Personen, die eine umfangreiche und dichte soziale Vernetzung besitzen, mehr und grössere soziale Unterstützung aus ihrem Umfeld erhalten als Personen mit geringeren und weniger intensiven sozialen Beziehungen. Dabei ist anzunehmen, dass das primäre Netz, d. h. Partnerschaft und familiale Beziehungen eine wichtigere Rolle für die soziale Unterstützung spielen als die Beziehungen des sekundären Netzes.

Im Schweizer Haushalt-Panel wurden die Befragten gebeten, für die bereits beschriebenen sechs Teilnetze – Partner, Kinder (über 15 Jahre) im selben Haushalt, Verwandte und Kinder ausserhalb des Haushaltes, Nachbarn, gute

Freunde sowie Arbeits- und Freizeitkollegen – anzugeben, wie gross die potentielle praktische und emotionelle Unterstützung ist, die sie bei Bedarf bei den einzelnen Teilnetzen finden können. Für die Einstufung des Ausmasses sozialer Unterstützung wurden den Befragten ein 11-stufige Skala von 0 (überhaupt keine Unterstützung) bis 10 (sehr viel Unterstützung) vorgelegt.

Abbildung 6: Praktische und emotionale Unterstützung aus sechs sozialen Teilnetzen, 1999/2000, Prozentanteil der Befragten die viel oder sehr viel Unterstützung erhalten (Skalenwerte 8–10)

Teilnetz	Praktische Unterstützung		Emotionale Unterstützung	
	1999	2000	1999	2000
Partnerschaft	73.5 %	72.3 %	82.4 %	81.1 %
Kinder über 15 (im Haushalt)	50.7 %	n. a.	70.8 %	n. a.
Verwandte und Kinder ausser Haus	44.9 %	45.8 %	57.5 %	61.7 %
Enge Freunde	47.9 %	46.0 %	63.0 %	61.9 %
Nachbarn	32.9 %	31.5 %	38.0 %	34.7 %
Arbeits- und Freizeitkollegen	21.9 %	19.5 %	31.0 %	29.0 %

Anmerkungen: Potentielle praktische und emotionale Unterstützung, die bei Bedarf bei den einzelnen Teilnetzen gefunden werden kann (11-stufige Skala von 0 = überhaupt keine Unterstützung bis 10 = sehr viel Unterstützung). Die in der Tabelle aufgeführten Prozentwerte beziehen sich auf den Anteil der Befragten, die Skalenwerte zwischen 8 und 10 angeben.
Stichprobe und Gewichtung: Schweizer Haushalt-Panel, Längsschnittstichprobe 1999–2000, Personen-Querschnittsgewichtung; Stichprobengrösse: *Praktische Unterstützung:* Partnerschaft (1999: N = 4550, 2000: N = 4811), Kinder über 15 im eigenen Haushalt (1999: N = 1970), Verwandte und Kinder ausserhalb des Haushalts (1999: N = 5380, 2000: N = 5506), Freunde (1999: N = 5313, 2000: N = 5291), Nachbarn (1999: N = 3895, 2000: N = 3954), Arbeits- und Freizeitkollegen (1999: N = 3748, 2000: N = 3691). *Emotionale Unterstützung:* Partnerschaft (1999: N = 4553, 2000: N = 4811), Kinder über 15 im eigenen Haushalt (1999: N = 1971), Verwandte und Kinder ausserhalb des Haushalts (1999: N = 5404, 2000: N = 5513), Freunde (1999: N = 5314, 2000: N = 5291), Nachbarn (1999: N = 3893, 2000: N = 3953), Arbeits- und Freizeitkollegen (1999: N = 3748, 2000: N = 3690).

In Abbildung 6 sind für jedes soziale Teilnetz die Prozentanteile der Befragten aufgeführt, die angeben, viel oder sehr viel Unterstützung zu erhalten (Skalenwerte 8–10). Wie erwartet, leistet das familiale Sozialnetz, d. h. die Partnerschaft und die Kinder deutlich mehr Unterstützung als das sekundäre

Netz. So geben über 70 % aller Befragten (mit Partner bzw. Partnerin) an, im Bedarfsfall sehr viel praktische Unterstützung vom Partner zu erhalten; bei der emotionalen Unterstützung sind es gar über 80 %. Bei den (älteren) Kinder, die im eigenen Haushalt leben, ist die emotionale Unterstützung sehr viel wichtiger als die praktischen Hilfeleistungen (71 % vs. 51 % mit sehr viel Unterstützung). Ähnliches aber in deutlich geringerem Ausmass trifft auch auf gute Verwandte und enge Freunde zu, die beiden wichtigsten Teilnetze des sekundären Netzes: 60 % der Befragten erhalten aus diesen Beziehungen sehr viel emotionale Unterstützung, während ca. 45 % angeben, viel praktische Unterstützung zu geniessen. Deutlich weniger wichtig sind die Teilnetze der Nachbarschaft und der Arbeits- und Freizeitkollegen, wo lediglich eine Minderheit, nämlich zwischen 20 % und 38 %, angibt, im Bedarfsfall mit einer grossen Unterstützung rechnen zu können. Im Unterschied zu allen anderen Teilnetzen halten sich bei der Nachbarschaft die praktischen und emotionalen Aspekte sozialer Unterstützung die Waage – Nachbarschaftskontakte sind demnach im Vergleich zu den anderen Netzen stärker auf die alltagspraktische Unterstützung ausgerichtet.

Wie bei den formalen Aspekten der sozialen Vernetzung zeigen sich auch bei der sozialen Unterstützung grosse Unterschiede zwischen Männern und Frauen. So fühlen sich Frauen erheblich besser durch ihr soziales Umfeld unterstützt – dies sowohl in praktischer wie in emotionaler Hinsicht. Dies gilt für alle sozialen Teilnetze mit einer Ausnahme: der Partnerschaft. Insbesondere bei der emotionalen Unterstützung ist der Anteil der Männer, die sich durch ihre Partnerin sehr gut unterstützt fühlt (Indikator: Skalenwerte 8–10 der 11-stufigen Skala) deutlich höher als dies bei den Frauen der Fall ist (1999: 88 % vs. 77 %, Chi-Quadrat: 99.5, $p < .001$; 2000: 87 % vs. 75 %, Chi-Quadrat: 205.8, $p < .001$). Männer sind demnach in emotionaler Hinsicht stärker auf die Partnerschaft ausgerichtet als Frauen, für die andere soziale Teilnetze ebenso wichtig sind für die emotionalen Unterstützung – neben der Partnerschaft sind dies insbesondere Kinder, Freundinnen und Freunde sowie Verwandte.

Neben diesen geschlechterspezifischen Unterschieden haben die verschiedenen Teilnetze im Lebenslauf eine unterschiedliche Bedeutung für die soziale Unterstützung. Für die unter 40jährigen ist die soziale Unterstützung durch den Freundeskreis sehr viel wichtiger als für die älteren Menschen. Ähnliches, aber weniger ausgeprägt, gilt auch für die Arbeits- und Freizeitkollegen sowie – eher überraschend – für die Verwandtschaft. Demgegenüber nimmt die emotionelle und praktische Unterstützung der eigenen Kinder mit dem Alter zu – am wichtigsten ist sie für die über 65jährigen. Die soziale Unterstützung aus der Nachbarschaft ist für die mittleren Altersgruppen (30–64jährige) wichtiger als für die Jungen und die Senioren. Keine Altersunterschiede gibt es hingegen beim wichtigsten Teilnetz, der Partnerschaft: Die praktische und emotionale Unterstützung durch die Partnerin bzw. den Partner ist für alle Altersgruppen hoch und auch gleich bedeutsam.

Abbildung 6 scheint darauf hinzudeuten, dass das Ausmass der Unterstützung im Zeitverlauf sehr stabil geblieben ist. Die einzige Ausnahme bildet die emotionale Unterstützung aus dem Teilnetz der Verwandtschaft, wo die Veränderungen (auf aggregierter Ebene) etwas grösser sind (von 58 % auf 62 %). Die in Abbildung 7 dargestellten detaillierten Analysen der Veränderungen auf der individuellen Eben zeigen jedoch, dass bei allen Netzen relative grosse Veränderungen stattfinden. Im Unterschied zu den formalen Aspekten des sozialen Netzes, sind jedoch starke Veränderungen die Ausnahme. Hinzu kommt, dass bei der sozialen Unterstützung Veränderung im Verlaufe von 12 Monaten durchaus plausibel sind. Dies gilt insbesondere für die soziale Unterstützung aus den weniger engen Kontakten des sekundären Netzes. Tatsächlich ist die soziale Unterstützung im Teilnetz der Partnerschaft sehr viel stabiler (42 % ohne Veränderung) als dies bei den Teilnetzen der Kollegen (20 % ohne Veränderung), Nachbarn (22 % ohne Veränderung), Verwandten (27 % ohne Veränderung) und Freunden (28 % ohne Veränderung) der Fall ist.

Lassen sich die Veränderungen im Ausmass der sozialen Unterstützung zwischen 1999 und 2000 durch bestimmte Ereignisse oder Veränderungen der Lebensumstände der Befragten erklären? Wie bei den Analysen zu den individuellen Netzveränderungen ist dies im Rahmen des vorhanden Datensatzes mit lediglich zwei Jahren nur ansatzweise möglich. Zwar lassen sich einzelne statistisch signifikante Faktoren eruieren – so führt die Beendigung einer engen Beziehung zu einer Verminderung der emotionalen Unterstützung durch die Partnerschaft, der Tod einer nahestehenden Person trägt bei zu einer Erhöhung der emotionalen Unterstützung in den meisten Teilnetzen und eine Zunahme (Abnahme) in der Grösse eines Teilnetzes begünstigt in der Regel eine Zunahme (Abnahme) der sozialen Unterstützung. All diese Modelle weisen jedoch eine verschwindend kleine Erklärungskraft auf (R^2_{adj} = 1 %). Wir erklären dies mit den Schwierigkeiten, die tatsächliche Veränderungen zwischen den zwei Erhebungszeitpunkten von Erhebungsfehlern und -ungenauigkeiten unterscheiden zu können (Reliabilitätsproblem).

Abbildung 7: Individuelle Veränderungen der emotionalen Unterstützung aus den verschiedenen Teilnetzen zwischen 1999 und 2000

Veränderung der emotionalen Unterstützung 1999–2000	Partner-schaft	Verwandte + Kinder ausser Haus	Freunde	Nachbarn	Kollegen
Keine Veränderung	42 %	27 %	28 %	22 %	20 %
Geringe Zunahme	23 %	20 %	23 %	18 %	16 %
Mittlere Zunahme	6 %	9 %	9 %	11 %	10 %
Starke Zunahme	1 %	2 %	2 %	3 %	4 %
Geringe Abnahme	21 %	25 %	27 %	32 %	38 %
Mittlere Abnahme	6 %	13 %	9 %	11 %	11 %
Starke Abnahme	1 %	4 %	2 %	3 %	2 %
N	4612	5369	5264	3878	3673

Anmerkungen: Veränderung der potentiellen emotionalen Unterstützung, die bei Bedarf bei den einzelnen Teilnetzen gefunden werden kann (11-stufige Skala von 0 = überhaupt keine Unterstützung bis 10 = sehr viel Unterstützung). Keine Veränderung: gleiche Indexwerte 1999 und 2000, geringe Zunahme: Zunahme um 1–2 Indexpunkte zwischen 1999 und 2000, mittlere Zunahme: Zunahme um 3–5 Indexpunkte zwischen 1999 und 2000, starke Zunahme: Zunahme um 6–10 Indexpunkte zwischen 1999 und 2000, geringe Abnahme: Abnahme um 1–2 Indexpunkte zwischen 1999 und 2000, mittlere Abnahme: Abnahme um 3–5 Indexpunkte zwischen 1999 und 2000, starke Abnahme: Abnahme um 6–10 Indexpunkte zwischen 1999 und 2000.
Stichprobe und Gewichtung: Schweizer Haushalt-Panel, Längsschnittstichprobe 1999–2000, Personen-Längsschnittgewichtung.

Wir haben weiter oben darauf hingewiesen, dass die ressourcentheoretische Perspektive einen engen Zusammenhang zwischen den formalen Aspekten sozialer Vernetzung und dem Ausmass sozialer Unterstützung annimmt. Die Anzahl vorhandener Teilnetze, die Grösse der sozialen Netze und die Intensität sozialer Beziehungen müsste entsprechend in einem engen Zusammenhang mit sozialer Unterstützung stehen. Tatsächlich weisen alle oben beschriebenen Indikatoren der sozialen Vernetzung hohe (bivariate) Korrelationen mit dem Ausmass der praktischen und emotionalen Unterstützung auf. Die engsten Beziehungen bestehen dabei zwischen der Anzahl der vorhandenen Teilnetze, sowie der Grösse und Intensität des sekundären Netzes.

Die oben erwähnten alters- und geschlechtsspezfischen Unterschiede sozialer Unterstützung deuten jedoch darauf hin, dass weitere Faktoren miteinbezogen werden müssen. Neben wichtigen Kontrollvariablen (neben Alter und Geschlecht gehören dazu insbesondere soziale Schicht, Nationalität, Erwerbsstatus, Konfession, Sprachregion) ist denkbar, dass eine Reihe weiterer Faktoren das Ausmass sozialer Unterstützung beeinflussen. So könnte z. B. argumentiert werden, dass mehr verfügbare Freizeit, die für Sozialkontakte verwendet werden kann, förderlich für eine gute soziale Unterstützung ist. Des weiteren könnte der lokale Gemeindekontext eine Rolle spielen – so wird im allgemeinen davon ausgegangen, dass in kleinen ländlichen Gemeinden die gegenseitige soziale Unterstützung grösser ist als in den anonymeren Grosstädten.

Eine solche detailliertere Analyse ist in Abbildung 8 dargestellt. Abhängige Variable dieser multiplen linearen Regressionsschätzung ist die gesamte soziale Unterstützung, die als Summe der praktischen und emotionalen Unterstützung berechnet wurde. Die Ergebnisse zeigen, dass der Umfang der sozialen Vernetzung, d. h. das Vorhandensein der einzelnen sozialen Teilnetze sowie die Grösse und Intensität des sekundären Netzes wichtige Faktoren für eine gute soziale Unterstützung bilden. Wie erwartet, bildet die Partnerschaft die wichtigste Quelle einer guten sozialen Unterstützung – sie erhöht die soziale Unterstützung um 1.3 (1999) bzw. 1.4 (2000) Indexpunkte. Das Vorhandensein von engen Freunden, Kollegen und Nachbarn bewirkt eine Erhöhung von je 0.7–1.1 Indexpunkten. Auch die erwähnten alters- und geschlechtspezifischen Unterschiede lassen sich bestätigen: So verringert sich in der zweiten Lebenshälfte (ab ca. 40 Jahren) das Ausmass der sozialen Unterstützung kontinuierlich: im Vergleich zu den 18–29jährigen verringert sich bei den über 80jährigen Befragten die soziale Unterstützung um 0.9 Indexpunkte (1999). Frauen geniessen eine deutlich stärkere soziale Unterstützung als Männer. Weitere Faktoren sind die Verfügbarkeit von Zeitressourcen, der Gesundheitszustand und die Erwerbstätigkeit. Der Vergleich zwischen den beiden Jahren zeigt, dass die wichtigsten Erklärungsfaktoren für soziale Unterstützung weitgehend stabil geblieben sind. Mit 30 % (2000) bzw. 26 % (1999) erklärter Varianz weisen die Modelle zudem einen guten Erklärungsgehalt auf.

Abbildung 8: Determinanten der gesamten sozialen Unterstützung 1999 und 2000 (lineare Regression, unstandardisierte Regressionskoeffizienten)

	1999		2000	
	b-Koeffizient	Irrtumswahrscheinlichkeit	b-Koeffizient	Irrtumswahrscheinlichkeit
(Konstante)	0.323	0.180	0.586	0.002
Geschlecht	–0.392	0.000	–0.237	0.000
Grösse des sekundären Netzes	0.25	0.000	0.341	0.000
Intensität des sekundären Netzes	0.341	0.000	0.278	0.000
Partner	1.261	0.000	1.395	0.000
Freunde	1.125	0.000	0.829	0.000
Nachbarn	0.722	0.000	0.772	0.000
Kollegen	0.94	0.000	0.902	0.000
Verwandte	n. s.	n. s.	0.709	0.000
Anzahl Kinder	0.05	0.025	n. s.	n. s.
Anzahl Teilnetze	0.171	0.004	n. s.	n. s.
Frei verfügbare Zeit	0.121	0.004	n. a.	n. a.
Gesundheitszustand	–0.164	0.000	–0.084	0.006
Vorhandensein von Sorgen	0.125	0.085	n. s.	n. s.
Alter 40 bis 49 Jahre	–0.164	0.004	–0.23	0.000
Alter 50 bis 59 Jahre	–0.389	0.000	–0.436	0.000
Alter 60 bis 69 Jahre	–0.587	0.000	–0.663	0.000
Alter 70 bis 79 Jahre	–0.753	0.000	–0.761	0.000
Älter als 80 Jahre	–0.925	0.000	–0.649	0.002
Mittlerer Bildung	0.086	0.040	n. s.	n. s.
Höhere Bildung	n. s.	n. s.	0.183	0.003
Beschäftigungsgrad: < 50 %	n. s.	n. s.	0.218	0.001
Beschäftigungsgrad: 50–90 %	n. s.	n. s.	0.18	0.028
Beschäftigungsgrad: > 90 %	0.124	0.018	n. s.	n. s.
R^2_{adj}	26.1 %		29.6 %	
F	74.429		106.824	
P	< .001		< .001	

Anmerkungen: Abhängige Variable: Gesamte praktische und emotionale Unterstützung aus fünf sozialen Teilnetzen (Partnerschaft, Verwandte und Kinder ausserhalb des eigenen Haushalts, enge Freunde, Nachbarn sowie Arbeits- und Freizeitkollegen).

Unabhängige Variablen: Geschlecht (0 : Frau, 1 : Mann), Grösse des sekundären Netzes (Summe der Anzahl Kinder (0 bis 17 Jahre alt) im eigenen Haushalt, Verwandten, Nachbarn, Freunden und Kollegen; nat. Logarithmus (ln(var + 1)), Intensität des sekundären Netzes (Summe

der Kontakthäufigkeiten mit Kindern, Verwandten, Nachbarn und Freunde; nat. Logarithmus (ln(var + 1)), Partner (0: ohne Partner, 1: mit Partner), Freunde (0: ohne enge Freunde, 1: enge Freunde vorhanden), Nachbarn (0: ohne Nachbarn, 1: Nachbarn vorhanden), Kollegen (0: ohne Kollegen mit enger Beziehung, 1: enge Kollegen vorhanden), Verwandte (0: ohne enge Verwandte, 1: mit engen Verwandten), Anzahl Kinder (Zahl der Kinder zwischen 0 und 17 Jahren), Anzahl Teilnetze (Vorhandensein von sechs sozialen Teilnetzen: Minimum = 0, Maximum = 6), Frei verfügbare Zeit (Anzahl frei verfügbarer Stunden pro Tag; nat. Logarithmus (ln(var + 1)), Gesundheitszustand (1 (sehr gut) bis 5 (überhaupt nicht gut)), Vorhandensein von Sorgen (0: manchmal bis immer, 1: selten bis nie), Alter (40 bis 49 Jahre, 50 bis 59 Jahre, 60 bis 69 Jahre, 70 bis 79 Jahre, 80 Jahre und älter; Referenzkategorie Alter: 18–29 Jahre), Bildungsgrad: Mittlere Bildung (Lehrabschluss oder Matura), Höhere Bildung (Fachhochschule, Universität), Referenzkategorie Bildung: obligatorische Schule, Anlehre; Beschäftigungsgrad (Teilzeitbeschäftigung unter 50 %, Teilzeitbeschäftigung 50–90 %, Vollzeitbeschäftigung, d. h. über 90 %; Referenzkategorie Beschäftigung: nicht erwerbstätig); n. a.: keine Angaben verfügbar; n. s.: kein statistisch signifikanter Zusammenhang.
Stichprobe und Gewichtung: Schweizer Haushalt-Panel, Längsschnittstichprobe 1999–2000, Personen-Querschnittgewichtung, N = 5900.

Wirkungen und Konsequenzen sozialer Netze: Soziale Unterstützung fördert das gesundheitliche Wohlbefinden

Soziale Netzwerke und soziale Unterstützung wirken in vielfältiger Weise auf andere zentrale Lebensbereiche des Menschen ein. Im Folgenden soll die Bedeutung sozialer Unterstützung für einen konkreten Bereich, die Gesundheit, genauer untersucht werden. Ausgangspunkt unser Analyse sind die in verschiedenen Studien beschriebenen positiven Wirkungen sozialer Vernetzung. Wie einleitend dargelegt, findet ein Teil der Studien direkte Effekte, während andere v. a. interaktive Effekte nachweisen können (d. h. nur beim Vorhandensein hoher Belastungen, negativer Lebensereignisse u. ä.).

Um die Gesundheitseffekte von sozialer Unterstützung zu prüfen, betrachten wir den Anteil der Befragten, die ihren Gesundheitszustand als mittelmässig oder schlecht bezeichnet, wobei wir zwischen einer ersten Gruppe mit hoher sozialer Unterstützung (oberhalb des Median) und einer zweiten Gruppe mit niedriger sozialer Unterstützung unterscheiden (unterhalb des Median). Die Ergebnisse zeigen statistisch signifikante, aber nicht besonders starke gesundheitsfördernde Wirkung sozialer Unterstützung: So liegt der Prozentanteil der Befragten, die ihren Gesundheitszustand als schlecht empfinden, in beiden betrachteten Jahren 4–5 % höher, wenn keine oder nur wenig soziale

Unterstützung vorhanden ist (16–17 % statt 12 %). Diese Effekte können jedoch nicht einseitig kausal interpretiert werden – auch aufgrund der weiter oben behandelten Ergebnisse (vgl. Abbildung 8) ist von einer gegenseitigen Beeinflussung zwischen sozialer Unterstützung und Gesundheit auszugehen.

Um zu prüfen, ob es sich bei diesen Gesundheitseffekten sozialer Unterstützung eher um direkte oder interaktive Wirkungen handelt, wird das Vorhandensein von Sorgen mit einbezogen. Sorgen können sich dabei auf soziale Beziehungen beziehen aber auch auf allgemeine Lebensumstände und -situationen (z. B. das Vorhandensein von Geldsorgen).

Aus den in Abbildung 9 dargestellten Resultaten sticht zunächst der starke negative Effekt der Belastung durch Sorgen auf die selbsteingeschätzte Gesundheit hervor. Erwartungsgemäss fühlen sich Befragte, die mit Sorgen belastet sind gesundheitlich deutlich schlechter (26–41 % im Vergleich zu 10–12 % wenn keine Sorgen vorliegen) – wobei von einer gegenseitigen Beeinflussung auszugehen ist. Eine überdurchschnittlich gute soziale Unterstützung verringert den Anteil der Befragten, die ihre Gesundheit als schlecht empfinden, erheblich. Dies gilt in besonderem Masse für Personen, die sich Sorgen machen: So sinkt der Anteil der Befragten mit schlechter Gesundheit von 41 % auf 34 % (1999; Chi-Quadrat: 10.6, $p = .001$) bzw. von 34 % auf 26 % (2000; Chi-Quadrat: 12.7, $p < .001$), wenn sich die Betroffen durch ihr soziales Umfeld gut unterstützt fühlen. Dies deutet darauf hin, dass der interaktive gesundheitsfördernde Effekt sozialer Unterstützung bedeutend stärker ist als der direkte Effekt. Der direkte Effekt lässt sich daran erkennen, dass bei niedriger sozialer Unterstützung der Anteil der Befragten mit schlechter oder mittelmässiger Gesundheit in allen Gruppen grösser ist als bei hoher Unterstützung. Der interaktive Effekt zeigt sich daran, dass dieser Unterschied bedeutend grösser ausfällt, wenn Sorgen vorhanden sind. So ist der Gesundheitseffekt der sozialen Unterstützung bei Personen ohne Sorgen statistisch nur schwach (1999) oder gar nicht signifikant (2000).[4]

4 1999: Anteil der Befragten mit schlechter Gesundheit und geringer sozialer Unterstützung 13.4 % vs. 9.6 % bei hoher Unterstützung (Chi-Quadrat 4.9, $p < .05$); 2000: Anteil der Befragten mit schlechter Gesundheit und geringer sozialer Unterstützung 12.1 % vs. 10.8 % bei hoher Unterstützung (Chi-Quadrat 1.6, $p = .109$).

Abbildung 9: Soziale Unterstützung und subjektives Gesundheitsempfinden 1999–2000, nach Belastungen durch Sorgen (Prozentanteil der Befragten, die ihre Gesundheit als mittel oder schlecht einstufen)

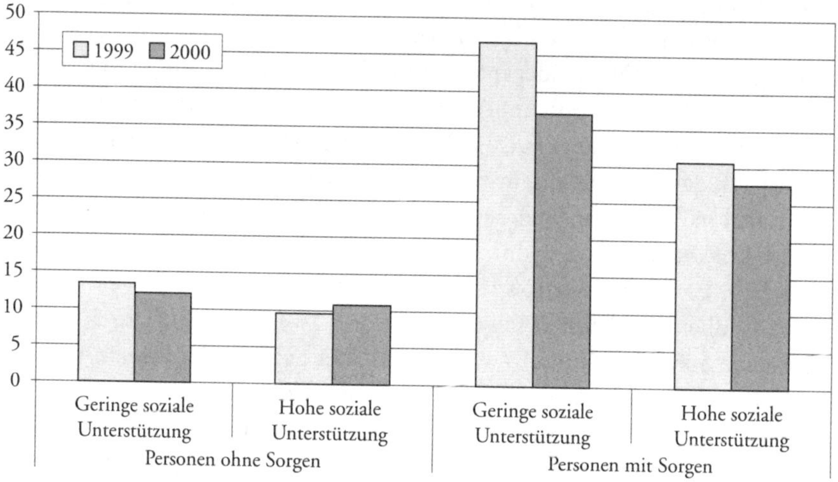

Anmerkungen: Gesundheit: Selbsteingeschätzter Gesundheitszustand (Prozentanteile der Befragten, die ihre Gesundheit auf als schlecht oder sehr schlecht einstufen); Soziale Unterstützung: gesamte praktische und emotionale Unterstützung aus fünf sozialen Teilnetzen (Partnerschaft, Verwandte und Kinder ausserhalb des eigenen Haushalts, enge Freunde, Nachbarn und Kollegen), geringe Unterstützung: unterhalb des Medianwertes, hohe Unterstützung: oberhalb des Medianwertes; Sorgen: Vorhandensein von Sorgen (ohne Sorgen: keine Sorgen oder nur selten; mit Sorgen: immer Sorgen oder zumindest manchmal).
Stichprobe und Gewichtung: Schweizer Haushalt-Panel, Längsschnittstichprobe 1999–2000, Personen-Querschnittsgewichtung; Stichprobengrösse: Geringe Unterstützung und ohne Sorgen (1999: N = 1792, 2000: N = 1819), hohe Unterstützung und ohne Sorgen (1999: N = 1914, 2000: N = 1978), geringe Unterstützung und mit Sorgen (1999: N = 218, 2000: N = 258), hohe Unterstützung und mit Sorgen (1999: N = 180, 2000: N = 230).

Umfassendere Analysen ergaben, dass diese Befunde sehr robust sind. So zeigten sich dieselben Ergebnisse, wenn anstelle der selbsteingeschätzten Gesundheit die allgemeine Lebenszufriedenheit verwendet wird. Auch in diesem Fall lassen sich starke interaktive Effekte und schwache direkte Effekte nachweisen. Desgleichen ergaben sich direkte und interaktive Effekte, wenn anstelle von allgemeinen Sorgen ein spezifischerer Indikator für das Vorhandensein von ernsthaften Meinungsverschiedenheiten verwendet wird (Angaben nur für 1999 verfügbar).

Schlussbemerkungen und Fazit

Im vorliegenden Beitrag wurden soziale Beziehungen und soziale Netz der Schweizer Wohnbevölkerung im Hinblick auf drei Aspekte untersucht: *Erstens* die formalen und strukturellen Charakteristika der sozialen Netze, *zweitens* der Zusammenhang zwischen sozialen Beziehungen und sozialer Unterstützung, und *drittens* die Wirkungen sozialer Unterstützung auf Gesundheit und subjektives Wohlbefinden.

Unsere Ergebnisse zu den formalen und strukturellen Aspekten sozialer Beziehungen zeigen, dass der grosse Teil der Bevölkerung in der Schweiz über eine breite soziale Vernetzung verfügt. Trotz Individualisierung und Pluralisierung der Lebensformen, trotz zunehmender Zahl von Einpersonenhaushalten und wachsenden Scheidungsraten kann von einer beziehungslosen Gesellschaft nicht gesprochen werden. So verfügen gegen 90 % der Schweizer Wohnbevölkerung über partnerschaftliche und familiäre Beziehungen, über gute verwandtschaftliche Kontakte oder über enge Freundesbeziehungen. Das umfangmässig grösste Teilnetz ist die Verwandtschaft, während die intensivsten Beziehungen (ausserhalb der Partnerschaft und des Zusammenlebens mit anderen Personen) zu den eigenen, nicht mehr im selben Haushalt wohnenden Kindern gepflegt werden.

Auf aggregierter Ebene haben sich die formalen Merkmale sozialer Vernetzung zwischen 1999 und 2000 kaum verändert – dies gilt insbesondere für das Vorhandensein der verschiedenen Teilnetze, aber auch für die Intensität der gepflegten Kontakte. Demgegenüber zeigen sich erhebliche Unterschiede zwischen den zwei Erhebungszeitpunkten, wenn Veränderungen auf individuellem Niveau betrachtet werden. Dies trifft in besonderem Masse auf die Grösse der sozialen Netze zu. Wir vermuten, dass es sich dabei grösstenteils um Erhebungsfehler (z. B. soziale Erwünschbarkeit) bzw. Messungenauigkeiten handelt und weniger um tatsächliche Veränderungen. So lassen sich die Veränderungen auf individuellem Niveau kaum durch die entsprechenden Ereignis- und Veränderungsfaktoren erklären, die sich in der beobachteten Zeitspanne ereignet haben (wie z. B. Trennung, Umzug, Stellenwechsel u. ä.). Offensichtlich wird die Frage nach der konkreten Anzahl von Beziehungspersonen (mit denen ein gutes Verhältnis gepflegt wird) situationsbedingt sehr unterschiedlich beantwortet.

Die sozialen Beziehungen – sowohl jene des primären wie auch jene des sekundären Netzes – spielen eine entscheidende Rolle für die soziale

Unterstützung. Dabei tragen die verschiedenen Aspekte sozialer Vernetzung unabhängig voneinander bei zu einer guten sozialen Unterstützung. Mit anderen Worten: Nicht nur das blosse Vorhandensein der verschiedenen sozialen Teilnetze, sondern auch die Grösse und die Intensität der Beziehungen verstärken die soziale Unterstützung. Die wichtigste Quelle für eine gute soziale Unterstützung bildet dabei die Partnerschaft sowie das Vorhandensein von engen Freunden, Kollegen und Nachbarn.

Die Bedeutung der verschiedenen Teilnetze für die soziale Unterstützung ist für Frauen und Männer sowie für die verschiedenen Altersgruppen unterschiedlich. So spielt für Männer die Partnerschaft eine wichtigere Rolle als für Frauen, v. a. für die emotionale Unterstützung. Männer weisen im allgemeinen ein breiteres Netz sozialer Beziehungen auf, doch verfügen Frauen über die intensiveren Kontakte und fühlen sich durch ihr soziales Umfeld in emotionaler und alltagspraktischer Hinsicht besser unterstützt.

Zwischen den zwei Erhebungszeitpunkten hat sich das Ausmass der sozialen Unterstützung auf dem individuellen Niveau zwar relativ stark verändert, auf dem aggregiertem Niveau ist es hingegen sehr stabil geblieben. Auch die wichtigsten Einflussfaktoren weisen zwischen den zwei Erhebungszeitpunkten eine hohe Stabilität auf.

Eine gute soziale Unterstützung fördert das gesundheitliche Wohlbefinden. Dabei wirkt die soziale Unterstützung und Vernetzung in erster Linie interaktiv: v. a. wenn persönliche Sorgen und soziale Belastungen vorhanden sind, lässt sich ein gesundheitsfördernder Zusammenhang mit sozialer Unterstützung feststellen. Soziale Beziehungen und soziale Unterstützung bilden damit eine wichtige persönliche Ressource im Alltag der Schweizer Bevölkerung.

Literaturnachweis

Andress, Hans-Jürgen, Gero Lipsmeier und Kurt Salentin (1995), Soziale Isolation und mangelnde soziale Unterstützung im unteren Einkommensbereich?, *Zeitschrift für Soziologie*, 24 (4), 300–315.

Antonucci, Toni C. (1990), Social Supports and Social Relationships, in: Robert H. Binstock und Linda K. George, Hrsg., *Handbook of Aging and the Social Science*, San Diego: Academic Press, 205–226.

Bourdieu, Pierre (1983), Ökonomisches Kapital, kulturelles Kapital, soziales Kapital, in: Reinhard Kreckel, Hrsg., *Soziale Ungleichheiten*, Göttingen: Schwartz, 183–198.

Cohen, Sheldon und S. Leonard Syme (1985), *Social Support and Health*, New York: Academic Press.

Coleman, James S. (1988), Social Capital in the Creation of Human Capital, *American Journal of Sociology*, 94, 95–121.

Due, Pernille, Bjorn Holstein, Rikke Lund, Jens Modvig und Kirsten Avlund (1999), Social Relations: Network, Support and Relational Strain, *Social Science & Medicine*, 48, 661–673.

Etzioni, Amitai (1993), *The Spirit of Community*, New York: Crown Publishers.

Granovetter, Mark (1973), The Strength of Weak Ties, *American Journal of Sociology*, 78, 1360–1380.

Granovetter, Mark (1983), The Strength of Weak Ties: A Network Theory Revisited, in: Randall Collins, Hrsg., *Sociological Theory*, San Francisco: Jossey Bass, 201–233.

Ibarra, Herminia (1997), Paving an Alternate Route: Gender Differences in Managerial Networks for Career Development, *Social Psychology Quarterly*, 60, 91–102.

Ibn Khaldoun, Abdurrahman (1934), *Les prolégomènes*, Paris: Librairie orientaliste Paul Geuthner.

Kawachi, Ichiro, Bruce Kennedy, Kimberley Lochner und Deborah Prothrow-Stith (1997), Social Capital, Income Inequality and Mortality, *American Journal of Public Health*, 87 (9), 1491–1498.

Kawachi, Ichiro, Bruce Kennedy und Roberta Glass (1999), Social capital and self-rated health: a contextual analysis, *American Journal of Public Health*, 89 (8), 1187–1193.

Lin, Nan (1999), Social Networks and Status Attainment, *Annual Review of Sociology*, 25, 467–487.

Lin, Nan und Walter M. Ensel (1989), Life Stress and Health: Stressors and Resources, *American Sociological Review*, 54, 382–399.

Meyer, Peter C. und Christian Suter (1993), Soziale Netze und Unterstützung, in: Peter Weiss, Hrsg., *Gesundheit in der Schweiz*, Zürich: Seismo, 194–209.

OECD (Organization for Economic Co-operation and Development) (2001), *The Well-being of Nations. The Role of Human and Social Capital*, Paris: OECD.

Putnam, Robert D. (1995), Bowling Alone: America's Declining Social Capital, *Journal of Democracy*, 6, 65–78.

Schilling, Oliver und Hans-Werner Wahl (2002), Familiäre Netzwerke und Lebenszufriedenheit alter Menschen in ländlichen und urbanen Regionen, *Kölner Zeitschrift für Soziologie und Sozialpsychologie*, 54 (2), 304–317.

Sprecher, Susan und Diane Felmlee (1992), The Influence of Parents and Friends on the Quality and Stability of Romantic Relationships: A Three-Wave Longitudinal Investigation, *Journal of Marriage and the Family*, 54, 888–900.

Thoits, Peggy A. (1995), Stress, Coping, and Social Support Processes: Where Are We? What Next? *Journal of Health and Social Behavior*, Extra Issue, 53–79.

Wellman, Barry und Scot Wortley (1990), Different Strokes from Different Folks: Community Ties and Social Support, *American Journal of Sociology*, 96 (3), 558–588.

3. Pratiques et modes de vie
Lebensstile

Parenté, mobilité familiale et modes de vie en Suisse*

Philippe Wanner** et Alexis Gabadinho***

Introduction

Soumise depuis quatre décennies à de profonds changements, la famille prend des formes de plus en plus diversifiées. Avec la diminution de la nuptialité et de la fécondité, l'accroissement de la divortialité, l'autonomie accrue des jeunes et la montée de la cohabitation hors mariage, des formes de vie familiales auparavant marginales ont progressivement pris de l'importance. La période de vie dans un ménage individuel concerne ainsi de plus en plus de jeunes et s'étend dans la durée; le ménage monoparental caractérise pour sa part un nombre croissant de femmes et d'enfants; la cohabitation non maritale est désormais la principale forme d'entrée dans une union conjugale (Gabadinho, 1998; Wanner, 2002). Ces évolutions, associées à la mobilité familiale en augmentation, ont peu à peu provoqué une modification du parcours de vie familiale. Alors que, dans le passé, une personne se retrouvait au cours de sa vie dans un nombre limité de configurations familiales (en règle générale d'abord dans le ménage parental, puis dans un couple marié avec enfant, enfin dans un couple marié sans enfant), il n'est pas rare qu'elle parcourt désormais un nombre plus élevé de situations familiales (une ou plusieurs expériences de vie de couple, de vie dans un ménage individuel, recomposé ou monoparental, etc.), vivant ce que certains auteurs

* Cette contribution fait partie de l'ouvrage collectif *Vivre en Suisse 1999-2000* (Erwin Zimmermann et Robin Tillmann (éds), Editions Peter Lang, Berne (2004)). Les analyses et résultats se basent sur les deux premières vagues de l'enquête longitudinale Vivre en Suisse réalisée auprès de 6 335 personnes interviewées en 1999 et 2000. La collecte des données, effectuée par M. I. S. Trend sous la responsabilité du Panel suisse de ménages de l'Université de Neuchâtel, a été financée par le PP Demain la Suisse du Fonds national suisse de la recherche scientifique (Subsides No. 5004-53205 / 5004-57894 / 5004-67304). Des informations complémentaires peuvent être obtenues sur le site www.swisspanel.ch

** Forum suisse pour l'étude des migrations et de la population, Rue St-Honoré 2, 2000 Neuchâtel, Philippe.Wanner@unine.ch

*** Panel suisse des ménages, Espace de l'Europe 4, 2000 Neuchâtel, Alexis.Gabadinho @unine.ch qualifient comme étant une «biographie choisie» (Beck et Beck-Gernsheim, 1996). L'allongement de la durée moyenne de vie et les modifications comportementales en matière de vie familiale ont contribué simultanément à cet accroissement du nombre d'expériences différentes (cf. Menthonnex, 2000).

Suite à cette mobilité familiale accrue, différentes questions se posent, dont certaines sont discutées dans ce texte. Elles ont trait en particulier aux déterminants des changements familiaux, que ceux-ci soient anticipés ou non. Quels sont les facteurs pouvant intervenir sur la survenance d'un événement familial? Certains groupes définis par leur appartenance à une catégorie socio-professionnelle présentent-ils une probabilité élevée d'observer un changement familial? Telles sont les questions auxquelles nous tenterons de répondre à partir des données du Panel suisse des ménages, en adoptant une approche quantitative et essentiellement descriptive.

Cette contribution s'articule autour de deux parties. La première, purement descriptive, décrit la situation des familles en 1999 et les changements[1] observés entre 1999 et 2000. La deuxième, plus analytique, discute les principales mobilités observées (mise en couple, naissance d'un enfant, rupture du couple), en comparant la probabilité de vivre cette mobilité en fonction de certaines caractéristiques socio-économiques.

Comme pour les autres contributions de cet ouvrage, les données du Panel suisse des ménages ont servi de base de données pour cette étude. A l'exception des données présentées au premier chapitre qui se réfèrent aux ménages, les analyses effectuées dans cette contribution reposent sur les informations individuelles et se limitent aux personnes rencontrées à chacun des deux premiers passages de l'enquête.

On relèvera d'entrée un biais relatif au type de données utilisées, qu'il convient de conserver à l'esprit au moment de la lecture des résultats des analyses: comme toute enquête longitudinale, la probabilité de «perdre» des personnes est plus élevée lorsque celles-ci vivent un changement familial. Il n'a en effet pas été toujours possible de repérer en 2000 les personnes ayant quitté le ménage dans lequel elles se trouvaient en 1999 (ne serait-ce que parce que certaines de ces personnes ont pu quitter la Suisse). L'interprétation des résultats obtenus doit être effectuée en ayant conscience de cette limite.

1 Nous parlerons dans ce texte de mobilité familiale, de transition familiale, ou de changement familial pour définir les modifications dans la structure et la composition du ménage observées d'une vague à l'autre.

1. Ménages, familles et mobilité familiale

1.1 Les ménages privés en 1999

Selon le PSM, la structure des ménages privés en Suisse présentait en 1999 et 2000 les caractéristiques suivantes (Tableau 1): légèrement plus de 26 % de couples avec enfants, la plupart ayant soit deux enfants, soit au moins un enfant de 16 ans et plus; près de 29 % de couples sans enfant, les deux tiers de ces ménages étant composés de conjoints âgés de 65 ans et plus; 27 % de ménages individuels, avec une majorité de personnes âgées entre 30 et 64 ans; légèrement moins de 6 % de ménages monoparentaux; environ 2 % d'autres ménages. Entre les deux vagues de l'enquête, très peu de changements dans la structure des ménages en Suisse ne sont observés, avec cependant un léger vieillissement des ménages, explicable par le fait que l'échantillon du PSM, non renouvelé, vieillit. Ainsi, les personnes vivant seules âgées de 65 ans et plus et les ménages parentaux et les couples avec enfant(s) âgés de 16 ans ou plus voient leur proportion augmenter. En revanche, la proportion des couples de 65 ans et plus sans enfant diminue entre 1999 et 2000, probablement en raison du risque de veuvage ou d'institutionnalisation aux âges avancés[2].

1.2 Les modifications familiales observées entre 1999 et 2000

Définie ici comme étant la transition, pour un ménage, d'une catégorie de ménage à une autre[3], la mobilité familiale concerne quelque 11 % des ménages interviewés en 1999 et rencontrés en 2000 (Tableau 2). La probabilité pour un ménage d'avoir changé de catégorie entre les deux premières vagues de l'enquête dépend étroitement de la structure initiale du ménage: la proportion de ménages ayant vécu une modification varie ainsi entre 0,7 % (couple avec 3 enfants ou plus) et 33 % (autres ménages non familiaux). Outre les couples ayant au moins 3 enfants, les personnes seules âgées de 65 ans ou plus sont les plus stables. Les personnes seules âgées de moins de 30 ans et les couples avec un enfant présentent, sans surprise, une mobilité familiale élevée.

2 Rappelons que l'enquête couvre les ménages privés.

3 La typologie des ménages utilisée dans le tableau 1 a été utilisée ici. On a cependant fait abstraction des changements dans le type de ménages provoqués par le passage d'une classe d'âges à une autre.

Tableau 1: Répartition en % des ménages en 1999 et 2000

Type de ménage		1999	2000
Individuel	65 ans et plus	7,5	8,1
	30-64 ans	15,3	15,8
	moins de 30 ans	4,1	3,4
Monoparental	enfant(s) moins de 16 ans	2,4	2,5
	enfant(s) 16 ans et plus	3,3	3,5
Couple sans enfant	moins de 65 ans	9,2	9,3
	65 ans et plus	19,8	18,9
Couple avec enfant	Un enfant	6,3	6,2
	Deux enfants	11,0	10,7
	Trois enfants ou plus	5,3	5,5
	Au moins un enfant de 16 ans et plus	13,7	13,9
Ménage non familial	Tous parents	1,3	1,4
	Sans lien de parenté	0,9	0,8
Total		100,0	100,0
Effectif		5074	4532

Source: Panel suisse des ménages 1999-2000. Fichier «Ménages».

Les principaux changements familiaux observés entre les deux vagues de l'enquête ont été la mise en couple pour les personnes âgées moins de 65 ans vivant seules en 1999 (et plus encore parmi les personnes âgées de moins de 30 ans), la formation d'un nouveau ménage familial (couple avec enfants) pour les ménages monoparentaux comprenant de jeunes enfants, la dissolution des ménages monoparentaux avec enfant(s) adulte(s) et des couples âgés de 65 ans et plus, suite au départ de l'enfant, respectivement au veuvage, l'agrandissement de la taille de la famille parmi les jeunes couples, et enfin le départ du foyer parental du dernier enfant parmi les ménages composés en 1999 d'un couple et d'un enfant adulte (Tableau 2).

Si l'on se réfère à l'âge, c'est entre 20 et 29 ans que la probabilité d'observer un changement dans son ménage est la plus élevée (Graphique 1). Ce changement peut se référer à son propre départ du ménage parental ou au départ d'un frère ou d'une sœur, plus tard à la mise en couple, ou encore à la naissance d'un enfant. Légèrement plus précoce chez les femmes que chez les hommes, cette mobilité – calculée, rappelons-le, entre deux vagues d'enquête séparées d'une année – concerne respectivement 13 % des femmes âgées entre 20 et 24 ans

Tableau 2: Proportions de ménages rencontrés en 1999 dont la structure du ménage s'est modifiée entre 1999 et 2000

Type de ménage en 1999	% de ménages ayant vécu un changement	Nombre de changements	Changement le plus fréquemment observé
Personne seule, 65 et plus	0,9	3	–
Personne seule, 30-64 ans	7,8	66	Mise en couple
Personne seule, moins de 30 ans	16,9	55	Mise en couple
Ménage monoparental aucun enfant adulte	9,3	19	Mise en couple avec enfants
Ménage monoparental, avec au moins un enfant adulte	11,4	17	Vit seul
Couple sans enfant, un conjoint âgé de 65 ans et plus	5,0	19	Vit seul
Couple sans enfant, moins de 65 ans	9,1	103	Couple avec un enfant
Couple avec un enfant	15,6	52	Couple avec 2 enfants
Couple avec deux enfants	6,0	71	Couple avec 3 enfants
Couple avec trois enfants et plus	0,7	18	–
Couple avec au moins un enfant adulte	8,5	50	Couple sans enfant
Autres ménages familiaux	14,1	8	–
Autres ménages non familiaux	33,0	12	–
Ensemble	11,0	493	–

Source: Panel suisse des ménages 1999-2000. Fichiers «Ménages». A l'exclusion des changements provoqués par l'avancement en âge.

et 8 % des hommes du même âge. Elle caractérise 16 % des femmes âgées de 25 à 29 ans et 15 % des hommes du même âge. Dès le groupe d'âges 35-39 ans, les probabilités de vivre un changement dans le ménage deviennent plus faibles, puisque l'on atteint alors des périodes de la vie où les comportements familiaux se stabilisent progressivement, et où les événements modifiant la composition ou la structure du ménage deviennent plus rares. On observe cependant une légère augmentation de la mobilité entre 55-59 ans, âges où les enfants quittent le foyer parental. Aux âges plus avancés, les femmes sont plus fréquemment concernées par les changements familiaux – la plupart du temps, il s'agit de femmes devenant veuves.

Graphique 1: Proportion de personnes ayant vu leur structure de ménage se modifier, selon l'âge

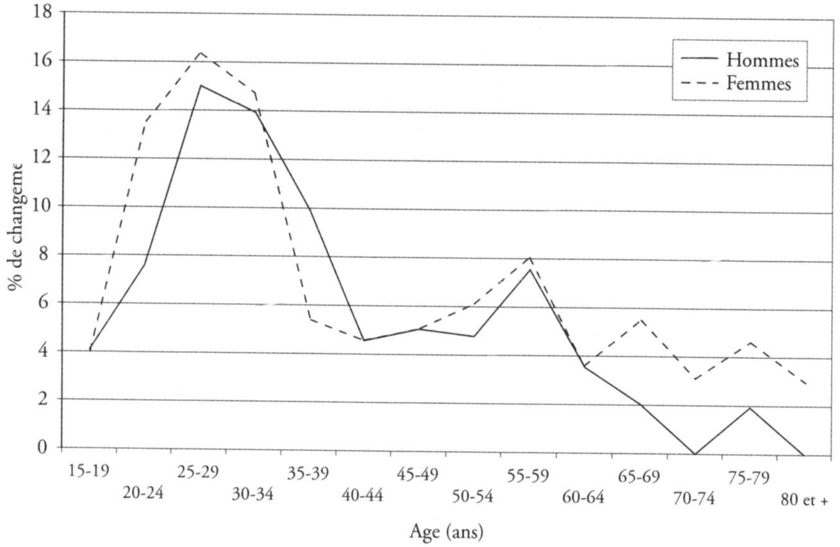

Source: Panel suisse des ménages, 1999 et 2000. Fichiers «Individus».

Les différences de calendriers observées entre homme et femme au moment de l'entrée dans la vie adulte ont été documentés par d'autres enquêtes, tels l'enquête suisse sur la famille de 1994/95 (Gabadinho, 1998) ou l'enquête suisse sur la population active de 1998 (Charton et Wanner, 2001a). Elles peuvent être mises en relation avec les rôles de l'homme et de la femme dans la société contemporaine, dont découlent des schémas bien établis: ainsi, dans une majorité des cas, la femme est plus jeune que l'homme au moment de la mise en couple.

1.3 Les changements familiaux sont-ils prévisibles?

On peut s'interroger sur le caractère prévisible et planifié des changements familiaux. Ceux-ci peuvent parfois être anticipés – par exemple dans le cas d'une volonté clairement établie de fonder une famille – mais aussi inattendus – dans le cas d'un décès soudain d'un membre du ménage, d'une séparation non anticipée, etc. En fonction du type de changement familial et de son éventuelle anticipation, les conséquences pour les membres de la famille peuvent d'ailleurs être très variées. S'il est prévu à l'avance et bien préparé, voire même désiré, le changement familial peut s'accompagner d'une faible mobilité socio-économique, et probablement d'un accroissement de la satisfaction générale. Dans le cas contraire, il peut être suivi d'une très rapide détérioration de la satisfaction de vie. Même si les données des deux premières vagues ne permettent pas de mettre en évidence les conséquences du changement familial sur les membres du ménage – il faudrait en effet pour cela un nombre plus important de transitions et donc attendre le troisième ou le quatrième passage – on peut déjà s'interroger sur sa nature prévisible ou non.

La première vague du PSM interrogeait en effet la personne de référence du ménage[4] sur les changements possibles, au cours de l'année à venir, concernant la structure de la famille. Les réponses apportées à cette question, comparées avec la réalité observée douze mois plus tard, permettent d'appréhender dans quelle mesure le changement observé dans le ménage correspond à un événement planifié.

Au total en 1999, quelque 10,7 % des ménages s'attendaient à un changement dans leur structure pour l'année à venir, 6,1 % ont répondu qu'un tel changement était peut-être possible, 1,8 % ne savaient pas et 81,2 % ne prévoyaient pas de changement. Ces chiffres peuvent être mis en relation avec l'observation effectuée ci-dessus d'une mobilité pour 11 % des ménages.

Parmi les ménages ayant déclaré en 1999 n'avoir observé aucun changement, quelque 7,2 % en prévoyaient un, résultat qui signifie que la planification d'une modification familiale n'est pas systématiquement suivie d'une réelle transition.

Parmi les ménages rencontrés aux deux passages et ayant vécu un changement de structure, seuls 35 % anticipaient cette transition. Environ 11 % des ménages la considéraient comme possible, tandis que les 54 % restants ne l'attendaient pas. Ces chiffres pour l'ensemble de l'échantillon cachent des disparités très importantes en fonction de la nature du changement observé (Tableau 3).

4 Celle-ci était la personne désignée pour répondre aux questions touchant à l'ensemble du ménage.

Tableau 3: Comparaison entre les changements de structure du ménage observés, et la réponse à la question sur la possibilité d'un changement

	Changement planifié			
Changement observé	Oui	Peut-être, ne sait pas	Non	Ensemble
Aucun changement du type de famille	7,2	7,3	85,4	100,0
Changement type de famille	34,8	11,4	53,8	100,0
Parmi lesquels:				
Mise en couple personne vivant seule	52,6	24,8	22,5	100,0
Naissance d'un premier enfant du couple	74,2	2,4	23,4	100,0
Séparation couple sans enfant	2,1	18,6	79,3	100,0
Séparation ménage familial	16,1	5,9	78,0	100,0
Départ du dernier enfant du couple	43,9	31,2	24,9	100,0
Evolution du nombre d'enfants dans le ménage				
Diminution nombre d'enfants	45,3	20,1	34,6	100,0
Nombre identique d'enfants	7,6	7,5	84,9	100,0
Augmentation nombre d'enfants	57,2	6,9	35,9	100,0

Source: Panel suisse des ménages, 1999 et 2000; ménages rencontrés lors des deux passages de l'enquête.

En effet, l'arrivée d'un premier enfant au sein du couple (74 %), la mise en couple pour une personne vivant seule (53 %), et le départ du dernier enfant du couple (44 %) figurent parmi les événements les plus fréquemment anticipés. La diminution ou l'accroissement du nombre d'enfants dans le ménage sont d'autres événements également souvent anticipés. Notons par ailleurs que le départ d'un enfant du foyer parental est parfois considéré comme possible, sans qu'il soit attendu avec certitude. Ce résultat reflète très certainement le fait que, s'il est attendu dans un avenir plus ou moins proche, cet événement ne peut être daté de manière exacte, puisqu'il dépend de nombreux paramètres pas toujours «contrôlés» par le ménage (entrée dans une université ou haute école située loin du lieu de domicile, entrée sur le marché du travail, indépendance financière, opportunités sur le marché du logement, etc. – cf. Hullen, 1995; Buck et Scott, 1993).

En revanche, les événements de la vie de couple ayant une valeur ou signification le plus souvent négative, tels que la rupture d'un couple avec enfant(s)

(16 %) ou sans enfant (2 %) sont beaucoup moins fréquemment anticipés. La décision de mettre fin au couple est probablement plus réfléchie en cas de présence d'enfants puisque la décision a des conséquences plus étendues sur le fonctionnement du ménage: ceci explique certainement la plus forte proportion de ruptures de couples prévues dans le cas d'un ménage avec un ou plusieurs enfants.

2. Les facteurs de la mobilité familiale

Différentes variables ou caractéristiques socio-démographiques et économiques peuvent influencer la survenance de changements dans la composition du ménage. Identifier et analyser ces variables permet de discuter dans quelle mesure la mobilité familiale se produit avec la même intensité dans l'ensemble de la population, ou si elle concerne des groupes précis de personnes. Outre le sexe et l'âge, facteurs très étroitement associés, comme nous l'avons montré plus haut, à la mobilité familiale, il s'agit ici de mettre en évidence les autres variables pouvant intervenir sur cette mobilité.

Compte tenu de l'échantillon disponible et de la fréquence relativement faible de la mobilité familiale enregistrée au cours d'une année, des effectifs peu élevés de ménages et de personnes interrogés ont observé une mobilité entre 1999 et 2000 (cf. ci-dessus). Pour cette raison, dans l'attente de pouvoir prendre en compte d'autres vagues de l'enquête, seuls deux événements ont pu être analysés dans les détails: (1) la mise en couple pour des personnes qui, en 1999, vivaient sans conjoint; (2) la rupture du couple, qu'elle soit due à une séparation, à un divorce, ou à un veuvage. Quant aux autres événements comme la naissance d'un enfant (67 naissances enregistrées entre 1999 et 2000, dont 24 de rang 1), il faudra attendre d'autres passages avant de pouvoir les analyser.

Pour cette même raison, nous sommes contraints d'étudier des hypothèses très générales sur les facteurs intervenant sur les événements analysés, sans pouvoir les vérifier systématiquement par des modèles statistiques très détaillés. A l'issue de l'analyse effectuée, les tests de khi carré sont l'outil statistique le mieux adapté pour mettre en évidence l'association entre différents caractères individuels et le fait de vivre un changement familial.

2.1 La mise en couple

Rares sont dans la population celles et ceux n'ayant pas, au cours de leur vie, vécu dans une relation de couple et partagé un logement avec une ou un conjoint: des données biographiques pour la Suisse indiquent en effet que quelque 93 % des hommes nés entre 1945 et 1959 et 90 % des femmes de la même génération ont vécu au moins une épisode de vie de couple avant le 35e anniversaire (Gabadinho, 1998). Les deux premiers passages du PSM ne couvrant qu'une fraction du parcours de vie, ils n'autorisent cependant l'identification que d'une faible proportion des mises en couple, définie par le partage d'un même logement par deux personnes entretenant des liens conjugaux. Ainsi, parmi les personnes incluses dans l'échantillon longitudinal du PSM vivant en 1999 sans partenaire au sein du ménage (33 % de l'ensemble de l'échantillon), seules 4,4 % ont observé une mise en couple entre les deux premiers passages de l'enquête.

Compte tenu de la fréquence de cet événement, les données du PSM permettent surtout d'appréhender le rythme de mise en couple parmi des personnes vivant sans conjoint en 1999.

Trois variables semblent intervenir sur la probabilité d'avoir vécu une mise en couple (Tableau 4): celle-ci est en effet plus fréquente parmi les femmes pratiquantes de confession catholique, parmi les personnes actives, ainsi que parmi les personnes de nationalité suisse par rapport aux étrangers.

Ces résultats peuvent traduire toute une série de facteurs. Concernant le rôle de l'activité professionnelle sur la mise en couple, le fait d'avoir un emploi est souvent, pour les jeunes adultes, une condition nécessaire avant d'une part de quitter le foyer parental et d'autre part de débuter une relation de couple en tant que cohabitant. La proportion plus élevée de mises en couple parmi les actifs (4 fois plus élevée pour les hommes, 8 fois plus élevée pour les femmes), s'explique très certainement par ce besoin d'acquérir une indépendance financière vis-à-vis des parents avant de se mettre en couple. L'association entre statut d'activité et la mise en couple n'étonne donc pas, car elle s'inscrit dans le passage à l'âge adulte.

Les personnes étrangères ne vivant pas en couple en 1999 paraissent être pour leur part moins fréquemment concernées par une mise en union entre les deux premiers passages de l'enquête. Un éventuel projet de retour, la présence d'un conjoint vivant dans le pays d'origine et en attente d'un regroupement familial peuvent être des facteurs expliquant ces résultats. Une autre explication peut découler des relations entre la migration et la vie familiale: la migration concerne de plus en plus des couples ou des familles avec enfant. La constitution de la famille précédant le mouvement migratoire, celle-ci ne peut être enregistrée par l'enquête.

Quant au lien entre religion et mise en union, signalons que le modèle familial «traditionnel», dans lequel le couple est marié et vit ensemble, est probablement plus fréquent parmi les pratiquants catholiques que parmi les personnes non pratiquantes (Charton et Wanner, 2001b). Ce constat n'explique cependant que très partiellement la fréquence plus élevée des mises en couple parmi les femmes pratiquantes de confession catholiques. On suspectera cependant que cette catégorie vit moins longtemps en ménage seule ou hors couple, et se retrouve plus fortement incitée à entrer dans une union de cohabitation par sa famille, ses proches ou par la reproduction de normes de vie.

L'association entre la mise en couple et d'autres facteurs professionnels ou socio-culturels n'est en revanche pas vérifiée par le modèle. C'est le cas en particulier du niveau de formation ou des modèles de répartition des tâches au sein du couple, qui ne paraissent donc pas jouer un rôle déterminant (Tableau 4).

2.2 La rupture du couple

Avec l'accroissement de la divortialité observé en Europe et en Suisse, différents courants de recherches tant sociologiques ou démographiques ont cherché à comprendre les facteurs influençant, dans un sens ou un autre, la probabilité de terminer une union maritale par un divorce (cf. pour la Suisse Kellerhals, 1985). Sans vouloir dresser un état exhaustif des études entreprises au cours des dernières décennies, signalons que celles-ci mettent en relation le rôle de l'âge au mariage (Booth et Edwards, 1985; Kiernan 1986), de la biographie prémaritale et de la durée écoulée depuis le mariage. Pour Andersson (1997), la naissance d'enfants semble pour sa part diminuer le risque de divorce. Cependant, les liens entre natalité et divortialité sont relativement complexes, en raison du fait que la naissance d'un enfant peut être ressentie différemment d'un couple à l'autre: si l'arrivée de l'enfant peut modifier positivement ou négativement les relations du couple, l'absence de descendance peut aussi intervenir sur la solidité du couple. La pratique religieuse agit aussi, puisque le risque de divorcer est moins fréquent parmi les pratiquants de confession catholique, ainsi que dans les cantons catholiques (Charton et Wanner, 2001c). D'autres

Tableau 4: Proportion de personnes ayant débuté une mise en couple entre les deux passages de l'enquête, selon différentes caractéristiques socio-culturelles

	Hommes		Femmes	
	En %	signification	En %	signification
Ensemble	9,8		4,8	
Niveau de formation				
Sans maturité	9,6	ns	5,1	ns
Maturité ou supérieur	9,2		3,8	
Appartenance religieuse				
Catholique	10,3	ns	6,1	*
Autre	5,4		1,9	
Pratique religieuse				
Moins de 2 fois par mois	7,1	ns	6,8	*
2 fois par mois ou plus	11,0		3,3	
Présence d'un enfant				
Non	10,2	ns	4,8	ns
Oui	2,3		4,8	
Nationalité				
Etrangère	4,6	**	2,0	**
Suisse	31,5		26,2	
Statut dans la profession				
Non actif	2,6	*	1,0	**
Actif, étudiant	11,7		8,4	
Effectif pondéré	422		799	

Source: Panel suisse des ménages 1999 et 2000. Les degrés de signification sont calculés sur un test de Khi carré: * <0.05, ** <0.01, ns non significatif.

facteurs sont suspectés, même s'ils ne s'observent pas systématiquement: le rôle de la femme dans le couple et la société, le divorce éventuel des parents (Wolfinger, 1999), la présence dans le couple d'enfants nés avant le mariage, la durée de la cohabitation pré-maritale (Berrington et Diamond, 1999; Demaris et MacDonald, 1993), bien que le rôle exact de ce facteur soit parfois mis en doute (Axinn et Thornton, 1992), la nationalité des conjoints (pour la Suisse: Zingg, 1997), voire le niveau de formation (Hoem, 1997).

Face à l'abondance de cette littérature, le PSM permet de mettre en évidence que très partiellement les facteurs des séparations observées entre les deux vagues de l'enquête. Partant de l'information disponible, on peut identifier 1,6 % d'hommes et 3,5 % de femmes vivant en couple en 1999 qui se sont séparés durant l'année qui a suivi. Ainsi, bien qu'elle soit légèrement plus fréquente que dans le passé, en particulier parmi les couples mariés, la rupture du couple est un événement qui intervient encore rarement, plus rarement que la mise en couple ou que la naissance d'un enfant.

La rupture du couple regroupe de nombreuses situations de vie, puisqu'elle peut regrouper le divorce, le veuvage, la séparation d'un couple nouvellement formé ou la rupture d'une union ayant duré plusieurs années voire décennies; toutes ces situations n'ont pas les mêmes causes, ni les mêmes conséquences. En raison du faible nombre de cas (81 cas), ces événements ont cependant dû être rassemblés. Dans les trois quarts des cas, ces ruptures concernent une séparation ou un divorce au sein d'un couple marié.

Les principales variables associées à la probabilité de rupture du couple ont été testées par un test de khi carré. Les femmes déclarant recevoir un faible support en 1999 ont une probabilité significativement plus élevée de vivre une séparation entre 1999 et 2000, par rapport à celles ayant déclaré un support élevé. Sans être significative, la répartition jugée égalitaire des tâches entre hommes et femmes semble aussi prédire le risque de rupture, les couples ressentant une répartition non égalitaire étant également ceux qui présentent une probabilité supérieure de rupture. La durée de cohabitation joue également un rôle, puisque lorsque la durée est supérieure à cinq ans, le risque de rupture est plus faible.

On n'observe en revanche aucune association entre le risque de rupture et d'autres variables telles que la religion déclarée, la pratique religieuse, ou la présence d'un enfant. Pourtant, il s'agit là de variables pour lesquelles on peut suspecter un rôle sur la rupture du couple.

Tableau 5: Proportion de personnes ayant observé un agrandissement de la taille de la famille entre les deux passages de l'enquête, selon différentes caractéristiques socio-culturelles

	Hommes En %	Hommes signification	Femmes En %	Femmes signification
Ensemble	1,6		2,5	
Niveau de formation				
Sans maturité	1,8	ns	2,7	ns
Maturité ou supérieur	1,3		2,0	
Appartenance religieuse				
Catholique	1,8	ns	2,3	ns
Autre	1,4		2,6	
Pratique religieuse				
Moins de 2 fois par mois	1,8	ns	2,8	ns
2 fois par mois ou plus	1,2		1,8	
Jugement concernant la répartition du travail				
Répartition égalitaire	1,5	ns	2,2	ns
Répartition non égalitaire	2,2		3,8	
Support pratique de la part du conjoint				
Non, faible	2,1	ns	3,6	*
Oui, élevé	1,4		1,9	
Support émotionnel de la part du conjoint				
Non, faible	2,7	*	3,5	*
Oui, élevé	1,3		2,1	
Présence d'un enfant				
Non	1,4	ns	2,8	ns
Oui	1,9		2,0	
Nationalité				
Etrangère	3,0	**	2,2	ns
Suisse	1,3		2,6	
Durée de vie commune				
Moins de 5 ans	4,8	**	5,3	**
5 ans ou plus	1,3		2,2	
Statut dans la profession				
Non actif	0,0	**	2,3	ns
Actif, étudiant	2,0		2,6	
Effectif pondéré	2374		799	

Source: Panel suisse des ménages, 1999 et 2000. Les degrés de signification sont calculés sur un test de Khi carré: * < 0.05 ** < 0.01 ns non significatif.

Conclusion

La mobilité familiale ne représente qu'une parmi de nombreuses formes de mobilités en accroissement au cours de ces dernières décennies. Elle présente un intérêt particulier, dans le sens où cet accroissement s'accompagne d'une très forte diversification des types de transition. Avec la perte d'importance de la famille «traditionnelle», de nouveaux types de familles ont émergé, qui parfois sinon souvent ne durent que quelques mois ou années. La vie en couple non marié représente en effet toujours en Suisse – contrairement à la situation observée dans d'autres pays – une situation transitoire, pouvant certes s'étendre sur plusieurs années, avant qu'un mariage ne subvienne et que l'agrandissement de la famille ne soit observé. La vie en ménage monoparental est également limitée dans le temps, et peut se terminer par une recomposition familiale ou par le départ des enfants. Un net accroissement des événements pouvant modifier la composition et la structure du ménage est observé dans la société. Objets de la présente étude, ces événements ne peuvent être analysés précisément qu'à partir de données longitudinales.

L'approche d'analyse suggérée ici présente certaines limites, relatives en particulier à la faible incidence des transitions familiales. Compte tenu de la durée d'observation prise en compte, le nombre d'événements observés – une fois classés en catégories – est limité. Il n'a pas été possible, pour cette raison, de discuter les conséquences des événements familiaux sur différents domaines de la vie. On a dû se restreindre à analyser les facteurs associés à deux de ces événements, tout en restant modestes par rapport aux outils d'analyse et aux interprétations. Il n'en reste pas moins vrai que les panels représentent un instrument essentiel pour la compréhension des transitions – familiales, mais aussi professionnelles, migratoires, etc. – survenant dans la vie. De par leur nature, les panels gagnent avec l'allongement de la durée d'observation un pouvoir explicatif, grâce à la possibilité de regrouper des événements survenant rarement, enregistrés entre diverses vagues. Ainsi, les frustrations observées au cours de la présente analyse, relatives à la taille des échantillons, devraient progressivement s'atténuer à mesure que la durée d'observation des ménages augmente.

Malgré ces limites, on observera cependant quelques résultats intéressants. Ils ont trait la mesure d'une mobilité familiale caractérisant chaque année plus d'un ménage privé sur dix en Suisse, et à la relative incapacité de prédire dans le temps des événements familiaux, en particulier ceux ayant une connotation négative. L'analyse des facteurs intervenant sur la mobilité familiale montre pour sa part quelques pistes de discussion, relatives en particulier au rôle que peuvent prendre les facteurs socio-professionnels dans la formation et la dissolution du ménage. Il conviendra résolument de vérifier à mesure de la disponibilité des vagues suivantes du PSM dans quelle mesure les différents facteurs identifiés peuvent intervenir sur la mobilité familiale.

Références bibliographiques

Andersson G. (1997), «The impact of children on divorce risks of Swedish women», *European Journal of Population*, 13/2, 109-145.

Axinn P. R., Thornton A. (1992), «The relationship between cohabitation and divorce: selectivity or causal influence?» *Demography*, 29/3, 357-374.

Beck U., Beck-Gernsheim E. (1996), «Individualization and ‹precarious freedoms›: perspectives and controversies of a subject-orientated sociology». In *Detradionalization: Critical Reflections of Authority and Identity*, P. Heelas, S. Lash et P. Morris eds, Oxford, United Kingdom: Blackwell, 22-48.

Berrington A., Diamond I. (1999), «Marital dissolution among the 1958 British birth cohort: The role of cohabitation», *Population Studies*, 53, 19-38.

Booth A., Edwards J. N. (1985), «Age at marriage and marital instability», *Journal of Marriage and the Family*, 47, 67-75.

Charton L., Wanner P. (2001a), *Migrations internes et changements familiaux en Suisse. Analyse du module «mobilité» de l'enquête suisse sur la population active de 1998*. Neuchâtel: Office fédéral de la statistique.

Charton L., Wanner P. (2001b), «Entre mariage et cohabitation. Choix et devenir de la première union non maritale en Suisse», *Population*, 56(4), 539-568.

Charton L., Wanner P. (2001c), «Divorcer en Suisse: effet des facteurs individuels, de mise en couple et de couple», *Revue suisse de sociologie,* 27(2) 255-280.

Demaris A., MacDonald W. (1993), «Premarital cohabitation and marital instability: A test of the unconventiality hypothesis», *Journal of Marriage and The Family*, 55, 399-407.

Gabadinho A. (1998), *L'enquête suisse sur la famille 1994/95: Présentation, résultats commentés et tableaux*, Berne, Office fédéral de la statistique.

Hoem J. M. (1997), «Educational gradients in divorce risks in Sweden in recent decades», *Population Studies*, Vol. 51, No. 1, London, 19-27.

Hullen G. (1995), «Der Auszug aus dem Elternhaus im Vergleich von West- und Ostdeutschland: Ergebnisse des Family and Fertility Surveys (FFS) 1992», *Zeitschrift für Bevölkerungswissenschaft*, 20(2), 141-158

Buck N., Scott J. (1993), «She's leaving home: but why? An analysis of young people leaving the parental home», *Journal of Marriage and the Family*, 55(4), 863-874.

Kellerhals J. et al. (1985), «Statut social, projet familial et divorce», *Population*, 40 (6), 811-828.

Kiernan K. E. (1986), «Teenage marriage and marital breakdown: A longitudinal study», *Population Studies*, 40(1), 35-54.

Menthonnex J. (2002), «L'impact du vieillissement démographique sur la composition des ménages: Le cas de la Suisse». In AIDELF (eds), *Vivre plus longtemps, avoir moins d'enfants, quelles implications*. AIDELF: Paris, 341-354.

Wanner P. (2002), «Changements dans les configurations familiales et les modes de vie des familles: une analyse statistique», *Démos*, 2/2002, Neuchâtel: Office fédéral de la statistique.

Wolfinger N. H. (1999), «Trends in the intergenerational transmission of divorce», *Demography*, 36(3), Silver Spring, Maryland, 415-420.

Zingg W. (1997), *Le mariage et le divorce depuis 1987*, Démos, 4/97, Berne, Office fédéral de la statistique.

Pratiques culturelles et de loisirs*

Caterina MODETTA, Pascale GAZARETH et Katja BRANGER

Introduction

Les pratiques de loisirs, et tout particulièrement celles liées aux activités culturelles, dépendent de nombreux facteurs comme l'offre existante ou les ressources financières et temporelles des individus. Plus profondément, elles découlent de divers *goûts et dégoûts* dont Bourdieu (1979) indique qu'ils sont, dans une très large mesure, structurés en fonction d'inégalités de capitaux (économique: revenu et fortune; et culturel: formation au sens large dont la scolarisation est un élément central) et de position dans l'espace social. Dans cette perspective, la consommation de biens culturels constitue un acte bien moins individuel que social.[1] De même, analysant les enquêtes sur les *Pratiques culturelles des Français* (4 sondages entre 1973 et 1997), Donnat (1998/1) relève l'influence prépondérante du capital culturel (milieu d'origine et formation) et de l'âge,

* Cette contribution fait partie de l'ouvrage collectif *Vivre en Suisse 1999-2000* (Erwin Zimmermann et Robin Tillmann (éds), Editions Peter Lang, Berne (2004)). Les analyses et résultats se basent sur les deux premières vagues de l'enquête longitudinale Vivre en Suisse réalisée auprès de 6 335 personnes interviewées en 1999 et 2000. La collecte des données, effectuée par M. I. S. Trend sous la responsabilité du Panel suisse de ménages de l'Université de Neuchâtel, a été financée par le PP Demain la Suisse du Fonds national suisse de la recherche scientifique (Subsides No. 5004-53205 / 5004-57894 / 5004-67304). Des informations complémentaires peuvent être obtenues sur le site www.swisspanel.ch

1 A la fin du 19e siècle, Veblen (1970) mettait déjà en évidence l'utilisation des loisirs dans les stratégies de différenciation des classes sociales supérieures. De même, Moeschler (2000) écrit que «les individus, structurés par l'ordre social de manière différentielle, consomment des produits culturels différents (ou n'en consomment point). La culture ou production symbolique se trouve – de même que sa consommation – fragmentée en divers sous-ensembles concurrents et de légitimité inégale» (p. 8). Illustrant ce phénomène, il mentionne la distinction courante entre *culture cultivée* (ou *savante* ou *légitime* ou *établie*: musées, théâtres, musique classique, danse), valorisée socialement et opposée à la *culture de masse* ou à la *culture populaire*, sans parler des activités reléguées au rang de simples loisirs.

alors que le capital économique, bien qu'influent, apparaît nettement secondaire. Ces éléments se retrouvent globalement en Suisse.[2]

L'analyse des pratiques culturelles dans le long terme fait apparaître une assez forte stabilité qu'il faut relier à l'influence des éléments de capital culturel: se modifiant peu, ces éléments favorisent la constance des goûts et dégoûts au cours de l'existence et leur transmission de génération en génération. Certaines évolutions sont toutefois perceptibles, qui tiennent en particulier au développement des nouvelles technologies de l'audiovisuel et de l'internet (voir Donnat, 1998/2). L'analyse des deux premières vagues du PSM se prête cependant mal à l'analyse de ces évolutions lentes.

Par ailleurs, l'influence de l'âge mise en avant par Donnat laisse supposer que différents éléments liés au cycle de vie[3] amènent des changements dans les pratiques culturelles individuelles. La situation professionnelle et familiale ou la santé peuvent ainsi générer des modifications au niveau des goûts et dégoûts ou du moins de leur traduction dans les pratiques. Elles jouent également sur les ressources disponibles (temps et argent), ce qui là aussi influence les pratiques. Les changements peuvent se traduire par l'abandon ou l'adoption de certaines activités ou par des variations dans la fréquence à laquelle elles sont menées. Etant donné l'inertie des goûts et dégoûts, on peut s'attendre à ce que les écarts de fréquence soient les plus courants.

Ce second type d'évolution se prête cette fois bien à l'analyse à court terme que suppose la comparaison des deux premières vagues du PSM. Nous nous attacherons donc dans cette contribution à dresser le bilan de la situation en matière de pratiques culturelles sur la base des données 2000 (analyse transversale). Nous analyserons ensuite les principaux changements survenus depuis

2 Voir notamment Lamprecht et Stamm (1994). En Suisse, la recherche sur les pratiques culturelles reste peu développée. Les enquêtes menées ces dernières années sont rares et se limitent en général à un contexte régional ou à un domaine spécifique. La dernière grande enquête nationale remonte à 1988 (Microrecensement OFS). D'une manière générale, le problème de délimitation de la notion de culture amène ces enquêtes à adopter une conception large de la notion de pratiques culturelles débordant plus ou moins sur celle de loisirs. Ainsi, à côté de la fréquentation des théâtres et galeries d'art, trouve-t-on également des questions sur les sorties au restaurant ou l'usage récréatif d'Internet.

3 A concevoir comme la succession des différentes étapes qui marquent la vie sociale d'un individu: enfance, période d'adolescence vécue entre formation et émancipation familiale, entrée dans le monde du travail, fondation de son propre foyer, arrivée puis départ des enfants, et retrait de la vie professionnelle, pour citer les principales étapes identifiables dans la société suisse actuelle.

1999 (analyse longitudinale), en examinant les facteurs individuels qui les ont favorisés. Nous tiendrons compte pour cela d'éléments de positionnement social et de cycle de vie (genre[4], âge, nationalité, domicile, situation familiale, activité principale[5], position socioprofessionnelle et santé) à la fois dans leurs aspects statiques (p. ex. profession exercée, lieu de domicile) et dynamiques (p. ex. mise en ménage, évolution du revenu du ménage).

Etat de la situation en 2000

Comportements en matière de pratiques culturelles et de loisirs en 2000

Cette première section donne une vue d'ensemble des comportements en matière de loisirs ainsi que de leur appréciation sur la base de la seconde vague du PSM.

Le tableau 1 présente les douze activités de loisirs figurant dans le PSM en 1999 comme en 2000 selon la fréquence à laquelle elles sont exercées.[6] La lecture y occupe une place importante: 70 % de la population s'y adonne quotidiennement. Pratiquées au moins une fois par semaine par 74 % de la population chacune, des activités à l'extérieur telles que se promener ou rencontrer des amis sont également très fréquentes. A l'opposé, la fréquentation de cours ainsi que des activités plus expressives telles que faire de la musique et aller danser arrivent en dernier.

Une première analyse exploratoire fait ressortir des catégories sociales exerçant certaines des activités à des intervalles particulièrement fréquents. Ainsi, les catégories de revenus, les niveaux de formation et l'origine sociale[7]

4 Nous privilégions ici la notion de genre à celle de sexe dans la mesure où les résultats de nos analyses démontrent assez clairement que les pratiques culturelles varient en fonction des différences de rôles et positions sociales entre hommes et femmes et non de leur spécificité biologique. En effet, on retrouve globalement les mêmes oppositions entre employés à plein temps d'une part et employés à temps partiel ou actifs au foyer d'autre part qu'entre hommes et femmes. La même interprétation doit être faite de la notion d'âge, qu'il faut relier à différents rôles et positions spécifiques de certaines phases du cycle de vie.

5 Etre en formation, au foyer, professionnellement actif, ou encore retraité.

6 Question posée: *Voici une liste d'activités de loisirs. A quelle fréquence les pratiquez-vous?*

7 Mesurées sur 5 niveaux (école obligatoire, secondaire II professionnel et général, tertiaire professionnel et universitaire), ces deux dernières variables ont globalement une influence similaire quelle que soit l'activité de loisirs considérée (l'origine sociale est évaluée par

Tableau 1: Activités de loisirs selon la fréquence à laquelle elles sont pratiquées (en % de la population de 15 ans ou plus)

	chaque jour	au moins une fois par semaine	au moins une fois par mois	moins d'une fois par mois	jamais
Lecture	70,0	18,7	4,6	3,4	3,2
Rencontrer des amis, connaissances, collègues	11,7	62,4	20,5	3,9	1,5
Pratiquer un sport individuel ou de groupe	6,2	52,2	9,2	3,7	28,6
Se promener	23,1	50,7	14,8	4,6	6,8
Aller dans un bar, pub, restaurant	3,7	44,1	31,9	10,5	9,8
Bricoler, travail manuel, jardiner	13,1	37,6	15,6	7,2	26,4
Aller au théâtre, à l'opéra, à une exposition	0,1	2,0	21,8	42,0	34,1
Aller au cinéma	0,0	2,8	26,8	36,4	33,9
Fréquenter des cours (langue, bricolage, cuisine, ...)	0,4	11,3	4,2	9,9	74,2
Faire de la musique, p. ex. jouer d'un instrument, chanter	8,3	15,3	4,0	3,0	69,4
Aller en disco, dans un dancing	0,1	7,2	11,9	14,9	65,9
Fréquenter des événements sportifs	0,1	7,4	16,9	21,0	54,6

Panel suisse de ménages 2000, échantillon transversal. Pondération transversale au niveau des individus. N = entre 7058 et 7065.

paraissent avoir une influence univoque sur la fréquence à laquelle les activités formatives, sportives ou liées au monde des arts (théâtre, opéra, exposition, cinéma) notamment sont pratiquées: plus le revenu du ménage et le niveau de formation sont élevés, plus la fréquence de ces pratiques tend à augmenter. Quant à la position socioprofessionnelle, on y retrouve les caractéristiques liées à la formation et au revenu: ainsi, contrairement aux personnes exerçant des professions manuelles, celles des professions libérales, managériales ou

le plus haut niveau de formation des parents). Elles contribuent par ailleurs à expliquer d'autres éléments comme la profession exercée ou le revenu qui se révèlent ainsi également souvent explicatifs mais rarement de manière autonome.

académiques s'adonnent davantage à la lecture et aux pratiques liées au monde des arts.

Les écarts les plus manifestes sont cependant à rapporter aux différentes catégories d'âge. Comparée à la population dans son ensemble, la part de jeunes de moins de 25 ans rencontrant des amis ou faisant de la musique quotidiennement est nettement plus élevée, de même que la part de jeunes fréquentant les bars, cinémas ou discothèques au moins une fois par semaine (différence de plus de 30 % par rapport à la population totale[8]). Dans le même ordre d'idées et avec les mêmes écarts par rapport à l'ensemble de la population, les personnes âgées de 65 ans ou plus sont plus nombreuses à faire des promenades, du jardinage ou du travail manuel quotidiennement ainsi qu'à aller au théâtre, à l'opéra ou à des expositions une fois par semaine. On retrouve ici des résultats proches des enquêtes citées dans l'introduction (p. ex. Donnat, 1998/1).

Une comparaison des pratiques sélectionnées s'avère néanmoins difficile, les différentes activités étant par essence exercées à des rythmes différents (si un grand nombre de personnes lit ou va se promener quotidiennement, on ne trouvera guère des personnes qui vont au théâtre ou au cinéma tous les jours). C'est pourquoi nous avons procédé à la création d'une variable exprimant le degré d'activité des personnes pour chaque activité de loisirs. Cette procédure nous permet par ailleurs, par addition du nombre d'activités activement menées, d'évaluer la diversité des pratiques pour chaque individu et d'identifier ainsi les groupes de population recourant à des activités particulièrement diversifiées.[9]

> *Répartition des modalités de fréquence dans les catégories «actif» et «non actif»:* pour chaque activité de loisirs, la catégorie de réponse la plus souvent citée – la valeur modale – a été groupée avec les catégories plus fréquentes pour former la catégorie «actif» (par ex. «au moins une fois par semaine» avec «chaque jour» si cette première possibilité de réponse est la plus souvent citée). Les autres catégories de réponse (dans cet exemple, «au moins une fois par mois», «moins d'une fois par mois», «jamais») ont été réunies dans la

8 I. e. le rapport «proportion de jeunes concernés / proportion de personnes concernées dans la population totale» dépasse 130 % ou alors est inférieur à 70 %.

9 Ces indicateurs globaux sont créés sur le modèle de travaux antérieurs de l'Office fédéral de la statistique. En particulier: *Les personnes âgées en Suisse*, Neuchâtel: série *Données sociales – Suisse*, 2000.

Figure 2: Part de la population pratiquant activement les activités de loisirs considérées, en %

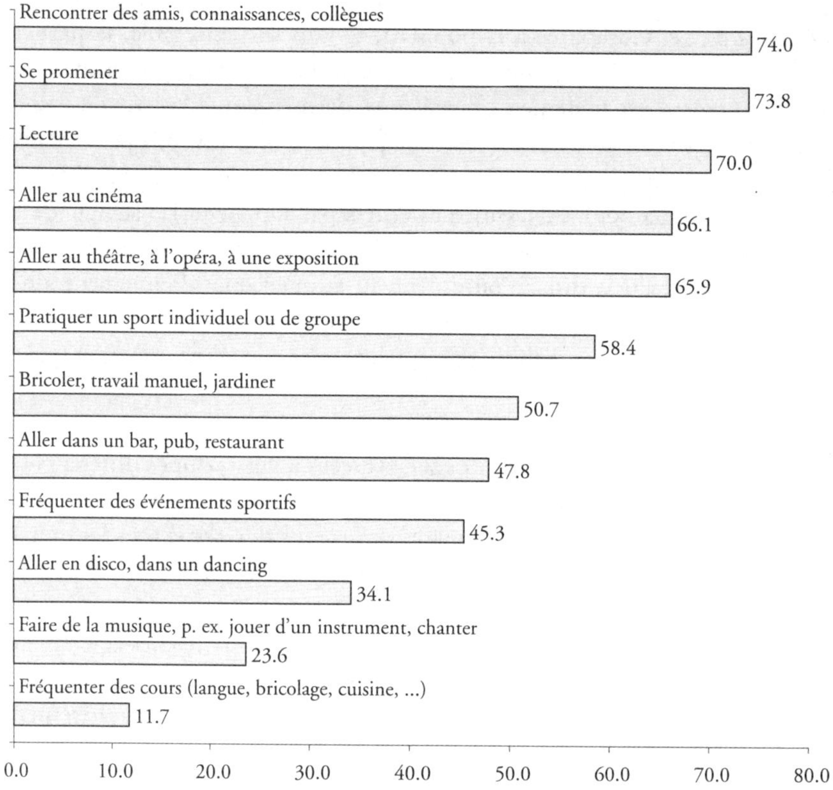

Panel suisse de ménages 2000, échantillon transversal. Pondération transversale au niveau des individus. N = entre 7058 et 7065.

catégorie «non actif». Le nombre de pratiques exercées activement a ensuite été résumé dans une nouvelle variable exprimant la diversité des activités auxquelles la personne recourt.

Si les rencontres avec des amis, les promenades ainsi que la lecture restent prépondérantes (cf. figure 2), ce regroupement permet néanmoins de relever l'importance des activités culturelles dans un sens strict à l'exemple d'aller au cinéma, au théâtre, à l'opéra, à des expositions. L'identification de catégories sociales particulièrement actives ou ayant des activités plus diversifiées que d'autres s'en trouve aussi facilitée.

Figure 3: Proportion d'actifs dans les différents types de loisirs

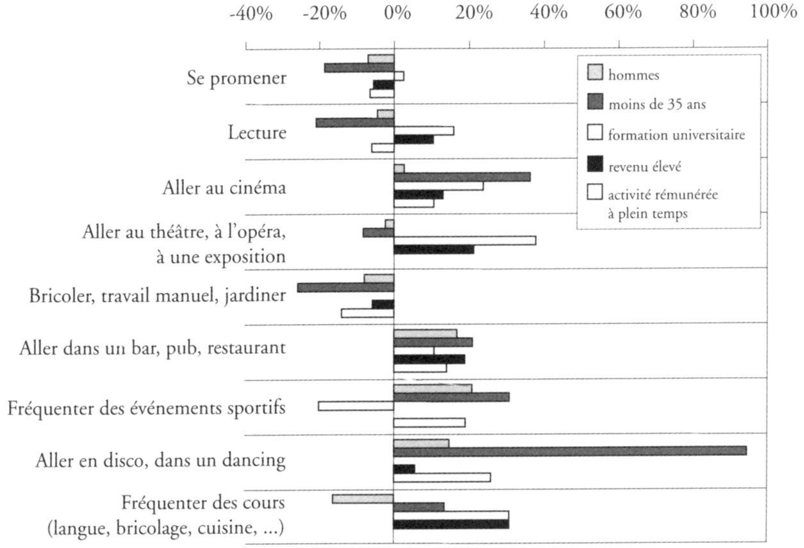

Panel suisse de ménages 2000, échantillon transversal. Pondération transversale au niveau des individus. Seules les valeurs statistiquement significatives sont prises en considération. N (total) = entre 7058 et 7065.

La figure 3 illustre les écarts de la part d'actifs dans quelques catégories particulièrement intéressantes par rapport à celle dans la population totale.[10] Les différences selon les classes d'âge sont particulièrement frappantes, ce qui n'étonnera guère. Les écarts par rapport au niveau de formation et à la catégorie de revenu sont également apparents: au chapitre des activités culturelles précitées notamment, les composantes économiques et culturelles semblent peser de tout leur poids. Inversement, on notera que le genre n'a qu'une incidence limitée sur les comportements en matière de loisirs, tout comme les variables géostructurelles (différences entre ville et campagne), qui ne sont pas illustrées dans le graphique.

10 En pourcentage: le calcul a été effectué en divisant la part de personnes actives dans les catégories sociales sélectionnées par celle dans la population totale. Cette dernière est indexée à 100 % et forme le point zéro. Les barres indiquent donc la différence du pourcentage d'actifs dans chacune des catégories par rapport à la population totale.

Quant à la largeur de l'éventail, la grande majorité de la population (64 %) exerce activement entre 5 et 8 activités parmi les 12 activités de loisirs proposées. Seuls 0,4 % ne sont actifs dans aucune des rubriques proposées (ce qui n'exclut pas une activité intense dans d'autres domaines non pris en compte ici, comme l'internet).

A l'opposé, 14 % de la population peut se prévaloir d'être active dans 9 domaines ou plus. Les personnes vivant dans un ménage aisé, celles bénéficiant d'une formation supérieure (niveau secondaire II général et plus), mais surtout les personnes âgées de moins de 35 ans comptent parmi les principaux groupes de population utilisant activement une large palette d'activités de loisirs (différences de 29 % ou plus par rapport à la population totale[11]).

Les quatre dimensions des activités de loisirs en 2000

Au-delà de la diversité des pratiques, il est utile d'examiner comment ces différentes activités se combinent: est-il possible de les réduire à quelques groupes relevant de dimensions communes? Une réponse est proposée au moyen d'une analyse exploratoire en composantes principales. Cette analyse permet de dégager quatre groupes apparentés. En effet, l'analyse divise les 12 activités de loisirs selon 4 composantes principales qui expliquent 51 % de la variance totale.[12] Les résultats en sont présentés dans le tableau 4.

> *L'analyse en composantes principales:*
> l'approche de l'analyse en composantes principales vise à expliquer la plus forte proportion de la variance des variables observées par un nombre aussi restreint que possible de dimensions latentes. A partir des corrélations entre toutes les variables se dégagent plusieurs groupes de variables fortement corrélées les unes avec les autres, et autant de variables

11 I. e. le rapport «proportion de personnes concernées dans le groupe de population analysé/ proportion de personnes concernées dans la population totale» dépasse 128 % ou alors est inférieur à 72 %.

12 L'analyse en composantes principales des variables de loisirs avec les données 1999 aboutit à la même structure générale des facteurs. Seuls les deux items qui ne sont pas attribués clairement à un facteur se trouvent associés à une autre dimension: *Aller au théâtre, à l'opéra, à une exposition* en 1999 se joint au facteur 3 et *bricoler, travail manuel, jardiner* au facteur 2. Puisque la structure est stable nous nous limitons à présenter les résultats de l'année 2000, qui constitue également la base pour l'analyse transversale.

Tableau 4: Analyse factorielle: Loadings des différentes variables de loisirs sur les quatre premières dimensions

	Facteur 1: Sociabilité et divertissement à l'extérieur	Facteur 2: Régénération et culture	Facteur 3: Activités expressives	Facteur 4: Activités liées au sport et manuelles
Aller au cinéma	0,70			
Aller dans un bar, pub, restaurant	0,65			
Aller en disco, dans un dancing	0,64	–0,39		
Rencontrer des amis, connaissances, collègues	0,55			
Lecture		0,69		
Se promener		0,60		
Aller au théâtre, à l'opéra, à une exposition	0,35	0,54	0,35	
Faire de la musique, p. ex. jouer d'un instrument, chanter			0,75	
Fréquenter des cours (langue, bricolage, cuisine, …)			0,56	
Fréquenter des événements sportifs				0,75
Pratiquer un sport individuel ou de groupe				0,55
Bricoler, travail manuel, jardiner	–0,38	0,35		0,38
Variance expliquée	17 %	13 %	11 %	10 %

Seules les valeurs dépassant 0,30 figurent dans le tableau.
Panel suisse de ménages 2000, échantillon transversal. Pondération transversale au niveau des individus. N = 7043.

synthétiques indépendantes (les *facteurs*) illustrant la dimension latente de chaque groupe, c'est-à-dire l'information commune aux variables de chaque groupe.

La mesure de Kaiser-Meyer-Olkin (KMO) est un indice de l'adéquation de la solution factorielle de l'échantillon. Un KMO élevé (i. e. d'une valeur de 0,5 ou plus, en général) indique qu'il existe une solution factorielle statistiquement acceptable qui représente les relations entre les variables. La valeur de KMO pour la solution de l'analyse en composantes principales présentée dans ce chapitre s'élève à 0,71, de sorte que cette solution peut être considérée comme adéquate.

Le premier facteur est déterminé par des variables comprenant les contacts sociaux à l'extérieur (rencontrer des amis, des connaissances, des collègues) ainsi que la fréquentation de cinémas, de discothèques ou de dancings, de bars, pubs et restaurants. La dénomination *sociabilité et divertissement à l'extérieur* sera par la suite utilisée pour résumer ces activités. L'item «bricoler, travail manuel, jardiner», dont le poids négatif s'élève à –,38, constitue le pôle opposé de ce facteur. Il désigne une activité effectuée principalement dans un cadre privé et moins liée à des contacts sociaux.

Le deuxième facteur représente la *régénération et culture* et réunit les activités «lecture», «se promener» ainsi que «aller au théâtre, à l'opéra, à une exposition». L'item «bricoler, travail manuel, jardiner» caractérise également ce facteur; son poids de 0,35 est cependant nettement inférieur à celui des trois variables précitées. A l'opposé de cette dimension, la fréquentation de discothèques revêt un poids relativement important (–0,39).

Les variables «fréquenter des cours, tels des cours de langue, de bricolage, de cuisine» ainsi que «faire de la musique, p. ex. jouer d'un instrument, chanter» sont prédominantes dans le troisième facteur. Il s'agit essentiellement d'*activités expressives*. Le poids de la fréquentation de théâtres, d'opéras et d'expositions est également relativement élevé sur cette dimension.

Les deux activités de loisirs liées au sport ainsi que le bricolage et jardinage forment le quatrième facteur, *activités liées au sport et manuelles*. Les items «fréquenter des événements sportifs» et «pratiquer un sport individuel ou de groupe (p. ex. fitness, jogging, football, volley-ball, tennis)» y possèdent des poids élevés. Le loading de l'autre activité contenant une composante physique, «bricoler, travail manuel, jardiner», est également le plus élevé dans cette dimension-ci, mais son poids y est cependant comparativement bas.

La localisation des pratiques de loisirs en 2000 et la satisfaction retirée

En plus de la pratique effective des loisirs, il est intéressant d'en examiner la localisation ainsi que la perception qu'en ont les gens.

De nouveau, l'âge s'avère fortement déterminant de la localisation des loisirs[13]: les personnes âgées de moins de 35 ans sont nettement plus nombreuses à les exercer à l'extérieur que la moyenne de la population (27 %, contre 17 % dans la population totale). Inversement, les personnes âgées de 65 ans ou plus pratiquent leurs loisirs davantage à la maison (37 %, contre 28 % dans la population totale). A l'instar de la population dans son ensemble, la majorité des personnes les exerce cependant de manière égale autant à la maison qu'à l'extérieur dans toutes les classes d'âge.

L'analyse des autres catégories sociodémographiques ne donne pas de résultats aussi prononcés.

Quant à la perception des loisirs, deux questions permettent de l'évaluer, l'une ayant trait au nombre d'heures de temps libre à disposition, l'autre aux activités exercées pendant ce temps.[14] De manière générale, la population est plutôt satisfaite du temps à disposition: le degré de satisfaction moyen se monte à 7,3 sur une échelle de valeurs allant de 0 à 10. Si la part de personnes très satisfaites (valeur 10) atteint 29 %, un quart de la population se dit néanmoins plutôt insatisfait (valeurs de 0 à 5 sur l'échelle). S'agissant de l'évaluation de l'organisation de ce temps, cette proportion diminue à 14 %, la valeur moyenne de 8 et un pourcentage de haute satisfaction de 32 % renforçant l'impression que de manière générale, les gens sont légèrement plus satisfaits des activités entreprises que du temps à disposition.

Les catégories sociales portant un jugement particulièrement négatif sur leurs loisirs sont illustrées dans le système de coordonnées ci-dessous (figure 5). L'axe horizontal se rapporte à la satisfaction par rapport au temps à disposition, l'axe vertical à la satisfaction par rapport aux activités exercées pendant ce temps. On remarque qu'une évaluation négative du temps à disposition ne doit pas nécessairement aller de pair avec une insatisfaction par rapport

13 Question posée: *Passez-vous vos loisirs le plus souvent à votre domicile, le plus souvent hors de votre domicile ou au domicile et hors du domicile de manière égale?*

14 Questions posées: *Dans quelle mesure êtes-vous satisfait(e) du nombre d'heures de temps libre dont vous disposez, si 0 signifie «pas du tout satisfait» et 10 «tout à fait satisfait»? Dans quelle mesure êtes-vous satisfait(e) des activités que vous avez pendant vos loisirs, si 0 signifie «pas du tout satisfait» et 10 «tout à fait satisfait»?*

Figure 5: Part de personnes insatisfaites par rapport au temps libre à disposition et aux loisirs pratiqués

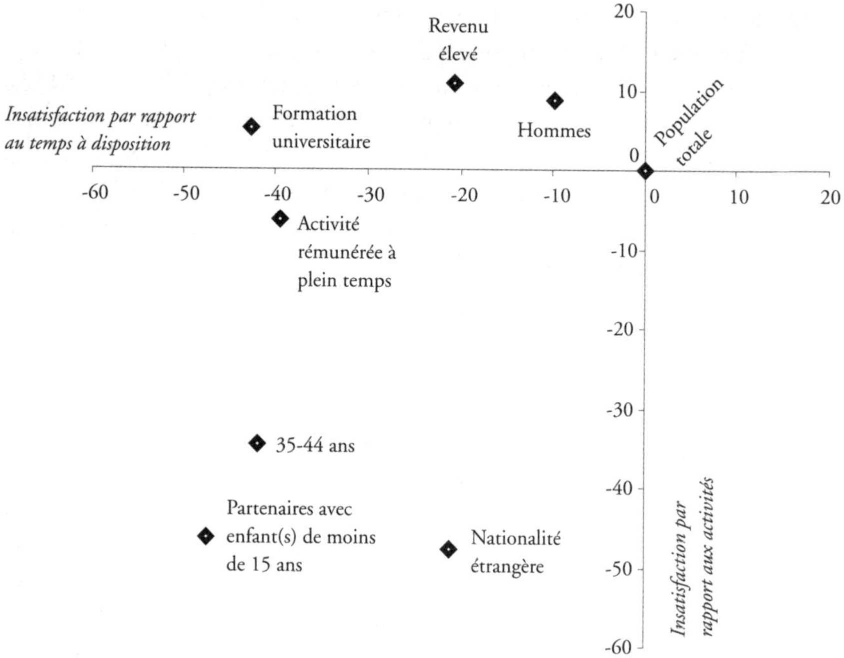

Les points indiquent la relation (en pourcentage) entre la part d'insatisfaits dans les différents groupes et celle dans la population totale. Cette dernière est indexée à 100 % et forme le point zéro: les points relatifs aux groupes sociaux s'obtiennent en y soustrayant à chaque fois le ratio «part d'insatisfaits dans le groupe / part d'insatisfaits dans la population totale».
Exemple de lecture: les personnes avec un niveau de formation universitaire sont proportionnellement moins satisfaites du temps libre à disposition que la population dans son ensemble (la part d'insatisfaits dans ce groupe dépasse de 43 % celle dans la population totale, cf. axe horizontal). Par contre, elles s'avèrent légèrement plus satisfaites de leurs activités de loisirs que la population totale (différence de 5 % sur l'axe vertical).

Panel suisse de ménages 2000, échantillon transversal. Pondération transversale au niveau des individus. Seules les valeurs statistiquement significatives sont prises en considération. N = 7062 (satisfaction par rapport au temps à disposition) et 7059 (satisfaction par rapport aux activités).

aux activités effectuées. Ainsi, l'insatisfaction relativement supérieure à la moyenne des universitaires, des personnes actives à plein temps ou vivant dans un ménage aisé se rapporte principalement au nombre d'heures à disposition pour leurs loisirs, leur appréciation des activités pratiquées ne divergeant à peine de celle de la population totale. Les ressortissants étrangers par contre se montrent particulièrement insatisfaits quant à leurs activités. Les partenaires avec enfants et les personnes en âge actif (35-44 ans notamment) semblent constituer les catégories sociales qui se différencient le plus par rapport à la population totale, tant au niveau du temps à disposition qu'au niveau des pratiques exercées.

Changements entre 1999 et 2000

La fréquence des activités culturelles et de loisirs

Comme indiqué en introduction, les analyses présentées ici portent sur l'impact de différents événements sur l'évolution des activités culturelles et de loisirs. Etant donné l'écart temporel étudié (une année), on peut supposer que cet impact concerne davantage la fréquence à laquelle ces activités sont menées plutôt que le choix de les mener ou non. Cette première hypothèse est clairement confirmée. En effet, lorsqu'on observe les changements intervenus en une année entre les personnes pratiquant au moins une fois de temps en temps et celles ne pratiquant jamais les 12 activités étudiées, on s'aperçoit que ceux-ci restent faibles: entre 4 % de la population (lecture) et 28 % (fréquenter des cours) ont soit commencé soit arrêté de pratiquer (moyenne des 12 activités: 17 %). Ceci indique une certaine stabilité des choix de pratiques, conforme à l'influence du capital culturel sur ces choix. En utilisant le nombre de pratiques menées de façon active[15] comme une première mesure des changements de fréquence, il ressort que seules 23 % des personnes interrogées sont restées actives dans le même nombre de pratiques en 2000 qu'en 1999.

15 Pratiques actives vs non actives: voir 1ère partie de cette contribution.

Tableau 6: Evolution du nombre d'activités activement menées en 2000 par rapport à 1999

	En % de la population
Au moins 3 activités actives en moins	7,5
1-2 activités actives en moins	26,6
Autant d'activités actives qu'en 1999	23,1
1-2 activités actives en plus	33,5
Au moins 3 activités actives en plus	9,3

Panel suisse de ménages 2000, échantillon longitudinal. Pondération longitudinale au niveau des individus. N = 6345.

L'évolution survenue en une année se mesure donc bien au niveau de la fréquence à laquelle les différentes activités sont pratiquées davantage qu'à celui du choix de pratiquer ou non. Elle se caractérise en outre par des mouvements à la hausse comme à la baisse, les premiers étant toutefois plus importants. Ceci indique que l'évolution n'est pas unidirectionnelle. Ces constats se retrouvent lorsqu'on analyse les changements intervenus au niveau des douze pratiques isolément. Faire de la musique et aller en discothèque apparaissent alors comme les activités qui ont le moins changé entre 1999 et 2000, contrairement au bricolage et jardinage où une majorité de la population a modifié la fréquence de sa pratique.[16] Pour toutes les activités considérées, les changements se font à la hausse comme à la baisse et restent le plus souvent de faible amplitude. Le bilan est globalement à la hausse (hausses plus importantes que les baisses) pour la fréquentation des bars et restaurants, se promener, rencontrer des amis, aller au théâtre, aller en discothèque et faire de la musique; il est logiquement à la baisse dans les autres activités.

Les changements en terme de fréquence étant les plus importants, la suite de l'analyse s'y limite. Elle consiste à mesurer l'influence de différents éléments de positionnement social et d'événements de vie sur ces changements. L'hypothèse principale de cette phase d'analyse suppose que les aspects dynamiques

16 Cette pratique a fait l'objet de 2 questions en 1999 et une seule en 2000. Une partie des changements observés pourraient s'expliquer par cet élément méthodologique.

Figure 7: Fréquence des activités: Evolution 2000 par rapport à 1999 en % de la population

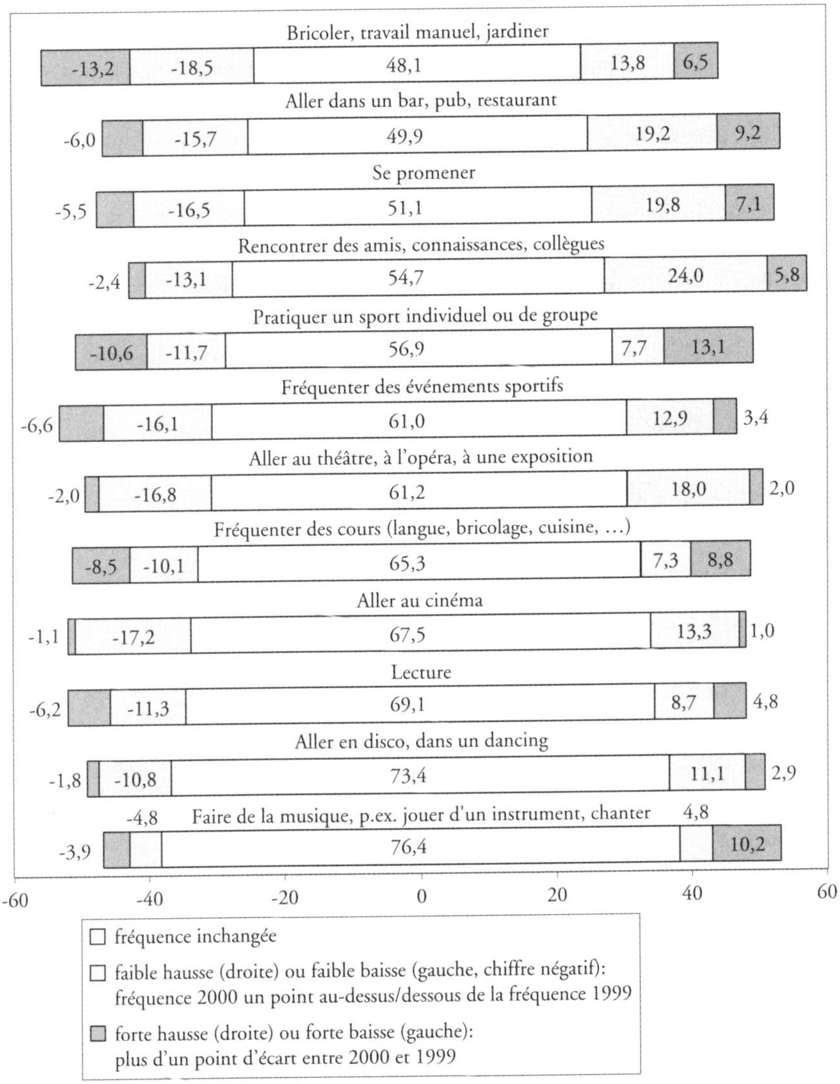

Rappel: fréquence mesurée sur une échelle de 5 points allant de 1 = tous les jours à 5 = jamais (voir tableau 1).
Panel suisse de ménages 2000, échantillon longitudinal. Pondération longitudinale au niveau des individus. N = entre 6313 et 6337.

(événements de vie[17]) sont plus influents que les aspects statiques. Pour tester cette hypothèse, nous avons créé des «indicateurs de changement important» permettant de tester la propension au changement selon différentes caractéristiques individuelles et la survenance des événements de vie retenus. Les changements se faisant à la hausse comme à la baisse, ces indicateurs opposent simplement les personnes ayant connu un changement à celles n'en ayant pas connu. La même démarche a été appliquée aux quatre groupes de pratiques issus de l'analyse factorielle et à l'ensemble des douze pratiques examinées. L'analyse se concentre sur les situations où un changement s'observe dans plus de la moitié des pratiques de chaque groupe (changement important), soit au moins 3 pratiques dans le groupe Sociabilité et divertissement à l'extérieur, 2 pratiques dans les groupes Régénération et culture, Activités expressives et Activités liées au sport et manuelles, et 7 pratiques pour l'ensemble. Elle compare la proportion de personnes connaissant une propension importante au changement telle qu'ainsi définie. Le tableau 8 en annexe présente le détail de ces analyses.

En concentrant notre commentaire au niveau des 12 pratiques en général, on relèvera tout d'abord que les groupes présentant une proportion de personnes connaissant un changement important (7 pratiques et plus) significativement supérieure à la moyenne de la population sont les suivants:

- les hommes,
- les personnes les plus jeunes et jusqu'à 44 ans,
- les personnes de nationalité étrangère,
- les partenaires avec enfants et les fils/filles vivant chez leurs parents,
- les personnes vivant avec un enfant de moins d'un an ou entre 5 et 17 ans,

17 Nous avons pris en compte les événements suivants survenus au cours de l'année écoulée: *santé* du répondant en tant qu'elle limite la possibilité d'effectuer certaines pratiques (évolution de son état de santé, maladie ou accident qu'il a personnellement connu, menaces ou agressions dont il a été victime), relations avec ses *proches* (mise en ménage, fin d'une relation étroite, problème avec un enfant, conflit avec un proche, maladie ou accident d'un proche, décès d'un proche), *activité professionnelle* (entrée ou sortie du marché de l'emploi (personnes occupées vs non occupées), changements de job ou d'employeur, problèmes ou conflits au travail), *revenu du ménage* (évolution) et *domicile* (déménagement). D'autres événements disponibles dans le PSM comme le changement de nationalité ou d'état civil n'ont pas été pris en considération pour des raisons d'effectifs trop réduits. Il en va de même des naissances, rarement signalées en tant que telles mais pour lesquelles la présence dans le ménage d'un enfant de moins d'un an offre une bonne estimation.

- les personnes ayant connu un changement dans leur situation familiale (mise en couple ou séparation, autres changements), ainsi que celles ayant vécu la fin d'une relation étroite (rupture sentimentale),
- les personnes n'ayant pas poursuivi d'études au-delà de la scolarité obligatoire,
- les personnes professionnellement actives, en particulier celles travaillant à plein temps, et celles en formation,
- les personnes occupant une profession intermédiaire ou non qualifiée,
- les personnes qui sont entrées sur le marché du travail (anciens chômeurs ou nouveaux arrivants), celles qui ont changé d'emploi ou d'employeur ainsi que celles ayant connu des problèmes ou conflits au travail,
- les personnes qui ont vu le revenu de leur ménage s'améliorer,
- les personnes qui ont vu leur état de santé s'améliorer ainsi que celles qui ont été victimes de menaces ou d'agression.

D'une manière générale, on constate que les événements de vie n'ont pas forcément plus ou moins d'influence que les éléments statiques, et que les différences se situent davantage entre domaines (vie familiale, santé, etc.) qu'entre éléments dynamiques et statiques. Ainsi, notre hypothèse à ce propos apparaît comme infirmée.[18]

Les critères qui influencent le plus la propension au changement sont largement liés entre eux. En particulier, la proportion de personnes connaissant une forte propension au changement est similaire parmi les jeunes (15-24 ans), les fils/filles vivant chez leurs parents et les personnes en formation.[19] En

18 Certains éléments empêchent en effet de rejeter clairement cette hypothèse. Les événements de vie n'impliquent souvent qu'un nombre restreint de personnes et leur marge de significativité est donc très large, rendant difficile l'établissement de différences avérées avec la population totale. De plus, l'âge ou l'âge du plus jeune enfant sont des éléments dynamiques même s'ils ne constituent pas un événement de vie. Enfin, l'écart d'une année peut être trop faible pour mesurer certaines influences.

19 Ceci s'explique si l'on tient compte du fait que: 90 % des personnes en formation ont moins de 25 ans et 72 % des 15-24 ans sont en formation; et que: 100 % des personnes vivant chez leurs parents ont moins de 25 ans (l'âge contribue à définir cette catégorie) et 78 % des moins de 25 ans vivent dans cette situation. Dans la même logique, seuls 14 % des retraités ont moins de 65 ans (5,8 % si on considère 62 ans pour les femmes et 65 ans pour les hommes). Un lien très clair existe également entre le genre et l'occupation principale (les hommes travaillent à plein temps, les femmes travaillent à temps partiel ou sont femmes au foyer).

contrôlant l'effet spécifique de ces éléments par régression logistique, il ressort que les modèles ne sont pas meilleurs s'ils tiennent compte des trois éléments à la fois, ou de l'âge uniquement.[20] C'est donc bien ce dernier élément qui est déterminant pour expliquer la forte propension au changement. Son effet est clairement decrescendo: la tendance au changement est la plus forte parmi les plus jeunes et la plus faible parmi les plus âgés.

La présence d'enfants dans le ménage est un second élément fort. La propension au changement est surtout marquée lors de l'arrivée des enfants (naissance) puis lorsqu'ils grandissent et s'autonomisent. Les choses sont sans doute similaires dans les familles monoparentales mais leurs effectifs sont trop restreints pour que des différences significatives apparaissent. La vie de couple joue également un rôle. Mises en ménage et ruptures sentimentales sont propices à modifier ses pratiques culturelles et de loisirs. Il en va de même des événements de la vie professionnelle (nouvel emploi, conflits, etc.).

La nationalité est également influente. Toutefois, son effet disparaît à formation égale.[21] La formation joue ainsi un rôle discret mais réel dans les changements de pratiques culturelles. Il en va de même du genre, dont l'influence est facilement masquée par d'autres éléments mais néanmoins réelle.

D'un autre point de vue, l'influence d'éléments comme le domicile (habiter à la ville ou à la campagne, avoir déménagé), la maladie ou accident pour soi ou pour un proche ou le décès d'un proche, ou encore des problèmes avec un enfant est clairement restreinte voire nulle. Ceci s'observe au niveau des 12 pratiques comme au sein des quatre groupes d'activités.

Beaucoup des résultats observables au niveau des 12 pratiques se retrouvent en effet dans les quatre groupes d'activité. Au moins l'influence de l'âge, de la nationalité (sous réserve d'un effet caché de la formation), de la situation familiale et de l'occupation principale est clairement récurrente. Ceci laisse entendre que la propension au changement est assez indépendante des

20 La complexité de ces modèles restant importante, nous ne les présentons pas dans le détail mais utilisons leurs constats pour préciser certains résultats.

21 La régression logistique laisse effectivement apparaître qu'à formation égale, la différence entre personnes de nationalité suisse ou étrangère disparaît. Elle laisse également percevoir que l'opposition principale se fait entre les personnes n'ayant pas poursuivi d'études au-delà de la scolarité obligatoire et celles au bénéfice d'une formation de niveau secondaire II général ou universitaire. De fait, à une formation plus généraliste correspond une moindre tendance au changement. Ceci pourrait être lié à un capital culturel imposant une très forte stabilité des goûts et dégoûts.

différentes pratiques et développe des effets globaux. Certains liens spécifiques sont toutefois observables en fonction de la nature de certaines activités. L'exemple le plus manifeste est l'influence de la formation et de l'origine sociale dans le groupe 3 (activités expressives). Ce groupe réunit la pratique musicale et la fréquentation de cours de formation continue. Aller au théâtre, à l'opéra ou à une exposition, bien que rattaché au groupe 2, y participe également, secondairement.[22] Or ces trois activités figurent parmi les plus liées au capital culturel. Il est donc logique que la formation et l'origine sociale y soient influentes, alors qu'elles n'ont que peu ou pas d'impact sur les autres groupes d'activités, moins socialement typés.

De la même manière, l'impact de certains facteurs n'est perceptible que pour une seule et unique pratique. Typiquement, le fait d'avoir déménagé, élément totalement non influent au niveau global comme des quatre groupes de pratiques, a un effet positif sur le bricolage et jardinage. On peut y voir l'effet très spécifique des travaux qu'occasionne un changement de domicile, tant pour remettre l'ancien logement en état que pour aménager le nouveau.

En se concentrant sur ce niveau détaillé aux douze pratiques étudiées, il ressort que les difficultés liées aux proches (maladie ou décès d'un proche, conflits, problèmes avec les enfants) ou le domicile du répondant (commune urbaine ou rurale, déménagement) ne sont qu'exceptionnellement explicatives des changements observés. Ceci confirme leur faible impact sur l'évolution en général des pratiques culturelles et de loisirs. A l'inverse, l'activité principale est explicative pour toutes les pratiques de loisirs considérées mais dépend largement d'autres éléments comme l'âge (formation, retraite) ou le genre (emploi à temps partiel, personnes au foyer). D'une manière générale, les éléments les plus explicatifs des changements observés restent l'âge, la situation familiale au sens large (position dans le ménage, vie de couple et âge du plus jeune enfant dans le ménage), la nationalité et le genre. La formation (et l'origine sociale, ces deux éléments exerçant globalement une action similaire) est également régulièrement influente. Enfin, les éléments liés à l'activité professionnelle (entrée ou sortie du marché du travail, changement d'emploi, conflits et problèmes au travail), au revenu ou à la santé du répondant (maladie ou accident, évolution de l'état de santé, menaces et agression) jouent un rôle secondaire dans le

22 En répétant l'analyse factorielle sur les données 1999, cette activité se retrouve d'ailleurs dans ce 3e groupe de pratiques, ce qui montre son ambivalence.

sens où ils n'interfèrent que dans une minorité de changements. Ces constats recoupent largement ceux établis précédemment.

En tenant compte de l'orientation des changements (hausse ou baisse), les plus jeunes (15-24 ans et jusqu'à 34 ans) se caractérisent par une propension au changement clairement bidirectionnelle en plus d'être nettement supérieure à la moyenne. Les personnes qui se sont mises en ménage entre les deux vagues d'enquête marquent un repli sur la sphère privée (réduction des sorties au cinéma, en dancing et aux manifestations sportives, hausse de la lecture et des promenades)[23], tandis que celles ayant connu une rupture sentimentale tendent pour une part à augmenter leurs pratiques de loisirs (réinvestissement de pratiques abandonnées lors de la mise en couple ou rôle exutoire) et pour une autre à les réduire (repli sur des activités plutôt intérieures et régénératrices). L'impact d'une naissance, mesuré à travers la présence d'un enfant de moins d'un an dans le ménage, laisse apparaître – sous réserve des effectifs restreints – une réduction des sorties (à l'exception de la fréquentation des bars et restaurants et des manifestions sportives) et une hausse des promenades et de l'activité sportive.

En résumé, il est rare que l'influence d'un facteur induise des modifications unidirectionnelles dans la fréquence des activités de loisirs. La plupart du temps, des hausses comme des baisses sont observables pour chaque groupe de la population. En outre, il est parfois difficile d'interpréter ces influences (pourquoi les personnes avec un revenu plutôt faible ont-elles davantage augmenté leurs sorties au cinéma que les autres?). De fait, l'information la plus pertinente se situe dans la plus ou moins forte propension des différents groupes à modifier ou non la fréquence de leurs loisirs. De ce point de vue, l'âge joue un rôle déterminant, à travers la très forte propension au changement des plus jeunes et la grande stabilité des plus âgés. Enfin, les mouvements observés dépendent largement du niveau initial des pratiques: une hausse est difficilement observable lorsque l'activité est très fréquemment menée. De fait, les baisses s'observent essentiellement parmi les personnes qui pratiquaient activement en 1999, et les hausses parmi celles qui pratiquaient non activement.[24] Toutefois, le fait de

23 Attention: peu de personnes ont connu cet événement de sorte que ces résultats ne peuvent prétendre à une quelconque valeur statistique. Comme pour la présence d'enfants de moins d'un an dans le ménage (voir ci-après), nous les présentons néanmoins vu leur intérêt sociologique mais ils appellent une confirmation ultérieure.

24 Pratique active vs non active: voir 1ère partie.

retrouver à peu près les mêmes groupes au niveau de l'analyse des changements qu'au niveau de l'analyse transversale laisse supposer que les changements ont surtout lieu lorsqu'il existe une pratique (relativement) importante.

La localisation des pratiques de loisirs et la satisfaction retirée

La localisation principale des pratiques (domicile vs extérieur) est restée inchangée dans 60 % des cas. Les changements s'observent de manière assez équilibrée vers l'extérieur (21 %) comme vers l'intérieur (19 %).[25] Ici, l'âge n'est pas déterminant (on relève juste une moindre tendance au changement parmi les classes d'âge moyen et une tendance vers l'intérieur plus marquée passé 75 ans), contrairement à la nationalité (mouvements plus prononcés parmi les personnes de nationalité étrangère), l'âge du plus jeune enfant (sans surprise: fort mouvement vers l'intérieur lorsque l'enfant a moins d'un an et plutôt vers l'extérieur lorsqu'il a 1 an et entre 11 et 14 ans), la vie de couple (comme déjà vu: repli sur l'intérieur lors de la mise en ménage commun et, en cas de séparation, fort mouvement vers l'extérieur accompagné d'un mouvement inverse moins intense) et l'évolution de l'état de santé (mouvement vers l'intérieur en cas de dégradation de l'état de santé et vers l'extérieur en cas d'amélioration).

Enfin, globalement, la satisfaction exprimée par rapport au temps libre à disposition d'une part et aux activités menées durant ce temps d'autre part a évolué de manière similaire. 56 % des réponses concernant le temps libre et 59 % concernant les activités sont globalement équivalentes en 2000 à celles fournies en 1999.[26] Les changements se mesurent davantage à la baisse (26 % et 23 %) qu'à la hausse (18 % et 19 %), et restent le plus souvent faibles (2 à 3 points d'écart).

25 Nous avons regroupé tous les changements impliquant un déplacement vers l'intérieur respectivement l'extérieur. Ainsi, une personne est cataloguée vers l'intérieur si elle a répondu *majoritairement à l'extérieur* en 1999 et *majoritairement à l'intérieur* ou *autant à l'intérieur qu'à l'extérieur* en 2000.

26 La satisfaction étant mesurée sur une échelle de 0 à 10, nous avons considéré les réponses variant d'un seul point comme équivalentes. Ainsi, une personne ayant donné un score de 7 en 1999 et de 8 en 2000 est tenue pour exprimer le même degré de satisfaction les deux années.

Conclusion

L'analyse des données du PSM rend compte des mêmes clivages dans les pratiques culturelles et de loisirs que d'autres enquêtes similaires menées en Suisse ou dans certains pays limitrophes. L'interprétation de Bourdieu en termes de capitaux et de positionnement dans l'espace social s'applique ainsi largement, de même que l'influence de l'âge mise en avant par Donnat. Inégalités de capitaux, clivages sociaux et cycle de vie déterminent ainsi les grandes lignes des inégalités d'accès aux différentes activités culturelles et de loisirs.

S'il n'est guère étonnant de retrouver ces différents éléments dans l'analyse transversale, ça l'est davantage dans l'analyse longitudinale dont on aurait pu penser qu'elle aurait été davantage marquée par les événements de la vie quotidienne. Ainsi, la propension à modifier ou non ses pratiques de loisirs reflète elle aussi ces inégalités. Seconde surprise: ces changements se font souvent à la hausse comme à la baisse, suggérant que cette propension n'est pas orientée mais indique simplement une plus ou moins grande variabilité dans l'organisation de ses loisirs.

Au-delà de ces éléments, la jeunesse apparaît comme le principal vecteur de changement. L'âge intervient cependant rarement seul: il agit le plus souvent conjointement à divers éléments tant familiaux que professionnels qui caractérisent différentes phases du cycle de vie contemporain (voir introduction). C'est donc en ces termes qu'il faut l'interpréter. Les pratiques culturelles et de loisirs reprennent ici encore l'habit de pratiques socialement inégales reflétant les stratégies de différenciation des diverses catégories d'âge. D'autres clivages sociaux, comme ceux liés au genre, sont encore perceptibles selon les activités. Enfin, la santé joue logiquement un rôle en influençant la capacité physique à effectuer certaines activités. Mais ce rôle se révèle complexe, générant des effets contraires à ceux auxquels on se serait attendu et stimulant autant qu'il limite certaines pratiques.

Les résultats présentés dans cette contribution devront toutefois être confirmés par d'autres analyses. En effet, l'intervalle d'une année sur lequel ils reposent nous amène à formuler deux réserves. Tout d'abord, certains résultats peuvent n'avoir qu'une portée limitée, qui ne se retrouverait pas à l'avenir. Ensuite, les effectifs sont parfois trop restreints pour évaluer de manière fiable l'influence de certains facteurs, en particulier au niveau d'événements rares comme la naissance d'un enfant. Il s'agira donc de mesurer la durabilité et par là la solidité des résultats présentés en réitérant ces analyses sur la base des prochaines vagues du PSM.

Bibliographie succincte

Bourdieu, Pierre (1979), *La Distinction: Critique sociale du jugement,* Paris: Minuit.

Donnat, Olivier (1998), *Les pratiques culturelles des Français. Enquête 1997,* Paris: La documentation française.

Donnat, Olivier (1998), Les pratiques culturelles des Français. Evolution 1989-1997, *Développement culturel,* 124.

Lamprecht, Markus, Stamm, Hanspeter (1994), *Die soziale Ordnung der Freizeit,* Zürich: Seismo.

Moeschler, Olivier (2000), *Publics de la culture à Lausanne: enquête sur la fréquentation des institutions culturelles,* Lausanne: Service des affaires culturelles.

Meier-Dallach, Hans-Peter, et al. (1991), *Die Kulturlawine: Daten, Bilder, Deutungen,* Chur, Zürich: Verlag Rüegger.

Veblen, Thorstein (1970), *Théorie de la classe de loisirs,* Paris: Gallimard.

Tableau 8: Part des personnes ayant connu un changement important entre 1999 et 2000, selon le groupe de pratiques

Aide à la lecture: 18,34 % des hommes ont connu un changement important au niveau des 12 activités.

[gris clair] = % significativement plus bas par rapport à la population totale
[gris foncé] = % significativement plus haut par rapport à la population totale
ns = écart non significatif

Comme dans l'ensemble de la contribution, la significativité est mesurée à l'aide d'intervalles de confiance avec un seuil de 95 %.

Petitesse de l'échantillon: chiffres en italique = <30 observations; ( ) = <10 observations.

Panel suisse de ménages 2000, échantillon longitudinal. Pondération longitudinale au niveau des individus. N = entre 2592 et 6345.

		Ensemble des douze pratiques	Groupe Sociabilité	Groupe Régénération	Groupe Activités expressives	Groupe Sport et bricolage
N		6255	6305	6326	6310	6327
Population totale	(N = 6345)	15,98	16,47	35,11	9,58	41,91
Sexe	(N = 6345)		ns	ns	ns	ns
femmes		13,91				
hommes		18,34				
Age	(N = 6345)					
15-24 ans		27,86	22,10	50,29	13,66	52,18
25-34 ans		21,18	20,70	40,56	11,80	43,49
35-44 ans		19,34	20,45	35,36	11,30	44,67
45-54 ans		14,49	15,89	31,85	10,10	40,11
55-64 ans		9,92	12,35	29,98	8,16	38,21
65-74 ans		6,64	8,74	28,34	*4,46*	36,46
75+ ans		4,08	*6,82*	23,59	( )	32,16
Nationalité	(N = 6345)					ns
suisse		15,11	15,03	33,63	10,35	
étrangère		19,97	23,06	41,87	6,04	
Situation familiale	(N = 6345)					
personnes seules		12,89	13,74	33,61	8,44	37,56
partenaires (ménage de 2 personnes)		11,00	13,03	29,73	7,22	39,27
partenaires avec enfants (le plus jeune: 0-14 ans)		19,46	19,72	35,64	11,22	45,69

N	Ensemble des douze pratiques 6255	Groupe Sociabilité 6305	Groupe Régénération 6326	Groupe Activités expressives 6310	Groupe Sport et bricolage 6327
Population totale (N = 6345)	15,98	16,47	35,11	9,58	41,91
Partenaires: autres	14,25	15,75	33,83	11,22	35,95
Fils/fillles (15-24 ans) vivant chez leurs parents	29,99	24,04	53,08	13,82	51,34
Personnes élevant seules des enfants	*21,32*	*27,30*	40,92	*8,45*	49,83
Age du plus jeune enfant (N = 2592)					
moins d'un an (= naissance dans l'année)	28,83		46,19		
1 an	18,27				
2-4 ans	20,49				48,37
5-10 ans	20,40	21,75		12,80	47,52
11-14 ans	20,91				
15-17 ans	24,03			13,43	
Changement de situation familiale (N = 6345)			ns	ns	ns
aucun changement	14,97				
mises en couple	*29,38*	*29,71*			
ruptures de couple	*25,20*				
autres changements	25,59				
Fin d'une relation étroite (N = 6339)		ns		ns	
oui	21,20		44,29		49,97
non	15,65		34,51		41,42
Formation (N = 6343)					
école obligatoire	18,47		39,46	6,80	
secondaire II professionnel	14,86			7,73	
secondaire II général	15,20	12,41		16,17	
tertiaire professionnel	17,41			12,58	
tertiaire universitaire	13,61		30,00	13,47	36,06
Origine sociale (N = 5740)	ns	ns			ns
école obligatoire				5,81	
secondaire II professionnel				9,97	

N	Ensemble des douze pratiques 6255	Groupe Sociabilité 6305	Groupe Régénération 6326	Groupe Activités expressives 6310	Groupe Sport et bricolage 6327
Population totale (N = 6345)	15,98	16,47	35,11	9,58	41,91
secondaire II général				15,85	
tertiaire professionnel			29,57	12,69	
tertiaire universitaire				11,99	
Occupation principale (N = 6345)					
emploi à plein temps	19,14	19,15	39,20	10,69	44,23
emploi à temps partiel	16,09	16,64	29,82	13,05	41,11
formation	28,16	23,14	49,09	11,92	51,55
au foyer	12,49	14,18	31,16	8,41	39,50
retraite	6,15	8,31	26,11	3,61	35,32
actifs occupés: total	18,31	18,09	36,76	11,26	43,85
non actifs: total	11,31	13,21	31,79	6,12	38,21
Modification du statut d'emploi (N = 6337)		ns			ns
actifs occupés restés occupés	17,75			11,44	
entrées sur le marché du travail	27,35		49,26		
retraits du marché du travail	*16,85*				
non actifs restés non actifs	12,87			6,82	
Catégorie socio-professionnelle (N = 4019)		ns	ns		
professions libérales et managériales	15,61				
autres indépendants	18,44				
professions académiques	14,94			14,74	35,97
professions intermédiaires	20,23			13,97	
professions qualifiées non manuelles	16,88				
professions qualifiées manuelles	21,64				52,04
professions non qualifiées	22,49				49,45
Changement d'emploi (N = 4287)		ns	ns		ns
oui	20,72			14,11	
non	18,05				

N	Ensemble des douze pratiques 6255	Groupe Sociabilité 6305	Groupe Régénération 6326	Groupe Activités expressives 6310	Groupe Sport et bricolage 6327
Population totale (N = 6345)	15,98	16,47	35,11	9,58	41,91
Problèmes ou conflits au travail (N = 6345)		ns	ns	ns	ns
oui	22,60				
non	15,89				
Revenus du ménage (N = 6345)	ns	ns	ns	ns	ns
faibles					
moyens					
élevés					
Evolution du revenu du ménage (N = 6325)		ns	ns	ns	ns
dégradation	16,87				
inchangé	14,79				
amélioration	19,62				
Domicile (N = 6345)	ns	ns	ns	ns	ns
ville					
campagne					
Déménagement (N = 6345)	ns	ns	ns	ns	ns
oui					
Maladie, accident personnel (N = 6345)	ns	ns	ns	ns	ns
oui					
Evolution de l'état de santé (N = 6343)		ns	ns	ns	ns
dégradation	17,54				
inchangé	15,27				
amélioration	18,78				
Menaces, agression durant l'année écoulée (N = 6343)		ns	ns	ns	ns
oui	23,50				
non	15,78				

	Ensemble des douze pratiques	Groupe Sociabilité	Groupe Régénéra-tion	Groupe Activités expressives	Groupe Sport et bricolage
N	6255	6305	6326	6310	6327
Population totale (N = 6345)	15,98	16,47	35,11	9,58	41,91
Problème avec un enfant (N = 3863)	ns	ns		ns	ns
oui			32,04		
non			31,37		
Conflit avec un proche (N = 6341)	ns	ns	ns	ns	ns
oui					
non					
Maladie, accident d'un proche (N = 6343)	ns	ns	ns	ns	ns
oui					
Décès d'un proche (N = 6341)	ns	ns	ns	ns	ns
oui					

Attitudes et pratiques religieuses: la perméabilité du religieux privé et public*

Irene BECCI et Claude BOVAY

Introduction: L'étude des pratiques et attitudes religieuses à l'intérieur du débat sur la modernité

Les changements qui affectent le champ religieux au cours du 20e siècle font l'objet de plusieurs lignes d'interprétation dans les sciences sociales. Nous envisageons la transformation de la place de la religion comme une des expressions des grands changements qui caractérisent la post-modernité. L'évolution religieuse est en grande partie liée à des processus qui concernent la société dans son ensemble: migrations, changement social, mondialisation économique, sociale et culturelle. La religion se présente aujourd'hui simultanément comme une affaire privée et comme une affaire publique. L'individu construit et oriente ses préférences dans le marché religieux: la pluralisation du paysage religieux, la connaissance accrue de religiosités non-traditionnelles par les voyages, les pratiques et la littérature mystique ont multiplié ses possibilités de choix. Cependant, contrairement à l'image moderniste d'une religion personnelle, profondément intime, le processus de construction individuelle/collective d'un soi religieux advient dans un contexte social par lequel il est informé. Notre compréhension de l'évolution accentue donc moins le repli de la religion que son adaptation au contexte social contemporain et la continuation, sous une autre forme, de sa présence dans le domaine public.

* Cette contribution fait partie de l'ouvrage collectif *Vivre en Suisse 1999-2000* (Erwin Zimmermann et Robin Tillmann (éds), Editions Peter Lang, Berne (2004)). Les analyses et résultats se basent sur les deux premières vagues de l'enquête longitudinale Vivre en Suisse réalisée auprès de 6 335 personnes interviewées en 1999 et 2000. La collecte des données, effectuée par M. I. S. Trend sous la responsabilité du Panel suisse de ménages de l'Université de Neuchâtel, a été financée par le PP Demain la Suisse du Fonds national suisse de la recherche scientifique (Subsides No. 5004-53205 / 5004-57894 / 5004-67304). Des informations complémentaires peuvent être obtenues sur le site www.swisspanel.ch

C'est dans cette optique que nous avons affronté dans la présente contribution les données du Panel Suisse des Ménages (PSM) qui traitent des comportements et des attitudes dans le domaine religieux. Nous jetons un triple regard sur les résultats des enquêtes de 1999 et 2000 en discutant les différents types d'indicateurs religieux présents dans le PSM: la pratique et l'appartenance, la discussion et la tolérance. Après une description des résultats principaux, nous les situons dans leur contexte social et culturel, puis nous nous intéressons spécifiquement à leur évolution longitudinale. Notre analyse tente d'interpréter les résultats du point de vue de la place attribuée à la religion et à la pluralité religieuse dans les choix qui se présentent comme personnels ainsi que dans l'espace public.

La mesure des attitudes et pratiques religieuses dans le PSM

La présente enquête réunit une série d'informations standards au sujet des pratiques individuelles et collectives. Dans l'ensemble, le PSM interroge trois dimensions de la problématique de la religion:

- trois variables classiques traitent du profil religieux: appartenance, participation à des services religieux et pratique de la prière. Elles ont fait l'objet d'une reprise dans les deux questionnaires envisagés[1];
- trois questions abordent les échanges au sujet de la religion: si les personnes discutent de religion en famille et avec des ami-e-s, s'il y a eu des désaccords importants en matière de croyances dans le ménage (notamment dans le questionnaire de 1999);
- trois questions sont en relation avec la tolérance en matière d'expression publique de la religion: les jeunes filles portant le voile à l'école pour des raisons religieuses, les nouveaux mouvements religieux présentant leurs idées publiquement et les programmes scolaires incluant un enseignement touchant les principales traditions religieuses (questionnaire 1999).[2]

1 Les questions du PSM et leur emplacement ont en partie changé entre 1999 et 2000. Les données ont été récoltées par un questionnaire adressé au ménage et par un questionnaire individuel. Dans le questionnaire ménage de la première année il n'y a pas de questions au sujet de la religion. Elles se trouvent toutes dans le questionnaire individuel.

2 Ces thèmes sont également traités dans différentes enquêtes quantitatives représentatives de la population vivant en Suisse. La plus récente est intitulée «Religion et lien social».

Le traitement de ces données s'opérera en trois temps. Le premier sera consacré à une discussion des résultats du PSM, en situant pour chaque variable son intérêt pour la connaissance et la compréhension du rapport à la religion des personnes interrogées. Nous analyserons les interactions entre les variables de l'appartenance et celles de la prière, de la pratique religieuse, et de la tolérance religieuse. Nous tenterons de dégager des profils de cet ensemble de pratiques, de comportements et d'attitudes, en considérant les jeux de tension selon que l'accent est mis sur la religion comme une affaire privée ou comme intérêt public.

Nous essaierons ensuite d'interpréter les réponses aux variables religieuses en fonction de diverses variables socio-démographiques. Nous explorerons ainsi l'influence de variables telles que l'orientation politique, la taille du ménage ou la profession par exemple.

Finalement, nous aborderons l'analyse diachronique. La variable retenue ici est celle de la pratique religieuse collective. Cet indicateur est en effet celui qui varie le plus entre 1999 et 2000. La prière et l'appartenance affichent une bien plus grande stabilité. Notre analyse cherchera à dégager des logiques sociales qui peuvent être à l'origine d'une évolution des comportements, tout autant que l'influence possible des circonstances biographiques ou conjoncturelles.

Appartenance

Parmi les tendances caractérisant l'évolution au cours du siècle dernier, la grande majorité de la population résidante a conservé un lien d'appartenance à une tradition ou à une communauté religieuse, alors que les déclarations de non-appartenance marquent un accroissement notable (Bovay 1997).

Les modifications principales concernent la représentation proportionnelle des groupes religieux dans la population globale ainsi que dans les cantons. On est passé d'une situation bipolaire où la Suisse se composait d'un ensemble d'états cantonaux dans lesquels l'appartenance religieuse était fortement territorialisée à une pluralisation des appartenances qui s'est étendue progressivement à l'ensemble des cantons.

Financée par le Fonds National Suisse pour la Recherche Scientifique et la Fédération des Eglises Protestantes de Suisse, cette recherche a été menée entre 1998-2000 par une équipe composée de Diane Barraud, Irene Becci, Claude Bovay et Raphaël Broquet, sous la direction de Roland Campiche.

Même si les deux traditions religieuses historiques conservent une position majoritaire, un nombre croissant de groupes, courants ou communautés religieuses constituent autant de minorités religieuses nouvelles en regard de celles qui composaient la scène religieuse au début du 20e siècle.

Tableau 1: L'évolution de l'appartenance religieuse en Suisse depuis 1970 selon les résultats du recensement fédéral[3]

		Année de recensement			
		1970	1980	1990	2000
0	Sans indication	,39 %	1,09 %	1,48 %	4,33 %
111	Eglise évangélique réformée	46,42 %	43,87 %	38,51 %	33,04 %
112	Eglise évangélique méthodiste	,17 %	,09 %	,15 %	,12 %
113	Eglises évangéliques libres et autres communautés protestantes	,42 %	,37 %	1,32 %	1,44 %
120	Eglise catholique romaine	49,39 %	47,60 %	46,15 %	41,82 %
130	Eglise catholique-chrétienne	,32 %	,26 %	,17 %	,18 %
140	Eglises chrétiennes-orthodoxes	,33 %	,58 %	1,04 %	1,81 %
151	Eglise néo-apostolique	,49 %	,46 %	,45 %	0,38 %
152	Témoins de Jéhovah	,17 %	,23 %	,28 %	,28 %
153	Autres Eglises et communautés chrétiennes (Mormons, Adventistes, ...)	,05 %	,30 %	,12 %	,20 %
200	Communauté de confession juive	,33 %	,29 %	,26 %	,25 %
300	Communautés islamiques	,26 %	,89 %	2,21 %	4,26 %
400	Eglises et communautés religieuses restantes	,12 %	,19 %	,42 %	0,78 %
500	Aucune appartenance	1,14 %	3,79 %	7,43 %	11,11 %
		100,00 %	100,00 %	100,00 %	100,00 %

Selon le recensement fédéral de la population 2000, le nombre de personnes qui indiquent n'appartenir à aucune communauté religieuse a massivement augmenté: de 7,4 % en 1990 à 12 % (873 600). Le nombre de musulman-e-s a plus que doublé, passant de 152 000 à 310 000 (4,3 %). Des estimations parlent d'environ 40 000 personnes de nationalité suisse se réclamant de l'Islam (Gerber, 2002).

3 Les tableaux et graphiques dans cet article ont été réalisés par Raphaël Broquet.

La répartition des appartenances confessionnelles entre protestant-e-s et catholiques dans l'échantillon du PSM reflète assez bien les statistiques nationales évoquées précédemment[4]. Environ 40 % de la population se dit appartenir au protestantisme, 41 % au catholicisme, 11 % n'appartiennent à aucune religion et le reste appartient à une autre religion.

Dans l'échantillon du PSM, on remarque la sous-représentation de deux groupes par rapport au recensement fédéral: les musulman-e-s et les orthodoxes. Celle-ci est due à la sous-représentation des personnes étrangères vivant en Suisse, notamment de celles dont l'immigration est récente.

Les pratiques religieuses

La participation aux services religieux constitue une dimension centrale pour la compréhension du rapport des membres déclarés avec leur groupe religieux. L'appartenance et la pratique ont originellement été utilisées pour suivre le processus de sécularisation et la perte d'emprise des Eglises sur la vie sociale: ainsi on observe généralement une diminution de la pratique religieuse en Europe occidentale depuis l'après-guerre (en termes de participation aux services religieux).

En mettant la limite entre pratique régulière et occasionnelle à une fréquence mensuelle, et en considérant comme non pratiquantes seulement les personnes qui disent ne jamais participer aux services religieux, nous voyons qu'en Suisse une grande partie de la population se situe dans les pratiquants occasionnels. Ce sont des personnes qui participent aux services religieux à l'occasion des fêtes religieuses ou des cérémonies familiales mais n'ont pas une pratique cultuelle régulière. Dans cette tranche de la population il y a une bonne partie de «sans appartenances». En effet, ne pas appartenir signifie rarement ne pas pratiquer du tout (des 683 «sans appartenance» seulement 23,4 % ne participent jamais à un service religieux).

4 En comparaison avec la population résidante totale, l'échantillon de la population considérée par le PSM est probablement plus traditionnel si l'on considère notamment la majorité d'appartenance aux deux confessions protestante et catholique. Le PSM offre malgré tout un échantillon intéressant par le fait qu'il n'a pas été recruté sur la base d'un intérêt pour les questions d'ordre religieux. Le positionnement vis-à-vis de la religion ne peut donc pas influer sur les résultats de l'enquête. Il est en effet possible que les personnes hostiles à la religion renoncent à prendre part à des enquêtes qui sont annoncées comme portant sur la question religieuse.

L'analyse de la prière est à considérer comme le complément indispensable à l'étude de l'appartenance et de la pratique collective. En effet cette analyse éclaire une des composantes individuelles de la pratique religieuse. Par individuel nous n'entendons pas nécessairement les contenus de la prière qui peuvent être des prières classiques apprises par cœur à l'occasion d'un catéchisme par exemple. Nous mettons plutôt l'accent sur le fait que ce comportement relève, davantage que la pratique collective, d'un choix personnel dont la fréquence peut être considérée comme l'indice de l'intensité du besoin religieux, sans que ce dernier reflète nécessairement le lien à un groupe ou à une tradition organisée.

En ce qui concerne la prière, notre échantillon se présente comme divisé. Soit on prie plutôt souvent, ou on ne prie pas ou pratiquement pas. Seule une petite minorité, 8,5 %, disent prier une fois par mois. Un tiers de l'échantillon dit ne jamais prier et un tiers prie quotidiennement ou presque. Si l'on mesurait le degré de religiosité sur la base de la prière, on pourrait difficilement parler de sécularisation.

Tableau 2: Régularité de la pratique collective et de la prière selon l'appartenance religieuse[5]

Confession ou religion	Pratique/Prière			
	Pratique/Prière régulières	Pratique régulière/Prière irrégulière	Pratique irrégulière/Prière régulière	Pratique/Prière irrégulières
Protestant	17,0 %	4,8 %	26,2 %	52,1 %
Catholique R.	29,5 %	6,8 %	25,0 %	38,7 %
Autres Chr.	69,8 %	0,7 %	17,3 %	12,2 %
Juif	17,6 %	17,6 %	11,8 %	52,9 %
Musulman	13,0 %		30,4 %	56,5 %
Autre	45,1 %	7,4 %	21,3 %	26,2 %
Sans religion	3,4 %	0,1 %	14,6 %	81,8 %
Total[6]	22,6 %	5,1 %	24,2 %	48,1 %

5 Nous avons créé deux variables dichotomiques. Pour considérer une pratique comme régulière, nous avons mis la limite à au moins une fois par mois.

6 Données non pondérées.

Les liens entre les trois variables considérées sont multiples. L'analyse statistique montre qu'il existe une corrélation positive entre participation à des services religieux et prière. De manière générale, plus on participe régulièrement aux services religieux plus on a tendance à prier. Par contre, comme signalé auparavant, cette relation n'est pas nécessaire. En ce qui concerne environ la moitié de l'échantillon (48,1 %), il s'agit de personnes qui ne prient quasiment pas ni ne participent à des services religieux. Le quart des personnes interrogées déclarent prier régulièrement (hebdomadairement au moins) et participer régulièrement à des services (mensuellement au moins); un cinquième prie régulièrement mais ne pratique que peu ou pas du tout, alors que seulement 5 % de pratiquants réguliers disent ne prier que peu ou pas du tout. Même certains «sans confession» (14,6 %) disent prier de manière régulière, sans fréquenter les services religieux.

Alors que pour la participation aux services religieux une tendance à la baisse est visible, la prière semble la grande gagnante de la modernité.

L'expression de la religiosité peut donc s'exprimer sur un mode individuel ou collectif, et elle relève d'un processus social et non seulement d'un choix personnel. Les personnes «jouent» avec les deux dimensions privée et publique de la religion.

En ce qui concerne l'appartenance, un facteur que l'on peut considérer comme institutionnel, elle corrèle également avec la pratique. D'un point de vue confessionnel le croisement de ces dimensions révèle des particularités intéressantes. Les protestant-e-s en Suisse affichent dans tous les sondages des niveaux de religiosité globalement moins élevés que les catholiques ou les autres confessions chrétiennes. Ceci est le cas encore aujourd'hui. Cette affirmation est toutefois nuancée par le fait que les protestant-e-s ont souvent un niveau de prière régulière élevé sans avoir une pratique collective régulière et les personnes qui pratiquent collectivement plus qu'elles ne prient sont en majorité catholiques.

Il faut relever ici que la pratique collective n'a pas la même signification selon les différentes confessions ou religions. Ainsi, il est plus important pour un-e catholique de participer aux messes pour donner un contenu à sa foi, que pour un-e protestant-e dont la tradition considère que la lecture de la Bible est bien plus significative. Historiquement, le milieu catholique a toujours été plus compact ce qui ne permettait jadis pratiquement pas de vie religieuse en dehors de la communauté ecclésiale. Comme l'écrit Lucian Hölscher c'est «pourquoi l'abstention de la pratique religieuse impliquait en même temps, beaucoup plus que dans le protestantisme, une rupture avec la foi religieuse» (Hölscher, 2000: 49).

Sur la seule base des quelques indicateurs considérés, il serait abusif de conclure que l'appartenance – acquise en grande majorité par la transmission familiale – implique automatiquement un type de comportement, elle va probablement plutôt l'orienter. Le type de religiosité mesurée auprès d'une grande partie de protestant-e-s est en tendance plus privé. Leur pratique religieuse valorise moins l'expérience collective.

Pour les personnes d'autres confessions chrétiennes, la pratique cultuelle régulière ne se conçoit pas sans une pratique régulière de la prière. Même si dans notre échantillon les minorités religieuses sont sous-représentées, nous pouvons dire que juifs-juives et musulman-musulmanes s'opposent sur ces questions: un-e musulman-e prie plus facilement sans pratiquer, et un-e juif-ve pratique plus facilement sans prier. La prière et la participation à des services religieux ne sont pas des critères neutres. En effet, pour un-e musulman-e la prière est tout aussi importante que la participation à la messe pour un-e catholique et elle est souvent tout aussi collective qu'individuelle.

L'appartenance à un groupe religieux ainsi que la régularité de la pratique collective (participation à des services religieux) et de la pratique individuelle (la prière) constituent trois des indicateurs majeurs de la sociologie de la religion. Leur mesure et leur comparaison longitudinale dans différents contextes nationaux ont longtemps constitué le critère principal du changement du paysage religieux en Occident.

Les analyses qui précèdent montrent que les variables religieuses peuvent ouvrir un champ complexe d'interactions entre les différentes dimensions religieuses. Il y a un phénomène de «believing without belonging» en Suisse, comme Grace Davie l'a nommé, mais il y aussi l'inverse, c'est-à-dire que l'appartenance peut se maintenir sans pratique collective ni prière (Davie et Martin, 1994).

Discussion au sujet de religion

La modernité a signifié un recul de l'influence de la religion dans les affaires publiques, et la quasi disparition de manifestations religieuses en public, mouvement que l'on qualifie souvent de privatisation de la religion. On observe pourtant que la religion, paradoxalement, est devenue un des objets d'intérêt public à travers le traitement proposé par les médias des changements qui la concernent. Il est dès lors intéressant de s'interroger sur la place occupée par la religion dans les échanges interpersonnels, par exemple le voile, ce que les media appellent les sectes, les fondamentalismes religieux, les voyages du Pape, l'engagement des Eglises dans des questions sociales comme la paix, etc. La question se pose à savoir si la privatisation varie selon qu'il s'agit de la mise en discussion de sa «propre» religion ou de celle des «autres».

L'idée que la religion est une affaire privée de laquelle on ne parle pas facilement est dominante en Suisse. Il reste à vérifier s'il s'agit d'un objet dont on débat avec son-sa partenaire ou ses ami-e-s. Si la réponse était oui on aurait un indice de la place occupée par la religion dans les échanges entre proches et du rôle du milieu dans la construction de l'opinion en la matière.

Dans notre évaluation, nous avons fait l'hypothèse que si une représentation strictement privée de la religion prévalait chez une personne, elle allait probablement se limiter à en parler avec les personnes les plus intimes (notamment le ou la conjoint-e), alors que si la religion était perçue comme une composante significative de la marche de la société et de la culture, l'échange s'étendrait aussi aux ami-e-s.

La comparaison des réponses aux deux questions indique que si les personnes interviewées ne parlent pas ou très peu avec leurs ami-e-s, il en va de même avec leur partenaire et que, globalement, elles échangent plus volontiers avec leur partenaire. Cela signifie que la perception de la religion comme une affaire privée voire intime reste dominante et que les occasions de débattre de sujets religieux sont plus fréquentes dans l'espace domestique que dans le cercle amical.

La religion est le plus souvent abordée comme sujet de discussion par les personnes qui sont plus religieuses sur les deux plans, celui de la prière et celui de la participation aux services religieux. L'appartenance et la pratique ensemble ont également une influence intéressante sur la discussion. En effet, parmi les membres d'une communauté religieuse ce sont les pratiquant-e-s qui abordent le plus souvent le thème de la religion dans leurs discussions. Les personnes «sans appartenance» discutent moins souvent de religion avec leurs proches.

Globalement, la religion ne semble pas être un enjeu de discussion important dans les couples, indépendamment du niveau d'éducation. Ceci est confirmé par une question supplémentaire concernant les causes de disputes entre les couples. Là nous voyons que seulement le 4,4 % des couples disent avoir eu des désaccords importants au sujet de croyances.

Il est important de ne pas en déduire trop rapidement, que la religion ne peut pas constituer un sujet contentieux à l'intérieur d'un couple. Cette problématique mériterait d'être travaillée en regard de l'appartenance des deux membres du couple, dans la mesure où l'on assiste à l'accroissement constant, en Suisse, de la proportion de couples dont les deux partenaires n'appartiennent pas à la même religion (Bovay, 2000). On note en particulier que le taux d'endogamie varie fortement entre les groupes religieux. L'endogamie catholique est plus constante (30,9 % des nouveaux couples déclarés à l'Etat Civil en 1995) que l'endogamie protestante (19,4 % la même année) qui affiche la diminution la plus importante, alors que la proportion de couples biconfessionnels, bireligieux ou dont un-e seul-e conjoint-e déclare une appartenance ne cesse de croître.

Tolérance en matière religieuse[7]

Depuis la Réforme, la Suisse connaît la pluralité confessionnelle. Jusqu'au 19e siècle, les différents groupes confessionnels vivaient repliés en de véritables enceintes confessionnelles, chacune souvent étroitement liée au pouvoir politique. Dans chaque canton, de tradition catholique ou protestante, un accord régnait: le pouvoir politique garantissait protection, droits et facilités financières aux Eglises, les Eglises offraient légitimation symbolique au pouvoir politique et certains services sociaux à la société (éducation, social...) (cf. Loretan, 1995). Cette dualité entre Eglises et Etat s'est installée progressivement et de manière différente dans les 26 cantons qui forment depuis 1848 une Confédération. Les divisions confessionnelles imprégnèrent les rapports sociaux en Suisse et menèrent au Kulturkampf tout au long du 19e siècle et en partie même après.

Aujourd'hui le cadre constitutionnel fédéral assure à chaque personne la liberté de conscience et limite les prétentions à la vérité religieuse des institutions politiques. La Constitution laisse aux cantons la compétence de définir les arrangements institutionnels selon leurs traditions et rapports de force particuliers. Dans la majorité des cantons, la proximité de l'Eglise catholique

7 La notion de tolérance peut connoter toute une série d'attitudes, des plus paternalistes à l'idée de reconnaissance véritable. Les données que nous avons à disposition ne sont bien évidemment pas suffisantes pour refléter cette diversité.

ou de l'Eglise protestante avec les institutions politiques est affirmée au niveau juridique (reconnaissance publique des Eglises, leur statut de droit public, etc.) et économique (salaires des ministres, subventions diverses, facilités fiscales, etc.). Seuls les républiques et cantons de Neuchâtel et de Genève ont opté pour une séparation institutionnelle entre l'Etat et les Eglises.

Au cours des vingt dernières années, à plusieurs reprises et dans différents cantons, la rupture de tout lien fut régulièrement traitée en votations populaires, sans obtenir l'assentiment de la majorité. La religion a continué à faire partie de la sphère publique selon le partage de pouvoir avec l'Etat. Il est donc important, de prendre en considération le rôle de l'Etat lorsque nous interprétons les changements religieux individuels ou collectifs en Suisse.

Pour cela nous avons posé, dans le PSM, trois questions concernant des thèmes dont on a débattu largement dans l'espace public ces dernières années: la question du voile, l'enseignement religieux dans les écoles publiques et l'expression de nouveaux mouvements religieux dans l'espace public[8].

Les deux premières questions concernent l'école qui se trouve au centre de nombreux débats autour de la diversité religieuse. C'est à l'école, de par son caractère public et obligatoire, que l'on rencontre une grande diversité religieuse et ceci sur différents plans, celui de l'appartenance, des pratiques, des attitudes, etc. A l'école se pose toute une série de questions sur comment construire un climat de respect réciproque et promouvoir les valeurs du pluralisme et de la participation sociale nécessaires au fonctionnement de la démocratie. La question du voile des filles à l'école semble être celle qui regroupe le plus d'accords, même si le panorama est très partagé dans son ensemble. Il y a presque autant de personnes qui n'acceptent absolument pas le voile que celles qui l'acceptent sans hésitations. Cependant, la balance penche vers la tolérance du voile des filles.

Un des arguments souvent mentionné pour expliquer le développement de l'intolérance religieuse est celui de l'analphabétisme religieux (Becci, 2000, Hutmacher, 1999). Dès lors, à qui revient le rôle de transmettre aux enfants futur-e-s citoyen-ne-s une éducation concernant les différentes religions? Notre deuxième question visait à comprendre si la population en Suisse

8 La question du voile est souvent prise comme une référence en matière de tolérance religieuse pour la France et celle concernant l'école pour l'Allemagne. cfr. à ce sujet Fetzer et Soper, 2003, plus largement cfr. Zouari, 2002, Mayer, 2000, Hutmacher, 1999.

attend de l'Etat qu'il accomplisse cette tâche. Les réponses montrent une forte hésitation. Il y a clairement une grande partie de la population qui ne semble pas souhaiter que l'Etat organise un enseignement concernant les grandes traditions religieuses, et une tranche plus petite, mais tout de même significative de personnes qui souhaite l'inverse, c'est-à-dire un rôle actif de l'Etat dans l'enseignement sur la religion. L'analyse du débat autour de cette question a montré qu'elle implique plusieurs registres: politique, social, historique, etc. C'est probablement cela qui fait qu'une grande partie des positions est hésitante.

Actuellement la présence d'un enseignement religieux est garantie dans toutes les écoles du pays, sauf dans les deux cantons de Neuchâtel et Genève. Parfois il est organisé et pris en charge par les Eglises, d'autres fois par le canton ou en concomitance entre les deux instances. Dans certains cantons l'enseignement religieux est œcuménique, dans d'autres nous trouvons des professeur-e-s d'histoire donnant une grande importance aux religions, d'autres cantons abordent certaines questions sur la tolérance, la connaissance de l'autre etc. d'un point de vue éthique par exemple. Il est probable que dans ces cas, le besoin de (plus) d'enseignement religieux ne soit pas ressenti. Certaines positions de désaccord peuvent se rapporter au fait qu'on continue à considérer l'enseignement religieux comme une tâche des communautés religieuses elles-mêmes ou à la peur que des communautés religieuses n'utilisent la place de l'école pour faire du prosélytisme.

Le sujet de la tolérance religieuse a aussi été abordé par une question centrée sur le droit des nouveaux mouvements religieux (NMR) de présenter leurs idées publiquement. Le graphique comparatif est très clair à ce sujet. Une grande majorité des personnes interviewées ne veut pas voir les idées et opinions des nouveaux mouvements religieux affichés en public. On peut considérer cette opinion comme paradoxale dans un contexte où la diversité des courants religieux fait l'objet d'une mise en paroles et en images à une vaste échelle par les médias électroniques. Cette médiatisation souvent spectaculaire et voyeuse du religieux «nouveau» ou «exotique» peut cependant susciter un effet simultané de fascination et de rejet.

Figure 1: Fréquences comparées des réponses aux trois questions relatives à la tolérance religieuse[9]

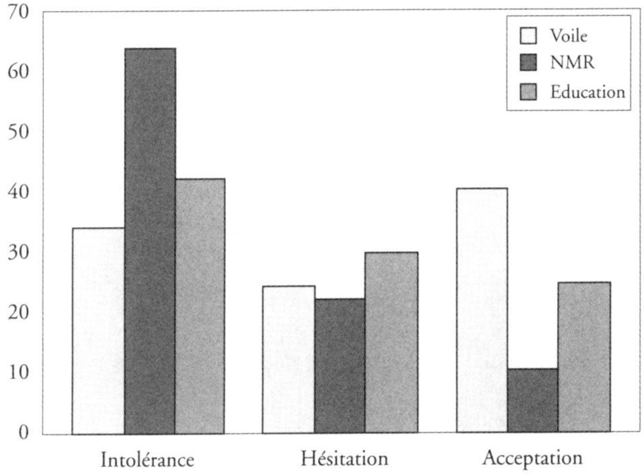

Les trois questions tendent à mesurer ensemble une dimension de tolérance générale face à la diversité religieuse[10]. Même si sur chaque objet les réponses varient fortement, comme l'indique l'histogramme ci-dessus, l'analyse comparative[11] montre qu'elles forment presque une échelle de tolérance. Il semble ainsi que la tolérance religieuse est différenciée. On est plus tolérant lorsqu'il s'agit de jeunes filles portant le voile que de nouveaux mouvements religieux présentant leurs idées en public.

La comparaison des réponses à ces trois questions montre qu'il existe une tendance vers la non tolérance dans la population étudiée dans le cadre de ce programme de recherche[12] mais que le degré de rejet varie selon l'objet pris

9 Nous avons regroupé les réponses de 0 à 2, de 3 à 7 et de 8 à 10 pour former les trois groupes d'intolérance, d'hésitation et d'acceptation.

10 Les trois variables sont significativement corrélées.

11 Analyse de type cluster.

12 Les remarques que nous avons fait préalablement concernant la composition de l'échantillon sont tout particulièrement à prendre en considération ici. En effet, une plus forte présence de minorités religieuses dans l'échantillon et de personnes très actives aurait probablement donné lieu à de résultats légèrement différents.

en considération. Le voile est accepté plus facilement mais cette acceptation n'implique pas l'acceptation d'autres aspects de pluralité religieuse. Par contre son rejet va entraîner aussi le rejet sur d'autres plans de tolérance.

Figure 2: Groupes d'opinion en matière de tolérance religieuse

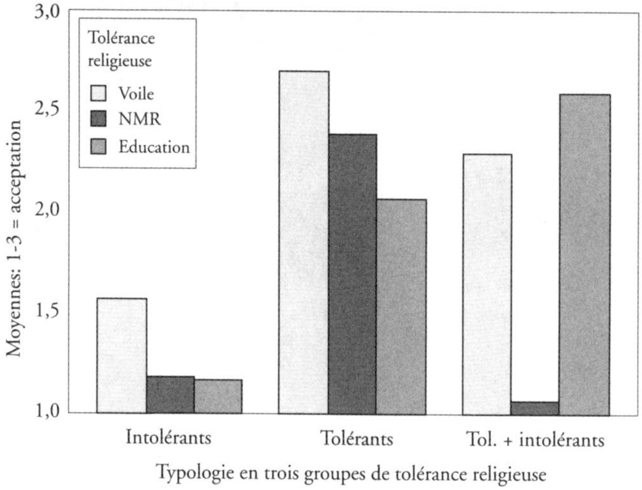

Deux groupes d'opinion se font face: les personnes «intolérantes» qui rejettent les trois propositions (il s'agit de 42,2 % du total) et celles qui ont un seuil de tolérance plus élevé. Ce dernier groupe peut être subdivisé en deux, car il regroupe deux attitudes très différentes. A côté des «tolérants» sur les trois objets pris en considération, on remarque en effet un groupe de personnes (29,7 %), dont la tolérance est sélective. Elles expriment le plus fort désaccord avec la présence de nouveaux mouvements religieux dans l'espace public, mais acceptent le plus volontiers d'inclure dans les programmes d'éducation un enseignement sur la religion.

Figure 3: Groupes d'opinion en matière de tolérance religieuse selon la régularité de la pratique collective

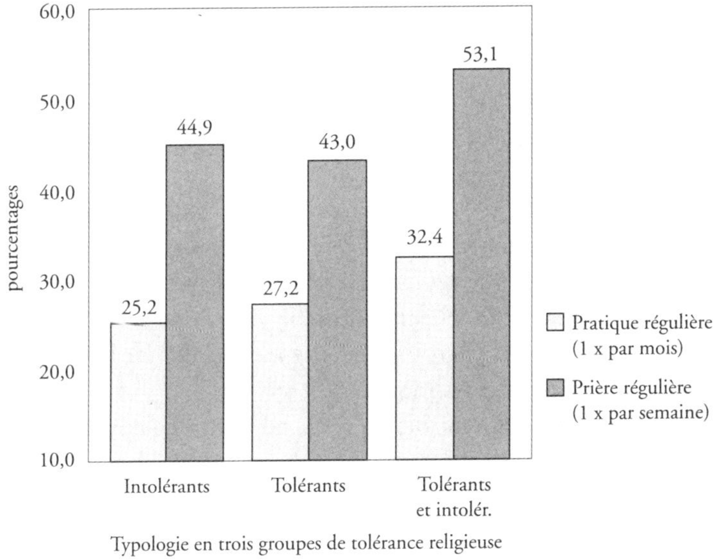

La tolérance de la pluralité religieuse est associée positivement à la pratique collective et à la discussion. La fréquentation de services religieux a un effet positif léger sur la tolérance de la pluralité religieuse en général, et particulièrement sur celle concernant l'enseignement religieux donné à l'école.

Prière et tolérance religieuse sont liées de manière non univoque. La prière a un effet négatif sur la tolérance des nouveaux mouvements religieux, mais un effet positif sur la tolérance concernant l'éducation religieuse. Cette attitude différenciée caractérise notre troisième groupe, celui que nous avons appelé «les tolérants sélectifs».

Les personnes qui discutent souvent de religion avec leur partenaire, sont plus tolérantes concernant les trois niveaux de tolérance mentionnés, le voile, les mouvements religieux et l'éducation religieuse.

Sachant que presque toutes les personnes participant régulièrement à des services religieux dans notre échantillon sont catholiques ou protestantes, nous pouvons faire l'hypothèse que le lien que ces deux confessions entretiennent avec l'Etat au niveau fédéral ou cantonal inspire une certaine confiance concernant l'enseignement religieux à l'école publique. En effet, ces deux Eglises ont toujours été fortement présentes dans les écoles. Ces mêmes personnes, pourtant, ne désirent pas trop élargir la présence de nouveaux mouvements religieux dans l'espace public.

Religion et profils sociaux

La compréhension du champ religieux doit prendre en compte le contexte social. Selon des études récentes sur les indicateurs du processus de sécularisation (Campbell et Curtis: 1994), les facteurs qui pèsent avec le plus de force sur les pratiques religieuses sont les valeurs culturelles d'une société, les caractéristiques socio-démographiques (l'âge, le sexe, l'origine sociale), l'urbanisation, l'industrialisation et l'orientation politique.

Pour donner une profondeur sociologique au tableau religieux que nous venons d'esquisser, nous avons exploré les liens avec les variables sociales et individuelles du PSM en recourant à l'étude des correlations. En d'autres termes, nous nous demandons dans quelle mesure on peut opérer un lien entre les pratiques et attitudes religieuses d'un côté, les pratiques et attitudes sociales de l'autre. Il s'agit par conséquent de poser la question de l'appartenance, des pratiques et de la tolérance religieuse dans son rapport aux autres types d'appartenance que connaissent les individus et qui travaillent la sphère collective.

En résumé, l'analyse a mis en évidence que leur influence sur les pratiques et attitudes religieuses de la population prise en considération montrait des tendances comparables à ce que l'on a pu étudier par d'autres recherches au niveau national. Parmi les variables sociales et culturelles qui se sont avérées significatives[13], on retrouve en effet: le niveau de formation, l'âge, le sexe, l'état civil, la classe socio-économique, la taille du ménage, l'insertion dans un réseaux associatif, le positionnement politique. La comparaison avec les caractéristiques individuelles en termes de santé ou de profil psychologique ont mis en évidence le lien possible avec l'état d'esprit général de la personne (degré de satisfaction, dépression).

13 Le poids d'un facteur tel que la nationalité (par rapport à l'appartenance et la pratique notamment) n'apparaît pas, en raison de la composition de l'échantillon.

Pratique collective et prière

Ni les appartenances, ni les degrés de participation religieuse collective ne s'expliquent de manière univoque par l'influence des groupes sociaux d'appartenance. Certains facteurs sociologiques peuvent toutefois être dégagés.

Les personnes qui déclarent une appartenance religieuse et qui assistent régulièrement à des services religieux se situent plus à droite politiquement, font partie d'un ménage composé d'un nombre plus important de personnes et sont plutôt âgées. On remarque également qu'il y a beaucoup de personnes sans partenaire parmi les pratiquant-e-s. Ce sont aussi des personnes qui ont un niveau plutôt élevé de satisfaction dans la vie en général.

Si nous nous interrogeons ensuite sur le profil social de celles et ceux qui déclarent prier, nous trouvons que les femmes prient plus que les hommes, que plus on est âgé, plus on prie et que plus souvent on est déprimé ou anxieux, plus on prie. Prient davantage aussi les personnes d'un ménage avec un nombre plus important de personnes. Elles se situent à droite politiquement, ont un revenu familial moins élevé et de manière moins significative un niveau de formation moins élevé. Le niveau d'éducation influence négativement la prière. En effet, moins on est éduqué, plus on prie. Si l'on introduit dans l'analyse le lien entre régularité de la prière et tolérance, nous pouvons mettre en évidence que les femmes catholiques, notamment celles plus âgées, semblent être des «tolérantes sélectives». Elles se déclarent plus tolérantes envers les jeunes filles portant le voile, mais moins tolérantes envers la présentation en public des idées des nouveaux mouvements religieux.

Quant à la pratique collective on note des écarts moins importants entre les genres: 25,3 % des hommes déclarent fréquenter un service religieux mensuellement ou plus, alors que cette féquence concerne 31 % des femmes. On notera ici qu'il s'agit de fréquences légèrement supérieures aux moyennes nationales (voir infra la comparaison longitudinale).

Certaines variables sociales influencent aussi bien l'intensité de la pratique individuelle que de la pratique collective. Ceci est le cas notamment du niveau de formation et du positionnement politique. Les personnes les plus religieuses sont plus au centre ou à droite politiquement: un tiers pratique et la moitié prie régulièrement, alors que la pratique régulière n'attire qu'un cinquième des partisan-e-s de gauche et que ces dernier-ère-s sont 41,3 % à prier régulièrement.

Figure 4: Régularité de la pratique collective et de la prière selon l'orientation politique

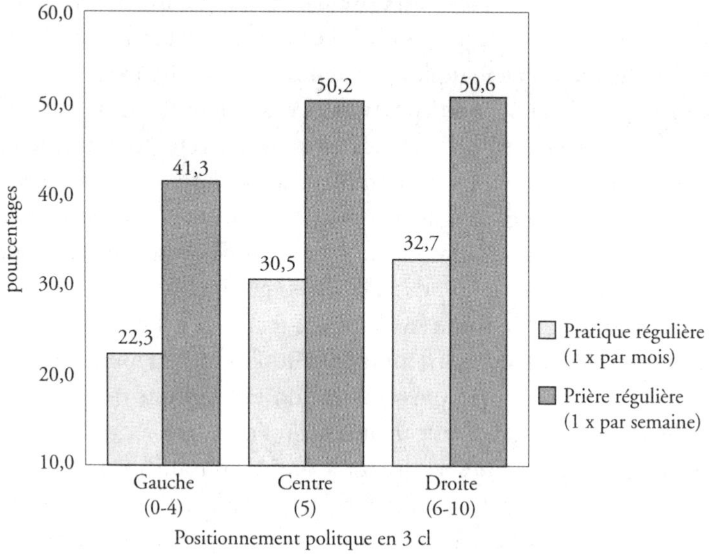

Le niveau de formation permet également de repérer des différences en matière de pratique collective et individuelle. Un niveau de formation plus élevé caractérise le groupe des «sans appartenance», alors que moins on est éduqué, plus on pratique. Ainsi par exemple, plus de la moitié des personnes dont le niveau de formation est bas prient une fois par semaine au moins (55,6 %) contre 41,1 % des personnes qui déclarent un niveau de formation élevé. Les personnes de niveau moyen se placent quant à elles à un niveau de pratique de la prière intermédiaire entre ces deux extrêmes (47,5 %).

Nous avons dit que le nombre de personnes vivant dans le même ménage joue un rôle important pour la pratique collective. Cette variable nous informe souvent aussi de la classe sociale et il n'est pas très étonnant de voir que c'est dans les familles nombreuses que nous trouvons le niveau de pratique le plus élevé. Il n'est de plus pas improbable que le nombre d'enfants dans le ménage ait à voir avec des convictions et un engagement religieux. Les petites familles pratiquent encore moins que les personnes vivant seules ou en couple. Notons dans l'histogramme que la croissance de la taille du ménage ne correspond pas de façon aussi linéaire avec la fréquence de la prière, ce qui confirme, encore une fois, qu'il s'agit d'une dimension plus personnelle de la religion.

Figure 5: Régularité de la pratique collective et de la prière selon la taille du ménage

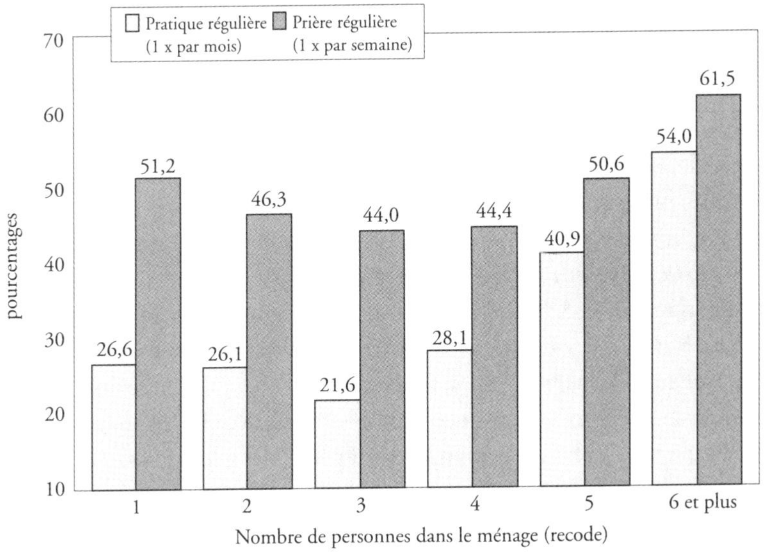

S'agissant d'une étude spécifiquement dédiée aux ménages, il est certainement intéressant de relever que le milieu de socialisation primaire constitue un espace pour l'expression de religiosité. Non pas, comme on l'a vu à propos des échanges dans le couple, qu'il s'agisse nécessairement ou principalement d'un indice de privatisation. Loin s'en faut. L'espace du ménage représente une des formes de l'expérience sociale, dans laquelle il est possible de faire appel individuellement ou collectivement à des ressources religieuses. Mais il est aussi possible de négocier ou d'affirmer des pratiques ou des attitudes individuelles qui ne seraient partagées avec le milieu (parents, conjoints, enfants, etc.). A cela s'ajoute que toutes les études convergent pour signaler le rôle important, sinon décisif, du ménage comme lieu de la transmission aux enfants d'un soi religieux ou plus simplement d'une posture vis-à-vis de la religion.[14]

14 Voir à ce sujet Hervieu-Léger: 1997.

Il nous semble par conséquent intéressant d'envisager l'extension de l'investigation à la comparaison des comportements et des attitudes des couples ainsi qu'à leurs enfants, dans le but notamment d'intégrer la problématique de la transmission et de la socialisation religieuse et celle de l'influence de la mixité sur le soi religieux.

La religion en public

Les personnes qui discutent avec le plus de régularité de religion sont nombreuses dans leur ménage, sont plus âgées et ont un revenu plutôt bas. Plus on est éduqué, plus on discute de religion avec son partenaire. Un trait particulièrement intéressant des personnes qui ont souvent la religion comme sujet de discussion est leur intérêt plus grand pour la politique. L'analyse du lien avec la variable intérêt dans la politique révèle pourtant d'une interaction complexe. Le fait de discuter souvent de religion avec les ami-e-s, et non pas seulement avec le ou la partenaire, indique que pour les personnes intéressées à la politique, la religion est un sujet qui peut être évoqué en dehors de la sphère strictement privée. Ces personnes sont plus que la moyenne confiantes dans le gouvernement fédéral et dans les partis politiques, plus que la moyenne satisfaites de la démocratie en Suisse. C'est pourquoi probablement elles se caractérisent aussi par le fait de parler en moyenne moins de politique. Ce sont des personnes plutôt à droite. Par ailleurs, les données du PSM montrent que les personnes faisant confiance au gouvernement fédéral acceptent plus facilement que l'Etat dispense un enseignement religieux dans les écoles[15]. Plus on est intéressé à la politique, plus on tolère les nouveaux mouvements religieux dans la place publique et plus on soutient un enseignement religieux à l'école.

Plusieurs questions restent en suspens après ces explorations. L'une d'elle concerne la logique plus large qui soutient ces caractéristiques. Une double hypothèse peut être dessinée: d'un côté il semble qu'une représentation de la religion comme affaire privée détermine souvent les opinions, les attitudes et

15 La corrélation est significative même si elle est contrôlée par le niveau de pratique et de prière: r = 0,081, p = 0,00.

les comportements des personnes concernant la religion. D'un autre côté, le fait de considérer la religion comme une affaire privée peut fortement varier en fonction d'autres facteurs conjoints, notamment le niveau d'éducation et le genre.

L'analyse longitudinale: les changements religieux

Les questions concernant la prière, la pratique et l'appartenance ont été posées en 1999 et 2000. L'analyse montre que ni les changements de groupe d'appartenance ni les variations de fréquence de la prière ne sont significatifs. Par contre, la fréquence de la participation à des services religieux se traduit par des variations non négligeables. Nous allons en examiner l'importance et la signification.

Ce qui frappe à première analyse, c'est de constater que la moitié environ des répondant-e-s déclare un rythme de pratique différent d'une année à l'autre. Il y a en effet 30,2 % de personnes qui ont diminué leur pratique. Mais il y a aussi 23,2 % de personnes qui l'ont augmentée. Seule une minorité, 47,5 %, déclare donc le même rythme de fréquentation des services religieux. Ces proportions peuvent sembler considérables, mais si nous prenons en compte certains éléments méthodologiques importants, elles s'estompent.

Tout d'abord, il faut relever que l'échelle proposée dans la réponse était très détaillée quant aux types de fréquence possibles. Il s'agit de mesures très fines, qui peuvent concerner le simple passage d'un rythme hebdomadaire à un rythme mensuel de pratique. La moitié environ des variations enregistrées par le PSM, concerne des changements d'un ou deux points sur une échelle qui comporte 7 points. Certains s'opèrent vers le haut (15,4 %), d'autres sont orientés vers une baisse de pratique (21,5 %). On ne peut donc parler à ce propos de bouleversement, mais plutôt d'inflexion.

Pour ce qui concerne la Suisse, l'étude la plus récente qui compare à 10 ans d'intervalle la pratique collective (1989 et 1999) fait état d'une diminution importante de la fréquentation régulière (mensuelle ou supérieure).[16]

16 Pour l'année 1989 nous nous référons à l'enquête présentée dans l'ouvrage *Croire en Suisse?* (Campiche et alii, 1989).

Tableau 3: Evolution de la pratique collective en Suisse entre 1989 et 1999

		Année d'enquête		
Pratique religieuse en 3 classes		Croire en Suisse 1989	Religion et lien social 1999	Total
Au moins une fois par mois		451	382	833
	%	34,3 %	24,5 %	29,0 %
Quelques fois par année		365	438	803
	%	27,8 %	28,1 %	27,9 %
Jamais		492	739	1231
	%	37,4 %	47,3 %	42,8 %
Sans réponse		7	2	9
	%	0,5 %	0,1 %	0,3 %
Total		1315	1561	2876
		100,0 %	100,0 %	100,0 %

Le tableau ci-dessus indique clairement que l'on ne semble pas assister à un report de la pratique régulière vers des rythmes irréguliers mais bien à une réduction massive, de telle sorte que près de la moitié de la population résidante peut être considérée comme non pratiquante.

Il est important d'analyser les changements mesurés par le PSM à la lumière des études comparatives qui enregistrent des tendances sur des périodes longues. En effet – comme nous l'avons mentionné dans l'introduction – l'intervalle d'un an mesuré par la première vague du PSM ne saurait nous donner les éléments nécessaires pour observer des mutations structurelles profondes. Il nous paraît dès lors pertinent de cibler l'étude longitudinale sur le passage à un taux bas de pratique collective qui se trouve à la fois représenter un mouvement significatif dans notre échantillon (8,6 %) et refléter une tendance nationale lourde[17].

Notre questionnement va viser à déterminer si ce recul de pratique est homogène dans l'ensemble de la société ou si nous nous trouvons face à un phénomène qui concerne une partie seulement de l'échantillon, par exemple un groupe d'âge. S'agissant d'une évolution annuelle, même dans l'hypothèse

17 Reste cependant que 6,9 % ont augmenté de plus trois points ou davantage. L'analyse ne permet pas d'opérer un lien entre les variables sociales et l'augmentation réelle de la pratique entre 1999 et 2000. L'analyse par régression sur les moyennes de pratique fait aparaître un lien entre le positionnement le plus à droite de l'échiquier politique et l'augmentation effective de la pratique.

où le changement apparaîtrait lié à une caractéristique sociale, nous devrons vérifier ce qu'il en est de la conjoncture individuelle des personnes concernées (état de santé, déménagement, etc.), afin d'éviter tout risque de réductionnisme. Nous verrons que cette option méthodologique est adaptée à la nature des résultats pris en considération.

Tout d'abord il faut préciser ce que l'on entend par diminution du niveau de la pratique collective. Si l'on s'en tient à la catégorie des personnes qui ne fréquentent jamais les services religieux, celle-ci est stable et n'augmente que de 0,3 %. Par contre, si l'on considère que le passage à un ‹niveau bas de pratique› inclut une participation limitée aux cérémonies de famille ou aux fêtes religieuses, le déficit de pratique augmente de façon significative de 1999 à 2000. De plus, on observe une baisse importante de la proportion de personnes qui déclarent un niveau élevé de pratique (au moins toutes les deux semaines). Nous ferons donc porter l'analyse longitudinale principalement sur la recherche d'explications du passage entre 1999 et 2000 d'une pratique régulière à une pratique basse, soit le 12,4 % de la population prise en considération par le PSM qui a passé à un niveau bas de pratique entre 1999 et 2000.

Une analyse de régression linéaire a été effectuée sur la base d'une variable dichotomique qui distingue les personnes qui ont passé à un bas niveau de pratique (12,4 %, N = 775). Les résultats rejoignent ceux effectués à l'aide d'une analyse logistique, à savoir que les personnes qui ont passé au niveau bas de pratique (venant d'un niveau plus élevé) entre 1999 et 2000 se caractérisent par des traits tels qu'un niveau d'engagement associatif bas (moins engagé dans une association culturelle en 1999), une augmentation du support émotionnel des ami-e-s entre 1999 et 2000, une augmentation du niveau de formation entre 1999 et 2000 ou encore se sont un peu désengagé-e-s d'une association d'environnement entre 1999 et 2000. A vrai dire, ces résultats sont quelque peu déroutants. Ils semblent en effet sinon expliquer un désengagement (religieux) par un autre (associatif), du moins davantage indiquer une tendance générale au retrait qu'en donner les raisons. Cette analyse n'est pas infirmée par le constat que sur le plan de l'appartenance confessionnelle, les protestant-e-s (contrairement aux catholiques et autres confessions chrétiennes) sont davantage passés au bas niveau de pratique.

A l'inverse, les personnes qui discutent davantage de sujets religieux passent moins au bas niveau de pratique. Si notre hypothèse est juste cela indique qu'une conception moins privée de la religion continue à s'exprimer en termes de pratique collective.

Une autre analyse par régression logistique effectuée sur l'ensemble de celles et ceux qui ont annoncé un recul de pratique collective (30,2 %, N = 1881), montre que les personnes concernées par une diminution de la pratique se retrouvent davantage parmi celles et ceux qui possèdent des caractéristiques telles qu'un âge supérieur (voir la figure 6), l'absence de partenaire en 1999, l'appartenance à un ménage nombreux, la nationalité étrangère, la non appartenance à une «autre confession chrétienne», la possession d'un niveau bas de formation.[18]

Par ailleurs, il semble aussi que les personnes de nationalité étrangère abandonnent avec l'âge le haut niveau de pratique, qui peut-être au début de leur immigration en Suisse était un élément d'intégration sociale. Ces caractéristiques (à part le fait d'être étranger et de ne pas être d'une confession chrétienne autre que catholique ou protestante) sont aussi des éléments explicatifs d'un niveau de pratique en 1999. On peut donc en conclure que ceux qui avaient les plus hauts niveaux de pratique en 1999 sont aussi ceux qui ont le plus diminué leur pratique.

Figure 6: Pourcentage de pratiquants bimensuels en 1999 et en 2000, selon l'âge

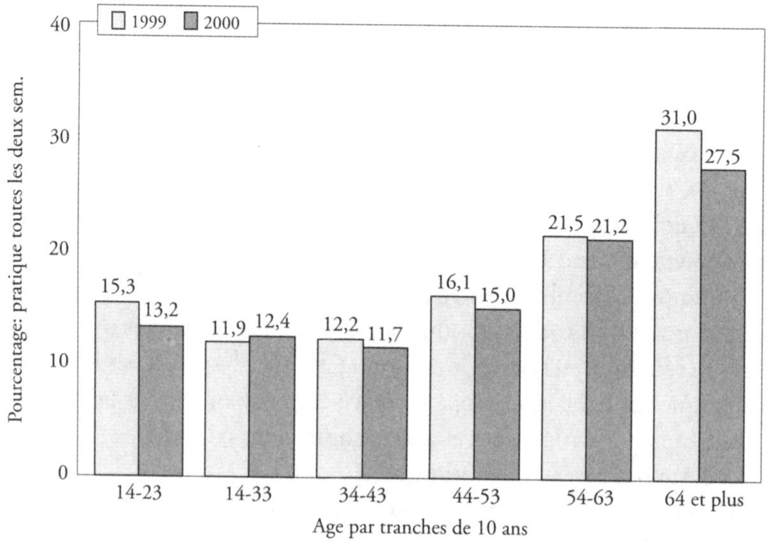

18 La régression logistique a été faite après une analyse backward et l'élimination des variables non significatives.

Nous avons vu que les personnes âgées (plus de 64 ans), qui ont un niveau de pratique plus élevé, ont davantage diminué leur pratique. Mais est-il possible de trouver des explications propres à un âge élevé? Une piste intéressante s'est peu à peu manifestée en confrontant ces éléments avec les réponses qui on trait à l'état de santé. Il se trouve en effet que les répondant-e-s de plus de 63 ans qui répondent que leur état de santé est bon en 2000, la proportion de pratiquant-e-s régulier-e-s est stable par rapport à celle de 1999. Par contre, celles et ceux dont l'état de santé n'est pas très bon se distinguent par une nette baisse du taux de pratiquant-e-s régulier-e-s, qui passe de 37,7 à 29,2 %.

Le schéma suivant illustre la tendance repérée parmi les personnes âgées, d'un lien entre état de santé médiocre et baisse de la pratique régulière. Les personnes qui affirment avoir un état de santé médiocre en 2000 (pouvant altérer les possibilités de déplacement) ont davantage diminué leur pratique.

Figure 7: Diminution de pratique régulière selon les groupes d'âge et la détérioration de l'état de santé en 2000

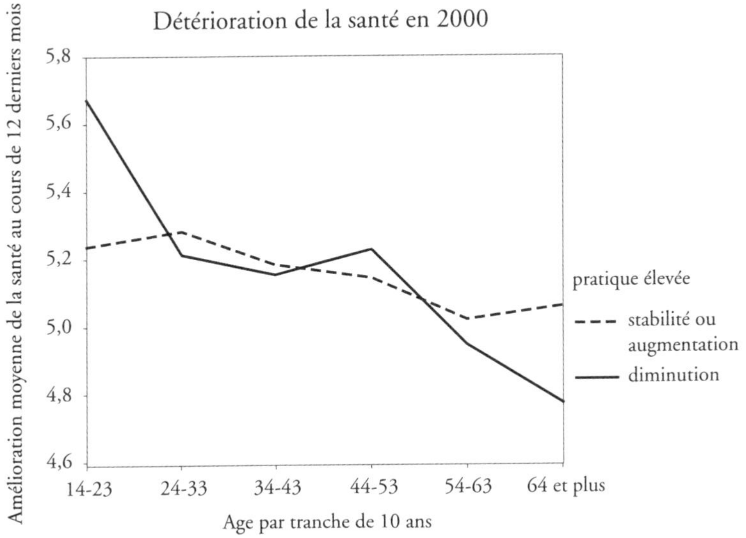

Sur l'échelle de 0 à 10, les valeurs de moins de 5 correspondent à une détérioration de la santé lors des 12 derniers mois. Contrairement aux personnes âgées qui n'ont pas diminué leur pratique, celles qui pratiquent moins affirment que leur état de santé «s'est détérioré» lors des 12 derniers mois.

Le rôle du niveau de formation est plus complexe à analyser. Selon l'analyse qui a porté sur la tendance à la diminution dans son ensemble, les personnes d'un bas niveau de formation – qui pratiquent plus en général – ont davantage diminué leur pratique. Cela nous confirme la logique selon laquelle les personnes qui avaient les plus hauts niveaux en 1999 ont le plus diminué leur pratique.

Figure 8: Diminution de pratique régulière selon le niveau de formation

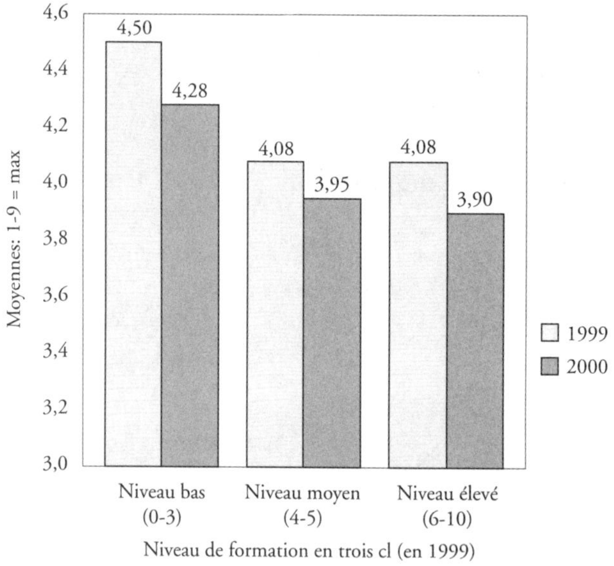

Par ailleurs, l'analyse de régression révèle une corrélation entre le passage à un bas niveau de pratique et l'augmentation du niveau de formation entre 1999 et 2000. Graphiquement cela peut être représenté de la manière suivante:

Figure 9: Progression du bas niveau de pratique collective en 2000 selon l'augmentation du niveau de formation

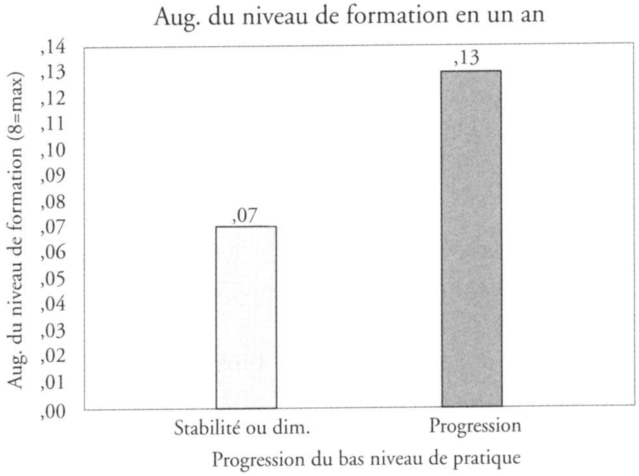

Globalement, le niveau de formation a légèrement augmenté entre 1999 et 2000. Mais cette augmentation a été un peu plus forte pour les personnes ayant passé au bas niveau de pratique. On peut donc conclure qu'une augmentation supérieure du niveau de formation a accéléré la diminution de la pratique.

Deux phénomènes distincts semblent se manifester et s'influer mutuellement ici:

1. L'augmentation du niveau de formation comporte une tendance à la diminution de la moyenne de pratique collective.
2. Les personnes ayant globalement (sur plusieurs variables) un niveau de pratique élevé – ce qui est le cas notamment des personnes âgées ou moins formées – diminuent davantage leur pratique que les autres. Cette tendance apparaît comme générale, sans que l'on puisse l'expliquer par des facteurs biographiques précis. La détérioration de l'état de santé est pourtant un facteur explicatif important mais pour les personnes très âgées uniquement.

Conclusion

Les variables religieuses retenues par le PSM ne cernent pas la religiosité individuelle des personnes interrogées (leurs systèmes de croyances), ni les rapports entre religion et morale. L'intérêt se concentre sur certains aspects personnels, interpersonnels et sociaux du rapport de l'individu à la religion. Tenant compte des caractéristiques de l'échantillonnage du PSM, les analyses effectuées confirment et illustrent les tendances dominantes de l'évolution du paysage religieux helvétique. On ne peut pas parler d'une sécularisation massive ou inéluctable. On observe plutôt une évolution marquée par une diminution de la religiosité institutionnelle (pratique collective) au profit de choix individualisés (prière, discussion, ...).

Les réponses enregistrées au sujet de certaines expressions publiques de la religion montrent que le religieux est aussi composé de frontières internes et externes que les acteurs sociaux peuvent rendre perméables. L'évolution sociale et démographique à l'origine de la pluralisation religieuse interroge nécessairement le statut public des groupes religieux ainsi que la définition des droits religieux individuels et collectifs. Cette interrogation est présente dans les questionnements sur le religieux mais les réponses sont très variées et hésitantes.

Le questionnaire du PSM ouvre d'intéressantes perspectives d'analyse sur le lien entre la conception du soi religieux et des variables de comportement ou d'attitude dans le domaine de l'engagement social et politique, de même qu'avec le profil social des personnes interrogées. L'intérêt du PSM consiste à inaugurer la possibilité de mesurer en temps «réel» des évolutions de comportements et d'attitudes auprès d'une même population. On a vu que pour ce qui concerne la pratique collective, les données disponibles mettent en évidence les mouvements annuels qui concernent une majorité de la population, même s'ils ne sont pas tous de la même importance. Quant aux traitements statistiques, ils n'expliquent pas tous ces changements, mais ils offrent de sérieuses pistes sociologiques qui méritent d'être explorées et poursuivies sur les prochaines récoltes de données.

Dans le mouvement de la modernité, un moyen – probablement le plus plausible – de conceptualiser la religion, consiste à considérer cette dernière comme un des répertoires de significations pour la conception de soi des individus et des groupes sociaux. L'analyse des données du PSM contribue à montrer pour qui et en quoi la religion peut servir d'ancrage social et/ou existentiel.

Cette perspective conduit à les considérer comme un apport à la compréhension des phénomènes de multiappartenance.

Références

Becci, I. (2000), Religionskundlicher Unterricht an der öffentlichen Schule: eine soziologische Einleitung zur Debatte, in: Kohler-Spiegel, H. et A. Loretan, éd. *Religionsunterricht an der öffentlichen Schule. Orientierungen und Entscheidungshilfen zum Religionsunterricht.* Zurich: NZN Verlag.

Bovay, C. (1997), *L'évolution de l'appartenance religieuse et confessionnelle en Suisse.* Berne: Office fédéral de la statistique.

Bovay, C. (2000), *Couples et appartenance religieuse en Suisse*, Diplôme de spécialisation en Sociologie de la religion, Université de Lausanne: polycop.

Campbell, Robert et Curtis James (1994), Religious Involvement across Societies: Analyses for Alternative Measures in National Surveys, in: *Journal for the Scientific Study of Religion* 33: 3, 217-229.

Campiche, R. J., A. Dubach, C. Bovay, M. Krüggeler et P. Voll (1992), *Croire en Suisse(s).* Lausanne: l'Age d'Homme.

Davie, G. et D. Martin (1994), *Religion in Britain Since 1945: Believing Without Belonging (Making Contemporary Britain).* Oxford: Blackwell Publishers.

Fetzer, J. S. et J. Ch. Soper (2003), The Roots of Public Attitudes Toward State Accomodation of European Muslim' Religious Practicies Before and After September 11, in: *Journal for the Scientficic Study of Relgion* 42: 2, 247-258.

Gerber, R. (2002), En marge couvent les conflits, in *La Suisse et le monde*, La revue du Département fédéral des affaires étrangères, Edition 3: 16-17.

Hervieu-Léger, D. (1997), La transmission religieuse en modernité, in *Social compass*, 44, 1: 131-143.

Hölscher, L. (2000), Les changements religieux. Etude d'histoire sociale et des mentalités (du XVIIIe siècle à 1945) in: Colonge, Paul et Rudolf Lill, dir. *Histoire religieuse de l'Allemagne.* Paris: Cerf.

Hutmacher, W., éd. (1999), *Culture religieuse et école laïque.* Rapport du groupe de travail exploratoire sur la culture judéo-chrétienne à l'école, Genève: Service de la recherche en éducation, Cahier 4.

Loretan, A. (1996), Brauchen die Kirchen den Staat noch?, in Ries, M. et W. Kirchschläger, *Glauben und Denken nach Vatikanum II*, Zurich: NZN Verlag.

Mayer, J.-F. (2000), Le «phénomène sectaire» en Suisse et dans le monde, in Bellanger, F., éd., *L'Etat face aux Dérives sectaires.* Bâle: Helbing et Lichtenhahn, 9-26.

Zouari, F. (2002), *Le voile islamique: Histoire et actualité, du Coran à l'affaire du foulard.* Lausanne: Favre.

4. Médias et politique
Medien und Politik

La Suisse en réseau*

Cristina MOLO-BETTELINI, Boris WERNLI et Maddalena ALIPPI

Internet, son utilisation et ses impacts

L'évolution et l'expansion rapide des télécommunications fait naître des interrogations à différents niveaux. Internet est la facette la plus médiatisée de ce phénomène. La complexité et l'interactivité de ses réseaux permettent des modes d'utilisation très différents, dont les conséquences sur le plan social, économique et psychologique sont seulement en partie prévisibles. Les possibilités de transformations sociales qui y sont liées sont l'objet de représentations qui peuvent varier considérablement, comme l'a montré notre première étude sur le sujet[1] qui nous a permis de mettre en relation certains indicateurs subjectifs avec des indicateurs objectifs relatifs aux modes d'utilisation effective de la part des personnes (Molo-Bettelini, Alippi et Wernli, 2001 a,b). La littérature sur les impacts de l'utilisation de ces technologies est désormais ample et on peut y trouver des hypothèses parfois surprenantes, mais pas toujours ancrées sur des données empiriques. Le but de cette partie de notre contribution, qui s'inscrit dans un projet de recherche plus large[2] concernant les impacts de l'utilisation de ces nouvelles technologies sur certains aspects spécifiques de la vie privée

* Cette contribution fait partie de l'ouvrage collectif *Vivre en Suisse 1999-2000* (Erwin Zimmermann et Robin Tillmann (éds), Editions Peter Lang, Berne (2004)). Les analyses et résultats se basent sur les deux premières vagues de l'enquête longitudinale Vivre en Suisse réalisée auprès de 6 335 personnes interviewées en 1999 et 2000. La collecte des données, effectuée par M. I. S. Trend sous la responsabilité du Panel suisse de ménages de l'Université de Neuchâtel, a été financée par le PP Demain la Suisse du Fonds national suisse de la recherche scientifique (Subsides No. 5004-53205 / 5004-57894 / 5004-67304). Des informations complémentaires peuvent être obtenues sur le site www.swisspanel.ch

1 Molo-Bettelini C. (1997-2000) «L'individu face aux nouveaux systèmes de télécommunication: représentations, utilisations sociales, processus de changement, impacts et besoins». Recherche conduite dans le cadre du Programme Prioritaire «Demain la Suisse», Fonds National Suisse de la Recherche Scientifique.

2 Molo-Bettelini C. (2000-en cours) «Les enjeux d'Internet. Utilisateurs, projets professionnels et vie privée». Recherche conduite dans le cadre du Programme Prioritaire «Demain la Suisse», Fonds National Suisse de la Recherche Scientifique.

et professionnelle des utilisateurs, est de faire la part des choses, en vérifiant l'utilisation d'Internet et certains de ses impacts sur les comportements des usagers dans trois régions linguistiques suisses, sur la base de données reconnues par la communauté scientifique.

La question des impacts de l'utilisation d'Internet sur les personnes a été évoquée sous plusieurs aspects.

L'uniformisation des informations engendrée par la mise en réseau à été reliée à des risques d'homogénéisation culturelle (Mattelart, 1999); la progression vers une civilisation de l'image et du son au détriment de celle de l'écrit à une réduction de l'autonomie intellectuelle et de la réflexion et à un accroissement de la passivité (Barber, 1999); le remplacement des contacts face-à-face à une plus grande solitude (Turkle, 1996; Kraut et al.; 1998, Nie et Erbring, 2000). D'autre part le réseau change les modes de communiquer et de maintenir les contacts (PEW, 2000) et rend possibles des contacts avec des personnes qu'on ne connaissait pas auparavant. Ces rencontres, bien que limitées par la distance et par l'anonymat, peuvent devenir en quelque sorte des relations stables (Serpentelli, 1993) et permettre de construire de nouvelles appartenances sociales (Hellerstein, 1985), dépassant les milieux sociaux, culturels et professionnels d'origine (Spears et Lea, 1992). Des impacts peuvent concerner aussi le contexte professionnel, et notamment des possibilités de travail et de formation à distance peuvent se développer et créer de nouvelles opportunités professionnelles. Le monde du travail connaît actuellement de profondes transformations par rapport aux modèles de parcours professionnels transmis par la génération précédente, surtout pour les jeunes qui se présentent sur le marché du travail, avec une diminution des possibilités d'obtenir un poste stable situé dans sa zone d'habitation, et des fluctuations au niveau de la rétribution, du temps de travail, du domaine d'activité. Ainsi changent les représentations concernant le travail, l'espace géographique associé à l'emploi et le statut de l'activité professionnelle. Ces changements ont touché de façon plus ou moins accentuée l'Europe entière. A coté de ceux qui n'ont pas pu trouver le travail qu'ils avaient imaginé pendant les études, il y a les autres qui ont choisi volontairement des formes de travail «atypiques». Le travail dépendant ne disparaît pas mais les formes changent. Et avec elles, surgissent des activités de petits indépendants ou semi-indépendants, des collaborations continues, le partage du travail (job sharing), etc. Le travail à distance, qui actuellement est encore marginalement diffusé, pourrait connaître un essor plus important. L'élargissement de la perspective régionale aux informations sans limitations de frontières qu'Internet offre (informations sur le marché, sur la recherche de personnel, sur des éventuelles possibilités de collaborations, sur les services, etc.) et l'interactivité peuvent contribuer à engendrer de nouveaux projets professionnels grâce à plus d'informations.

Parallèlement, le système multimédia tendrait à augmenter la stratification sociale existante (Castells, 1996). Selon cette thèse, l'exclusion/inclusion et les types de relations dans le réseau dessineront les processus dominants de nos sociétés, où les différences ne cesseront de s'accroître entre les exclus (pour leur distance physique, sociale, économique, culturelle et politique) et les inclus, et parmi ceux-ci entre ceux qui par leur formation et leur savoir-faire sauront choisir les circuits à leur avantage et ceux qui ne recevront que des options pré-conditionnées.

Deux hypothèses sous-tendent notre travail

Tout d'abord, certaines caractéristiques personnelles et du contexte influencent l'utilisation d'Internet selon une relation qui se modifie dans le temps. D'instruments d'élite, ces nouveaux systèmes se démocratisent rapidement, en faisant leur entrée dans un nombre croissant de ménages. Ce schéma, déjà vérifié pour nombre d'innovations technologiques dans le domaine des transports et télécommunications, veut que le rapport que l'on entretient avec ces instruments change donc aussi.

De plus, une utilisation importante de certains nouveaux services co-agit dans le processus de transformation de certains comportements des individus. Nous pensons tout particulièrement à des aspects comme la gestion du temps, les pratiques culturelles et de loisirs, l'utilisation des médias, certains aspects des relations interpersonnelles et certains projets et débouchés professionnels, relativement sensibles à l'utilisation du nouveau média.

Une série de questions en découlent, notamment:

- Quelles sont les caractéristiques des utilisateurs d'Internet en Suisse?
- Quelle est l'utilisation effective des différents services?
- Existe-t-il des différences régionales en Suisse?
- Peut-on relever des différences spécifiques entre hommes et femmes dans l'utilisation d'Internet?
- Quelle est la diffusion du phénomène en Suisse par rapport aux autres pays occidentaux?

- Quelle est l'évolution de tous les paramètres susmentionnés dans le temps?
- L'utilisation des nouveaux systèmes de télécommunication est-elle accompagnée de changements dans certains aspects de la vie des usagers, comme le réseau social, les activités dans le budget temps et loisirs, l'utilisation des autres médias, les situations et les débouchés professionnels?
- Quels sont les risques de sur-utilisation et de dépendance liés au Net?

Afin de répondre à ces questions, nous avons décidé de nous concentrer dans le cadre de la présente recherche sur l'analyse des données les plus exhaustives et actuelles disponibles en Suisse. Nous avons d'abord orienté nos efforts vers une analyse secondaire des données du Panel Suisse de Ménages (PSM), notamment pour vérifier les caractéristiques des différents types d'utilisateurs, les modalités d'usage et ses impacts. Nous utilisons en outre les données de l'enquête menée par REMP[3] pour mieux cerner les différences régionales et internationales et pour y confronter les indicateurs du PSM.

Le schéma d'analyse du travail que nous présentons ici se résume dans le plan de la figure 1.

Les caractéristiques socio-démographiques des personnes interviewées renvoient essentiellement à l'âge, au sexe, au niveau de formation, à la situation familiale, professionnelle et économique. Nous avons postulé que ces caractéristiques, et tout particulièrement le sexe, l'âge et le niveau de formation, ont une influence sur l'utilisation d'Internet, notamment sur l'intensité de l'utilisation, le lieu d'utilisation (à la maison, au travail, ailleurs), les services utilisés (courrier électronique, groupes de discussion, journaux, etc.), et les buts d'utilisation (ludique, utilitaire, etc.).

Parallèlement, voulant vérifier si l'utilisation d'Internet est susceptible de modifier certains aspects de la vie quotidienne des utilisateurs, les facteurs explicatifs du graphique sont dédoublés, car il est un élément supplémentaire dans l'analyse: le temps. Le schéma est dynamique: Tx est la situation de départ, tandis que Tx + y est celle qui est mesurée après 1, 2, 3 ou y année. Le

3 L'enquête menée en Suisse par REMP SA explore le monde des utilisateurs d'Internet à travers des entretiens téléphoniques (CATI) chaque six mois depuis fin 1997. L'univers pris en considération est celui de la population suisse âgée de 14 ans et plus. L'échantillon comprend chaque fois entre 10 000 et 13 000 personnes et offre les plus amples données existantes actuellement en Suisse concernant les profils des utilisateurs d'Internet et les types d'utilisation. Voir http://www.wemf.ch pour plus de détails.

Figure 1: Représentation graphique du plan d'analyse des données du PSM

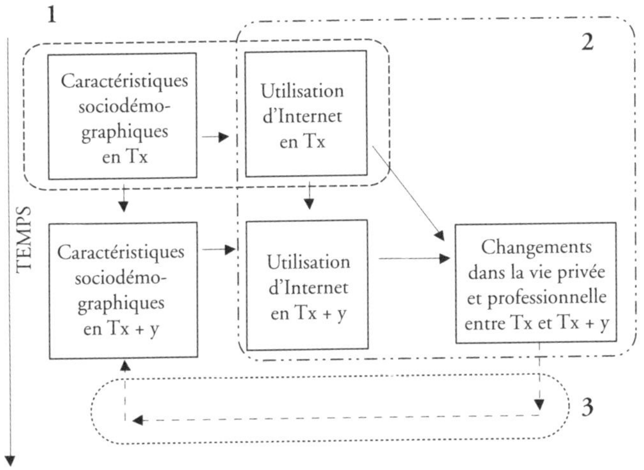

schéma se réplique ainsi vers le bas, illustrant l'effet successif de chaque état sur celui qui lui est postérieur.

Sur la figure 1, les cercles numérotés indiquent les différentes étapes de notre projet; dans la première phase (1997-2000), nous nous sommes principalement intéressés aux liens entre les caractéristiques socio-démographiques, l'utilisation d'Internet et les changements dans la vie de tous les jours. L'accent a été mis sur la zone du graphique entourée par le cercle 1, pour répondre à la question «qui utilise Internet et comment». La zone 2 a aussi été abordée, de manière moins exhaustive, en analysant l'impact d'une utilisation intensive sur la vie courante.

La seconde partie du projet (2000-2003) porte essentiellement sur les zones 2 et 3. L'idée est de mettre en évidence les changements à long terme de l'utilisation d'Internet en rapport avec les habitudes de vie des répondants. C'est dans cette deuxième partie que le temps est réellement mis en perspective, avec notamment l'utilisation de données de panel, alors que presque toute la première étape donne un point de vue transversal. La durée d'observation prévue par cette recherche concerne trois vagues du PSM: cette contribution présente les résultats relatifs aux deux premières.

Profil des utilisateurs en Suisse

Selon les données de la deuxième vague du Panel suisse de ménages[4], à la fin de l'année 2000 les utilisateurs d'Internet en Suisse représentent 47 % de la population âgée de 14 ans et plus, dont 51 % accèdent au réseau depuis leur lieu de travail, 17 % depuis l'école et 80 % depuis leur domicile. Parmi les utilisateurs, 21 % se connectent pendant moins d'une heure par semaine, 51 % de une à moins de quatre heures, 17 % de quatre à moins de huit heures et 11 % affirment l'utiliser huit heures ou plus hebdomadairement. Le temps moyen d'utilisation hebdomadaire est de 222 minutes, soit un peu moins de 4 heures. Les personnes très assidues sont rares, avec 5 % d'utilisateurs connectés 2 heures et plus par jour et 2 % 3 heures et plus par jour. Seulement 45 personnes (0,6 % de tout l'échantillon, 1,3 % des utilisateurs) ont affirmé utiliser Internet pendant plus de 4 heures par jour, dont 5 pendant en moyenne 8 heures par jour et 4 excédant les 10 heures. Les données du panel ne permettent malheureusement pas de savoir si l'usage massif de ces dernières personnes est de nature privée ou professionnelle.

On constate tout d'abord que l'utilisation est plus fréquente parmi les hommes (57 % d'utilisateurs) que chez les femmes (37 %).

Les classes d'âge sont aussi différemment représentées parmi les utilisateurs: si près des trois quarts (70 %) des jeunes de 30 ans et moins utilisent Internet, cette proportion décroît rapidement avec l'âge pour devenir très marginale chez les plus âgés (3 % des personnes de 70 ans et plus). Le niveau de formation a encore une influence: 67 % des répondants ayant accompli une formation supérieure utilisent Internet, contre 40 % des personnes avec un apprentissage ou une formation professionnelle et 34 % de celles avec un niveau de formation plus bas. On assiste aussi à une nette sur-représentation des actifs (60 %) et des étudiants (74 %), au contraire des personnes au foyer (24 %) et des rentiers (10 %).

Malgré des bases de calcul différentes, nos résultats sont très similaires à ceux de l'enquête REMP menée à la même époque (octobre 2000 – mars 2001), qui constitue un excellent standard de comparaison (environ 12 000 personnes interrogées); ainsi, nos 47 % d'utilisateurs se comparent aux 52 % de personnes s'étant connectés à Internet durant les 6 mois précédant l'enquête REMP, tandis que la distribution selon le genre et l'âge sont quasiment

4 7071 répondants. La première vague comptait 7 799 répondants.

Tableau 1: Profil des utilisateurs, fin 2000 – % d'utilisateurs et d'utilisateurs assidus dans les sous-groupes

	Tous les utilisateurs	Utilisateurs assidus (> = 14 h/semaine)
n	3285	175
% d'utilisateurs	47 %	2,5 %
Sexe	V de Cramer de ,19, p < ,001	V de Cramer de ,10, p < ,001
hommes	57 %	4 %
femmes	37 %	1 %
Age	V de Cramer de ,40, p < ,001	V de Cramer de ,08, p < ,001
moins de 31 ans	70 %	3 %
31 à 50 ans	54 %	3 %
51 à 70 ans	30 %	1 %
plus de 70 ans	3 %	0 %
Niveau de formation	V de Cramer de ,28, p < ,001	V de Cramer de ,10, p < ,001
formation obligatoire	34 %	1 %
formation professionnelle	40 %	2 %
formation supérieure	67 %	5 %
Occupation	V de Cramer de ,43, p < ,001	V de Cramer de ,11, p < ,001
travail à plein temps	60 %	4 %
en formation	74 %	2 %
au foyer	24 %	1 %
retraité	10 %	1 %
Etat-civil	V de Cramer de ,30, p < ,001	V de Cramer de ,07, p < ,001
célibataire	66 %	4 %

identiques. Ceci montre que le mode d'échantillonnage spécifique du panel (sélection de tous les membres du ménage, engagement d'une participation de long-terme à l'étude) ne péjore pas la représentativité des données.

Retournons sur les données du panel pour nous concentrer sur les plus gros utilisateurs d'Internet en l'an 2000, les personnes se connectant au moins quatorze heures par semaine (2 h./jour, y compris le week-end). L'analyse met en évidence le fait que l'on retrouve en plus accentuées certaines caractéristiques des utilisateurs toute intensité comprise: plus d'hommes et encore plus de personnes avec une formation supérieure et professionnellement actives à plein temps, mais aussi plus de personnes entre 30 et 50 ans, qui utilisent vraisemblablement[5] Internet aussi professionnellement.

On remarque donc dans les attributs des utilisateurs d'Internet, et particulièrement chez les utilisateurs les plus assidus, les caractéristiques d'un groupe relativement bien défini socialement (dominante masculine, niveau de formation élevé, jeune âge, actif ou aux études); nous verrons plus loin ce qu'il en est dans le temps, vu la diffusion rapide de ce média.

Services utilisés

Toujours avec les données du panel de 2e vague (fin 2000 – début 2001), la recherche d'informations précises est l'activité la plus répandue (96 %), un tiers des utilisateurs ayant affirmé utiliser Internet pour ce motif au moins une fois par jour, ce qui renvoie à l'appellation couramment utilisée «d'autoroute de l'information» du réseau.

Un autre aspect spécifique est la potentialité d'Internet en terme de communication: 84 % des répondants qui accèdent au réseau échangent des e-mails privés (37 % avec une fréquence journalière), 55 % échangent du courrier électronique professionnel (39 % quotidiennement) et, en considérant les deux types de courrier, 92 % des personnes ayant accès au Net expédient et reçoivent des messages électroniques.

Le Web est aussi utilisé pour se divertir (64 % des utilisateurs, 13 % chaque jour) et pour lire des journaux et des revues online (50 %, 12 % au moins une fois par jour)[6]. A ce propos, on remarque qu'en Suisse, selon Baromedia (2002), la lecture de la presse quotidienne sur papier est passée de 70 % en 1997 à 59 % en 2002, ce qui n'est peut-être pas étranger à la consultation des journaux online.

Finalement, l'utilisation d'Internet pour effectuer des paiements, des transactions et des achats est moins fréquente (32 % des personnes accédant au Net).

5 La deuxième vague du PSM ne faisait plus le détail du temps d'utilisation entre la semaine et le week-end.

6 Comme point de comparaison, selon les données REMP, calculées sur la base des utilisateurs réguliers (plusieurs fois par semaine), 45 % lisent des journaux ou des périodiques online, 29 % utilisent Internet pour le trafic électronique de paiements, 24 % pour consulter des petites annonces et 21 % pour effectuer des achats. Ces chiffres sont encore une fois très similaires à ceux du panel.

Internet ne connaît toutefois pas un usage homogène: les caractéristiques socio-démographiques des utilisateurs sont plus ou moins liées avec et expliquent avec plus ou moins de force la fréquence des différents types d'usages d'Internet, comme le montrent les régressions multiples du tableau 2.

Tableau 2: Explication de la fréquence des différents types d'usages d'Internet à la fin 2000 chez les utilisateurs interrogés par le PSM – Régressions multiples – coefficients de régression standardisés Beta et R2 ajusté – n= 3250 au maximum

	Information	Achats, paiements	Lecture journaux	Divertissement	Courrier privé	Courrier professionnel
Age	n.s.	n.s.	n.s.	–,29***	–,14***	n.s.
Sexe (fém.)	–,21***	–,08***	–,11***	–,12***	n.s.	–,10***
Formation	,08***	,06***	,08***	–,12***	,10***	,18***
Débutant	–,17***	–,23***	–,16***	–,13***	–,29***	–,11***
Actif	,09***	,08***	n.s.	n.s.	–,04*	,37***
R2 ajusté	,12***	,09***	,05***	,15***	,16***	,27***

n.s. non significatif, * p. < ,05, ** p. < ,01, *** p. < ,001

L'âge influence très fortement l'usage récréatif: plus les personnes sont jeunes, plus elles utilisent Internet pour s'amuser et se divertir. De même, mais dans une moindre mesure, pour le courrier électronique privé, qui est généralement d'ordre récréatif ou convivial. Par rapport aux autres types d'usages, l'âge ne ressort pas comme un élément discriminant.

Les femmes font généralement un usage moins intensif d'Internet que les hommes, sauf pour le courrier privé où il n'y a pas de différences liées au sexe.

Les personnes avec un niveau de formation élevé utilisent plus Internet dans presque tous les types d'utilisation. L'exception est notable: concernant l'usage récréatif, c'est le contraire qui prévaut, avec une utilisation plus fréquente au fur et à mesure que le niveau de formation baisse.

Le fait d'être actif professionnellement influence naturellement fortement l'envoi de courrier professionnel, mais n'a pas d'impact dans les autres types d'utilisation.

Finalement, l'utilisation des données longitudinales permet de mettre en évidence le fait que la fréquence d'utilisation d'Internet a tendance à augmenter dans le temps, et ceci dans tous les domaines; en effet, les personnes commençant à l'utiliser seulement en 2ᵉ vague du panel montrent toujours un usage moins fréquent que celles déjà connectées en première vague.

Une analyse factorielle exploratoire[7] confirme ces impressions en mettant à jour deux dimensions principales parmi les six types d'usages d'Internet du tableau 2; une dimension «utilitaire», surtout liée au courrier professionnel, à l'information et aux transactions, et une «ludique», corrélée avec le divertissement, le courrier électronique privé et la lecture des journaux. Le fait que cette dernière activité soit associée à un divertissement plutôt qu'à un outil de travail peut étonner à première vue; il ne faut toutefois oublier que la lecture de journaux online est relativement peu commode à l'écran et que les sites ne mettent à disposition qu'une partie, le plus souvent restreinte, du contenu rédactionnel, de sorte que le support informatique se prête plutôt mal à une lecture exhaustive de la presse. N'oublions pas en outre que dans la lecture des journaux, tant online que sur papier, les rubriques les plus lues sont les chroniques sportives, les faits divers et la météo (Pew, 2000), ce qui s'apparente plus à une activité ludique qu'utilitaire.

L'analyse basée sur les dimensions de cette analyse factorielle confirme que le niveau de formation et l'insertion professionnelle sont très liés positivement à un usage utilitaire, alors qu'ils sont liés négativement à un usage ludique.

On constate un résultat similaire avec l'âge, les personnes d'un certain âge faisant un usage plus utilitaire d'Internet, tandis que les jeunes l'utilisent essentiellement pour se divertir. Les femmes ont une utilisation moins intense dans les deux registres de même que les personnes ayant commencé à utiliser Internet plus récemment.

7 Rotation orthogonale varimax, eigenvalues supérieures à 1, KMO de ,69, 54 % de variance expliquée.

Comparaisons régionales

Pour effectuer nos comparaisons inter-régionales en Suisse, nous avons utilisé des données relatives à la langue d'interview et à la région de résidence (7 régions statistiques, selon la définition de l'OFS).

L'utilisation d'Internet est significativement plus répandue parmi les répondants de langue allemande (50 % d'utilisateurs) que chez les francophones (42 %) et surtout les italophones (32 %). Même constatation avec la région de résidence: de manière générale, en Suisse allemande et en Suisse centrale, Internet a plus d'émules qu'en Suisse romande, et surtout qu'en Suisse italienne[8], résultat qui reste valable sous contrôle du niveau de formation, de l'occupation, et de l'âge. Dans la région de Zurich (54 %) et les régions industrialisées du Nord-Ouest de la Suisse allemande (51 %) l'usage d'Internet est le plus répandu. Entre les régions suisses on ne constate pas de différences concernant le sexe, l'âge et le niveau de formation des utilisateurs.

Si l'usage d'Internet est moins répandu chez les latins, ces derniers, quand ils l'utilisent, le font plus longtemps que les alémaniques (en moyenne 261 minutes par semaine pour les répondants de langue française, 264 chez ceux de langue italienne et 205 pour ceux de langue allemande).

Comparaisons internationales

Les comparaisons internationales avec les pays de la CE et les Etats-Unis montrent que la Suisse est l'un des pays où l'utilisation d'Internet est largement répandue en l'an 2000.

Le pourcentage d'utilisateurs d'Internet en Suisse (47 %) est supérieur à la moyenne des Pays de la Communauté européenne où l'on compte 42 % d'utilisateurs (Gallup Europe 2000 N = 22 562). Bien évidemment la pénétration dans les Pays de la CE est très hétérogène, avec des pourcentages de plus de 60 % aux Pays Bas et en Scandinavie, de 44 % en Allemagne, 35 % en France, 33 % en Italie pour arriver à 19 % en Grèce.

En Suisse on se connecte plus depuis la maison (80 %, moyenne européenne 57 %) et au travail (51 %, moyenne européenne 40 %), par contre

8 La différence entre Tessinois et Suisses romands est à la limite de la significativité, en raison du nombre plus limité d'interviews.

l'accès à l'école (17 %) est légèrement au-dessous de la moyenne européenne (21 %). Le temps de connexion hebdomadaire est de 5,4 heures par semaine en moyenne dans la Communauté européenne (6,1 en Allemagne, 4,6 en Italie et 4,1 en France) chez les utilisateurs, ce qui est supérieur aux chiffres dont nous disposons pour la Suisse (3,7 heures). Dans les autres pays européens, les hommes constituent aussi la majorité des utilisateurs (56 %) dans une proportion semblable à celle en Suisse, de même que les jeunes (61 % des personnes entre 15-24 ans ont accès au réseau contre 11 % de celles de 55 ans et plus).

Les chiffres concernant l'utilisation sont plus difficilement comparables, car des bases de données différentes sont considérées. Durant les trois mois précédant l'enquête, 31 % des européens de la CE affirment avoir déjà fait des achats via Internet (proportion plus élevée qu'en Suisse selon les données REMP). 31 % des utilisateurs européens lisent online des journaux nationaux (48 % en Finlande, 43 % en Espagne, 25 % en Allemagne), significativement moins qu'en Suisse (50 %) et un quart (29 % des Suisses selon les données REMP) a effectué des opérations sur son compte bancaire à travers Internet.

Outre Atlantique, l'utilisation d'Internet est plus développée et les inégalités dans l'utilisation relatives à l'âge et au sexe ne sont pas constatées. Ainsi, aux Etats-Unis en 2001 (U.S. Department of commerce, 2002) 65 % des personnes entre 9 et 49 ans utilisaient Internet (sans différences relevantes parmi les groupes d'âge), et 37 % de celles de 50 ans et plus. Les femmes constituent le 51 % des utilisateurs. Aux USA aussi, l'activité la plus fréquente est le courrier électronique (84 % des utilisateurs), suivie par la recherche d'information sur un produit ou un service spécifique (67 %) et par la lecture de news, d'un bulletin météo ou de résultats de sport (62 %). Les achats online sont effectués par 39 % des internautes américains, le online banking par 18 % et la recherche d'un emploi en utilisant le Web par 9 %.

Les différences dans la diffusion d'Internet entre les pays sont souvent expliquées par des facteurs économiques, tels que le PIB (produit intérieur brut), la disponibilité en infrastructures, les prix et la structure du marché, mais pour rendre compte des inégalités, un autre élément explicatif est l'aspect culturel (Goodmann, Press, Ruth et Rutkowski, 1994; Maitland, 1998). En effet, la diffusion d'instruments nouveaux dépend largement de leur perception par les utilisateurs potentiels. La première dimension qui a été relevée est l'évitement de l'incertitude: dans les sociétés où l'accent est mis sur la réussite plus que sur la sécurité et l'évitement de l'incertitude est peu présent, les nouvelles idées sont non seulement tolérées mais considérées comme intéressantes et donc plus facilement adoptées. Un autre aspect est celui de l'égalité entre hommes et femmes: les pays à tendance plus égalitaires paraissent plus ouverts à la nouveauté car ils sont en mesure d'exploiter les potentialités d'un nombre plus élargi de population. L'effet de ces éléments culturels sur la diffusion d'Internet dans les différentes nations a été analysé (Maitland et Bauer, 1999) en le comparant avec le poids des variables économiques et d'infrastructure[9]: les résultats sur 28 pays montrent que les trois variables les plus fortement corrélées à la croissance nationale d'Internet sont le nombre de PC, l'égalité entre hommes et femmes (qui a un impact positif) et le score d'évitement de l'incertitude (qui a une influence négative). Ces éléments sont à notre avis susceptibles d'expliquer aussi la diffusion différente d'Internet dans les différentes parties de la Suisse.

Evolution de l'utilisation d'Internet en Suisse

La diffusion d'Internet a été considérable durant ces dernières années. Les données transversales des 1ère et 2e vagues du PSM (figure 2) montrent un accroissement rapide des utilisateurs qui sont passés en une année de 27 % à 47 % de la population, avec une augmentation numérique plus importante des femmes, bien que les hommes soient encore légèrement majoritaires.

En construisant une typologie des utilisateurs sur la base de l'échantillon longitudinal ayant pris part aux deux vagues du panel en automne – hiver 1999-2000 et en automne – hiver 2000-2001[10], 54 % des répondants n'utilisaient pas Internet tant en 1999 qu'en 2000, 25 % l'utilisaient durant les deux vagues, 1 % ont stoppé toute utilisation, tandis que 19 % ont commencé. Ceci signifie qu'une fois adopté, très peu de personnes y renoncent, en tout cas sur le court terme, tandis que l'on assiste à une augmentation relative de 73 % du pourcentage d'utilisateurs entre les deux vagues.

9 L'évitement de l'incertitude à été mesuré avec le UAI (Uncertainty Avoidance Score, Hofstede, 1995) et l'égalité avec le Gender Empowerment' Score (UNDP).

10 L'échantillon longitudinal du PSM est composé de 6335 personnes ayant complété un questionnaire individuel durant les deux premières vagues. Les membres de cet échantillon longitudinal sont représentatifs des échantillons de la première et de la deuxième vague en ce qui concerne les habitudes d'utilisation d'Internet et représentent donc une bonne base pour l'étude des changements dans son utilisation en Suisse.

Figure 2: Intensité hebdomadaire de l'utilisation (1999 N=7799, 2000 N=7071)

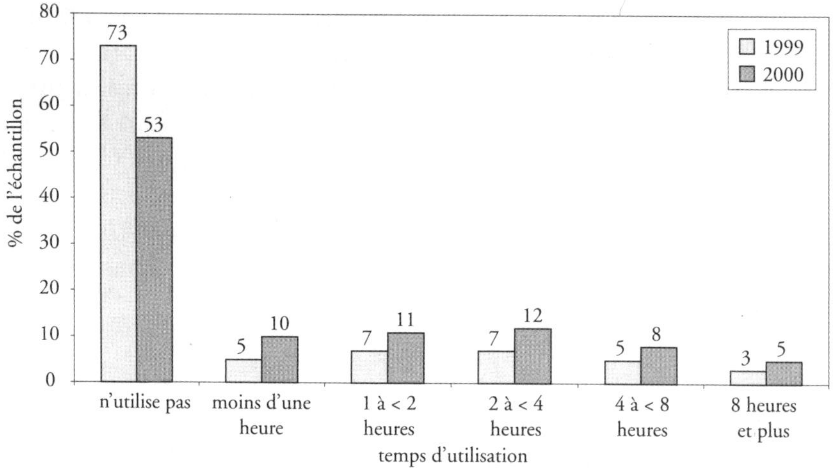

Les italophones, qui étaient déjà moins nombreux à utiliser Internet en 1999 (68 % ne l'utilisaient pas en 1999 contre 58 % des francophones et 52 % des germanophones), ont été aussi moins nombreux à commencer à l'utiliser au cours de l'année suivante (12 % contre 16 % et 21 %). Mêmes constatations pour les régions, Internet s'étant diffusé moins vite au Tessin que dans le reste de la Suisse, et surtout la Suisse allemande.

Les femmes sont nettement sur-représentées parmi les nouveaux utilisateurs par rapport aux anciens. Concernant l'âge, les nouveaux utilisateurs sont légèrement plus âgés que les anciens (39 ans en moyenne contre 37) et par rapport au niveau de formation, celui des nouveaux arrivants est plus bas. C'est un aspect de l'élargissement de la diffusion du nouveau média, qui était essentiellement masculin et réservé aux élites cultivées il y a quelques années, et qui dans tous les pays occidentaux s'étend à des couches plus larges de la société.

Les personnes qui arrêtent l'utilisation ne se distinguent de celles qui continuent que par le niveau de formation, les personnes ayant conclu leur formation par l'école obligatoire, un apprentissage ou une formation professionnelle ayant trois fois plus tendance à abandonner que celles avec une formation supérieure, et par le fait de ne pas avoir d'accès depuis la maison.

Figure 3: Utilisation d'Internet au moins une fois par jour

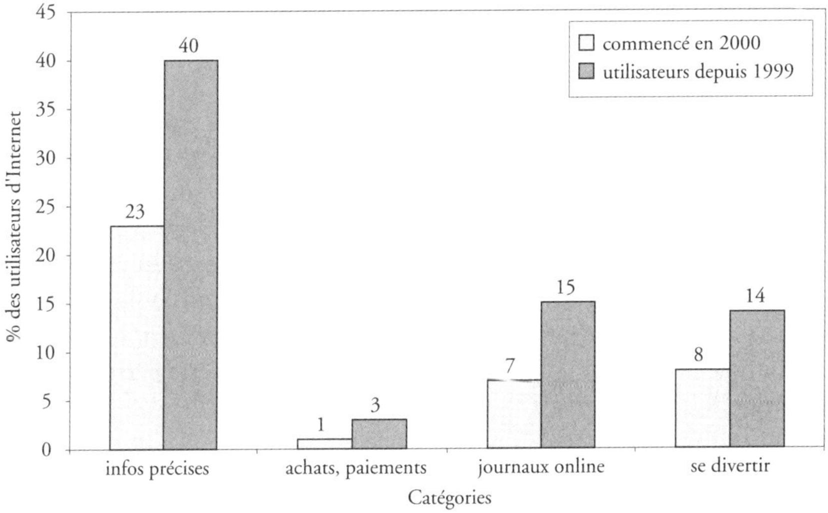

Figure 4: N'utilisant jamais Internet dans ce but

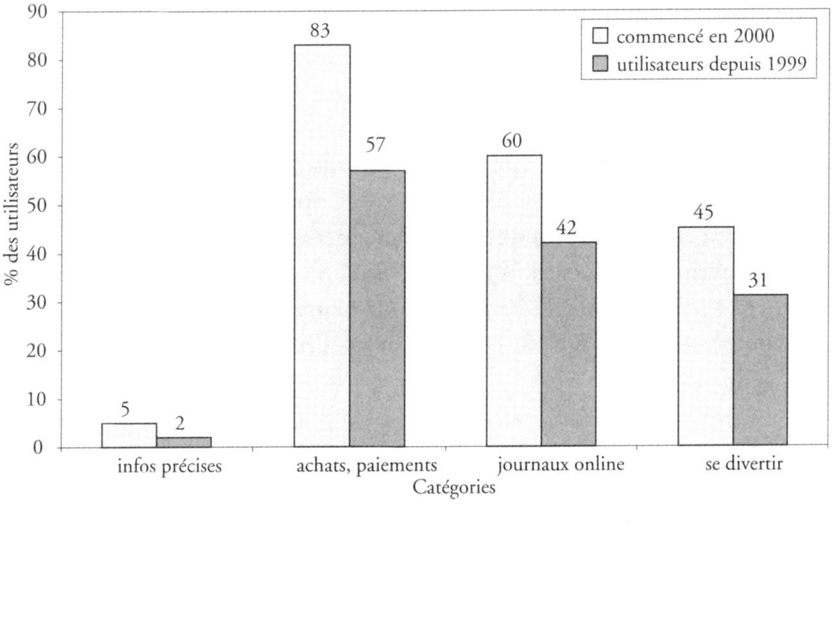

Globalement, les personnes qui ont utilisé Internet durant les deux vagues ont plutôt tendance à augmenter leur temps de connexion (52 %, contre 44 % de diminution et 4 % de stabilité, leur moyenne hebdomadaire passant de 218 minutes à 263 minutes), vraisemblablement en raison de l'habitude, et de la découverte de nouvelles possibilités.

La recherche d'informations précises, la lecture de journaux, l'utilisation du courrier électronique privé ou professionnel et l'usage de divertissement deviennent plus fréquents au fur et à mesure de l'ancienneté de l'utilisation (figures 3 et 4), ce que nous avions déjà constaté dans le tableau 2. Le retard de la part des nouveaux utilisateurs est plus marqué pour les transactions et les paiements, qui demandent une certaine habileté, mais aussi pour le courrier électronique privé, dont les avantages ne deviennent peut-être patents qu'avec l'habitude.

Changements dans la vie privée et professionnelle

Un des buts principaux de notre recherche était de mettre à jour les relations entre l'utilisation de ce nouveau système de télécommunication et les différents aspects de la vie des personnes, concernant le contexte familial, le réseau social, les loisirs, l'utilisation des autres médias, la situation et les conditions de travail, et les débouchés professionnels. Etant donné qu'à priori l'utilisation d'Internet durant la semaine sur le lieu de travail ne peut avoir que des conséquences limitées sur la vie privée et que la deuxième vague du panel ne collecte pas d'informations sur le moment de la connexion, nous nous sommes concentrés sur les utilisateurs assidus du week-end de la première vague (plus d'une heure par jour durant le week-end). A la fin 1999, 81 % des répondants n'utilisaient pas Internet le week-end, 17 % jusqu'à une heure par jour et seulement 2 % passaient plus d'une heure par jour sur Internet pendant le week-end[11].

11 Des analyses subséquentes montrent que les personnes non connectées en fin de semaine utilisent en moyenne Internet 3 minutes pendant les jours ouvrables, celles qui se connectent jusqu'à une heure par jour pendant le week-end y consacrent 28 minutes quotidiennement en semaine, tandis que les «utilisateurs assidus du week-end» le font en moyenne une heure et demie par jour. Ceci montre que les utilisateurs réguliers durant le week-end sont pour la plupart aussi des personnes utilisant Internet assidûment durant la semaine, tandis que le contraire n'est pas forcément vrai.

Ces utilisateurs assidus durant le week-end se révèlent être surtout des hommes jeunes, célibataires, vivant seuls, actifs à plein-temps ou étudiants. On compte aussi dans ce groupe une légère sur-représentation des étrangers et des enfants de personnes d'origine étrangère.

Tableau 3: Profil des utilisateurs assidus durant le week-end, en 1999 (> 1 h./jour)

n	185	
% d'utilisateurs assidus durant le W.-E.	2,4 %	
Sexe		V de Cramer de ,09, p < ,001
hommes	4 %	
femmes	1 %	
Age		V de Cramer de ,12, p < ,001
moins de 31 ans	5 %	
31 à 50 ans	2 %	
51 à 70 ans	1 %	
plus de 70 ans	0 %	
Occupation		V de Cramer de ,13, p < ,001
travail à plein temps	3 %	
en formation	7 %	
au foyer	0 %	
retraité	1 %	
Etat-civil		V de Cramer de ,10, p < ,001
célibataire	5 %	
Nationalité		V de Cramer de ,03, p < ,001
étrangère	3 %	

Concernant certains aspects de leurs opinions politiques, il s'agit de personnes qui s'intéressent moins à la politique, sont plus souvent antimilitaristes, favorables à l'intégration européenne, à la protection de l'environnement, ceci sous contrôle des principales variables socio-démographiques, notamment l'âge, le sexe, la nationalité, l'intégration professionnelle.

Les données du PSM, confirmées par différentes études internationales (Pew, 2000; Hampton, 2001; Kraut et al., 2002; UCLA, 2003), montrent que les utilisateurs assidus ont plus de contacts sociaux et voient plus souvent leurs amis (relations significatives sous contrôle du sexe, de l'âge et de l'activité professionnelle). Ceci ne signifie toutefois pas qu'Internet a provoqué cette augmentation des contacts sociaux. L'hypothèse la plus plausible est que ces utilisateurs assidus ont un mode de vie qui comprend une fréquence accrue des contacts sociaux, auquel l'usage d'Internet peut éventuellement contribuer, de par sa facilité d'emploi et son côté «branché». Rappelons que leur profil assez spécifique (jeunes hommes célibataires, bien formés, actifs, etc.) va dans le sens de cette explication.

Une augmentation du temps passé sur Internet n'est pas liée à des changements concernant les relations familiales (mésentente sur les aspects financiers, sur les idées, sur le partage des travaux domestiques, sur les projets de vie et l'éducation des enfants, sur l'aide et le soutien apportés par le réseau social, sur la satisfaction de la vie en famille), ni à des changements par rapport aux activités de loisirs, ni même à la satisfaction envers sa vie privée. Seul le fait d'avoir récemment eu des conflits graves avec ou entre ses proche est lié à une augmentation de l'intensité d'utilisation, Internet servant alors peut-être de refuge pour échapper à une réalité difficile.

Concernant la consommation de médias traditionnels, les données du PSM montrent que non seulement les utilisateurs habituels d'Internet sont des consommateurs plus assidus de radio et télévision, mais encore qu'une augmentation du temps de connexion ne diminue pas le temps dédié à ces médias, résultats confortés par des données internationales (Robinson, Barth et Kohut, 1997; UCLA, 2003; Huber et al., 2002).

Pour le reste, les résultats de nos analyses multivariées montrent que les utilisateurs assidus d'Internet ne se différencient pas significativement des autres catégories de personnes sur les différents aspects des loisirs, de la santé et de la vie sociale, conclusion similaire à celle d'une recherche de UCLA (2001), menée auprès de plus de 2000 ménages aux USA. De même, les changements dans la durée hebdomadaire d'utilisation d'Internet entre 1999 et 2000, indépendamment du lieu d'où l'on se connecte (à la maison, au travail ou ailleurs), ne sont pas significativement liés à des changements dans les activités de loisirs (satisfaction dans les loisirs, type et fréquence des activités), ce qui signifie qu'une personne augmentant son utilisation d'Internet, qu'elle soit un «ancien» ou un «nouveau» utilisateur, ne semble pas plus qu'une autre renoncer à d'autres types de loisirs ou changer significativement ses habitudes dans ce domaine.

Les utilisateurs assidus ne se distinguent pas particulièrement quant à leur activité professionnelle et à d'autres aspects y-relatifs, comme la satisfaction qu'ils en retirent. Tout au plus, ils font nettement plus d'heures supplémentaires que les non-utilisateurs mais moins que les utilisateurs moyens, et ont très souvent une connexion électronique avec leur employeur (63 %, contre 30 % en moyenne).

L'augmentation de l'utilisation d'Internet d'une année à l'autre, même nette, ne semble non plus s'accompagner de changements notables dans les habitudes de la vie privée et professionnelle des répondants. En fait, il est probable que les effets de l'utilisation soient importants chez les très gros utilisateurs, mais ces cas sont encore trop marginaux dans les données du PSM pour donner lieu à des analyses spécifiques.

Comme point de comparaison, on signalera toutefois que les trois quarts des répondants à une importante[12] enquête européenne menée au printemps 2000 sur les impacts de l'utilisation d'Internet ont affirmé que leur activité online les a amenés à réduire le temps dédié à la télévision; presque la moitié de ces utilisateurs européens disent avoir aussi soustrait du temps à la lecture de livres, tandis que, concernant les rapports sociaux, Internet aurait eu des effets négatifs sur le temps passé avec la famille (environ 30 % des cas) et les amis (24 %, avec d'importantes variations selon les pays).

Un résultat similaire était ressorti de notre enquête online, avec une diminution déclarée du temps consacré au temps de sommeil, aux médias traditionnels, aux loisirs, mais aussi dans une moindre mesure à la famille et aux amis chez les utilisateurs d'Internet interrogés (Molo-Bettelini, Alippi et Wernli, 2001a). Si une telle diminution n'était pas du tout perceptible pour 80 % des personnes se connectant moins de 2 heures par semaine, l'impact se faisait rapidement sentir au fur et à mesure de l'augmentation de l'usage, et ceci surtout pour les médias traditionnels et les heures de sommeil. Ainsi, pour une utilisation de 4 à 7 heures par semaine, 56 % des répondants disaient diminuer le temps consacré à la radio et la télévision, 35 % le temps de sommeil, 23 % celui dédié à la lecture de livres. Le temps dédié à la famille (14 % des répondants utilisant Internet 4 à 7 heures par semaine), aux amis (8 %) et aux sports et loisirs (12 %) baissait lui de manière moins brutale.

12 Echantillon de 16 000 personnes représentatives de la population âgée de 15 ans et plus des pays de la Communauté Européenne (European Commission 2000). La question de l'impact de l'utilisation sur le budget temps a été posée ici directement et n'est pas le résultat de confrontations et d'analyses comme dans notre étude.

Différences liées au genre

Les femmes rattrapent rapidement le retard qu'elles accusaient, avec une augmentation particulièrement rapide du nombre d'utilisatrices. A la fin de l'an 2000 les femmes représentaient le 45 % des utilisateurs, avec une augmentation de 10 % en une année. Cette réduction de l'écart laisse toutefois ouvertes des questions sur les éventuelles différences dans la façon d'utiliser le réseau. On remarque avec les données de la seconde vague du PSM une différence importante au niveau du temps d'utilisation (moyenne hebdomadaire de 4 h. 26 min. pour les hommes, et de 2 h. 31 min. pour les femmes). Les diversités entre les deux sexes concernant les choix de formation et d'activité professionnelle, les intérêts, le temps libre et le temps dédié aux travaux ménagers et au soin de la famille, peuvent sûrement expliquer en bonne partie cette disparité. En détaillant l'usage d'Internet en 2e vague du panel, nous avions noté en outre que la plupart des services sont plus utilisés par les hommes (sous contrôle des autres variables socio-démographiques et de l'intensité d'utilisation).

Selon plusieurs études (par exemple Weiser, 2000), entre autres notre recherche online effectuée au Tessin en 1999 (Molo-Bettelini et al. 2001), une différence particulièrement significative apparaît dans la participation aux listes de discussion[13], alors que pour d'autres activités telles que les chat-lines, la navigation, ou l'utilisation privée du courrier électronique, on ne recense aucune différence. Toujours selon les données de cette enquête online, confirmées par celles du PSM, les hommes effectuent plus de transactions financières et plus d'achats à travers Internet, et ils affirment plus fréquemment n'avoir pas de réticences envers ce type d'achat. Les femmes, plus méfiantes, sont proportionnellement plus nombreuses à prétendre ne vouloir rien acheter, même dans le futur, par ce moyen. Les motifs que les personnes citent pour justifier leur accès au réseau sont les mêmes (recherche d'informations, contacts, travail), sauf que les hommes affirment plus souvent utiliser Internet pour s'amuser.

13 Plusieurs recherches (Peterson, 1994; Cook et Stambaugh, 1997; Herring, 2000; King, 2000) ont montré que même lorsque les femmes sont présentes dans ces groupes, elles expédient beaucoup moins de messages. La raison de cette réticence semble être, selon les hommes comme les femmes interviewés à ce sujet, l'intimidation qu'on peut subir dans ces discussions et la différence de réaction aux agressions verbales, les hommes les acceptant comme un aspect normal de la discussion alors que les femmes ressentiraient une profonde aversion envers ce mode de communication.

Les opinions à l'égard de ce nouveau moyen de télécommunication constituaient aussi un pan privilégié de notre précédente enquête online; si nos résultats ont montré un ample consensus quant aux avantages perçus d'Internet, certains aspects semblent préoccuper de façon inégale[14] hommes et femmes. Les femmes mettent plus l'accent sur les risques induits par la consommation passive d'informations, sur le modèle de l'utilisation de la télévision, les hommes sur l'efficacité et l'utilité. En outre, les femmes se disent plus convaincues de la nécessité d'une censure à propos de certains contenus, indépendamment de la présence dans leur foyer d'enfants ou d'adolescents[15].

Les différentes façons d'utiliser et de concevoir ces nouveaux médias, n'impliquent pas un obstacle à leur appropriation. En effet, selon les résultats de notre enquête online, hommes et femmes, à parité d'âge et de formation, ne présentent aucune différence au niveau de la connaissance d'Internet et de ses potentialités, ainsi que dans la facilité perçue d'adaptation à cet instrument et dans la création de nouveaux projets professionnels inspirés par l'utilisation du Web.

Discussion et conclusions

Nos résultats ont montré que les utilisateurs d'Internet en Suisse, toute intensité d'utilisation comprise, sont à la fin 2000 en majorité des jeunes hommes, avec un niveau de formation supérieure, actifs à plein temps ou en formation; parmi les personnes qui l'utilisent tous les jours au moins deux heures on constate une sur-représentation des hommes professionnellement actifs et plus âgés, alors que les utilisateurs habituels du week-end sont surtout des hommes plus jeunes, célibataires, professionnellement actifs ou étudiants. Avec le temps, l'intensité d'utilisation augmente, et là aussi ce sont les hommes qui utilisent Internet plus longtemps. Une année après, on compte toutefois parmi les nouveaux utilisateurs un nombre élevé de femmes, de personnes moins jeunes et avec un niveau de formation plus bas, phénomène qui se produit de façon similaire aussi dans les autres pays.

14 Différences significatives en contrôlant les autres variables socio-démographiques, l'intensité d'utilisation et l'expérience sur le réseau.

15 Certaines études ont associé cette opinion au fait que les hommes semblent reconnaître une valeur plus élevée à la liberté d'expression, même si elle est agressive (Morahan-Martin, 1998; Herring, 2000).

Il est donc intéressant de constater que d'un côté Internet semble se «démocratiser» et toucher un nombre plus élargi et des couches plus amples de population, ce qui confirme la première partie de notre hypothèse; mais, d'autre part, les utilisateurs plus assidus montrent nettement des caractéristiques différentes et spécifiques qui en font des groupes assez homogènes, ainsi que d'autres données internationales le confirment (UCLA, 2003); parallèlement, un usage plus intense et plus expérimenté, porte à une utilisation en partie différente avec une meilleure exploitation des potentialités offertes et plus de services consultés.

La recherche d'informations est l'objectif principal de la grande majorité des personnes, de façon croissante pour les plus expérimentées et les plus formées, qui utilisent aussi plus le médium pour la lecture de journaux online, les achats et les transactions et le courrier électronique. Par rapport aux différentes utilisations nos analyses montrent des différences significatives aussi selon le sexe, l'âge et le fait d'être professionnellement actif. Ceci confirme l'hypothèse que non seulement l'intensité mais aussi les buts de l'utilisation de ces technologies dépendent de certaines caractéristiques des usagers.

Les services les plus utilisés sont le courrier électronique et tout particulièrement pour des raisons privées (plus de 60 % de la population connectée l'utilisant au moins une fois par semaine). Face à cette réalité, un sujet qui devrait être approfondi est celui de savoir si, par rapport à la communication privée par téléphone, on assiste seulement à un changement de canal ou si une modification apparaît dans les habitudes, les modes et les contenus et la sémantique de la communication, à même d'engendrer certaines retombées aussi au niveau des relations sociales. D'autre part, l'énorme diffusion du téléphone portable et l'élargissement de ses potentialités pourraient substituer, avec les SMS et MMS dans la communication privée, une partie de la fonction de maintien et de renforcement des relations attribuée à la poste électronique (Boneva, Kraut et Frohlich, 2001), avec des aspects similaires par rapport à la communication qu'il serait intéressant d'approfondir.

Par contre la deuxième partie de notre postulat, relative aux changements dans les habitudes de la vie quotidienne des usagers liés à l'utilisation d'Internet, n'est en grande partie pas confirmée, ce qui contredit plusieurs thèses de la littérature. Le manque de relations entre plusieurs aspects de la vie privée et professionnelle et l'utilisation, même assez intensive, d'Internet n'exclut pas le fait que des changements se produisent, mais plus au niveau de la façon de faire les choses, dans la manière de chercher les informations, dans la façon de communiquer, qu'en rapport à des impacts plus généraux concernant les habitudes de vie. Ceci nous pousse à esquisser une explication.

Tout d'abord on pourrait penser qu'une année de follow-up est insuffisante pour percevoir des changements importants. A ce propos, l'enquête longitudinale HomeNet Project (Kraut et al., 1998 et 2002) montre que les changements liés à l'utilisation d'Internet sont très différents après une année et après plusieurs années d'observation, notamment à cause du fait que l'environnement d'Internet change dans le temps, avec plus de services potentiellement utilisables et plus de personnes connectées.

Mais la thématique est probablement plus complexe. Plusieurs recherches (European Commission, 2000; Huber et al., 2002; Molo-Bettelini, Alippi et Wernli, 2001a) utilisant des indicateurs subjectifs (questions posées directement à l'interviewé dans le but de savoir à quelles activités il a soustrait le temps dédié à Internet) ont montré que les individus perçoivent des impacts dus à une utilisation régulière d'Internet, et ceci à plusieurs niveaux de leur vie privée et professionnelle. Par contre, les données du panel et d'autres recherches basées sur des critères objectifs ne montrent pas de variations patentes dans ces mêmes activités. Une explication pourrait venir du fait que les indicateurs objectifs sont construits à partir des réponses données séparément aux différents items, réponses qui, sur un sujet comme «le temps qu'on dédie en moyenne à...» sont nécessairement approximatives; vu que les variations attendues dues à l'impact de l'utilisation d'Internet ne sont à priori pas spectaculaires, de par le fait aussi que les utilisateurs très intensifs sont en nombre très limité, ces approximations pourraient en partie estomper les différences.

D'autre part, il a aussi été montré que dans plusieurs domaines tels que l'utilisation des médias traditionnels, certaines activités de loisir et relatives au travail, l'usage des nouveaux médias est plutôt complémentaire que substitutif. Concernant le temps, il a aussi été remarqué que l'utilisation d'Internet remplit certains temps morts (Gershuny, 2002).

Mais, plus fondamentalement, peut-on parler d'impacts généraux d'Internet sur l'individu? Les techniques n'existent pas indépendamment des personnes et de l'utilisation qu'elles en font. Notre société est une société technique au point qu'il est difficile d'opérer une distinction entre société, culture et technique. Ainsi, le rapport entre la technologie, qui produirait des impacts, et la société et les individus, qui en subiraient les effets, n'est pas causal et unidimensionnel, mais il s'agit d'une relation complexe entre un grand nombre d'individus qui pensent et utilisent de façons différentes les techniques, avec des implications sociales qui peuvent varier selon une multiplicité de facteurs.

Les techniques, en tant que produits d'une société donnée, ouvrent certaines possibilités qui peuvent être ou ne pas être développées par les individus. Elles ne sont pas déterminantes (Lévy, 1999), mais elles peuvent fournir des potentialités de changement culturel et social selon une condition d'interprétation individuelle. Il est clair que nous ne sommes pas complètement libres face aux techniques et que certains modes d'usage sont imposés par la société et par la machine; toutefois, les caractéristiques du réseau, l'interactivité, la logique en réseau, la possibilité d'agir sur l'information, sont à même de donner de larges marges d'autonomie où des idées et des projets peuvent naître. Il s'agit donc moins d'évaluer des impacts globaux, mais d'essayer de comprendre les conditions dans lesquelles ces technologies permettent de voir et de saisir des opportunités et rendre possibles des projets, qui dérivent d'une utilisation et d'une appropriation réussie du moyen.

Souvent les analyses ne considèrent pas suffisamment le contexte des utilisateurs, leurs caractéristiques et les différents modes d'usage. En effet, il est utile de différencier les modes d'utilisation d'Internet selon le niveau d'implication et d'interactivité. L'utilisation peut se faire dans une relation unidimensionnelle avec la machine, où l'utilisateur est dans une condition de réceptivité directe et sans discrimination avec le moyen (Maragliano, Martini et Penge, 1994), une relation bidimensionnelle, qui implique une réceptivité active et sélective où la personne recourt à l'élaboration volontaire en posant des questions et en organisant des stratégies de réponse, et une modalité d'appropriation tridimensionnelle de l'interactivité, où le sujet agit en modifiant l'objet de connaissance, il n'est pas seulement influencé mais il influence l'information. Les compétences nécessaires sont de type technique (modes d'usages), encyclopédique (questions qu'on pose à la technique, tirer des informations pertinentes) et liées à l'expérience (habitudes, possibilité de lier les informations aux expériences).

La limite principale du travail que nous présentons ici concerne justement cet aspect. S'agissant d'une exploitation secondaire des résultats de recherches existantes, nous avons dû baser nos analyses sur les données disponibles, qui ne permettent pas d'explorer de façon plus fine les modes d'utilisation d'Internet dans le but de mieux en vérifier facteurs d'influence et éventuels changements[16]. C'est-à-dire pour mieux comprendre pour quelles personnes et à quelles conditions les données véhiculées dans la toile deviennent des informations, et quelles significations les informations prennent (Döring, 1999) pour les personnes.

Car les thématiques fondamentales concernant l'utilisation de ces nouvelles technologies sont les transformations et les différences sociales qu'elles peuvent engendrer. Pour diminuer les différences d'opportunités, il est nécessaire de fournir aux personnes, notamment aux jeunes, les instruments qui peuvent contribuer à élargir leurs possibilités de trouver des solutions appropriées aux parcours souhaités. Concernant les nouvelles technologies de la communication, la question a été posée en termes d'égalité des citoyens par rapport à l'accès, ce qui implique l'extension des connexions physiques du réseau. Un problème ultérieur est celui des barrières culturelles inhérentes à cette technologie et l'apprentissage continu pour maîtriser les nouveautés et s'y adapter que certains usages comportent (Communauté d'étude pour l'aménagement du territoire, 1997). L'augmentation de la complexité et la vitesse des progrès ne facilitent pas pour tout le monde les possibilités de comprendre et de choisir. Différents types d'usage ne requièrent pas les mêmes niveaux de compétences.

L'aspect qui mérite une réflexion plus approfondie est de mieux comprendre qui, comment et à partir de quelles conditions sait s'approprier des progrès de ces techniques en termes de satisfaction de ses besoins cognitifs (d'information et de connaissance), affectifs, d'intégration personnelle et sociale et d'évasion (Cho et al., 2003). Comme aussi nos résultats l'ont montré, pour la plupart des utilisateurs du Net ne disposant pas d'un haut niveau de formation et d'expérience sur le réseau se connecter constitue une activité ludique sans autre implication. Pour ce qui concerne l'information, le risque est que devant les innombrables messages qui apparaissent à l'écran, la connaissance, qui implique une hiérarchie des informations accompagnée par l'attribution de sens, soit troquée contre de simples amas de données éparses et non structurées.

16 Dans le but de vérifier certains aspects du «Digital divide», lors de notre enquête online avec les jeunes ayant terminé l'université effectuée cette année dans le cadre du même projet faisant partie du PP «Demain la Suisse» nous avons développé de façon plus approfondie les thématiques des modes d'utilisation, certains facteurs personnels et quelques informations supplémentaires concernant le contexte, en reformulant en partie notre hypothèse, dans le sens que certaines caractéristiques individuelles (socio-démographiques, culturelles et psychologiques) sont prédictives de certains modes d'utilisation, et que ces deux domaines de facteurs coagissent avec des éléments du contexte dans une exploitation positive des potentialités d'Internet en termes de projets professionnels.

On parle souvent du fait que ces nouvelles technologies tendent à renforcer les différences entre le monde des utilisateurs et celui des autres personnes qui, pour des raisons diverses, ne les utilisent pas. Mais une division ultérieure, et probablement tout aussi marquée, apparaît par rapport aux modes d'appropriation des possibilités offertes par ces technologies; devenir des intéracteurs (Castells, 1996), et non seulement des intéragis, dépend de plusieurs facteurs parmi lesquels les plus importants sont l'expérience sur le réseau (de Haan, 2003), la formation et l'âge (Cho et al., 2003). Ces nouvelles inégalités, qui souvent correspondent aux hiérarchies sociales existantes en les creusant davantage, pèsent plus que la différence d'accès dans la création d'une catégorie de personnes à même de tirer profit de ces technologies[17] pour se sentir intégrées et accéder à de meilleures chances dans notre société qui change rapidement (de Haan, 2003).

C'est à ce niveau qu'il sera utile d'approfondir les différents aspects touchant la formation en général et notamment l'utilisation des différents potentiels de ses nouveaux médias, afin de renverser le problème et ne plus penser en terme de ce que la technique peut faire de nous, mais en ce que nous pouvons faire de la technique (Galimberti, 1999).

Bibliographie

Barber, B. R. (1999). Culture McWorld contre démocratie. *Manière de voir 46* (Le Monde Diplomatique), Juillet-Août , 70-74.

Baromedia (2002). *Résultats 2002 du baromètre des médias suisses* http://www.webdo.ch/baromedia/baromedia_2002/baro2002_f.pdf.

Boneva, B., Kraut, R. et Frohlich, D. (2001). Using E-mail for Personal Relationships: The Difference Gender Makes. *American Behavioral Scientist, 45* (3): 530-549.

Castells, M. (1996). *The Rise of the Network Society.* Oxford: Blackwell Publishers.

Cho, J., De Zúñiga, H. G., Rojas, H. et Shah, D. V. (2003). Beyond Access: The Digital Divide And Internet Uses And Gratifications. *IT&Society, 1* (4): 46-72 <http://www.ITandSociety.org>.

17 La disparités dans l'habilité d'usage de l'ordinateur et d'Internet et dans la capacité à exploiter un bon nombre de ses applications n'est pas sans conséquences importantes dans la vie des personnes. En effet les bénéfices économique liés aux instruments informatiques sont considérables: Ono et Zavodny (2003) rappellent que les personnes sachant utiliser un ordinateur gagnent 15 % de plus que les travailleurs avec la même formation et la même expérience professionnelle mais sans familiarité avec l'informatique; en outre elles ont plus de possibilités d'être embauchées lors d'une recherche d'emploi.

Cook, K. J. et Stambaugh, P. M. (1997). Tuna Memos and Pissing Contests. Doing Gender and male Dominance on the Internet. In C. Rambo Ronai, B. A. Zsembik et J. R. Feagin (eds.), *Everyday Sexism in the Third Millenium*. New York London: Routledge.

Communauté d'études pour l'aménagement du territoire (1997). *Nouvelles technologies de la communication et politique*, Rapport intermédiaire Programme «Technology assessment».

Döring, N. (1999). *Sozialpsychologie des Internet*. Göttingen: Hogrefe.

European Commission (2000). *Measuring Information Society 2000. A Eurobarometer survey.* http://europa.eu.int/comm/public_opinion/archives/eb/ebs_141_en.pdf.

Galimberti, U. (1999). *Psiche e techne*, Milano: Feltrinelli.

Gallup (2000). *Internet et le Grand Public,* Flash Eurobarometre, N° 88 (10-30/10/2000) – Rapport.

Gershuny, J. (2002). Social leisure and home it: a panel time-diary approach. *IT&Society, 1* (1): 54-72. <http://www.ITandSociety.org>.

Goodman, S. E., Press, L. I., Ruth, S. R. et Rutkowski, A. M. (1994). *The Global Diffusion of the Internet: Patterns and Problems*, <http://som.csudh.edu/fac/lpress/sy.htm>.

de Haan, J. (2003). IT and social inequality in the Netherlands *IT&Society, 1*, (4): 27-45. <http://www.ITandSociety.org>.

Hampton, K. N. (2001). *Living the wired life in the wired suburb:netville, glocalization and civil society.* Toronto: Department of sociology, University of Toronto.

Hellerstein, L. N. (1985). The Social Use of Electronic Communication at a Major University. *Computers and the Social Sciences, 1*: 191-197.

Herring, S. C. (2000). Gender Differences in Cmc: Findings and Implications. *Computer Professionals for Social Responsibility Newsletter*, 18 (1), Winter 2000.

Huber, M., Cosandey, F., Täube, V. G., Arvanitis, S., Bonfadelli, H., Bütschi, D., Hollenstein, H., Marr, M., Perret, J.-F., Sabo, M. et Trechsel, A. H. (2002). *La société de l'information en Suisse. Etat des lieux et perspectives.* Neuchâtel: OFS/GSR/OFCOM.

King, L. (2000). Gender Issues in Online Communities. *Computer Professionals for Social Responsibility Newsletter*, 18, (1), Winter 2000.

Kraut, R., Kiesler, S., Boneva, B., Cummings, J., Helgeson, V. et Crawford, A. (2002). Internet Paradox Revisited. *Journal of Social Issues*, 58 (1): 49-74.

Kraut, R., Lundmark, V., Patterson, M., Kiesler, S., Mukopadhyay, T. et Scherlis, W. (1998), Internet paradox. A social technology that reduces social involvement and psychological well-being?, *American Psychologist*, 53 (9): 1017-1031.

Lévy, P. (1999). *Cybercultura. Gli usi sociali delle nuove tecnologie.* Milano: Feltrinelli.

Maitland, C. (1998). Global Diffusion of Interactive Networks. The Impact of Culture, in C. Ess et F. Sudweeks (eds). *Proceedings Cultural Attitudes Towards Communication and Technology.* University of Sydney, Australia, 268-286.

Maitland, C. et Bauer, J. (1999). *Global Diffusion of the Internet.* Dept. of Economics of Infrastructure Delft University of Technology, The Netherlands et Dept. of Telecommunication, Michigan State University, USA.

Maragliano, R., Martini, O. et Penge, S. (1994). Dall'uomo alla macchina in tanti modi diversi. In R. Maragliano., O. Martini et S. Penge (a cura di), *I media e la formazione* (15-25). Roma: La Nuova Italia Scientifica.

Mattelart, A. (1999). Dangereux effets de la globalisation des réseaux. *Manière de voir* 46 (Le Monde Diplomatique), Juillet-Août, 54-57.

Molo-Bettelini, C., Alippi, M. et Wernli, B. (2001a). Représentations et réalités liées à la diffusion d'Internet. *Schweizerische Zeitschrift für Soziologie*, 27: 131-149.

Molo-Bettelini, C., Alippi, M. et Wernli B. (2001b). Wahrnehmungen und Auswirkungen des Internet im Privat- und Berufsleben. IN: *Das Internet-Potenzial und Grenzen aus sozialwissenschaftlischer Sicht*. Bern: SAGW.

Morahan-Martin, J. (1998). *Women and Girls Last: Females and The Internet*. IRISS International Conference: 25-27 March 1998, Bristol, UK <http://www.sosig.ac.uk/iriss/papers/paper55.htm>.

Nie, N. H. et Erbring, L. (2000). *Internet and Society. A preliminary report*. Stanford Institute for the Quantitative Study of Society SIQSS, Stanford University. <http://www.stanford.edu/group/ siqss/Press_Release/Preliminary_Report.pdf>.

Ono, H. et Zadovny, M. (2003). Gender and the Internet. *Social Science Quarterly*, 84 (1): 111-121.

Peterson, R. (1994). Harassment by Electronic Mail. *Synthesis: Law and Policy in Higher Education (Winter/Spring)*, 402-403.

Pew Research Center (2000). *Tracking online life: How women use the Internet to cultivate relationships with family and friends*. The Pew Internet et American Life Project. Washington, DC <http://www.pewinternet.org/reports>.

Robinson, J. P., Barth, K. et Kohut, A. (1997). Social Impact Research: Personal Computers, Mass Media, and Use of Time. *Social Science Computer Review* 15(1): 65-82.

Serpentelli, J. (1993). *Conversational structure and personality correlates of electronic communication*. Haverford University <ftp://ftp.lambda.moo.mud.org/pub/MOO/papers/conv-structure.txt>.

Spears, R. et Lea, M. (1992). Social influence and the influence of the social in computer-mediated communication. In L. Lea (éd.), *Contexts of computer-mediated communication* (30-65). Harvester Wheatsheaf: Hemel Hempstead.

Turkle, S. (1996). *Virtuality and its discontents: searching for community in cyberspace*, <http://epn.org/prospect/24/24turk.html>.

U. S. Depertment of Commerce (2002). *A Nation Online: How Americans Are Expanding Their Use of the Internet*, <http://www.ntia.doc.gov/ntiahome/dn/anationonline2.pdf>.

UCLA (2001). *The UCLA Internet Report. Surveying the Digital Future*. UCLA Center For Communication Policy <http://ccp.ucla.edu/pdf/UCLA-Internet-Report-2001.pdf>.

UCLA (2003). *The UCLA Internet Report – Year Three – Surveying the Digital Future*. UCLA Center For Communication Policy <http://ccp.ucla.edu/pdf/UCLA-Internet-Report-Year-Three.pdf>.

Weiser, E. (2000). Gender differences in Internet use patterns and Internet application preferences: A two-sample comparison. *CyberPsychology & Behavior*, 3 (2): 167-177.

Changements dans les comportements, attitudes et opinions politiques entre les deux premières vagues du PSM*

Boris Wernli

Introduction

Cet article est consacré au changement politique de court-terme, étant donné qu'il base ses analyses empiriques sur un horizon-temps d'environ une année, celle qui sépare les 1ère et 2e vagues du PSM. Il convient toutefois d'introduire la problématique du changement politique de manière plus générale, afin de poser les jalons de fond de nos analyses et de les inscrire dans un contexte plus ample. Les lignes suivantes exposent quelques généralités de la vie politique suisse de ces dernières années.

Les données du PSM sont prometteuses pour l'étude du comportement politique notamment parce que le paysage politique suisse a connu de profonds changements depuis environ une trentaine d'années. L'impression laissée par l'étude de la politique suisse depuis les années 1960 est celle d'un monde en profonde mutation, voire d'une fin de règne (Kriesi 1995: 2).

Plusieurs indicateurs font état de cette mutation.

On constate tout d'abord que les partis «bourgeois» de centre droit, les Démocrates-chrétiens (PDC) et les Radicaux (PRD), ont connu une baisse régulière de leurs résultats électoraux depuis les 20 dernières années. Cette perte de pouvoir s'est faite au profit des formations se situant aux extrémités

* Cette contribution fait partie de l'ouvrage collectif *Vivre en Suisse 1999-2000* (Erwin Zimmermann et Robin Tillmann (éds), Editions Peter Lang, Berne (2004)). Les analyses et résultats se basent sur les deux premières vagues de l'enquête longitudinale Vivre en Suisse réalisée auprès de 6 335 personnes interviewées en 1999 et 2000. La collecte des données, effectuée par M. I. S. Trend sous la responsabilité du Panel suisse de ménages de l'Université de Neuchâtel, a été financée par le PP Demain la Suisse du Fonds national suisse de la recherche scientifique (Subsides No. 5004-53205 / 5004-57894 / 5004-67304). Des informations complémentaires peuvent être obtenues sur le site www.swisspanel.ch

du spectre politique, les Socialistes (PSS), sur la gauche, et les Démocrates du centre (UDC), sur la droite, qui privilégient actuellement une politique de rupture, au détriment des pratiques consensuelles ayant caractérisé la politique suisse depuis des décennies (Lijphart 1984). Malgré le changement progressif des rapports de force au Parlement fédéral, la composition du Conseil fédéral, l'exécutif au niveau national, resta inchangée[1] entre 1959 et 2003, en raison d'une série de règles informelles[2], mais aussi d'arrangements institutionnels[3] privilégiant le statu quo.

Outre une tendance à délaisser progressivement les partis du centre pour se tourner vers les extrêmes, les électeurs montrent un comportement de plus en plus volatil, en changeant plus facilement de parti d'une élection à l'autre. Les liens moins serrés entre les partis et les citoyens se traduisent aussi par une nette baisse[4] au niveau de l'identification partisane. Cette baisse est synonyme d'une indépendance accrue des électeurs vis-à-vis des partis politiques et de joutes électorales plus compétitives (Joye et Papadopoulos 1986: 57-9; Kriesi 1995: 155); actuellement, la plupart des votants prennent la liberté de personnaliser leur bulletin de vote dans les cantons à plus d'un siège, alors que les bulletins modifiés étaient l'exception dans les années d'avant-guerre.

Outre une indépendance accrue, on observe que la population porte un regard de plus en plus critique sur les autorités politiques, ce qu'illustre la forte baisse de la confiance à leur égard (Papadopoulos 1997).

Si une partie des électeurs deviennent moins fidèles envers les partis et moins confiants dans les institutions politiques, de plus en plus ne se déplacent tout simplement plus aux urnes. La forte hausse de l'abstentionnisme au niveau de la Suisse entière, illustre ce propos, avec une moyenne nationale de participation électorale pour les élections fédérales qui est passée de taux dépassant 65 % dans les années 60, à un peu plus de 40 % en 1999. Le désintérêt pour les élections fédérales ne se traduit pas forcément par un retrait complet de

1 Deux sièges pour les Radicaux, les Démocrates-chrétiens et les Socialistes, et un siège pour l'Union démocratique du Centre (UDC). L'UDC obtint un second siège à fin 2003, au détriment du PDC.

2 «Formule magique», répartition des sièges selon les critères régionaux, linguistiques, de sexe, etc.

3 Election de l'exécutif fédéral par l'Assemblée, élection des Conseillers fédéraux l'un après l'autre, et pas en bloc, pas de responsabilité du Gouvernement devant l'AF, etc.

4 37 % des Suisses s'identifient à un parti lors des élections fédérales de 1999, contre 63 % en 1971.

la vie politique: il a été accompagné par une augmentation[5] des activités non électorales, que l'on observe aussi dans les autres pays européens (Topf 1995: 52-91). L'augmentation quantitative du recours à la démocratie directe depuis la fin des années 1960 (Kriesi 1995: 80-123), atteste aussi de la volonté populaire de chercher d'autres formes plus efficaces d'expression politique.

Toutes ces indicateurs vont dans le sens d'une émancipation accrue des électeurs par rapport aux partis; une partie des électeurs se transforment en «citoyens-consommateurs», qui jugent au cas par cas, en évaluant l'offre politique disponible, quitte à privilégier les partis offrant les solutions les plus spectaculaires et les plus tranchées. Ces changements sont notamment dus à la profonde mutation culturelle ayant suivi la seconde guerre mondiale, mutation culturelle résultant des transformations structurelles de notre société. La mobilité accrue des biens, des personnes, l'urbanisation, l'accroissement générale du niveau de formation, du niveau de vie, les changements dans l'économie (développement du tertiaire au détriment des secteurs secondaire et primaire, globalisation, etc.) ont peu à peu entrainé un affranchissement dans nombre de domaines (politique, mais aussi religieux, social, sexuel, etc.), prélude à une sorte de redistribution des cartes, favorable à certains groupes sociaux, remettant en cause les acquis d'autres tranches de la société.

Des auteurs comme Kriesi (1993) ou Kitschelt (1995), postulent plus ou moins explicitement que c'est chez les citoyens des couches inférieures et laborieuses, désécurisés par le processus de modernisation industrielle, voyant dans les minorités raciales et la main d'œuvre immigrée une menace pour leur statut social et leurs acquis, que se développeraient un corpus de valeurs plutôt réactionnaires, une pensée manichéenne et une tentation pour les solutions simples, extrémistes et non consensuelles (vote pour l'extrême-droite, augmentation du potentiel protestataire). Au contraire, les gagnants du processus de modernisation (nouvelle classe moyenne, ainsi que les indépendants ayant réussi à tirer parti de la globalisation) développeraient des valeurs d'ouverture vers l'étranger, défendues par les partis de la gauche et ceux de la droite libérale, ouverte au monde extérieur.

5 La participation à des manifestations s'est accrue, passant de 8 % des électeurs suisses en 1976 à un niveau avoisinant les 15 %, en 1988-89 et 1995.

Hypothèses de recherche

De manière générale, les analyses de ce chapitre sont consacrées aux changements dans les comportements, attitudes et opinions politiques et tentent de répondre aux questions suivantes: qui change, comment, et pourquoi?

Bien conscient qu'avec des données distantes d'une année il est un peu illusoire de vouloir tester des théories structurelles du changement, on peut vérifier si la baisse de la confiance dans le système politique et ses acteurs, le recours à des activités protestataires, l'adoption de positions extrémistes ou le choix d'acteurs politiques présentant des options radicales et peu nuancées entre la 1ère et la 2e vague du panel, sont liés à une dégradation des conditions de vie objectives des interviewés ou de leur évaluation subjective de celles-ci.

Une autre hypothèse est celle de la polarisation des électeurs suisses, liée au durcissement du discours et des options des partis se situant sur les extrêmes de l'échiquier politique. L'intérêt est ici mettre en évidence si, oui ou non, les électeurs les plus modérés sur certains enjeux, notamment relatifs à l'ouverture de la Suisse sur le monde, sont tentés de délaisser les partis de la gauche, respectivement de la droite nationaliste, formations dans lesquelles ils ne se reconnaîtraient plus.

Confrontation des données du PSM de 1ère vague

Validons tout d'abord les données de 1ère vague du panel en les confrontant avec d'autres sources. L'analyse descriptive de quelques variables politologiques de la 1ère vague du PSM autorise quelques comparaisons, notamment avec les données collectées après les élections fédérales de 1999 dans le cadre du projet Selects[6] 1999. Cette dernière enquête ne portant que sur les électeurs suisses, j'ai aussi adopté cette base de comparaison dans le tableau 1.

6 Selects, qui signifie Swiss Electoral Studies, est un projet subventionné par le Fonds national suisse de la recherche scientifique joignant les forces des départements de sciences politiques des Universités de Genève, Berne et Zurich. Deux études ont déjà été réalisées dans ce cadre, focalisées autour des élections fédérales de 1995 et 1999.

Tableau 1: Confrontation des données du PSM de 1ère vague

	Electeurs du panel (Suisses âgés de 18 ans au moins)	Selects 1999	différence électeurs-selects	test de t	force effective des partis au niveau suisse lors des élections fédérales de 1999 – source OFS
n maximum	5952	2048			
	moyenne	moyenne			
Confiance dans le Conseil fédéral, 0 à 10	5,78	6,18	–0,39	***	
Confiance dans les partis politiques, 0 à 10	4,44	5,35	–0,91	***	
Participation sur 10 votations fédérales	7,17	7,00	0,17	***	
Positionnement sur l'axe gauche-droite, 0 à 10	4,87	5,21	–0,34	***	
Pas d'armée-armée forte, 1 à 5	3,20	3,28	–0,08	***	
Augmenter-diminuer les dépenses sociales, 1 à 5	2,70	2,94	–0,25	***	
Sans-avec énergie nucléaire, 1 à 5	2,38	2,35	0,02	n.s.	
Adhésion-non-adhésion à la CE, 1 à 5	2,69	2,67	0,02	n.s.	
Egalité-non-égalité des chances pour les étrangers, 1 à 5	2,79	3,06	–0,26	***	
Protection de l'environnement-croissance économique, 1 à 5	2,58	2,49	0,09	***	
Augmenter-diminuer les taxes sur les hauts revenus, 1 à 5	2,08	2,17	–0,09	***	
Choix partisan en cas d'élection	%	%			%
Gauche	39%	33%	6%		29%
Centre	3%	3%	0%		3%
Droite traditionnelle	35%	34%	1%		39%
Droite nationale	22%	29%	–8%		27%
Autres formations	1%	1%	0%		2%
Total	100%	100%			100%

*** p. < ,001; ** p. < ,01; * p. < ,05; n.s. non significatif

Le tableau 1 montre que les électeurs suisses interrogés par le PSM sont moins confiants envers le Conseil fédéral et les partis politiques que ceux de l'enquête Selects 1999. Si le déficit de confiance envers le Conseil fédéral reste modéré (,39 sur une échelle allant de 0 à 10) chez les pannelisés, quand il s'agit des partis politiques la différence devient conséquente (,91). Concernant la participation aux votations fédérales, indicateur à la fiabilité plutôt faible[7], la différence est très restreinte, avec une assiduité aux urnes légèrement plus forte chez les répondants du PSM (différence de ,17 sur une échelle allant de 0 à 10). Le positionnement sur un axe idéologique allant de 0 (gauche) à 10 (droite) voit les pannelisés se situer généralement plus à gauche (,34 de différence) que les répondants de l'enquête électorale 1999. La prise de position sur une série de valeurs confirme cette orientation de l'échantillon du PSM, avec des positions plus favorables à l'augmentation des dépenses sociales (,25 de différence sur une échelle allant de 1 à 5) et à l'égalité des droits entre Suisses et étrangers (,26). Les autres valeurs montrent des différences plus faibles, voire inexistantes, mais allant généralement encore dans le même sens. Idem concernant le parti choisi en cas d'élections[8], avec les 39 % de votes pour des partis de gauche (socialistes, écologistes, verts, alternatifs et popistes) des pannelisés, contre 33 % avec Selects, le corollaire étant une sous-représentation de 8 % du vote pour la droite nationale (UDC, Démocrates suisses, UDF, Parti de la liberté, Lega) dans l'échantillon des électeurs du PSM. Cette sur-représentation de la gauche ressort aussi de la comparaison avec les résultats officiels des élections, le score des partis[9] aux élections fédérales de 1999 étant d'ailleurs le seul repère objectif de notre population-mère.

Pour résumer, les électeurs du PSM montrent une orientation légèrement plus à gauche que ceux de l'enquête électorale 1999, tant au niveau de l'auto-positionnement idéologique, que du vote et des valeurs, mais aussi une défiance plus forte envers les autorités et surtout des partis politiques.

A quoi tiennent ces différences? Les période et méthode d'interview étant similaires, ainsi que la formulation des questions, les écarts tiennent probable-

7 Le taux moyen déclaré dépasse les 70 % tant pour Selects que le PSM alors qu'il s'établit dans la réalité autour de 45 %.

8 Pour le PSM, il s'agit du parti pour lequel on voterait en cas d'élections au moment de l'interview, pour Selects il s'agit du parti pour lequel ont voté les votants et de celui pour lequel auraient voté les abstentionnistes. J'ai considéré ici les groupes de partis.

9 Proportion des suffrages, et des non des sièges.

ment à des biais dans l'échantillonnage liés à la non-réponse aux enquêtes, qui n'est pas distribuée au hasard. Pour le panel, cette non-réponse a été corrigée par une pondération sur différents critères, comme le sexe, l'âge, le niveau de formation, le revenu, la taille du logement; d'autre part, la validation externe des données Selects a montré une très forte représentativité quant à des critères comme l'âge et le sexe. Malgré tout, le choix électoral des participants à l'enquête électorale étant en conformité avec les résultats officiels des élections fédérales de 1999, il y a lieu de penser que le léger biais vers la gauche des données du PSM a trait à des critères subjectifs, pour lesquels aucune pondération n'est possible. En définitive, l'échantillon de 1ère vague du panel semble très légèrement déformé en raison d'une sur-représentation de personnes plus ouvertes aux enquêtes sociales, plus conscientes de leur utilité et donc plus disposées à consacrer de leur temps à unc enquête assez astreignante.

Le fait que la confiance envers les autorités et institutions soit plus basse dans l'échantillon du PSM relève à mon sens d'un autre facteur, car il n'y a pas de lien[10] entre la confiance et le positionnement idéologique. On peut penser à cet égard que les personnes méfiantes envers le système politique et ses acteurs sont sous-représentées dans les sondages axés sur les élections comme Selects, auxquels elles refusent plus souvent de participer de peur de se faire instrumentaliser, tandis qu'elles sont moins rebutées par une enquête pluridisciplinaire et non focalisée sur la vie politique, comme le PSM.

Le changement net entre 1ère et 2e vague du PSM

Les pages suivantes se focalisent sur l'étude du changement politique, passant outre la description des indicateurs à notre disposition, ce qui n'apporterait rien de nouveau par rapport aux connaissances actuelles en la matière.

Le fait de disposer de deux vagues successives d'interviews menées avec le même questionnaire et espacées d'une année permet de mettre en évidence le changement net, à savoir dans quelle mesure la distribution de nos indicateurs varie ou non pour l'ensemble de l'échantillon, et par inférence pour la population-mère.

10 R de Pearson de ,05, $p < ,001$, avec la confiance envers les partis, relation non significative ($p = ,50$) avec la confiance envers le Gouvernement, soit une relation très faible dans le premier cas, non significative statistiquement dans le second.

Pour des raisons pratiques et d'harmonisation des différents chapitres de cet ouvrage, la comparaison se fait sur la base de l'échantillon longitudinal du panel, qui comprend seulement les individus ayant répondu aux deux premières vagues d'interviews. L'avantage de cette pratique est qu'elle mesure le changement net indépendamment du hasard lié aux tirages successifs d'échantillons différents; l'inconvénient est que l'échantillon longitudinal n'est pas forcément représentatif de la population-mère, en raison de l'atrition non aléatoire entre les deux vagues. Les individus ayant certaines caractéristiques sociales et politiques peuvent avoir une probabilité plus forte de quitter le panel. Ce problème ne nous a pas échappé: les analyses relatives au changement net ont aussi été effectuées avec les échantillons transversaux de 1ère et 2e vague, en obtenant les mêmes résultats, ce qui montre que la pondération utilisée pour corriger l'atrition est efficace, et ceci aussi pour les analyses politologiques.

Le tableau 2 permet d'observer quelques changements, généralement très faibles.

Tableau 2: Analyse du changement net 1ère-2e vague du PSM – échantillon longitudinal pondéré

Vague du panel	1ère (1999-2000)	2e (2000-2001)	
n maximum	6335	6335	
	moyenne	moyenne	Eta
Intérêt pour la politique, 0 à 10	5,17	5,41	,04***
Satisfaction envers le fonctionnement de la démocratie, 0 à 10	5,77	6,09	,08***
Sentiment d'influence politique, 0 à 10	3,17	3,45	,05***
Confiance dans le Conseil fédéral, 0 à 10	5,82	5,94	,03**
Participation aux votations fédérales, 0 à 10	7,22	7,44	,03***
Potentiel de boycott, 0 à 10	3,81	4,06	,04***
Potentiel de grève, 0 à 10	3,26	3,46	,03**
Potentiel de manifestation, 0 à 10	3,70	3,73	n.s.
Positionnement sur l'axe idéologique gauche-droite, 0 à 10	4,71	4,72	n.s.

Vague du panel	1ère (1999-2000)	2e (2000-2001)	
	%	%	V de Cramer
Armée forte	39	37	,06***
Adhésion à la CE	60	54	,06***
Augmentation des dépenses sociales	44	47	,05***
Egalité des chances pour les étrangers	57	64	,07***
Croissance économique (vs protection de l'environnement)	17	12	,08***
Augmentation des taxes pour hauts revenus	69	72	,03**
Pas d'énergie nucléaire	65	63	,03*
Choix électoral en cas d'élections	%	%	V de Cramer
Gauche	24	23	
Centre	2	1	
Droite traditionnelle	18	18	
Droite nationale	11	9	
Autre partis	1	0	
Aucun parti cité	44	49	
Total	100	100	
			,06***

*** p. < ,001; ** p. < ,01; * p. < ,05; n.s. non significatif

Globalement, on constate que l'échantillon du panel est très légèrement plus intéressé par la politique, plus satisfait et confiant dans le fonctionnement des institutions, tout en ayant un activisme conventionnel et un potentiel protestataire très légèrement plus fort en 2000 qu'en 1999. Aucun changement significatif n'est constaté quant au positionnement sur l'axe idéologique gauche-droite, alors que les valeurs politiques montrent des évolutions contrastées. Si les répondants adoptent globalement des positions légèrement plus de gauche[11] concernant l'égalité des chances entre Suisses et étrangers, les dépenses sociales, l'armée et la protection de l'environnement, on constate aussi une baisse des attitudes favorables à l'adhésion à l'Union européenne. Concernant le choix électoral, on constate surtout une légère augmentation

11 En faisant référence aux positions prises par le parti socialiste suisse.

du nombre de personnes ne favorisant aucun parti, ce qui peut être dû au fait que 1999 étant une année électorale la question était alors plus concrète qu'une année plus tard. Soulignons ici que tous les changements susmentionnés sont très faibles et qu'ils sont significatifs statistiquement parce que nous utilisons des échantillons très grands, dont la marge d'erreur est très faible.

A quoi tiennent les changements observés, si minimes soient-ils?

Etant donné que ce changement est mesuré auprès des mêmes personnes, le hasard de deux échantillonnages successifs ou un phénomène d'atrition non aléatoire n'entrent pas en ligne de compte. On note qu'une bonne partie des variations vont dans le sens d'une citoyenneté plus active, plus intéressée, plus satisfaite, plus consciente de ses pouvoirs, moins méfiante. Serait-ce un retour à la normale, après une année 1999 marquée par les élections fédérales et des campagnes électorales plus agressives et délétères que jamais, qui ont pu saturer une partie des électeurs? Ou alors, suite à la poussée spectaculaire de l'UDC le sentiment que les choses peuvent changer, après des décennies d'inertie, suscite-t-il des espoirs? Concernant les valeurs, peut-être que ce petit pas vers la gauche est-il le pendant de la poussée de l'UDC lors des élections fédérales de 1999. Que dire alors de la prise de recul par rapport à la question européenne, qui va plutôt dans le sens contraire (54 % des répondants sont pour l'adhésion en 2e vague, contre 59 % en 1ère)? On pourrait arguer du fait que l'acceptation en votation populaire le 21 mai 2000 des accords bilatéraux entre la Suisse et l'UE, ainsi que l'élargissement de cette dernière, rendent l'adhésion moins vitale et attractive aux yeux de la population. De même, la question européenne ayant été largement mise au centre du débat des dernières élections fédérales, nombre de personnes ont peut-être saisi l'occasion de mener une réflexion à ce propos, en se distançant des mots d'ordres et slogans des partis. On remarquera qu'un tel mouvement est aussi perceptible dans les données VOX de la même période[12], avec une baisse[13] des personnes très favorables à l'ouverture de la Suisse dans le monde, tandis que, comme le montre aussi les données du panel, la proportion de personnes favorables à l'égalité des chances entre Suisses et étrangers augmente[14] dans le même laps de temps.

12 Juin 1999 à mars 2001 pour les enquêtes VOX, qui sont réalisées après chaque journée de votations fédérales.

13 On passe de 33 % de très favorables en juin 1999 à 24 % en mars 2001.

14 18 % en juin 1999, 28 % en mars 2001.

Concernant le choix électoral, et la légère augmentation de la proportion de personnes ne citant aucun parti, je l'attribue au fait que les élections fédérales de 1999 se sont déroulées contemporainement à la 1ère vague du PSM, faisant que la question du choix était d'actualité et que les partis jouissaient d'une certaine publicité, tandis qu'une année plus tard la situation était revenue à la normale.

Le changement brut entre 1ère et 2e vague du PSM

Les données du panel se distinguent surtout en permettant l'analyse du changement brut, c'est-à-dire l'étude des variations du comportement, attitudes et opinions politiques au niveau individuel.

Le tableau 3 nous présente les changements observés sur les variables quantitatives[15], en termes relatifs[16] et absolus, la corrélation entre les réponses de 1ère et 2e vague, ainsi que la proportion de données manquantes sur l'une ou l'autre des enquêtes.

On constate que pour la plupart des variables, les changements individuels inter-vagues sont modestes, voire très modestes, si l'on tient compte du fait que l'erreur de mesure sur une échelle allant de 0 à 10, lors d'une interview rapidement menée, peut être assez élevée. C'est le cas notamment pour l'intérêt pour la politique, la participation aux votations fédérales, le positionnement sur l'axe gauche-droite, où les réponses des deux vagues sont très corrélées (R de Pearson supérieur ou égal à ,70) et pour lesquels moins de 20 % des répondants connaissent un changement d'attitude de plus de deux unités dans un sens ou dans l'autre.

Le sentiment d'influence politique (,44), et de manière générale le potentiel d'activisme protestataire (R de ,53 à ,62) sont par contre les attitudes les plus fluctuantes, avec une proportion oscillant entre 30 % et 40 % de répondants montrant un changement d'attitude de plus de deux unités en valeur absolue, peut-être en vertu du fait qu'elles sont moins tangibles, s'agissant d'un potentiel non avéré.

15 Score en 2e vague – score de 1ère vague.

16 En termes relatifs, la différence garde son signe, et peut théoriquement aller de –10 à +10 sur les échelles, tenant compte ainsi de la force et de la direction de la différence, en termes absolus on fait ressortir l'écart par rapport à la position de l'année précédente, sans égard à la direction.

Tableau 3: Variables quantitatives – changements de comportements et d'attitudes entre 1ère et 2e vague du PSM – échantillon longitudinal pondéré (n max=6335)

changements en valeur relative («score» de 2000 – «score» de 1999)	% miss.	min	max	moyenne	écart-type	Percentiles 10	20	30	40	50	60	70	80	90	Corrélation
Intérêt pour la politique	0%	–10	10	0,23	2,04	–2	–1	0	0	0	0	1	2	3	,76***
Satisfaction du fonctionnement de la démocratie	7%	–10	10	0,29	1,97	–2	–1	0	0	0	1	1	2	3	,53***
Sentiment d'influence politique	7%	–10	10	0,22	2,84	–3	–2	–1	0	0	1	1	2	4	,44***
Confiance dans le Conseil fédéral	8%	–10	9	0,11	2,00	–2	–1	–1	0	0	0	1	2	2	,59***
Participation aux votations fédérales	25%	–10	10	0,25	2,16	–2	–1	0	0	0	0	0	1	2	,77***
Potentiel de boycott	5%	–10	10	0,25	3,54	–5	–2	0	0	0	0	1	3	5	,53***
Potentiel de grève	5%	–10	10	0,18	3,15	–3	–2	0	0	0	0	0	2	5	,60***
Potentiel de manifestation	3%	–10	10	0,02	3,09	–4	–2	0	0	0	0	0	2	4	,62***
Positionnement sur l'axe idéologique gauche-droite	25%	–10	10	0,02	1,73	–2	–1	0	0	0	0	0	1	2	,70***
changements en valeur absolue															
Intérêt pour la politique		0	10	1,36	1,54	0	0	0	1	1	1	2	2	3	
Satisfaction du fonctionnement de la démocratie		0	10	1,39	1,42	0	0	0	1	1	1	2	2	3	
Sentiment d'influence politique		0	10	2,02	2,01	0	0	1	1	2	2	3	4	5	
Confiance dans le Conseil fédéral		0	10	1,41	1,43	0	0	1	1	1	1	2	2	3	
Participation aux votations fédérales		0	10	1,21	1,80	0	0	0	0	0	1	2	2	4	
Potentiel de boycott		0	10	2,35	2,66	0	0	0	1	2	2	3	5	6	
Potentiel de grève		0	10	1,95	2,48	0	0	0	0	1	2	3	4	5	
Potentiel de manifestation		0	10	1,95	2,39	0	0	0	0	1	2	3	4	5	
Positionnement sur l'axe idéologique gauche-droite		0	10	1,07	1,36	0	0	0	0	1	1	1	2	3	

*** p. <,001

Le tableau 4 nous présente les changements de positionnement d'une vague à l'autre sur 7 enjeux concrets considérés comme ceux articulant le débat politique suisse par les études politologiques helvétiques comme Selects 1995 et 1999 (Mazzoleni 2003) ainsi que les enquêtes Vox. On dispose annuellement de 3 choix pour chaque item, à savoir celui d'une des deux prises de positions antagonistes ou l'indécision, que l'on considère comme une option intermédiaire. Les valeurs politiques en question ayant toutes été orientées dans le même sens, le changement d'opinion entre les deux vagues peut ainsi s'exprimer sur une échelle à 5 positions, allant d'un fort déplacement vers la gauche (–2), selon les prises de positions du parti socialiste suisse, à un fort déplacement vers la droite (+2), selon les positions de la droite nationale et de l'UDC en particulier. La position centrale (0) illustre la stabilité entre les deux vagues, qu'elle soit relative à une opinion de droite, de gauche ou indécise.

Tableau 4: Valeurs politiques – ampleur des changements d'opinions entre 1ère et 2e vague du PSM – échantillon longitudinal pondéré, n=6335 au maximum

	distribution en %							
	–2	–1	0	1	2	total		
	fort déplacement vers la gauche		stabilité des opinions		fort déplacement vers la droite nationale		V de Cramer	Gamma
Armée	2 %	16 %	65 %	15 %	2 %	100 %	,52***	,80***
Dépenses sociales	4 %	18 %	62 %	13 %	3 %	100 %	,39***	,63***
Adhésion à la CE	3 %	4 %	81 %	6 %	6 %	100 %	,54***	,92***
Egalité des chances pour les étrangers	11 %	9 %	67 %	7 %	6 %	100 %	,35***	,69***
Protection de l'environnement	5 %	20 %	58 %	15 %	3 %	100 %	,32***	,56***
Taxes sur les revenus élevés	4 %	11 %	72 %	9 %	3 %	100 %	,36***	,68***
Energie nucléaire	5 %	6 %	76 %	7 %	6 %	100 %	,45***	,83***

*** p.<,001

L'examen du tableau 4 montre que selon les items retenus, entre 58 % et 81 % des répondants campent sur leurs positions durant les deux vagues. Les retournements complets d'opinion (amplitude de 2 dans un sens ou l'autre) ne sont pas monnaie courante. Cette assez grande stabilité est confirmée par les deux dernières colonnes de la droite du tableau, qui montrent que la corrélation entre les positionnements des deux années est élevée à très élevée (Gamma de ,56 à ,92).

Finalement, le tableau 5 nous présente le croisement des choix électoraux en cas d'élection en première et seconde vague du panel.

Tableau 5: Choix électoraux en 1999 et 2000 – échantillon longitudinal pondéré, n=6335

		Choix électoral en 1ère vague du PSM					
		Gauche	Centre	Droite traditionnelle	Droite nationale	Autre partis	Aucun parti cité
Choix électoral en 2e vague du PSM	Gauche	69 %	13 %	5 %	4 %	22 %	8 %
	Centre	0 %	41 %	1 %	0 %		0 %
	Droite traditionnelle	4 %	14 %	62 %	14 %	12 %	9 %
	Droite nationale	2 %	2 %	4 %	54 %	2 %	3 %
	Autre partis	0 %	1 %	0 %	0 %	6 %	1 %
	Aucun parti cité	24 %	30 %	29 %	28 %	59 %	79 %
Total		100 %	100 %	100 %	100 %	100 %	100 %
	V de Cramer: ,50***						

*** p. < ,001

La corrélation est là encore élevée (V de Cramer de ,50). On constate avec la lecture de la diagonale que la stabilité entre les deux vagues est la plus grande pour les personnes n'indiquant aucun nom de parti, quelle qu'en soit la raison[17] (79 %); les partis de gauche ont les partisans les plus fidèles (69 % de ceux qui les choisissaient en première vague le font aussi lors de la seconde), suivis

17 N'irait pas voter, ne prendrait aucun parti, vote pour un candidat, pas pour un parti, ne sait pas, pas de réponse, etc.

par ceux de la droite traditionnelle (62 %). On constate que l'électorat de la droite nationale (UDC, Démocrates suisses, UDF, Parti de la liberté, Lega) est plus volatil (54 %), peut-être en vertu de son caractère plus hétéroclite et de sa récente et brutale poussée en 1999, ce qui fait qu'elle dispose de bases moins solides que les autres partis pour l'instant.

On remarque aussi que nombre (14 %) de ces supporters de la droite nationale en 1999 se tournent vers la droite traditionnelle (Radicaux, Démocrates-chrétiens, Libéraux) en 2000, dans une sorte de retour aux sources après l'expression d'un mécontentement lors des élections fédérales de 1999. On constate par contre peu de ralliements à la droite nationale en 2e vague, avec seulement 4 % des électeurs de la droite traditionnelle de 1999 tentés par les sirènes nationalistes en 2000.

Les déterminants du changement entre 1ère et 2e vague du PSM

La question abordée maintenant est celle des déterminants du changement politique de court-terme, avec l'étude des facteurs associés aux déplacements susmentionnés. Par une série d'analyses multivariées, il s'agit de répondre à la question suivante: qui change d'attitude, de comportement ou d'opinion, et dans quel sens.

Les attitudes politiques

Concentrons-nous ici sur les attitudes politiques connaissant les changements les plus importants dans le tableau 3, à savoir le sentiment d'influence politique et les indicateurs du potentiel d'activisme protestataire (boycott, grève, manifestation). Les autres indicateurs sont tellement corrélés d'une année à l'autre (par exemple, R de Pearson de ,76 pour l'intérêt pour la politique, de ,77 pour la participation aux votations fédérales) et la capacité explicative de nos modèles se montre de manière générale, nous le verrons dans les pages suivantes, si restreinte que rien ne ressort de leur analyse.

Au niveau du sens, ces indicateurs du sentiment d'influence politique et du potentiel d'activisme protestataire sont en fait liés; ils illustrent la perception subjective de la capacité qu'un individu a de faire changer les choses sur le plan politique, pour le sentiment d'influence politique, et la mesure avec laquelle il est prêt à adopter un comportement politique considéré généralement comme non conventionnel pour faire entendre sa voix.

Les trois indicateurs du potentiel d'activisme protestataire étant très liés[18] les uns aux autres, ils ont été regroupés dans une échelle additive.

Tableau 6: Explication du changement dans le potentiel protestataire des jeunes (25 ans et moins) – régression multiple – Coefficients de régression standardisés (Beta) et R^2 ajusté

	Beta
Augmentation de la satisfaction de la situation financière	–0,14 ***
Augmentation de l'intérêt pour la politique	0,10 **
Non-positionnement sur l'axe gauche-droite en seconde vague	0,10 **
R^2 ajusté	0,04
n	873

*** p.<,001 ; ** p.<,01 ; * p.<,05

Force est de constater que les changements dans le potentiel d'activisme protestataire entre la première et la seconde vague du PSM s'expliquent très mal (tableau 6) avec les variables à notre disposition, qui couvrent pourtant un très large répertoire des indicateurs socio-psycho-économiques. En se concentrant sur les jeunes de 25 ans[19] et moins, on parvient à expliquer tout au plus 4 % de la variance du changement[20] de potentiel protestataire. Cela peut s'expliquer par le caractère très subjectif et volatil de ce potentiel, déconnecté de tout contexte.

Le tableau 6 montre que seuls trois facteurs ont un impact significatif, bien que très limité.

18 Alpha de Cronbach standardisé de ,87 lors des deux vagues pour l'échelle additive constituée des trois items, corrélations de Pearson inter-items minimales de ,65.

19 Ce taux descend à 1 % si l'on considère l'ensemble des interviewés. Le modèle multivarié donne de meilleurs résultats auprès des jeunes de 25 ans et moins parce que cette période est celle de la socialisation politique, susceptible de connaître les plus grands changements dans le comportement individuel.

20 Différence entre l'échelle de potentiel protestataire de 2e vague et celle de 2e vague, qui a été présentée précédemment.

Quand la situation financière de la personne interrogée s'améliore entre les deux vagues, le potentiel de protestation a tendance à baisser (coefficient de régression standardisé Beta de –,14). Ce phénomène peut être interprété comme une sorte de «normalisation politique» chez les jeunes, qui sortiraient progressivement d'une phase protestataire liée à l'adolescence quand ils ont l'impression que leur situation financière s'améliore. Le potentiel protestataire augmente de pair avec l'intérêt pour la politique (Beta de ,10, p. < ,01), ce qui n'est pas pour surprendre, les recherches politologiques montrant généralement que l'apathie politique est généralement liée à un intérêt faible et que l'activisme augmente avec l'intérêt. Finalement, le non-positionnement sur l'axe idéologique gauche-droite en seconde vague du panel augmente légèrement (Beta de ,10), l'activisme protestataire, ce qui dénote le fait que les personnes s'y positionnant ont plus tendance à favoriser l'expression de leur opinion par des moyens conventionnels.

Concernant les changements dans le sentiment d'influence politique entre les deux premières vagues du panel (tableau 7), les résultats sont là encore très mitigés, avec quelques variables ayant un impact significatif, mais très limité (taux de variance expliquée du modèle entier de 4 %). La population retenue ici est l'ensemble des répondants.

Tableau 7: Explication du changement dans le sentiment d'influence politique – Régression multiple – Coefficients de régression standardisés (Beta) et R^2 ajusté

Augmentation de la satisfaction dans la démocratie	0,10	***
Augmentation de l'intérêt pour la politique	0,09	***
Augmentation de la confiance dans le Conseil fédéral	0,09	***
Non-positionnement sur l'axe gauche-droite en seconde vague	–0,03	*
R^2 ajusté	0,03	
n	5449	

*** p.<,001 ; ** p.<,01 ; * p.<,05

L'augmentation de la satisfaction dans la démocratie, de l'intérêt pour la politique et de la confiance dans le Conseil fédéral ont toutes un effet bénéfique de même importance (Beta de ,09 à ,10) sur le sentiment d'influence politique, ce qui n'est pas pour surprendre. On note encore l'effet très faible (Beta de –,03) du non-positionnement sur l'axe idéologique gauche-droite en 2e vague qui diminue le sentiment d'influence politique, à interpréter comme une sorte de résignation plus prononcée des personnes ne se retrouvant pas dans les repères traditionnels du système partisan.

Les opinions politiques

Concernant les opinions politiques, le tableau 4 mettait en évidence le fait que les changements étaient plutôt limités et qu'ils allaient généralement dans le sens d'un glissement vers la gauche, si l'on se réfère aux prises de position des partis politiques helvétiques.

Etant donné la faible ampleur de ces changements et le fait que ces opinions politiques sont généralement articulées autour de deux voire trois axes de valeurs structurant le débat politique suisse, ma première intention a été de réduire la complexité de l'information en dégageant les facteurs sous-jacents aux changements d'opinions. Le tableau 8, où toutes les variations sont orientées dans le sens gauche-droite, montre que cette stratégie est vouée à l'échec[21], avec des corrélations extrêmement faibles (R de Pearson de ,07 au maximum) voire inexistantes entre les changements d'opinions.

Je trouve assez déroutant que les changements d'opinion ne soient pas ou très peu corrélés entre eux, alors que les opinions le sont, comme le montrent le tableau 9[22] et les études politologiques suisses menées jusqu'à présent (par exemple Mazzoleni 2003).

Ceci signifie que si le positionnement à un moment donné est structuré, de manière semblable lors de chacune des deux vagues, les changements ne le sont quasiment pas et semblent obéir à une autre logique. Faute de structure commune, ces résultats m'ont poussé à analyser séparément le changement sur les différentes opinions politiques. Je ne présenterai ici aucun résultat, parce qu'aucune des régressions effectuées ne parvient à expliquer ne serait-ce que 1 % de la variance du changement d'opinion sur un des items considérés. Ainsi, en plus d'être relativement peu fréquents et quasiment indépendants les uns des autres, les changements d'opinion à court-terme restent inexpliqués.

21 Coefficient Kaiser-Meyer-Olkin de ,51, ce qui signifie que les données ne se prêtent pas à une analyse factorielle.

22 La structure des liens en 2e vague est quasiment identique à celle de 1ère vague du panel.

23 Au préalable, les variables indépendantes quantitatives ont été standardisées (transfor-

Tableau 8: Matrice des corrélations (R de Pearson) des changements d'opinions entre les 2 vagues

		Armée	Dépenses sociales	Adhésion CE	Egalité CH – étrangers	Croissance économique	Taxation revenus élevés
Dépenses sociales	Pearson Correlation	0,01					
	Sig. (2-tailed)	0,54					
Adhésion CE	Pearson Correlation	–0,02	0,00				
	Sig. (2-tailed)	0,15	0,98				
Egalité CH – étrangers	Pearson Correlation	0,00	0,02	0,00			
	Sig. (2-tailed)	0,73	0,15	0,91			
Croissance économique	Pearson Correlation	0,02	0,03	0,02	0,01		
	Sig. (2-tailed)	0,11	0,06	0,09	0,35		
Taxation revenus élevés	Pearson Correlation	0,04	0,07	0,01	0,03	0,03	
	Sig. (2-tailed)	0,01	0,00	0,46	0,05	0,01	
Energie nucléaire	Pearson Correlation	0,03	0,03	0,01	0,00	0,01	–0,02
	Sig. (2-tailed)	0,01	0,05	0,57	0,84	0,54	0,22

Tableau 9: Matrice des corrélations (R de Pearson) des opinions en 1999

1ère vague (1999)	Armée	Dépenses sociales	Adhésion CE	Egalité CH – étrangers	Croissance économique	Taxation revenus élevés
Dépenses sociales	0,25					
Adhésion CE	0,27	0,23				
Egalité CH – étrangers	0,29	0,21	0,33			
Croissance économique	0,22	0,15	0,06	0,15		
Taxation revenus élevés	0,12	0,21	0,03*	n.s.	0,11	
Energie nucléaire	0,25	0,13	0,08	0,10	0,25	0,11

p.<,001 dans tous les cas, sauf * = p<,05 et n.s. = non significatif

Le choix électoral

L'étude du changement d'orientation du vote est basée sur le choix électoral des répondants des deux premières vagues. Les faibles effectifs pour chaque formation ne permettent de faire des analyses qu'avec les regroupements de partis (gauche, droite traditionnelle, droite nationale, aucun parti cité).

La stabilité du choix électoral

Certains interviewés plébiscitent le même groupe de formations politiques durant les deux premières vagues du panel, et effectuent un choix qu'on peut qualifier de «persistant». Le tableau 10[23] présente les facteurs expliquant la stabilité du choix entre les deux vagues; les régressions logistiques effectuées tentent chaque fois d'expliquer le vote persistant pour une famille de partis politiques (ou pour aucune d'entre elles) plutôt qu'un autre choix, quel qu'il soit[24].

mation mathématique donnant à la variable une moyenne de 0 et un écart-type de 1) de manière à ce que les coefficients EXP(B), qui expriment le changement dans les *odds ratios* occasionné par l'augmentation d'une unité de la variable indépendante, soient comparables. Les variables dichotomiques et nominales n'ont pas été transformées, afin que leur impact soit interprétable. Dans mes commentaires j'inverserai parfois le sens des échelles utilisées, afin d'obtenir des odds ratios supérieurs à l'unité et comparables avec ceux des autres variables.

24 Vote persistant pour un autre groupe de partis, changement d'une vague à l'autre, etc.

25 A nouveau, les variables indépendantes quantitatives sont standardisées.

Tableau 10: Facteurs explicatifs de la stabilité du vote – Régressions logistiques – Exp(B) (ou odds ratios, calculés sur la base des variables quantitatives standardisées), n, Pseudo-R carré de Cox et Snell et de Nagelkerke

	vote persistant à gauche		vote persistant à droite		vote persistant pour la droite nationale		vote persistant pour aucun parti	
	Sig.	Exp(B)	Sig.	Exp(B)	Sig.	Exp(B)	Sig.	Exp(B)
Sexe (masculin)					0,000	1,688		
Niveau d'éducation	0,027	1,200						
Intérêt pour la politique	0,010	1,230			0,000	1,345	0,000	0,560
Confiance dans le Conseil fédéral			0,000	1,559	0,000	0,563		
Confiance dans les partis politiques	0,000	1,351	0,017	1,173	0,000	1,564	0,000	0,699
Participation aux votations fédérales	0,005	1,239					0,000	0,758
Non-participation aux services religieux	0,000	1,284						
Potentiel protestataire	0,000	1,368	0,000	0,798			0,000	0,872
Positionnement idéologique gauche-droite	0,000	0,236	0,000	1,856	0,000	2,308		
Armée forte	0,000	0,727	0,000	1,326				
Diminution des dépenses sociales	0,000	0,782	0,003	1,181				
Adhésion à la CE	0,000	1,793	0,000	1,300	0,000	0,483		
Pro-nucléaire			0,000	1,196				
Ouverture			0,000	1,271	0,000	0,750		
Inégalité des chances entre Suisses et étrangers					0,001	1,255		
Croissance économique			0,000	1,241				
Diminution taxation des revenus élevés			0,010	1,147				
Nombre de non-réponses sur les opinions pol.							0,000	1,374
Ménage ne reçoit pas d'aide sociale			0,039	1,448				
Typologie socio-professionnelle (basée sur les csp)	0,023		0,000					
dirigeants	0,041	0,372	0,090	0,535				
professions libérales	0,338	0,689	0,043	1,964				
autres indépendants	0,049	0,692	0,000	1,654				
prof. intellectuelles et d'encadrement	0,271	1,219	0,069	1,303				
intermédiaires	0,367	1,126	0,150	1,186				
employés qualifiés	0,857	0,974	0,427	1,108				
ouvriers qualifiés	0,075	1,496	0,026	0,594				
travailleurs non qualifiés	0,031	1,708	0,144	0,754				
étudiants	0,361	1,309	0,056	0,582				

	vote persistant à gauche		vote persistant à droite		vote persistant pour la droite nationale		vote persistant pour aucun parti	
	Sig.	Exp(B)	Sig.	Exp(B)	Sig.	Exp(B)	Sig.	Exp(B)
au foyer sans avoir jamais exercé d'activité professionnelle	c. r.	c. r.	c. r.	c. r.				
Langue d'interview					0,000			
Français					0,001	0,468		
Allemand					0,000	1,807		
Italien					c. r.	c. r.		
Confession					0,000			
Protestant					0,000	1,548		
Catholique					0,001	0,647		
Autres confessions					0,012	1,681		
Sans confession					c. r.	c. r.		
n	3892		4109		4770		5053	
Cox et Snell R Square	0,35		0,14		0,17		0,15	
Nagelkerke R Square	0,54		0,25		0,42		0,21	

c. r. = catégorie de référence dans les variables nominales

Vote persistant à gauche

L'équation de régression logistique est performante (pseudo-R^2 de Nagelkerke de ,54) quand il s'agit d'expliquer le vote persistant à gauche, c'est-à-dire le choix d'une formation de la gauche (socialistes, écologistes, verts, alternatifs et popistes) durant les deux vagues.

Le facteur le plus déterminant est le positionnement sur l'axe idéologique gauche-droite en première vague; la probabilité de vote durant les 2 vagues pour un parti de gauche augmente très fortement quand les personnes se positionnent nettement sur la gauche de l'échiquier politique (odds ratio de ,24 pour l'augmentation d'un écart-type sur l'échelle dans le sens gauche-droite ou de 4,24 si on l'inverse dans le sens droite-gauche). Evidemment, cela peut sembler tautologique, mais son inclusion permet de montrer l'influence des autres paramètres de l'équation indépendamment de ce paramètre, et de pouvoir comparer son impact entre les modèles d'explication.

Plusieurs variables ont un impact plus limité, comme le fait d'être favorable à l'adhésion à l'Union européenne (odds ratio de 1,79), d'être anti-militariste (1,38), d'être pour une augmentation des dépenses sociales (1,28), d'avoir confiance dans les partis politiques (1,35), d'avoir un potentiel d'activisme protestataire élevé (1,37), de participer souvent aux votations fédérales (1,24) mais peu aux services religieux (1,28), d'être intéressé par la politique (1,23) et d'avoir un niveau de formation élevé (1,20). On constate aussi que les dirigeants et les indépendants sont sous-représentés parmi ces personnes fidèles aux partis de gauche, au contraire des travailleurs non qualifiés; l'impact des autres catégories socio-professionnelles n'est pas significatif statistiquement (p. > ,05).

Vote persistant à droite

Le vote persistant pour une formation de la droite traditionnelle (radicaux, démocrates-chrétiens et libéraux) est expliqué de manière moins satisfaisante par le modèle présenté dans le tableau 10 (pseudo-R^2 de Nagelkerke de ,25), ce qui signifie que les facteurs utilisés sont globalement moins discriminants.

Naturellement, plus les personnes se situent à droite sur l'axe idéologique, plus elles ont tendance à favoriser les partis de la droite traditionnelle durant les deux vagues (odds ratio de 1,86), mais en comparaison avec son impact sur le vote persistant de gauche, on constate que ce facteur a ici environ deux fois moins d'importance (1,86 contre 4,24). Ceci montre que les partisans des formations de la droite traditionnelle ont tendance à se positionner de manière plus centrale que les électeurs de gauche.

La confiance dans le Conseil fédéral est aussi un facteur important (1,56), alors qu'il n'a pas d'impact significatif pour le choix d'un parti de gauche; ceci relève le fait que l'exécutif fédéral est d'orientation bourgeoise (deux radicaux, deux démocrates-chrétiens), avec en outre des représentants socialistes et agrariens généralement choisis pour leurs positions modérées par rapport à celles de leur parti. Au niveau des autres attitudes et opinions politiques, on remarque parmi nos électeurs fidèles de la droite traditionnelle une sur-représentation des personnes favorables à une armée forte (1,33), à l'adhésion à l'Union européenne (1,30), à l'ouverture plutôt qu'à la défense des traditions (1,27), à la croissance économique plutôt qu'à la protection de l'environnement (1,24), à l'énergie nucléaire (1,20), à la diminution des dépenses sociales (1,18) et de la taxation des revenus élevés (1,15).

La confiance dans les partis politiques a aussi un impact positif (1,17) pour ce vote fidèle en faveur des partis de la droite traditionnelle, de même que le fait d'avoir un potentiel d'activisme protestataire faible (1,25). On ajoutera encore une sur-représentation des indépendants (1,65), des professions libérales (1,96) et des ménages ne recevant pas d'aide sociale (1,45), ainsi qu'une sous-représentation des ouvriers qualifiés (,59 ou 1,68 si l'on inverse la variable) parmi nos fidèles électeurs potentiels des partis bourgeois. Là encore, rien de très original dans ces résultats, qui corroborent toutes les observations que l'on a pu faire dans les analyses politologiques précédentes ou en suivant le débat politique suisse.

Vote persistant pour la droite nationaliste

Concernant la fidélité pour la droite nationaliste (UDC, Démocrates suisses, UDF, Parti de la liberté, Lega), les variables utilisées et présentées dans le tableau 10 sont très discriminantes, comme pour les partis de la gauche, avec un pseudo-R^2 de Nagelkerke de ,42.

Les électeurs potentiels et fidèles de la droite nationale ont une nette tendance à se situer à droite (odds ratio de 2,31), à s'opposer à l'adhésion à l'Union européenne (2,07), à habiter en Suisse alémanique (1,81), à avoir une confiance limitée dans le Conseil fédéral (1,78) mais relativement importante dans les partis politiques (1,56). Indépendamment des facteurs susmentionnés, ils sont sur-représentés parmi les hommes (1,69), les protestants (1,55), les personnes intéressées à la politique (1,35), favorables à la défense des traditions plutôt qu'à l'ouverture du pays (1,33) et à ce que les Suisses soient favorisés par rapport aux étrangers (1,26).

Vote persistant pour aucun parti

Le vote persistant pour aucun parti durant les deux premières vagues du panel, quelle qu'en soit la raison, s'explique relativement mal (pseudo-R^2 de Nagelkerke de ,21) avec les variables à disposition.

Le manque d'intérêt pour la politique (odds ratio de 1,79), de confiance dans les partis politiques (1,43), le fait d'avoir un nombre élevé de non-réponses concernant les opinions politiques (1,37), de s'abstenir lors des votations fédérales (1,32) et d'avoir un potentiel protestataire faible (1,15) sont ici les facteurs les plus déterminants de ce vote persistant pour aucun parti.

La démobilisation

Outre la stabilité, les données du panel permettent de s'intéresser à divers types de changements dans le choix des partis. Les lignes qui suivent portent sur la «démobilisation», c'est à dire le fait de ne citer aucun parti en 2e vague après avoir exprimé un choix nominal en 1ère. Je parlerai ici de «démobilisés» de la gauche, de la droite traditionnelle et de la droite nationaliste.

Le tableau 11 présente les facteurs expliquant cette démobilisation entre les deux vagues; les régressions logistiques[25] effectuées essaient chaque fois de prédire la démobilisation au sein d'une famille de partis politiques plutôt que la fidélité à celle-ci en 1ère et seconde vague du panel.

Tableau 11: Facteurs explicatifs de la démobilisation pour les partis politiques – Régressions logistiques – Exp(B) (ou odds ratios, calculés sur la base des variables quantitatives standardisées), n, Pseudo-R carré de Cox et Snell et de Nagelkerke

	«démobilisés» de gauche		«démobilisés» de droite		«démobilisés» de la droite nationale	
	Sig.	Exp(B)	Sig.	Exp(B)	Sig.	Exp(B)
Adhésion à la CE	0,012	0,776			0,000	1,503
Pas d'armée			0,002	1,294		
Protection environnement			0,016	1,190		
Manque de confiance dans le CF			0,003	1,294		
Positionnement idéologique gauche-droite	0,000	1,927			0,001	0,670
Baisse du sentiment d'influence politique	0,001	1,307				
Diminution de la volonté d'adhésion à la CE	0,001	1,302				
Perte du positionnement idéologique gauche-droite	0,000	13,478	0,000	10,792	0,000	5,147
n	1273		1023		537	
Cox et Snell R Square	0,12		0,09		0,10	
Nagelkerke R Square	0,18		0,13		0,14	

Les «démobilisés» de la gauche

En premier lieu, on constate que la démobilisation pour les partis de la gauche s'accompagne très fortement d'une perte de positionnement sur l'axe idéologique gauche-droite entre la première et la seconde vague (odds ratio de 13,48). Evitons à dessein de parler de causalité, tant ce positionnement idéologique et le choix partisan peuvent sembler liés, ce paramètre étant inclus surtout pour des raisons de comparabilité entre les équations du tableau.

Plus intéressant, parmi les électeurs potentiels de la gauche, les personnes se situant le plus à droite sur l'axe idéologique en 1999 ont une probabilité très grande (1,93) de se démobiliser en 2e vague.

Encore plus intéressant, l'enjeu de l'intégration européenne se montre problématique pour la gauche helvétique: les personnes déjà sceptiques quant à une adhésion en 1ère vague (1,29), de même celles qui voient leur europhilie décliner entre les deux vagues (1,30) sont nettement plus susceptibles de se démobiliser que les autres.

Finalement, on constate que la baisse du sentiment d'influence politique entre les deux vagues se traduit aussi par une probabilité de démobilisation plus élevée (odds ratio de 1,31) chez les électeurs potentiels de la gauche.

Les «démobilisés» de la droite traditionnelle

Comme pour la gauche, la perte du repère sur l'axe idéologique gauche-droite est souvent fatale à la mobilisation pour la droite (odds ratio de 10,79).

Indépendamment de ceci, on constate encore que les électeurs potentiels de droite en 1999 les moins militaristes (1,29) et les plus attachés à la protection de l'environnement (1,19) en 1ère vague sont aussi plus susceptibles de se démobiliser. Il en va de même pour les moins confiants dans le Conseil fédéral en 1999 (1,29).

Les «démobilisés» de la droite nationaliste

La perte de positionnement sur l'axe idéologique gauche-droite entre les deux vagues reste déterminante mais est clairement moins préjudiciable à la mobilisation pour la droite nationaliste que pour les deux autres familles politiques précédentes (5,15 contre 10,79 pour la droite et 13,48 pour la gauche). Ceci est lié au caractère «attrape-tout» de ces formations politiques populistes et à leur volonté de se détacher des traditionnels clivages gauche-droite en mettant l'accent sur l'enjeu de l'ouverture du pays à l'extérieur et en cristallisant les mécontentements de toutes natures.

Les chiffres du tableau 11 montrent encore que les formations de la droite nationaliste ont une probabilité plus grande d'être désertées par leurs électeurs potentiels les moins réfractaires à l'intégration européenne (1,50) et les plus à gauche (1,49).

La mobilisation

Nous sommes aussi en mesure de nous pencher sur certaines formes de mobilisation politique, c'est à dire le fait de citer un parti pour lequel on voterait en 2e vague après ne pas l'avoir fait en 1ère.

Le tableau 12 est consacré aux déterminants de cette mobilisation entre les deux vagues, en faveur de la gauche, de la droite et de la droite nationaliste; les régressions logistiques prédisent chaque fois la mobilisation pour une famille de partis politiques en seconde vague plutôt que le fait de ne citer aucun parti durant les deux vagues. Les variables indépendantes quantitatives sont une nouvelle fois standardisées.

Mobilisation en faveur de la gauche

Parmi les interviewés n'ayant pas émis de préférence politique particulière en 1999, les personnes se situant le plus à gauche en 1999 (odds ratio de 1,93), celles ayant un potentiel protestataire élevé (1,36), celles opposées au nucléaire (1,34), celles intéressées par la politique (1,26) et plutôt favorables à l'adhésion à l'Union européenne (1,24), sont les plus susceptibles de se mobiliser pour les partis de la gauche helvétique en 2e vague du panel.

Tableau 12: Facteurs explicatifs de la mobilisation pour les partis politiques – Régressions logistiques – Exp(B) (ou odds ratios, calculés sur la base des variables quantitatives standardisées), n, Pseudo-R carré de Cox et Snell et de Nagelkerke

	«mobilisés» de gauche		«mobilisés» de droite		«mobilisés» de la droite nationale	
	Sig.	Exp(B)	Sig.	Exp(B)	Sig.	Exp(B)
Intérêt pour la politique	0,010	1,261	0,000	1,673	0,000	2,054
Potentiel protestataire	0,000	1,357	0,013	0,802		
Positionnement idéologique gauche-droite	0,000	0,519	0,000	1,949	0,001	1,732
Anti-nucléaire	0,002	1,335				
Adhésion à la CE	0,015	1,243			0,000	0,498
Egalité des chances entre Suisses et étrangers					0,030	0,758
Diminution de la satisfaction financière			0,002	1,249		
n	1472		1624		1381	
Cox et Snell R Square	0,08		0,06		0,07	
Nagelkerke R Square	0,14		0,11		0,19	

Mobilisation en faveur de la droite

Pour la mobilisation en faveur de la droite traditionnelle, le positionnement à droite (1,95), l'intérêt pour la politique (1,67), le fait d'avoir un potentiel protestataire bas et de voir la satisfaction envers sa situation financière baisser entre les deux vagues (1,25) sont les seuls facteurs déterminants.

Mobilisation en faveur de la droite nationale

La mobilisation en faveur de la droite nationale est surtout liée à l'intérêt pour la politique (2,05), à l'opposition à l'adhésion de la Suisse à l'Union européenne (2,01), à l'auto-positionnement à droite (1,73) et à la volonté de voir les Suisses favorisés par rapport aux étrangers dans notre pays (1,32).

Le changement de famille de partis politiques

Le passage de la droite nationale à la droite traditionnelle

Le seul changement de famille de partis politiques analysable dans de bonnes conditions (97 cas) est celui de la droite nationale à la droite traditionnelle entre 1999 et 2000. Les autres passages à «l'ennemi» sont trop rares et s'inscrivent dans des distributions trop asymétriques pour donner des estimations fiables.

Dans le tableau 13, qui oppose ces transfuges aux personnes restant fidèles à la droite nationale durant les deux vagues, on constate que les conversions sont le fait de personnes plutôt favorables à l'adhésion à l'Union européenne (odds ratio de 1,69), confiantes dans le Conseil fédéral (1,40) et qui voient leur niveau d'intérêt pour la politique augmenter entre les deux interviews (1,37).

Tableau 13: Facteurs explicatifs du passage de la droite nationale à la droite traditionnelle – Régression logistiques – Exp(B) (variables quantitatives standardisées), n, Pseudo-R carré de Cox et Snell et de Nagelkerke

	Sig.	Exp(B)
Augmentation de l'ntérêt pour la politique entre les deux vagues	0,012	1,372
Confiance dans le Conseil fédéral	0,007	1,398
Adhésion à la CE	0,000	1,698
n	467	
Cox et Snell R Square	0,08	
Nagelkerke R Square	0,12	

Fidélités et infidélités politiques

Des analyses dédiées à l'orientation du vote lors des deux vagues du panel on retient tout d'abord que la stabilité s'explique mieux que les changements (pseudo-R^2 de Nagelkerke de ,21 à ,54, contre ,11 à ,19). Ceci corrobore l'idée que le choix d'un parti est plutôt stable dans le temps (tableau 5).

Les analyses dédiées à la fidélité aux familles de partis politiques n'apportent pas de révélations dans le sens où elles confirment les travaux précédents consacrés à l'orientation du vote (Linder 1998, Holzer et Linder 2003, Mazzoleni

2003) en en exacerbant parfois les résultats, étant donné que nous avons affaire à des électeurs potentiels fidèles, ayant confirmé deux fois leur choix.

On y décèle ainsi un impact légèrement plus important des caractéristiques sociales et démographiques des citoyens que ne l'avaient montré les études électorales précédentes (Linder 1998, Schloeth 1998), avec une nette sur-représentation des hommes dans l'électorat de la droite nationale ou un niveau d'éducation supérieur parmi les électeurs de gauche. Le fait que les ouvriers soient sur-représentés dans les rangs de la gauche, à l'inverse des patrons et indépendants et que l'inverse soit vrai pour la droite bourgeoise n'est évidemment non plus pas une découverte. Que les partis de gauche recueillent surtout les suffrages de personnes peu actives religieusement ne surprend non plus pas, tout comme le fait que la droite nationale soit clairement sous-représentée dans la partie francophone du pays et dans l'électorat catholique.

Concernant les attitudes politiques, si les personnes fidèles aux trois familles de partis politiques considérées ont généralement confiance dans les partis, le fait que les partisans de la droite nationale aient une confiance très limitée dans le Conseil fédéral est symptomatique. Ceci rejoint les travaux de Trechsel (1994), qui parle de «clivage de confiance», politisé par les partis de la nouvelle droite et ensuite par l'UDC, qui critique la composition consensuelle du Conseil fédéral et y réclame un second siège, parallèlement à l'éviction des socialistes.

Au sujet des opinions politiques structurant le débat politique suisse actuel, on ne s'étonnera non plus pas de voir que les partisans de la gauche se distinguent par des opinions pro-européennes, anti-militaristes et opposés à la diminution des dépenses sociales. Que les personnes fidèles aux partis de la droite traditionnelle dans leurs intentions de vote soient aussi en général pro-européennes, mais par contre plutôt militaristes, pro-nucléaires, favorables à la diminution des dépenses sociales, à la croissance économique (au détriment de la protection de l'environnement) et à la diminution de la taxation des revenus élevés ne fait que refléter les prises de position de ces formations politiques. Toujours au niveau des opinions politiques, ce sont les enjeux de l'adhésion à l'Union européenne et de l'ouverture du pays qui opposent les tenants de la droite traditionnelle à ceux de la droite nationaliste, ces options étant défendues par les partis bourgeois traditionnels (PRD, PDC et Libéraux) et combattues par l'UDC et ses alliés.

Les déterminants de l'indifférence persistante vis-à-vis des partis durant les deux vagues ne sont non plus pas originaux et recoupent plusieurs de ceux habituellement mis en évidence pour l'abstentionnisme, à savoir le manque d'intérêt pour la politique, le manque de confiance et l'absence de prises de positions tranchées quant aux opinions politiques (Wernli 2001, Mazzoleni et Wernli 2002).

Ce qui est plus nouveau est l'étude des variations dans l'orientation du vote, autorisée par les données de panel. Les analyses consacrées aux «désertions» des trois grandes familles de partis politiques suisses, à savoir une préférence exprimée en première vague et non confirmée en seconde, laissent entendre qu'on se trouve en face d'une sorte de polarisation entre les deux enquêtes. Les partis de la gauche helvétique sont abandonnés par les personnes les moins à gauche et celles critiques par rapport à l'adhésion à l'Union européenne, ceux de la droite traditionnelle par les anti-militaristes et les personnes sensibles à la protection de l'environnement, tandis que la droite nationaliste tend à faire fuir les europhiles et ses votants potentiels les moins marqués à droite. Ce qu'il n'est pas possible de dire pour l'instant, c'est si le phénomène est lié aux élections fédérales de 1999 ou s'il s'inscrit dans le plus long terme. Dans la première des hypothèses, on pourrait penser qu'après les élections, les électeurs potentiels les plus atypiques des familles de partis politiques se démobilisent en raison de leurs prises de positions iconoclastes et qu'ils soient rameutés par la propagande au moment de chaque rendez-vous électoral, dans une sorte de processus d'activation déjà décrit par les précurseurs de l'école de Columbia (Lazarsfeld, Berelson et Gaudet 1968). Dans la seconde, ce phénomène serait une manifestation supplémentaire de la polarisation et du durcissement général du paysage politique suisse de ces dernières années, avec une gauche et une droite nationaliste conquérantes, toujours plus tranchées et réticentes aux compromis, les radicaux et démocrates-chrétiens perdant du terrain en raison de leurs options centristes.

Concernant les cas de mobilisation, on voit que les familles de partis politiques n'arrivent à rallier le vote potentiel que des personnes déjà prédisposées de par leurs positions politiques.

Pour le passage de la droite nationale à la droite traditionnelle, on remarque que les personnes changeant de camp avaient en fait des positions proches des partis bourgeois, notamment pro-européennes et une confiance élevée dans le Conseil fédéral. Ici, on peut hésiter entre deux interprétations, peut-être correctes toutes les deux, à savoir s'il s'agit de personnes ayant traditionnellement voté pour la droite traditionnelle et qui retournent vers celle-ci après une infidélité en faveur de la droite nationaliste, ou d'éléments agrariens modérés, effrayés par la dérive populiste et isolationniste de leur parti.

Conclusion

On retiendra tout d'abord que les indicateurs politologiques du panel offrent des distributions très comparables à ceux d'autres enquêtes, ce qui est un bon signe de validité.

Les variations des attitudes politiques entre les deux vagues sont généralement modestes et la stabilité du comportement individuel prévaut. Concernant les prises de positions sur des questions précises, la stabilité est aussi généralement de mise, avec une tendance à un léger déplacement sur la gauche, en vertu des prises de positions de la gauche helvétique, pour les personnes indécises et ayant des opinions de droite en 1ère vague. Un point se démarque de cette tendance générale, avec une légère diminution de la proportion de personnes favorables à l'adhésion à l'Union Européenne. Pour le choix partisan, la stabilité prévaut aussi, que ce soit parmi les personnes ne citant aucun parti, pour les partis de la gauche et de la droite traditionnelle, l'électorat de la droite nationale se montrant plus volatil, à mon sens en vertu de son caractère plus hétéroclite et de sa récente et brutale poussée en 1999.

Au niveau individuel, malgré le foisonnement d'hypothèses testées, les changements dans les attitudes et les opinions politiques s'expliquent très mal. La première hypothèse, qui veut qu'ils puissent être mis en relation avec les changements dans les conditions de vie des personnes, est clairement infirmée.

Au niveau des changements dans le choix partisan, les résultats deviennent plus probants, avec la mise en évidence d'une sorte de polarisation qui voient les familles de partis politiques être abandonnées par leurs votants potentiels les moins radicaux, sans que l'on puisse dire pour l'instant si ce phénomène est lié à une activation tous azimuts des sympathisants liée aux élections fédérales de 1999 ou à un durcissement du paysage politique suisse relatif à la poussée des socialistes et des démocrates du centre.

Une constante se dégage aussi de toutes les analyses: le caractère atypique de la question de l'adhésion à l'UE. C'est la seule opinion politique qui connaisse un léger glissement en direction des thèses de la droite nationaliste entre les deux vagues, celle où les prises de positions des tenants et des opposants sont les plus stables, une de celles qui voit la plus forte polarisation des indécis, celle qui est la plus déterminante pour expliquer la stabilité, la mobilisation et la démobilisation vis-à-vis des familles de partis politiques, enfin, celle qui sépare le plus la droite traditionnelle (PRD et PDC) de la droite nationaliste (UDC et petites formations d'extrême-droite). Si l'on ajoute le fait que la question de l'intégration européenne a engendré un taux de participation extrêmement élevé (78 %) lors des votations fédérales de décembre 1992 (adhésion à l'EEE), qu'elle constitue le point d'achoppement le plus important entre et à l'intérieur même des partis bourgeois représentés au Conseil fédéral et qu'elle explique largement le raz de marée victorieux de l'UDC aux dernières élections fédérales, on comprend que l'enjeu est hors du commun et revêt un caractère particulier dans la politique suisse actuelle et certainement des prochaines années.

Bibliographie sélective

Holzer, Thomas et Wolf Linder 2003. «Die Wahlentscheidung im Wechselspiel zwischen Parteiidentifikation und Sachfragenorientierung», in *Schweizer Wahlen 1999,* Pascal Sciarini, Sybille Hardmeier et Adrian Vatter (eds). Bern: Haupt.

Joye, Dominique et Yannis Papadopoulos 1986. «La mobilisation partisane est-elle en crise?», *Annuaire suisse de science politique* 26, 47-62.

Kitschelt, Herbert 1995. *The radical right in western Europe: a comparative analysis.* Ann Harbor: University of Michigan.

Kriesi, Hanspeter 1993. *Political mobilization and social change. The dutch case in comparative perspective.* Aldershot: Avebury.

Kriesi, Hanspeter 1995. *Le système politique suisse.* Paris: Economica.

Lazarsfeld, Paul F., Bernard Berelson et Hazel Gaudet 1968. *The people's choice.* New-York: Columbia University Press.

Lijphart, Arendt 1984. *Democracies.* New-Haven: Yale University Press.

Linder, Wolf 1998. «Parteien-, Persönlichkeits-, Europa- oder Traditionswahl? Eine systematische Untersuchung des Einflusses der Sachthemen auf den Wahlentscheid», in *Die Schweizer Wahlen 1995. Ergebnisse der Wahlstudie SELECTS,* Hanspeter Kriesi, Wolf Linder et Ulrich Klöti (eds). Bern: Haupt.

Mazzoleni, Oscar et Boris Wernli 2002. *Cittadini e politica.* Osservatorio della vita politica, Ufficio di Statistica.

Mazzoleni, Oscar 2003. «La dimension gauche-droite et le choix partisan. Une perspective comparée», in *Schweizer Wahlen 1999,* Pascal Sciarini, Sybille Hardmeier et Adrian Vatter (eds). Bern: Haupt.

Papadopoulos, Yannis 1997. *Les processus de décision fédéraux en Suisse.* Paris: L'Harmattan.

Schlöth, Daniel 1998. *Vor die Wahl gestellt. Erklärung des Wahlerverhaltens bei den Eidgennössischen Wahlen 1995.* Bern: Haupt.

Topf, Richard 1995. «Beyond electoral participation», in *Citizens and the state,* Hans-Dieter Klingemann et Dieter Fuchs (eds). Oxford: Oxford University Press.

Trechsel, Alexandre H. 1994. *Clivages en Suisse – Analyse des impacts relatifs des clivages sur l'électorat suisse lors des élections fédérales.* Mémoire de Diplôme d'Etudes Supérieures en science politique. Université de Genève.

Wernli, Boris 2001. *Contraintes institutionnelles, influences contextuelles et participation aux élections fédérales en Suisse.* Haupt: Berne.

5. Qualité de vie et santé
Lebensqualität und Gesundheit

Change and Stability of Satisfaction over One Year*

Annette Scherpenzeel

Introduction

Theories of Happiness and Life Satisfaction

The subject of happiness or life satisfaction has a long history of social research. It has especially evolved in the 1970's, when a growing stream of conferences, research institutes, surveys and reports appeared, referred to as the "Social Indicator Movement". This "movement" was directed to find new, non-materialistic indicators of welfare. Until then, mainly economic criteria were used to define welfare, both on the societal and individual level. Welfare was measured by, for example, the national product of a nation, the security of income, the degree of social-inequality, and, for individuals, by the material standard of living. These criteria indicate the "presumed" quality of living, as Veenhoven (1995) calls it. The "post-materialism" values shift called for a broader definition of welfare, and for measures of how well people are doing given their living conditions, or, in other words: the "apparent" quality of living. Happiness and satisfaction with life were introduced as indicators of this "apparent" quality of living or "subjective well-being". Landmark books were published, such as: "The quality of American life" by Campbell et al. (1976) and "Social indicators of well-being" by Andrews and Withey (1976). Even an international, specialised journal, "Social Indicators Research" was founded.

* The present article is part of the book *Living in Switzerland 1999–2000* (Erwin Zimmermann and Robin Tillmann (eds), Editions Peter Lang, Bern (2004)). The analyses and results are based on the first two waves of the longitudinal survey called Living in Switzerland in which 6,335 persons were interviewed in 1999 and 2000. On behalf of the Swiss Household Panel at the University of Neuchâtel, the data collection was carried out by M. I. S. Trend and financed by the PP Switzerland Towards the Future of the Swiss National Science Foundation (Grants No 5004-53205 / 5004-57894 / 5004-67304). Further information can be found on the website www.swisspanel.ch.

Part of the tradition of social research is the aim to develop a better society. The thought that happiness and satisfaction are changeable, that you could make people happier if you knew the necessary conditions, stimulated research into the causal mechanism of happiness and satisfaction[1]. The first, most general causal model re-introduces the economic factors described above, but this time as predictors of life satisfaction. The hypothesis on a societal level was that if the level and security of income, the degree of social-equality, and eventually the degree of democracy of a nation would increase, average satisfaction would also increase. On an individual level the expectation was that the higher a persons standard of living, level of education and social support, the more happy and satisfied he or she will be. On the societal level the theory holds to a certain extent: A rather strong relationship is often found between average life satisfaction in nations and income per head. The relationship is curvilinear: among poorer nations it is stronger than among richer nations. Average satisfaction also correlates quite strongly with societal characteristics such as social security, political and personal freedom, equality, etc. (Veenhoven, 1996). The curvilinear pattern is reflected on the individual level: Income is strongly related to life satisfaction within poor countries, in rich countries the relationship is very weak. In Western, rich countries the demographic variables age, gender, education and income have almost no relationships with life satisfaction at the individual level. Occupation is generally found to have a somewhat stronger correlation: professionals and managers tend to be the most satisfied in many nations. According to Veenhoven (1995) these demographic variables together never explain much more than 10 % of the variance in individual satisfaction in the richer nations. Veenhoven and Saris (1995) have, across 10 European studies, tested whether correcting for measurement error could increase this low level of explained variance. However, the correction did not make a difference. Their results confirmed what had been found before: Relationships are very weak in the richer Western countries in Europe, and stronger within the poorer

1 Some researchers use measures of happiness, others use measures of life-satisfaction. In theoretical discussions the terms are often intertwined, because they seem to denote basically the same construct. When happiness is conceived as *the degree to which an individual judges the overall quality of his life favourably* (Veenhoven, 1991), happiness can also be called 'life-satisfaction'. In the present paper we will make no theoretical distinction between the terms, and we use measures of satisfaction in our study.

East-European countries. Most recently, this pattern of interaction has once again been confirmed by Schyns (2002).

Another view on the relationship between living conditions and satisfaction comes from sociological theories about inequality. In this perspective, demographic variables are important for satisfaction, in the sense that they constitute one's position in society. Social positions are seen as essentially invariable and persistent, and that distinguishes this theory from the foregoing. In the second view, satisfaction changes little in time since social position changes little. However, all evidence cited above about the lack of relationships between demographic variables and satisfaction in rich countries challenge this second view as well. In addition, both living conditions and satisfaction do change over time in poorer, developing countries.

As a result of the lack of explicative power of demographic variables, other theories of happiness and satisfaction evolved. One kind of theories can perhaps be summarised under the name "Comparison" theories[2] and assumes that satisfaction is based on a comparison of ones life with subjective standards of how-life-should-be. Since the standard of comparison is chosen or constructed by each person self, it is subjective and arbitrary: It is not necessarily a realistic standard of comparison or even a good one for that person, according to objective criteria. Consequently, comparison theory implies that satisfaction has no relationship with actual living conditions. People living in objectively bad conditions can be as satisfied as or more satisfied than people living in better conditions. The same income, for example, can lead to different levels of satisfaction for different persons, dependent on the income of their neighbours. In addition, most comparison theories assume that the standards of comparison adjust when living conditions change: People adapt to the changed situation and shift their standard of comparison ("Adaptation" theory). In this view, changing living conditions have no long-term effect on satisfaction and it makes no sense to strive to improve general or individual satisfaction. The standards of comparison which have most been investigated are "important others" and one's own past condition. Michalos (1985), however, distinguished five different standards: what one "wants", what one "had" earlier in life, what

2 Under this general term we summarise theories called: "Relative Satisfaction" theory; "Relative Deprivation" theory; "Relative Standards" theory; "(Multiple) Discrepancy" theory; "Adaptation" theory.

one "expected" to have, what one thinks "other people" have and what one thinks is "deserved".

Comparison theory seems to hold only for individuals in the rich, Western societies. As described above, at the national level relationships exist between average life satisfaction and economical and societal conditions. Comparison theory would predict that people in poorer countries would adjust their standards of comparison and be equally happy as people in richer countries. In addition, income appears strongly related to life satisfaction within poor countries. Perhaps people in poor countries choose a different type of standards or choose their standards in a different way than people in rich countries, but in what way and why is not explained by comparison theory.

In contrast with sociology, the field of psychology tends to view satisfaction as a personality trait. This trait is a disposition to or outlook on life, which is either innate or acquired, but is stable and independent of living conditions. Someone having a pessimistic disposition will always take less pleasure from changes in life than someone having a happy disposition. A variation of the trait theory sees satisfaction rather as a "national trait": a collective outlook on life based on cultural norms, religion, and history. Both at the individual and the national level, trait theories assume that people stay as happy or unhappy as they are, independent of changes in life circumstances. Hence, happiness cannot be improved and is highly stable trough time. The national-level theoretical variation is mainly based on common sense ideas (i. e. "Italians are light-hearted, Swedes are worrywart"), and hardly any scientific proof exists for it. We saw above that, in contrast with the individual level, substantial effects of living conditions on satisfaction are found at the cross-national level. Veenhoven (1994) compared 30 countries and found that the quality of living conditions can explain up to 80 % of the variance in happiness between countries. In addition, economic growth in poorer countries is proven to be followed by increasing satisfaction (Veenhoven, 1994). Another falsification is found in the fact that East- and West Germans, who share the same language and for a large part the same culture, but live in different conditions, significantly differ in happiness (Landua, 1992). Finally, from national trait theory would follow that satisfaction within one nation is homogeneous. This is certainly not the case in poorer nations, as we saw before, but even within the richest countries, where living conditions do no longer relate to satisfaction, we still can observe satisfaction to vary over individuals. The latter phenomenon would lead to the theory of satisfaction as an individual personality trait. Evidence for trait theory on the individual level is found in studies that find satisfaction to be unrelated to living conditions; studies in which satisfaction is found to be stable over time and insensitive to changes in life; and studies showing that personality traits explain a considerable part of the variance in satisfaction. Veenhoven (1994) evaluates all evidence in a meta-analysis of longitudinal studies. We only briefly summarise some of the criticisms here, for the complete review we refer to Veenhoven. Firstly, as we have seen before, satisfaction is only independent of living conditions within the richest nations, in poorer countries relationships do exist. Secondly, Veenhoven finds that happiness indeed appears to be stable on the short term, but over the years it is not. Furthermore, most studies that have shown satisfaction to be insensitive to changes in life use life-changes which are part of the normal sequence of life, such as leaving school, getting married, taking a new job, moving to another house. However, when really dramatic events occur, such as cardiac attacks, dead of a spouse or a child, etc., satisfaction does seem to decrease. Finally, even though a correlation between personality and satisfaction cannot be denied, it does not explain *all* variance in satisfaction. Veenhoven (1994) argues that there is room for other factors to explain satisfaction as well. Recently, a model has been proposed in which effects of life-changes as well as a stable factor were both included: Ehrhardt et al. (2000) regarded the stable factor in their model not so much as a personality trait but as "stable stocks", which according to them include one's body, personality and social position. Using 11 years of German panel data, they found the effects of the "stable stocks" and the (summed) life-changes to be almost equally strong. They concluded that satisfaction with life is not primarily determined by stable personality traits or by stable social positions but contains as much stability as variability.

Goal of this Study

In this study we have tried to formulate the predictions of each of the theories described above with regard to changes in life satisfaction over time and defined a dynamic model to test these predictions. As was said above, living conditions are often unrelated to satisfaction scores on an individual level in cross-sectional studies. However, cross-sectional studies look at *differences* in living conditions and satisfaction between people and do not tell us whether a *change* in a living condition will cause a change in satisfaction. The uniqueness of a panel study like we use here is exactly the possibility of measuring the real changes in living conditions and satisfaction.

Our model is, in line with Ehrhardt et al. (2000), a structural equation model describing changes in satisfaction through time, effects of changes in living conditions and the effect of a stable component. Structural equation models can be seen as extended regression equations that allow measurement error in the explanatory as well as the dependent variables and correlations between the error components. They can also be viewed as factor analyses that permit direct and indirect effects between factors. Furthermore, they can include multiple indicators and latent variables. In short, only these type of models encompass all tools we need for our theory test, in which we want to test the existence of a (latent) stable component, specify both direct and indirect effects of the living conditions, and allow correlated errors to model the dependence between two identical variables at two different points in time.

We have extended the model of Ehrhardt et al. with a comparative evaluation of one's living situation, using as standard of comparison the situation of one year ago. We use measures of satisfaction (see footnote 1) and living conditions from the first two waves (1999 and 2000) of the Swiss Household Panel Survey.

Four possible results can be expected, each of which confirms one of the described theories and falsifies the others:

1. Satisfaction does not change; living conditions have not changed either. This result would confirm the theory of invariable socio-economical position determining life-satisfaction. However, it can also be due to a too short time-period to show any change, or it can be a ceiling effect in a very rich country where the needs of most people are met.
2. Satisfaction does not change; living conditions do show change. Trait theories would predict that changes in living conditions have no effect on satisfaction. The Trait theory can further be confirmed by the significance of the effects of a stable component.
3. Satisfaction changes, independently of (changes in) living conditions. This finding would be expected by Comparison theories: Living conditions have no direct effects on satisfaction. Finding a significant effect of the comparative measure in the model would further confirm Comparison theory.
4. Satisfaction changes causally related to changes in living conditions. It is unlikely that general demographic variables, like age, education, and

> income will show significant effects on (changes in) satisfaction in the present study, since this is generally not found in rich countries. However, if we can find other, more specific, or more relevant "objective" variables, we might find significant effects and that would than be in line with sociological theories of changeable happiness or "Social engineering". The proof of these theories would be complete when, in addition, neither the stable component nor the comparative measure would have any effect.

The problem of this study is, of course, the very short time-span of observation (one year). This means that if no changes in living conditions and no changes in satisfaction are found (result 1), we cannot decide between the different theories: It can be that satisfaction is stable and independent of living conditions, it can also be that satisfaction is dependent of societal position which changes little, or it can be that the time-span was too short to measure significant changes. However, if a significant effect of changing living conditions on satisfaction is found, we can say which theory is most probable. Moreover, we have two additional tests by including the stable component and the comparative measure in the model.

The model test is done several times, each time within a specific domain. That is: we will not relate general life-satisfaction to various aspects of life, but instead relate satisfaction with health to health status and other relevant health or illness variables, satisfaction with financial situation to income variables, satisfaction with work to working conditions, etc. We believe the relationships we search will be much stronger within the specific domains than on a general level, which allows better tests. Likewise, we have not used general demographic variables, such as age, gender, education and income, because these are known to have little relationships with satisfaction in rich countries. We have chosen more specific, domain-bound living conditions, for example: "job security" and "type of employment" as conditions for satisfaction with work. The general demographic variables are assumed to be "input" to these conditions, and as such they can eventually have indirect effects on satisfaction. However, this is not tested in our study, because we are more interested in testing the different theoretical predictions about satisfaction change by means of direct, substantial effects.

Method

The Domains and Living Conditions

Four major domains of life are selected for our model tests: Finances, Health, Work and Intimate Relations. Below, an overview is given of all relevant living conditions that were included in the model for each domain. Each condition is measured by asking the respondents themselves in a telephone interview.

Finances
- Equivalised, yearly net household income following the OECD definition
- Problems in payment of bills (no/sometimes/often)
- Financial situation manageable (scale from 0 to 10)
- Reception of financial help (yes/no)
- Number of (luxury) goods the household does not possess for financial reasons

Health
- Medication need (scale from 0 to 10)
- Impediment in every day activities (scale from 0 to 10)
- Number of health problems
- Number of days affected by health problems
- Number of doctor consultations
- Health event: illness or accident

Work
- Socio-economical classification scales
- Type of Job (management, teaching, production, etc.)
- Type of Employer (small/big, government, private, self-employed, etc.)
- Type of contract (permanent or a temporary, and for how long)
- Amount of overtime
- Daily commuting time
- Perceived risk of unemployment (scale from 0 to 10)
- Perceived job security (scale from 0 to 10)
- Correspondence of qualifications and job (correspond/do not correspond)

Full-or part-time work (percentage)
Event: change of job

Intimate relations
Partner (no/yes but not living together/yes living together)
Practical support from partner (scale from 0 to 10)
Emotional support from partner (scale from 0 to 10)
Event: death of a closely related person
Event: termination of a close relationship
Event: conflicts with or among related persons
Event: problems with own children

The Model

In figure 1, the model is depicted in a general and simplified form. At each of the two points in time, satisfaction is affected by a number of "objective" conditions, specific for the domain studied. The objective conditions are allowed to change over time. The model furthermore contains events that have occurred between the two panel waves, and the variable "relative situation". As was described in the introduction, the standards of comparison mostly used in satisfaction research are "important others" and one's own past condition. It is very difficult to measure comparison with others in social surveys. One has to rely on self-reported social comparisons, which are known to be very unreliable. Most people when asked report they do not use social comparison. Measures of comparison with people's (recent) past situation are much easier to include in a panel survey. Therefore, in the questionnaire of the second wave of the panel, questions were included asking people to evaluate their present (health-, financial-, work-) situation in comparison with a year ago: How much had it deteriorated or ameliorated, or had it stayed the same? The events are assumed to affect the evaluation of the relative situation, which then in turn affects satisfaction. Finally, the figure contains a "stable component". This component is a *latent* factor, represented by a circle, which means the factor is not a measured variable but a theoretical construct. In each domain we will estimate the model both with and without this factor, to see whether the "stable component" significantly improves the model of satisfaction. The model in principle resembles the "stable component model" of Ehrhardt et al., but differs from it in the sense that these authors use the *sum* of changes in living conditions as a single causal variable at each time point, while we include each event as a separate variable. Moreover, Ehrhardt et al. only include *changes* in living conditions, while we also look at living conditions that remain stable over time.

This basic model was varied somewhat in each domain, when the data made it necessary: A certain objective condition could, for example, turn out to have an indirect effect on satisfaction instead of the assumed direct effect, or two conditions could appear to influence each other. Non-significant parameters were in most cases deleted from the model, and likewise, variables with no significant effects at all were left out of the model. All model estimations were done with the AMOS program for linear structural equations (Arbuckle, 1997), a detailed description of the estimation procedure can be found in the technical appendix.

The model in figure 1 is a simplified, illustrative version of the model that in reality has to be specified for an analysis. To make the model complete and estimable, unique components, correlations and restrictions have to be added (see technical appendix). Moreover, some measures were very highly correlated and could be viewed as different dimensions of a single concept. In such cases, we specified a latent factor with a measurement model. Latent factors make the structural part of the model more parsimonious and give more possibilities for the correction of measurement error. In the paragraph "Results" the complete model of satisfaction with Finances is given as illustration, including a latent factor, error components and correlated error.

Data

The data used come from the first two waves of the Swiss Household Panel. The complete longitudinal sample (individuals interviewed in the first and second waves) comprises approximately 6,000 individuals. For our analysis, only individuals could be used who had valid data for all variables in the model in a certain domain. Individuals with missing data or, for example, a "don't know" answer to a relevant question were excluded from the analysis within that domain. Since individuals for whom data is missing in one domain can have complete data in another domain, the number of cases in the analyses can vary over the domains. The analysis in the domain Work, for example, has a much smaller number of cases than other analyses, since it includes only people who have a paid job.

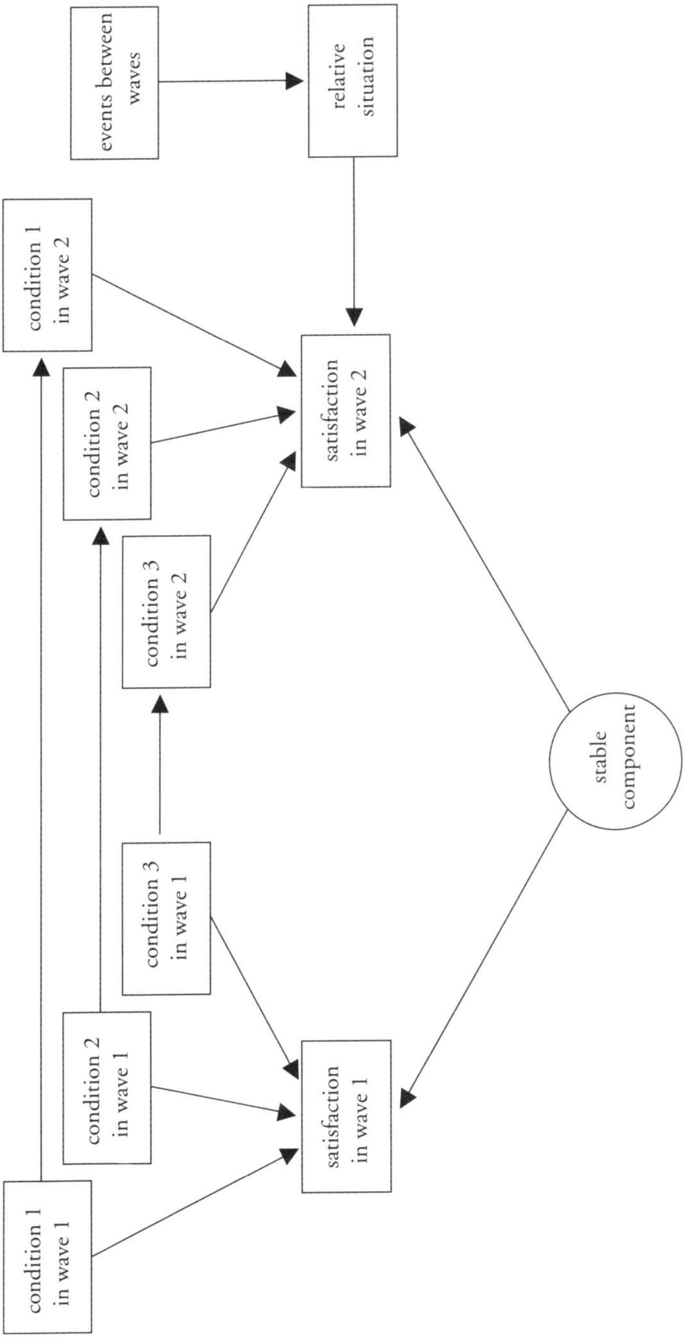

Figure 1: General two-wave causal model of satisfaction

Results

We will describe in some detail the complete model of satisfaction with finances and the results obtained with it, as an illustration of the approach we followed in all four domains. For the other three domains, the effects will only be summarised and compared across domains, to allow the test of the hypotheses described in the introduction. The detailed results obtained in each domain can be found in the appendix “estimated effects”.

Finances

The complete model of satisfaction with finances including the standardised parameter estimates is presented in figure 2, to illustrate the application of the general model of figure 1 to a specific domain. Satisfaction with financial situation is an uni-dimensional observed variable at both waves. The important objective conditions in the financial domain are income and expenses. As income measure, we have chosen the equivalised, yearly net household income following the OECD definition. We did not include the total of all expenses of a household as input variable, since de panel survey is not a pure economical survey and does not extensively ask about all possible expenses. Furthermore, we considered the concordance between income and expenses and resulting problems to be of more importance than the absolute level of expenses of a household. To represent this concordance, we chose the variables “Problems in payment of bills” (no/sometimes/often), “Financial situation manageable” (0–10) “Reception of financial help” (yes/no), and “Deprivation” (the sum of all goods the household does not possess for financial reasons). The three variables “Problems in payment of bills”, “Financial situation manageable” and “Deprivation” correlated very strongly and were defined to form one factor, labelled “Financial Problems”. The variable “Reception of financial help” had no significant effect on satisfaction. It was therefore deleted from the model.

Hence, the conditions affecting satisfaction both at the first and the second wave are “Financial problems” and “Equivalent income”. In addition, satisfaction in the second wave is influenced by the relative situation. No events in the financial domain were available in the panel data and thus not included in the model. The difference with figure 1 is that one of the conditions, “Financial problems”, is not an uni-dimensional observed variable, but a latent variable measured by the three items described above. In figure 2 is shown how this is

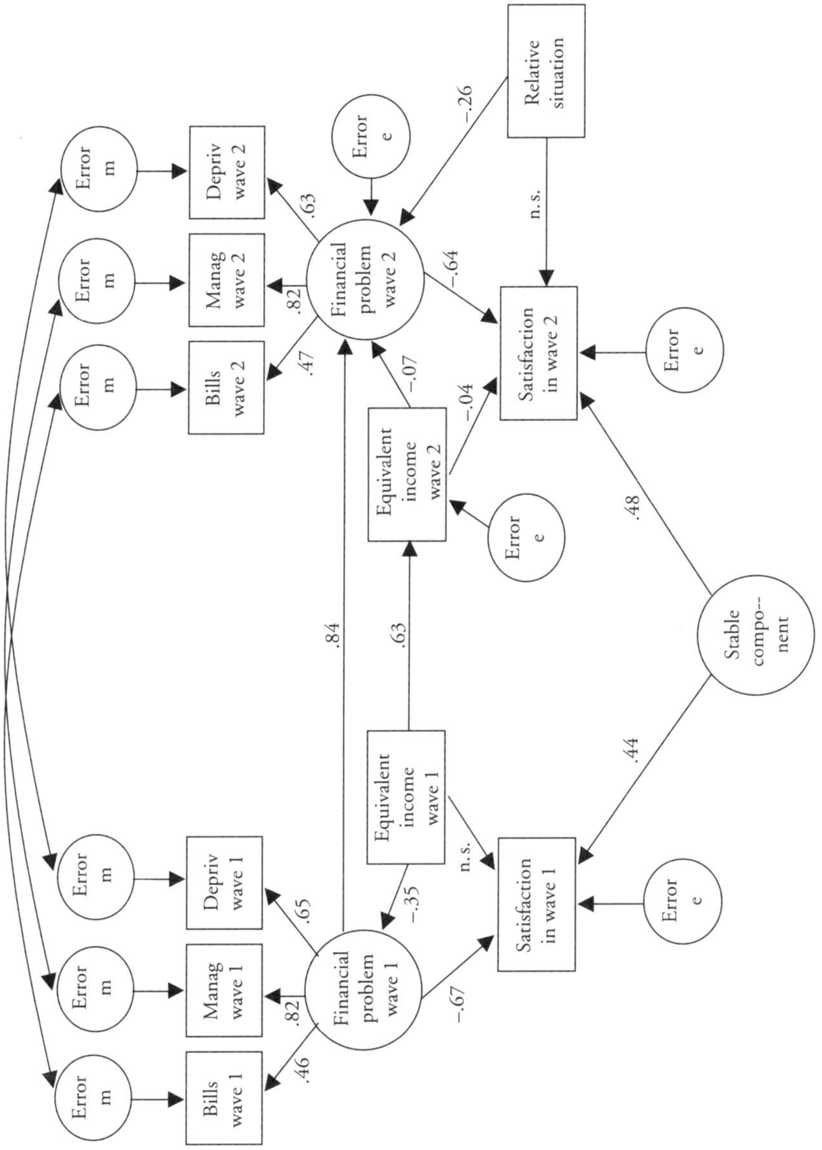

Figure 2: Two-wave causal model of satisfaction with finances

modelled. In addition, we now have depicted the error components as well: The circles labelled "Error m" represent the errors of measurement, which disrupt the relation between the latent and the observed variable. The components labelled "Error e" represent the errors in the equations, also called "unique components". As in a regression equation, these errors include variables that influence the dependent variable but are omitted from the equation.

The numbers next to each arrow in figure 2 are the effect estimates that resulted from the estimation of the model. These effect estimates have an interpretation comparable to the interpretation of the (standardised) B coefficients in a normal regression analysis: If we start with the effects of the two living conditions on satisfaction, for example, it is clear that "Financial Problems" has a much larger effect (–.67 in the first wave, –.64 in the second wave) than "Equivalent Income" (not significant in the first wave, –.04 in the second wave). People with a low income are, of course, more likely to have financial problems, but in principle people with a relatively high income can also experience problems when they expense more than they have. It seems that such problems are the main determinant of satisfaction with finances, and not the absolute level of income. We assumed income and financial problems would be related, and indeed found significant effects of "Equivalent Income" on "Financial Problems" (–.35 in the first wave and –.07 in the second wave). We could conclude that income only has an "indirect" effect on satisfaction with finances. As described, the relative situation was included in the model (Financial situation deteriorated or ameliorated since first interview), which was for the financial domain measured on the household level[3]. This relative variable had no effect on the satisfaction in the second wave, but did have a substantial effect (–.26) on the financial problems reported in this wave. Satisfaction with finances is significantly affected by the latent, stable component: The effects are .44 and .48.

To test the different theories of satisfaction as described in the introduction, we not only need estimates of the effects of living conditions on satisfaction, but also estimates of the change in living conditions over time. Such an estimate is given in figure 2 by the effect of the condition "Equivalent Income" in the first wave on "Equivalent Income" in the second wave, which is .63. This effect can be viewed as an estimate of the stability of "Equivalent Income". The square of the

3 The reference person in the household answered the question about the relative financial situation of the household, and his or her answer was imputed for all members of the household.

stability estimate indicates the proportion stable variance in this living condition, here: $(.63)^2 = 40$ %, the complement of this proportion indicates the amount of change, here: 60 %. Similarly, the stability estimate of "Financial Problems" is .83, which means there is $(.83)^2 = 69$ % stable variance and 31 % change.

To summarise, satisfaction with financial satisfaction is for the main part dependent on the objective conditions and for a somewhat smaller part a stable state. Problems in paying bills, managing one's finances and obtaining goods are the main determinants of satisfaction with one's financial situation. Both income and the relative financial situation have only indirect effects on satisfaction, through the factor "financial problems". Satisfaction with finances also contains a significant portion stable variance, but it is not as large as the amount of variance attributable to the living condition "Financial Problems". Having financial problems seems to be a rather stable situation over a one-year period, although some amount of change exists even within this short time. These results are in line with predictions of sociological change theory and with trait theory. Comparison theory is falsified within this domain by the lack of direct effect of the relative variable on satisfaction.

Comparison across Domains

To test the importance of the different causal factors, a series of nested models was specified within each domain: (1) model of satisfaction with only living conditions and events as input variables, (2) model with living conditions, events and relative situation, (3) model with living conditions, events, relative situation and stable component. The third model is the complete model described above and was used to obtain the results presented below. The tests showed that the third model, including all factors, is the best model in all domains: Both the relative situation and the stable component significantly improve the fit of the models (see technical appendix for a description of the tests and the fit of the models).

Figure 3 presents, for each of the domains, the variance in satisfaction explained by the different factors in the second wave. This explained variance is obtained by taking the square of the estimated effect of each factor[4], as it

4 The estimated effects are the numbers presented next to each arrow in figure 2, the paragraph "finances" explains their meaning. A table containing all estimated effects can be found in the appendix "effect estimates".

was estimated with the model, and sum up the squares over the various living conditions and events.

Figure 4 shows the estimates of stable variance of all living conditions included in the different models. These estimates are obtained by taking the square of the stability estimate of each living condition, as it was described in the paragraph "Finances".

Figure 3: Contribution of the different factors to the explanation of satisfaction in the second wave: Percentage of explained variance

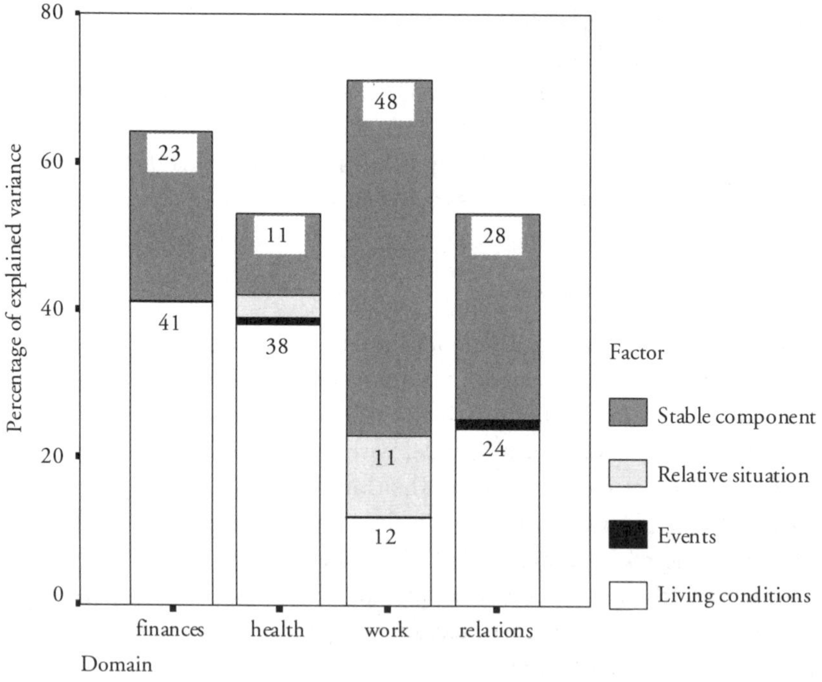

First of all, we see in figure 3 that the total amount of variance explained in each of the domains is relatively high in comparison with many studies of satisfaction. Secondly, we see that in all domains, either the living conditions or the stable component are most important: Events and relative situation never are the strongest factors. For satisfaction with finances and health, the living conditions clearly make the largest contribution. The results in the finance domain were described above. In the health domain, two latent factors were constructed from the health measures in the panel survey: A latent factor we called "Everyday health", measured by the items: "Medication need", "Impediment in every day activities", and "Number of health problems". This factor "Everyday health" had a rather high stability (76 % stable variance, figure 4). The second latent factor represented the "Health events" and was measured by "Number of days affected by health problems" and "Number of doctor consultations". The factor "Health events" was, logically, less stable than the factor "Everyday health" (figure 4). In the second wave, the event "Illness or accident between the two waves" was added to the other conditions. Satisfaction with health did show change in the short time span measured, and appeared to be strongly determined by the everyday health condition (figure 3, see also the appendix "estimated effects"). It was influenced slightly by health events and the relative health situation. The effects of the stable component were significant and larger than the effects of "Health events", but much smaller than the effects of "Everyday health". Although trait theory and comparison theory are not wholly falsified by this result, the effects point stronger towards sociological theories in this domain.

In contrast with all other domains, the stable component in the work domain clearly explains more variance than all living conditions together. It is also in this domain only that the relative situation has a rather large effect. Satisfaction with work at the first and the second wave was represented in the model by two latent factors, each measured by three items: "Satisfaction with income from work", "Satisfaction with working conditions", and "Satisfaction with the atmosphere at work". These three items appeared to represent different dimensions of work satisfaction. Satisfaction with work was influenced by only a few of the many conditions we tested. None of the socio-economical classification variable CAMSIS, ISCO, Wright, Goldthorpe, CSP had any significant effects on job satisfaction. Similarly, neither of the two job classification variables "Type of Job" (management, teaching, production, etc.) and "Type of Employer" (small/big, government, private, self-employed, etc.)

5 It has to be noted that both the socio-economical classification variables and the job classification variables were very unstable across the two waves. The unstability was so high, that it is not very likely to reflect real job changes. Some sort of measurement error or unreliability must be present in this data, which could attenuate effects that these variables

had any effects[5]. Other working conditions which had no significant effects on job satisfaction were: having a permanent or a temporary contract (and for how long); the average amount of overtime one has to do; and the commuting time daily needed to reach work. Four working conditions did have significant effects: "Security of work"; "Correspondence of qualifications and job"; and "full-or part-time work". The condition "Security of work" is a latent factor, constructed from the observed variables "Perceived risk of unemployment" and "Perceived job security". This latent factor had the strongest effect on work satisfaction. The other two working conditions had significant but rather small effects on satisfaction. The event "Change of job between the two waves" had no direct effect on satisfaction at the second wave, but it did have a significant effect on the variable "Relative situation". Hence, one could argue that "Change of job" had an indirect effect on satisfaction by influencing the evaluation of the present working situation compared with the year before, which in turn affects satisfaction with work. We can conclude that satisfaction with work is for a large part a stable trait. It is not very strongly related to the working conditions we tested, but the relative work situation and, indirectly, changes in job had substantial effect. These results are in line with the trait theory, as well as the comparison theory and, to a smaller degree, also the sociological change theories. The sociological theories about invariant position in society, however, are falsified in this domain by the fact that none of the socio-economical scales had any effect, if we assume that at least some of these scales are valid indicators of position in society.

For the domain of intimate relations, we selected the subpopulation of people who have a partner, either living together with this partner or not. Within this domain, we analysed satisfaction with communal living, which is constructed from the variables "satisfaction with living alone" for the one-person households and "satisfaction with living with other household members" for households with more than one person. As input variables, we chose the variables: "Partner situation" (not living together/living together) and "Support from partner" (0–10). "Support from partner" is a latent factor, consisting of two very highly correlated observed variables: practical support

might have on job satisfaction. For a more detailed discussion and analysis of the unreliability in these variables we refer to a panel research note (research note "Measurement error in the Work module", Scherpenzeel, 2002).

from the partner and emotional support from the partner[6]. In addition to the input variables, we included events within the intimate relations domain which happened between the first and second wave. No variable representing the relative situation could be included in the model of satisfaction with communal living, because in this domain, the comparative question was not asked (it is rather difficult to formulate such a question in this domain). The results showed that the partnership situation and, even more, the amount of support one gets from a partner are important determinants of satisfaction with one's communal living form: People who are living together with a partner are more satisfied than people who have a partner with whom they do not live together (see appendix "estimated effects" for the detailed effects of each of these factors). The amount of support received from one's partner substantially increases satisfaction with communal living. Two of the four social events we originally included in the model had some additional, smaller effects: "Termination of a close relationship" and "Conflicts with or among related persons". People who experienced (one of) these two events tended to be less satisfied with their communal living than others. The events "Problems with own children" and "Death of a closely related person" had no significant effects on satisfaction. The stable component had rather strong effects, comparable to the size of the effects of the living conditions in this domain (figure 3). In conclusion, satisfaction in the domain of intimate relationships is for a rather large part dependent on living conditions. At the same time it contains a large amount of stable variance. The living conditions do show some change over the one-year time period (figure 4). Like the results of the models of health- and financial satisfaction, this result seems to point to a combination of sociological change theory and trait theory. Comparison theory cannot be tested in this domain, since no relative variable was present.

6 For readers interested in measurement matters, we would like to remark that the measure of emotional support loads higher on the latent support-factor than the measure of practical support.

Figure 4: Stability of the living conditions: Percentage of stable variance

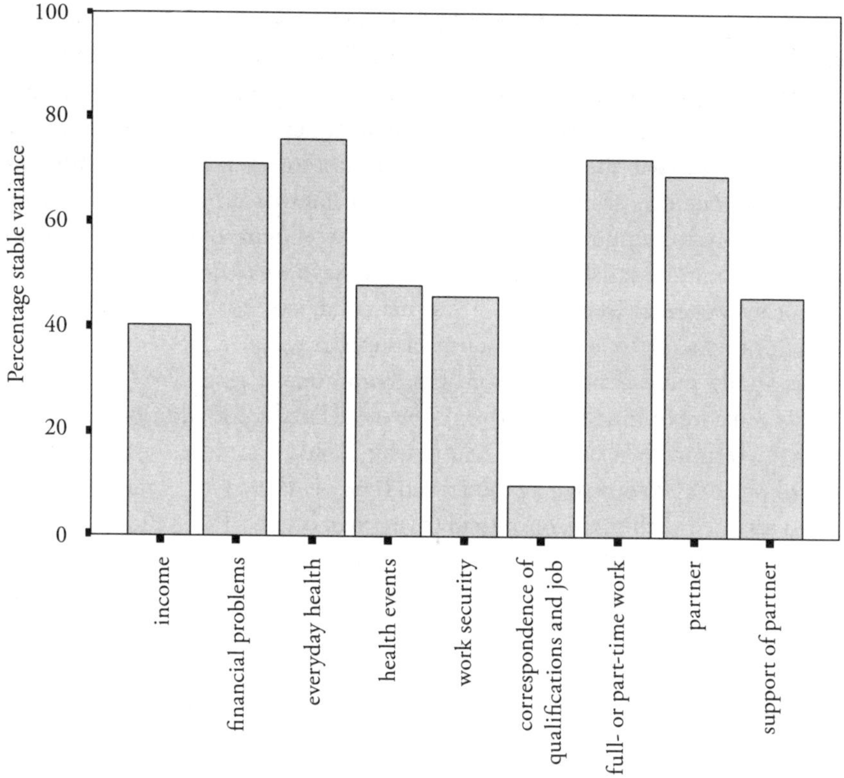

Discussion

We will now evaluate in how far each of the four possible results described in the introduction has been found and in how far each of the theories described has been confirmed or falsified. The first possible result we described was that no change would be observed in satisfaction or in living conditions, which would be expected by the sociological theory of invariant societal position determining satisfaction. It can easy be seen that this result is not found. In all domains, the stability estimates found for the different living conditions show that at least some change exists and sometimes even quite a lot, considering the short time period of the study. It could be argued that the instability found merely reflects random error ("unreliability") in the measures of living conditions. This would be a valid argument if we had used the simple correlation or regression coefficients of the living conditions as measure for stability. However, exactly for this reason have we chosen to use structural equation models: In all models we were able to define latent factors for some of the living conditions, which allows a correction of random measurement error variance. In fact, estimates of reliability are incorporated into the model by using latent factors. Since we still found instability in the living conditions while including such corrections, it is likely that the living conditions really changed.

As a second possible result we saw that living conditions would change, but satisfaction would not. Completed with the significance of a stable component of satisfaction, this result could be seen as the full proof of the Trait theory of satisfaction. The first part of this prediction is refuted by this study: The living conditions do change but they also affect satisfaction. Relevant events weakly but significantly affect satisfaction as well. Finally, the stable component never explains more than 50 % of the variance in satisfaction, which means satisfaction does change over the one-year period. On the other hand, the effects of the stable component are significant, they do improve the fit of the model and add substantively to the explanation of satisfaction in all the domains. In one domain the stable component even is the most important explicative factor. Consequently, although Trait theory cannot fully explain satisfaction, it cannot be fully falsified either.

The third possible result was that satisfaction and living conditions would change, but independently. Living conditions were expected to have no effects on satisfaction. In combination with a significant relationship between satisfaction and the comparative measure, this result would confirm the Comparison theory. Again, the first part of this prediction is disproved by our findings: Living conditions do have effects on satisfaction in all domains. The second point, however, seems to be at least partially right: The measure of comparison with one's past does have effects in two of the three domains that it was tested in. In addition, the events in a domain generally affected the comparative measure more than they directly affected satisfaction, suggesting that events (changes in life) influence satisfaction only because they influence the comparison with the past. Hence, we conclude that comparisons do contribute to satisfaction, but are by no means the only (or most) important factor. A point of critic that comparative theorist could make is that we have only included one standard of comparison. It is well possible that other comparative measures, such as comparison with important others or with what someone thinks is "deserved", would have explained much more of satisfaction than the measure we have chosen. However, even if we would have found such effects, the rather large effects of the living conditions and the stable component would probably exist as well, which would still suggest a combination of theories.

The fourth result described was that satisfaction would change as a result of changes in living conditions, predicted by sociological theories of changeable satisfaction or "Social engineering". Contrary to most other studies of satisfaction in rich, Western nations, we found satisfaction to be highly related to living conditions, and thus to confirm these theories.

To explain the difference with the findings of other studies, it has to be emphasised again that we did not use, as most studies do, the very general demographic variables such as age, sex, and education as explicative variables. Instead, we used different, very specific conditions within each domain, such as "problems in paying bills" for satisfaction with finances, and "correspondence of qualifications and job" for satisfaction with work. As it appears, this type of conditions is much stronger related to domain-satisfaction than the more general variables. Of course, one could also argue that the variables we used are in fact subjective variables instead of "objective" living conditions, because they are measured by questions about people's own subjective perceptions of their situation. The fact that the same person answers both questions about satisfaction and his/her subjective living situation could create an "artificial" correlation between these variables, representing his/her personality, outlook on life, or style of answering survey questions. However, although all variables we used were subjective in the sense that they were measured by asking the people themselves, many of them asked for quite factual, almost "objective" information, for example "Number of doctor consultations" or "Full-or part-time work (percentage)". This type of variables also had substantial effects on satisfaction. Moreover, the general demographic variables age, education and income, which are used in other studies, are usually also assessed by asking respondents themselves.

A second difference with other studies is that we used domain-satisfaction. It can very well be that the normally-used demographic variables have weak effect on general life satisfaction, as is usually found, but would also have strong effects on domain-satisfaction. However, Veenhoven compared the effects of gender, age, education, and income on satisfaction in different specific domains across four different countries and found only weak effects of these general demographics on domain-satisfaction too. The large difference that the choice between a general or a more specific input variable can make, is perhaps best illustrated by the result we found in the domain Finances: Not the absolute level of income determined satisfaction with finances, but the reported financial problems. As was said earlier, people with a relatively high income can just as well have financial problems as people with a low income, when this income does not fit their way of living.

There is one additional problem concerning the stable component. Since this is a latent component, we can give it any label we like. The component as it is specified represents some variance that the two measures of satisfaction have in common. However, whether this really is the stable personality trait we see in it is not absolutely sure. It could also represent, for example, a stable manner of responding to telephone questions, or a stable bias in the satisfaction question, or even the effect of an underlying, omitted variable. There is some argument against the first two possibilities: In the domain Work, satisfaction with work was defined as a latent factor, measured by three items: "Satisfaction with income from work", "Satisfaction with working conditions", and "Satisfaction with the atmosphere at work". In this model, we specified correlations between the error components of the repeated, identical measures of the same satisfaction variable at the first and the second wave. Hence, between for example "Satisfaction with income from work" at the first wave and "Satisfaction with income from work" at the second wave. These correlated or "systematic" errors can represent artificial correlations due to the repeated use of a certain interview method, scale, formulation, etc. In other words: they model exactly the stable systematic error or bias which was described above. The stable component was the most important factor in the model of satisfaction with work even though such bias was corrected by the inclusion of the correlated errors. Consequently, the stable component is unlikely to represent only systematic error or bias. However, the argument that it could represent some omitted other variable, for example an unknown living condition affecting satisfaction at both points in time, remains valid. The findings in the work domain even point in that direction: The stable component is largest in this model that has the weakest effects of living conditions of all domains. We could ask ourselves whether we have included the right living conditions in the work domain. It is imaginable that we have simply not yet found the relevant working conditions and that the effect of the stable component would decrease if we would find those conditions. This possibility cannot be excluded at this stage of our research. One argument against this alternative interpretation of the stable component can be found in literature: The explicative power of a stable component in a model of change in satisfaction has been shown before by Ehrhardt et al. (2000). Furthermore, we hope to obtain more conclusive evidence with the help of future data from the same panel, as is described below.

Conclusion

If we adhere to our interpretation of the stable component, the conclusion of the model tests is that Trait theory, Comparison theory, and Sociological Change theory all three explain a significant part of satisfaction. Our model combined different factors representing the different theories, for the purpose of testing these theories. The goal was to eliminate some of these factors and ultimately prove the effect of only one type of factor. However, satisfaction turns out to be optimally explained by a combination of the factors, and the test-model in its complete form seems to be the best model. We propose to use this model for the explanation of satisfaction and call it the "Composite model", because it defines satisfaction as a composition of living conditions, comparison with standards and stable traits. Saris (1995) has earlier proposed a mixed model of satisfaction, combining Comparison theory and Sociological change theory. However, this model does not include the Trait theory and is basically different from ours since it was designed to explain the contradictory finding of strong correlations between living conditions and satisfaction at the aggregate level and the lack of such relations at the individual level.

Our "Composite model" is the best model for satisfaction over a very short time period in a single, Western country. Evidently, it should also be tested with data from other countries. In the near future, we will extend the model with the third and the fourth wave of Swiss panel data, to test whether the composite model still is the best model of satisfaction over a longer period and more measurement points. We might, for example, find a higher number of events over a longer period, which could strengthen the effects of the events in the model. It is exactly this possibility to observe *change* in living conditions over time and its effects, which make a panel survey indispensable. It is also the possibility to observe *change*, and separate it from random variation over time, which demonstrates the utility of a causal structural equation model.

Moreover, it has been made clear that the possibility of including direct and indirect effects and latent (stable component) factors enables a more adequate explanation of satisfaction than the usual regression analyses that estimate only the direct effects of uni-dimensional, observed variables or the often used descriptive analyses that split up satisfaction scores into univariate subgroups. The composite model, even though it does need some more testing before it can be generalised, offers a much more promising contribution to the comprehension of satisfaction and to the prediction of changes in satisfaction.

References

Andrews, F. M. and Withey, S.: 1976, Social indicators of well-being. American Perceptions of life-quality. Plenum Press, New York.

Arbuckle, J. L.: 1997, Amos 3.62. Copyright 1994–1997 SmallWaters Corporation, Chicago.

Campbell, A., Converse, P. E. and Rodgers, W. L.: 1976, The quality of American life. Russel Sage Foundation, New York.

Ehrhardt, J. J., Saris, W. E. and Veenhoven, R.: 2000, 'Stability of life-satisfaction over time. Analysis of change in ranks in a national population'. Journal of Happiness Studies 1, p. 177–205.

Landua, D.: 1992, 'Satisfaction changes', Social Indicators Research 26, p. 221–241.

Michalos, A. C.: 1985, 'Multiple discrepancies theory (MDT)', Social Indicators Research 16, p. 347–413.

Saris, W. E.: 1995, 'Integration of data and theory: a mixed model of satisfaction', In: Saris, W. E., Veenhoven, R., Scherpenzeel, A. C., Bunting, B. (eds.), A comparative study of satisfaction with life in Europe. Eötvös University Press, Budapest, p. 281–97.

Saris, W. E., Satorra, A. and Sörbom, D. (1987). The detection and correction of specification errors in structural equation models. In: Clogg, C. C. (ed.). Sociological methodology 1987. Washington D. C., American Sociological Association.

Schyns, P.: 2002, 'Wealth of nations, individual income and life satisfaction in 42 countries: A multilevel approach', Social Indicators Research 60, p. 5–40.

Veenhoven, R.: 1991, 'Is happiness relative?', Social Indicators Research 24, p. 1–34.

Veenhoven, R.: 1994, 'Is happiness a trait?', Social Indicators Research 32, p. 101–160.

Veenhoven, R.: 1995, 'The study of life-satisfaction', In: Saris, W. E., Veenhoven, R., Scherpenzeel, A. C., Bunting, B. (eds.), A comparative study of satisfaction with life in Europe. Eötvös University Press, Budapest, p. 11–48.

Veenhoven, R. and Saris, W. E.: 1995, 'Satisfaction in 10 countries: summary of findings', In: Saris, W. E., Veenhoven, R., Scherpenzeel, A. C., Bunting, B. (eds.), A comparative study of satisfaction with life in Europe. Eötvös University Press, Budapest, p. 223–230.

Appendix I. Estimated Effects

The numbers in the table are the effect estimates that resulted from the estimation of the model in each domain. For the domain finances, the same estimates are shown next to the arrows in figure 2. These effect estimates have an interpretation comparable to the interpretation of the (standardised) B coefficients in a normal regression analysis.

Table of standardised effect estimates and stability estimates in each domain

Domain	Factor	Effect on satisfaction wave 1	wave 2	Stability w1 – w2
Finances				
	Equivalised yearly net household income	n. s.	–.04	.63
	Financial Problems	–.67	–.64	.84
	Relative Situation		n. s.	
	Stable Component	.44	.48	
Health				
	Everyday health	.80	.62	.87
	Health events	.09	–.11	.69
	Relative situation		.16	
	Stable component	.31	.33	
Work				
	Security of work	–.41	–.32	.68
	Correspondence of qualifications and job	.08	.09	.32
	Full-or part-time work	–.05	–.09	.85
	Change of job between w1–w2		n. s.	
	Relative situation		.33	
	Stable Component	.75	.69	
Intimate relations				
	Partner situation	.25	.22	.83
	Support Partner	.50	.44	.68
	End of a relationship between w1–w2		–.04	
	Conflict with relatives between w1–w2		–.09	
	Stable component	.51	.53	

n. s. = not significant. Only significant effects are given, and only variables with at least one significant effect on satisfaction are shown in the table.

Technical Appendix

Model Estimation

All model estimations were done with the AMOS program for linear structural equations (Arbuckle, 1997), using Maximum Likelihood estimation. All variables are standardised, except the disturbance variables, which are normally not standardised. We assume, as is normally done, that the correlations between the disturbance variables and the explanatory variables in each equation and across equations is zero. The living conditions at the first wave are assumed to be exogenous variables, being correlated among each other and having no unique component. The living conditions at the second wave are endogenous, determined by the conditions at the first wave (the lagged variables) and having unique components. All satisfaction variables and many of the living conditions were measured on the 0 to 10 scale. A few living conditions, mostly in the Work domain, were nominal in nature: The categories of these variable were recoded into dummy variables before they were used in the structural equation model. The events were dichotomous: each of them could take the value 0, meaning the event did not happen, or the value 1, meaning the event did happen.

Correlated errors are introduced in the model between identical measures of a latent factor in the first and the second wave. Such correlations often improve the fit of measurement models, which is at such not a good reason to introduce them. However, in this case there is theoretical justification for them: They model the systematic error that may exist in repeated measures of the same variable (artificial correlation caused by using the same method, measure, formulation, scale, etc. See also the paragraph "Discussion"). Hence, we do not introduce correlations between *all* error components in the model, but only between the error components of identical measures at the first and the second wave.

Test of Nested Models

The Maximum Likelihood procedure provides a chi-square test of the fit of a model. Our large sample size, however, can influence the evaluation of the absolute fit as indicated by this test[7]. Therefore, we will use the chi-square

7 The power of the chi-square test is related to sample size and the size of the parameter estimates (Saris et al., 1987).

statistic primarily to compare the *relative* fit of the models with and without the factors of interest. The difference in chi-square statistic between two nested models is itself chi-square distributed, and can therefore be used to evaluate the relative fit of the models. To test the importance of the different causal factors, a series of nested models was specified within each domain: (1) model of satisfaction with only living conditions and events as input variables, (2) model with living conditions, events and relative situation, (3) model with living conditions, events, relative situation and stable component. The chi-square tests of all three models in each of the domains are shown in the table below. The tests show that the third model, including all factors, is the best model in all domains: Both the relative situation and the stable component significantly improve the fit of the models. It can also be seen that, even with these factors, the model still has a bad (absolute) fit in all domains. However, exploration of all theoretically interpretable corrections of the model did not reveal any important mis-specifications, given the available data. We have to conclude that the model with relative situation and stable component, although not a perfect description of the data, apparently is the best approximation we can get at the moment. The chi-square statistic is possibly very sensitive to small specification errors in this model due to the large sample sizes.

Contribution of the different factors to the fit of the model: Chi-square tests

Domain	Model: N	Only living conditions and events		With relative situation		With relative situation and stable component	
Finances	4661	811	(37)*	805	(36)	370	(35)
Health	6125	1228	(68)	958	(67)	844	(66)
Work	2846	1196	(122)	954	(121)	571	(120)
Intimate Relations	2337	506	(38)			201	(37)**

* Degrees of freedom are given in brackets.

** In the domain Intimate Relations with stable component, but no relative situation.

Changing Health in Switzerland – 1999–2000*

Aggregate Stability and Individual Fluctuations

Erwin ZIMMERMANN and Claudine BURTON-JEANGROS

> "[...], *research and policy aimed at understanding the determinants of, and ensuring improvements in, health must recognize that intervening mechanisms and risk factors can be understood and effectively modified only in the context of the larger social environment in which they occur.*"
> (David R. Williams and Chiquita Collins, 1995, p. 380)

Background and Research Questions

Over the course of the 20th century, life expectancy has steadily improved in Switzerland as in most industrialized countries. Since 1999, this country has enjoyed the highest life expectancy at birth of all European countries[1] and it has positioned itself among the top-countries in terms of number of years spent in good health. Over 80 % of the residents of Switzerland, interviewed periodically since 1992 by the Swiss Health Survey[2] and annually from 1999 by the Swiss Household Panel, report their health to be excellent or good (Figure 1). Since the mid 1980s, the self-reported health status of the Swiss population has remained remarkably stable (Weiss 1993). In comparison to other countries, the proportion of population in good or excellent health is amongst the highest worldwide (Cavelaars 1998).

* The present article is part of the book *Living in Switzerland 1999–2000* (Erwin Zimmermann and Robin Tillmann (eds), Editions Peter Lang, Bern (2004)). The analyses and results are based on the first two waves of the longitudinal survey called Living in Switzerland in which 6,335 persons were interviewed in 1999 and 2000. On behalf of the Swiss Household Panel at the University of Neuchâtel, the data collection was carried out by M. I. S. Trend and financed by the PP Switzerland Towards the Future of the Swiss National Science Foundation (Grants No 5004-53205 / 5004-57894 / 5004-67304). Further information can be found on the website www.swisspanel.ch.

1 In 2001, 77.2 years for men at birth, 82.8 for women at birth (source: Swiss Statistical Encyclopedia, http://www.jahrbuch-stat.ch/f/auswahl.htm).

2 The Swiss Health Survey SHS is conducted periodically by the Swiss Federal Statistical Office. Over 15,000 persons randomly sampled from the permanent resident population of Switzerland have been interviewed in 1992, 1997 and 2002.

Figure 1: Levels of Self-Assessed Health in the Swiss Population since 1992[3]

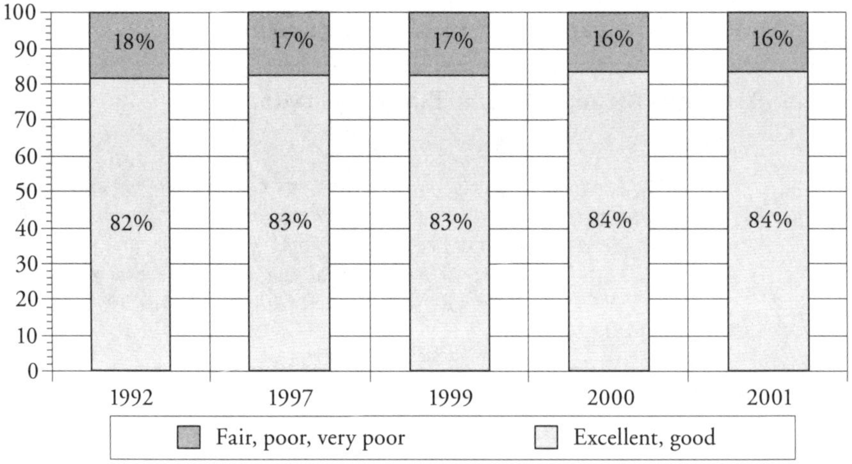

This constant level of good health in the general population of Switzerland over the last decade may give rise to misleading conclusions that a) the individual health status remains stable over time and b) the 'constant stock of illness' in society relates to a chronically ill minority. This static image might mask changes in health at the individual level and in specific population subgroups. Firstly, individual health changes are likely to be quite frequent, as a consequence of the occurrence of an illness, an accident or other significant health relevant life events. Secondly, research on health inequalities suggest that health is not evenly distributed among the whole population. Here, we examine the impact of social determinants on the Swiss population health in general, and on individual health fluctuations in particular.

Despite improved living conditions and access to medical care, inequalities in health have rather increased in modern Western societies (Adler and Ostrove 1999, House 2001, Williams 1990). Various determinants are discussed in the literature.

3 Data for 1992 and 1997 is based on the Swiss Health Surveys, for 1999 to 2002 on the Swiss Household Panel. The question was identical in both surveys: *We are going to talk about various aspects of your health. How do you feel right now?* Answers were attributed by the interviewer to one of the following response categories: (1) very well, (2) well, (3) so, so average, (4) not very well, and (5) not well at all.

Differences in *health status* are related to *gender* and could be summarised as follows: women get sicker but men die quicker (Annandale and Hunt 2000, Ross and Bird 1994). Research on gender and health argues that such differences are not determined by nature but should be viewed in the context of "socially structured gender roles, identities, and inequality in opportunities and resources (that) shape men and women's lives and in turn affect their health" (Rieker and Bird 2000, p. 98; Arber and Khlat 2002). Socio-economic inequalities particularly structure that context (Matthews and Power 2002, Moss 2002).

Health status is inversely related to *age* (Blaxter 1991, Lynch and Kaplan 2000). As a consequence of normal biological processes, health deteriorates with age – especially after ages 50 and 75 years – (Waite and Hugues 1999). Beyond these processes, the relationship between age and health interacts with socio-economic status (SES): among higher SES persons the onset of health problems is usually postponed until rather late in life, while health declines are prevalent in lower SES groups by middle age (House et al. 1994, p. 213).

Socio-economic status (SES) is positively associated with health (Adler and Ostrove 1999). Well-educated, upper socio-economic status people enjoy longer lives in good health (Lantz et al. 2001, Williams 1990), but also consistently report better health and higher satisfaction with health (Thiede and Traub 1997). Ross and Wu (1995, 1996) conclude from the analysis of two large U. S. data sets that educational attainment improves health directly, and indirectly through work and economic conditions, socio-psychological resources and healthy lifestyle. Besides education, occupation and income are also quite consistently associated with health status.

The relationship between *ethnicity* and health is more complex. In the United States, non-white persons have considerably lower life expectancy and worse health (Williams 1999), but they also encounter poorer education, have lower socio-economic status and have less access to appropriate health care (Ostrove and Feldman 1999). In addition, ethnicity is linked to migration with positive or negative selection effects based on education and socio-economic background such that foreign immigrant groups may be in better or worse health than the resident population (Williams and Collins 1995).

Health may also vary between *regions* within a single country. Despite quite homogeneous living conditions across Switzerland, differences in health among the three major regions – defined by their own language and culture, ie German, French and Italian – have been observed: the Swiss Health Surveys

1992 and 1997 have consistently shown poorer self-reported health in the Swiss Italian region (Calmonte, Koller and Weiss 2000).

Life events and chronic strains have been related in a wide range of studies to mental and physical health outcomes (Thoits 1995). Following Brown and Harris (1978, 1989) studies have consistently shown the significant negative effects of life events on *physical* and *mental health* (Creed 1985, Thoits 1983).

The favourable impact of *social networks and social supports* on health has been evidenced in a large number of studies (Berkman 1984, Berkman and Glass 2000, Ross 1990, Thoits 1995, Zimmermann and Haour 1988). Social networks not only provide the basis for social control and support but also a sense of belonging and responsibility towards others. Social support is a particularly valuable coping resource in the case of adverse life events. The availability of *emotional support* appears to have a major buffering effect with regard to health.

For Switzerland, results based on the Swiss Health surveys consistently confirm the empirical relevance of the above social determinants of health. The slowdown of the Swiss economy during the 1990s, accompanied by rapidly deteriorating job security and increased short and long-term unemployment, has led to increasing inequalities in health among different population groups (Calmonte, Koller and Weiss 2000).

Changes in health status over time will be analysed here at the light of those previous findings on health determinants. The data derived from the Swiss Household Panel (SHP) offers a unique opportunity to study the impact of gender, age, socio-economic status, ethnicity, life events, cross-sectionally and prospectively, assessing changes over time. They are expected to explain not only differences in health within the Swiss population but also individual health changes over time since we hypothesise that individuals experiencing precarious situations are more likely to report fluctuating health states, which would reflect the lack of stability in their living conditions.

The present contribution addresses the following research questions:

- To what degree inequality in ill-health based on gender and socio-economic status (SES – education, income and occupational class) can be observed in the SHP data?
- How does self-assessed health status change over a one year period at the individual level?

- How much of the observed deterioration of individual health over a one-year period can be explained by illness, accident and other negative life events?
- To what extent can individual health changes be attributed to *gender*, *ethnicity* and *socio-economic status* (SES) while controlling for *age*, *health at baseline* and health relevant *life events*?

Methods

Measuring Health

Three aspects of health will be considered: health status, health impediments and chronic health conditions.

a) Health status 1999/2000 is measured by two indicators: self-rated 'physical' health and mental health.

For self-rated 'physical' health[4] the question was: *We are going to talk about various aspects of your health. How do you feel right now?* For the analysis, the answers are dichotomised in two categories of well (very well, well) and less than well (so, so average, not very well and not well at all). Self-rated ill-health amounts to 17% in 1999 and 16% in 2000.

Mental health was measured by the current mood: *Do you often have negative feelings such as having the blues, being desperate, suffering from anxiety or depression, if 0 means 'never' and 10 'always'?* People with scores of five and higher are considered to suffer from mental health problems (12% in 1999 and 14% in 2000).

4 Self-rated health is a measure that is regularly used and has been found predictive of future health events including mortality (for recent review see: Idler and Benyamini 1997). However, self-rated health is likely to be affected by mood and distress at the moment of the interview. Analysing data from four different samples Tessler and Mechanic (1978) show that perceived health status is associated with psychological distress, even after controlling for a variation in physical health status, though the latter has a stronger relationship to perceived health than does the former. Based on the National Health and Nutrition Examination survey using the first two waves of panel data spanning approximately 10 years (n=6,833), Farmer and Ferraro (1997) also show that distress remains a strong predictor of perceived health at wave 2 even after controlling for perceived health at wave 1. Similarly, in the present study, physical symptoms such as backaches and headaches are more strongly associated with self-rated health and to a lesser extent with mental health.

Figure 2: Regression Model of Relationships among the four Health Dimensions in 1999

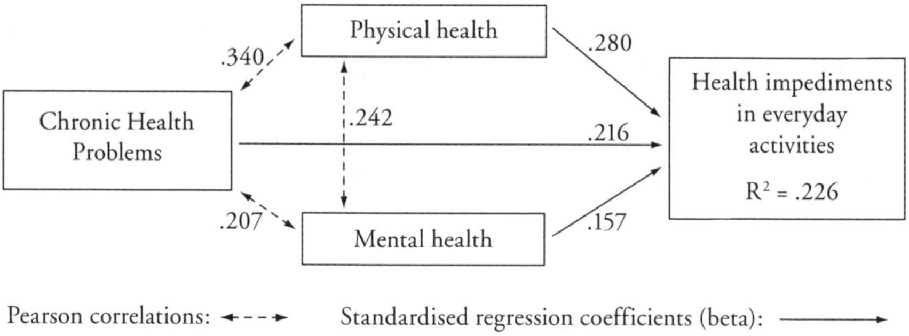

b) Health impediments 1999/2000 are accounted for by the question: *Please tell me to what extent, generally, your health is an impediment in your everyday activities (in your housework, your work or leisure activities), if 0 means 'not at all' and 10 'a great deal'?* People with scores of five and higher are considered to experience a notable handicap in their everyday activities (17 % in 1999 and 16 % in 2000).

c) Chronic health conditions have been assessed only in the first interview wave (1999) by the means of the following question: *Are you suffering from a long-term health problem or disability of a psychological or physical nature?* An affirmative answer was obtained from 21 % percent of the respondents.

As expected, the four health measures overlap to some extent because every single health aspect may affect all the others ($.20 \leq r \leq .40$). In a one-directional causal perspective, chronic health problems condition physical and/or mental health status which in turn lead to impediments in every day activities (Figure 2).

Chronic health problems affect negatively physical and mental health, the effect of physical ill-health being stronger. In turn, health impediments in every day activities are the consequence of chronic health problems, physical and mental ill-health. Here again, the impact of physical ill-health is more pronounced. In this model, health impediments appear more clearly influenced by the presence of chronic problems and physical ill-health than by mental health.

Social Characteristics

The following standard social characteristics are taken into account[5]:

a) *Age* is used as a categorical variable with seven age groups corresponding to major stages in the life cycle: 1 thru 24 years old (childhood-adolescence); 25 thru 34 years (young adulthood); 35 thru 44 years, 45 thru 54 and 55 thru 64 (adulthood); 65 thru 74 (elderly); 75 and over (old old).

b) *Socio-economic status (SES)* comprises *education*, *household income* and *occupational position*.

Education is measured by the highest level of education achieved in 1999 and is used as an ordinal variable from lowest to highest: compulsory, secondary and higher education.

Household income has been obtained by adding up individual incomes of all household members if available, or alternatively by the total household income as indicated by the reference person. As a result of refusals and data entry problems, income was obtained for 80 percent of the households. The equalised yearly household net income is categorised as quintiles of roughly equal size[6].

Occupational position is based on the professional activity carried out in 2000 or 1999, or on the last prior activity if not active in 2000 or 1999. The original eight professional positions have been grouped into only six categories[7]: (1) *Unqualified non-manual and manual collar workers*, (2) *Qualified manual professions*, (3) *Qualified non-manual professions*, (4) *Intermediate self-employed professions*, (5) *Intermediate wage earning professions* and (6) *Management, liberal, academic professions*.

c) *Ethnicity* is measured by two indicators: *nationality of origin* and *cultural region*.

5 See Appendix, Table 1 for detailed weighted and un-weighted distributions.

6 The definition of the quintile income boundaries is based on the weighted SHP-1st wave 1999 household level data and is applied to the longitudinal 1999–2000 individual basis.

7 As both *higher management* and *liberal professions* make up for only 3.6 % of all professions, they have been put together with *academic professions and senior management* to form the highest level category. For full presentation of occupational positions, see Joye et al. (2002).

Nationality of origin differentiates five major regional origins: (1) *Switzerland* (no indication of an other nationality), (2) *Northern Europe*, (3) *Eastern Europe*, (4) *Southern Europe* and, (5) *other regions*.[8]

Cultural region is based on the language used in the household interviews and roughly defines the three major cultural regions of Switzerland: *German*, *French* and *Italian*.[9]

Measures of Negative Life Events Occurring between the Interviews 1999 and 2000

To assess *negative life events* which may have occurred in-between the two interviews, eight kinds of events were probed (see items in Table 2). The question asked for the first event was: *Since (month, year of the last interview), have you had an illness, an accident or another serious health problem?* Illness or accident of a close person and death of a close one are the most frequently cited negative events, with about 20 % of the population reporting each of them (Table 1, col. 3). Illness or accident of self has been reported by one person out of six. The impact over time of these negative events is unevenly distributed (Table 1, col. 4): besides the heterogeneous category of other life events, the most lasting difficulties relate to problems with children, illness or accident of a close person, conflicts with close persons. Forty-six percent of the respondents reported no event, 31 percent mentioned one event and 23 percent mentioned at least two.

An *illness or an accident of the respondent* is most likely to affect his or her perception of his/her health status. Therefore, it will be treated separately from the other life events. A *life event incidence index* is created by summing the positive mentions on the events 2 through 8 for each respondent; this index is used here in its categorical form (no event: 52 percent; one event: 30 percent, two and more events: 18 percent).

8 Swiss bi-national citizens are classified as foreign, including the rather few Swiss citizens who have acquired a foreign nationality by marriage or a prolonged stay in a foreign country.

9 Though interviewees could choose between German, French and Italian as interview language, the great majority (from 85 up to 99 percent) of the interviews were conducted in the language of the corresponding region. E. g. In the exclusive Italian speaking Ticino comprising a significant proportion of German speaking residents, only seven percent of the interviews were realised in German.

Table 1: Negative Life Events Occurring during the Period 1999–2000

Negative Life Event	Incidence during the year 1999–2000 (percentages / n)	Still suffering from events in 2000 (mean scores on 0–10 scales / n)
1. Illness, accident (self)	14.2% (n=6,335)	4.2 (n=901)
2. Illness, accident (close person)	21.7% (n=6,333)	4.8 (n=1,375)
3. Death of close person	19.9% (n=6,332)	4.2 (n=1,262)
4. Termination of close relationship	6.1% (n=6,327)	4.1 (n=385)
5. Conflicts with/ among close persons	7.6% (n=6,330)	4.5 (n=482)
6. Problems with children	6.5% (n=3,856)	5.0 (n=413)
7. Threat or attack on self	2.6% (n=6,335)	2.5 (n=167)
8. Other negative life events	6.9% (n=6,332)	5.2 (n=436)

Logistic regression models are used to estimate the associations between various dimensions of poor health and the hypothesized determinants. In order to account for the simultaneous effects of more than one independent variable, adjusted odds Ratios (aOR) and corresponding 95 percent confidence intervals (CI) are recorded in the various tables. Statistically insignificant effects ($p > .05$) are excluded from the models and the adjusted odds ratios re-computed. Odds ratios indicate the relative likelihood of ill-health of every response category compared to a defined standard risk. E. g. in Table 2, 1st column: (a) women are 1.4 times more likely to be in poor physical health compared to men, and (b) the elderly (75+ years) are five times more likely to be in poor physical health compared to the youngest age category (14–24 years). The Nagelkerke Pseudo R-Square indicates the model's goodness of fit, similar to the standard R^2 (proportion of explained variance) for ordinary least squares regression.

In all statistical analysis, *weights* are consistently applied. For panel designs, cross-sectional and longitudinal weights need to be distinguished. The cross-sectional weights are applied in order to improve the sample estimates for the population from which the sample is drawn (Cornali and Vonlanthen 2000; Naud and Latouche 2001ab). The longitudinal individual weights aim at maintaining the first wave sample characteristics over time, despite losses of original sample members.[10]

People who did not respond to the second interview because of severe illness and death could not be identified as such and are therefore excluded from our analysis as are other kinds of non-respondents. Consequently, worsening health occurring in between the two interview waves is underestimated and factors accounting for severe and fatal outcomes biased. As the focus of our analysis is on predictors of health changes within the general population of Switzerland and not within specific subgroups such as the elderly, the resulting biases are unlikely to be strong.

Social Determinants of Ill-Health

In this first section of results, the impact of indicators typically associated with health differences among groups of the population is assessed. The analysis considers health measures for the year 2000.

Physical ill-health, poor mental health and *impediments in daily life* are consistently related to *gender* and *education* and to a lesser extent to *income* and *cultural region. Occupational position* has no additional independent impact on health (Table 2).

Physical health declines as expected with age, significantly after age 44 and most strongly at old age (Table 2, col. 3). People over 75 are five times more likely to indicate poor physical health than are adolescents and young adults (ages 14 through 25). In poorer physical health are also women, persons having accomplished only compulsory schooling and persons from low to middle income households. Beyond these classical health determinants, people whose origins are *Eastern* or *Southern Europe* declare poor physical health significantly more often. Controlling for the above-mentioned characteristics, there remains no significant *regional* effect. More in depth analyses indicate that, a) the indigenous Swiss enjoy the best physical health in each of the three language regions (only about 17 percent show poor health), b) persons of Southern European origin report poor health much more often in the Swiss Italian part of Switzerland (27 percent), and c) the Southern European effect does not show up at all in the Swiss German region (16 percent) and only moderately in the Swiss French region (20 percent)[11].

For *health-related impediments in daily living* (Table 2, col. 5), the results are almost identical to those obtained for physical health. However, people living in

10 For the 6,335 persons interviewed at both of the first two waves, the standardized individual longitudinal weights vary from 0.48 to 4.08.

11 This results might be explained by differences in the social characteristics of the Southern European immigrants according to the three cultural regions of Switzerland. In the Swiss German part, immigrants from Southern Europe are mostly composed of longstanding immigrants from Northern Italy; in the Swiss Italian part, the less well-educated and more recent immigrants originate from Southern Italy (see in particular the works by Etienne Piguet within the NFP39 Immigration and integration since 1948: http://www.unine.ch/fsm/).

the French or Italian regions of Switzerland are almost twice as likely to suffer from health impediments (aOR= 1.7) compared to Swiss German people.

Contrary to the health dimensions already described, *mental health* is unrelated to age, but quite strongly to *gender*, *education* and *cultural region* (Table 2, col. 2). Women and persons with only compulsory education are twice as likely to suffer from mental health problems compared to men and the well-educated. Similar findings have already been reported for Switzerland in the past (Gognalons Nicolet 2000). Residents in the French part of Switzerland are two times more likely, residents in the Italian part almost three times more likely to suffer from poor mental health than Swiss German people.

Health Changes 1999–2000

This second section of results addresses the issue of changes in health status over time. After assessing the extent and dynamic of those changes, the impact of social determinants typically associated with health inequalities will be examined.

Amount and Dynamic of Change

When directly asked about changes in their health in between the 1999 and 2000 interviews[12], 76.2 % of the longitudinal respondents reported no change, 14.2 % considered that their health had improved and 9.6 % that it had worsened. In regards to self-assessed health dimensions, the overall picture is one of fairly high stability at the individual level (Table 3): for about 85 percent of the subjects the health level has not changed from 1999 to 2000.

12 *Since (month-year), has your health improved or worsened, if 0 means greatly worsened and 10 greatly improved?*

Table 2: Social Determinants of Ill-Health in 2000 (Multivariate Logistic Regression)[13]

	Dependent variables	Poor Physical Health 2000 (n=5,169)*		Poor Mental Health 2000 (n=5,176)*		Strong Health Impediments 2000 (n=5,170)*	
Characteristics	Categories	a OR	(95%CI)	a OR	(95%CI)	a OR	(95%CI)
Gender	Male	1.0	—	1.0	—	1.0	—
	Female	1.4	(1.1–1.7)	2.0	(1.6–2,3)	1.5	(1.2–1.7)
Age	14–24 years	1.0	—	n. s.		1.0	—
	25–34 years	1.4	(0.9–2.0)			1.7	(1.2–2.4)
	35–44 years	1.7	(1.2–2.4)			1.8	(1.2–2.6)
	45–54 years	3.3	(2.3–4.6)			3.0	(2.1–4.2)
	55–64 years	3.7	(2.7–5.2)			3.6	(2.5–5.0)
	65–74 years	3.7	(2.6–4.3)			2.9	(2.0–4.1)
	75+ years	5.0	(3.3–7.5)			4.6	(3.0–7.0)
Education	Higher	1.0	—	1.0	(1.1–1.8)	1.0	—
	Secondary	1.3	(1.0–1.6)	1.4	(1.1–1.8)	1.2	(1.0–1.6)
	Compulsory	1.6	(1.2–2.0)	1.9	(1.5–2.2)	1.6	(1.3–2.1)
Household Income-Percentiles	Very low	1.7	(1.3–2.2)	1.8	(1.3–2.4)	1.7	(1.2–2.2)
	Low	1.4	(1.1–1.8)	1.2	(0.9–1.6)	1.1	(0.8–1.5)
	Middle	1.4	(1.1–1.8)	1.7	(1.2–2.2)	1.5	(1.1–1.9)
	High	1.1	(0.8–1.5)	1.0	(0.7–1.4)	1.0	(0.7–1.4)
	Very high	1.0	—	1.0	—	1.0	—
Occupational position	Higher prof.	n. s.	n. s.	n. s.	n. s.	n. s.	n. s.
	Intermed. Prof.						
	Intermed. self-empl.						
	Qual. non-man prof.						
	Qual. manual prof.						
	Unqual. Workers.						
Nationality of Origin	Switzerland (only)	1.0	—	1.0	—	1.0	—
	Northern Europe	0.9	(0.6–1.5)	1.1	(0.7–1.7)	1.3	(0.9–1.8)
	Eastern Europe	1.8	(1.1–3.5)	1.3	(0.8–2.1)	2.2	(1.4–3.4)
	Southern Europe	1.3	(1.1–1.8)	1.7	(1.4–2.1)	1.3	(1.1–1.6)
	Other Countries	1.6	(0.8–3.2)	1.0	(0.5–1.9)	0.9	(0.5–1.7)

13 Social determinants of ill-health are evaluated simultaneously by including them all in the logistic regression procedure. Using the backward stepwise logistic regression procedure, statistically non-significant characteristics ($p<.05$) are excluded.

	Dependent variables	Poor Physical Health 2000 (n=5,169)*		Poor Mental Health 2000 (n=5,176)*		Strong Health Impediments 2000 (n=5,170)*	
Characteristics	Categories	a OR	(95%CI)	a OR	(95%CI)	a OR	(95%CI)
Cultural Region	German			1.0	—	1.0	—
	French	n. s.	n. s.	1.9	(1.5–2.2)	1.7	(1.4–2.0)
	Italian			2.7	(2.0–3.6)	1.7	(1.2–2.3)
Pseudo R^2	(Nagelkerke)	.081	—	.110	—	.089	—

* n < 6,335 mainly because 19 percent of the respondents have no valid information on the household income.

n. s. = not significant at the p ≤ .05 level (not included in the stepwise selection).

a OR = adjusted odds ratios for all variables in the model.

Table 3: Health Changes 1999–2000

Self-reported Health	Response items (6320 ≤ n ≤ 6335)	1999 (w1)	2000 (w2)	Health Changes 1999–2000 worse	same	better	Correlation 1999–2000 (Pearson r)	Paired T-Test Score 1999/2000 p-value
Physical health	% ill-health (scores 3 to 5)	16.9 %	15.9 %	7.4	84.2	8.3	0.425* (n=6332)	.060
Mental Health	% negative mood (scores 5 to 10)	11.8 %	14.0 %	8.2	85.6	6.1	0.366* (n=6324)	.000
Health impediments in every day activities	% health impediments (scores 5 to 10)	17.2 %	15.7 %	8.0	82.5	9.5	0.460* (n=6327)	.004

* p ≤ .001

Figure 3 illustrates how rates of health at the population level appear stable, despite changes at the individual level. For *physical health*, *mental health* and *health impediments*, the proportion of those in good health changes very little over time. However, in the three cases, about half of those reporting ill-health in 1999 were in better condition a year later, whereas one out of ten feeling in good health at the first interview experienced a downgrading over this same period.

This dynamic of individual changes in health status over time will be further examined by analysing the single impact of negative life events on health deterioration; secondly by adding to the model social characteristics typically associated with health inequalities.

Negative Life Events as Determinants of Health Changes 1999–2000

Self-evaluated health change is strongly related to the occurrence of an *accident or a serious illness* during the period 1999–2000. The large majority of the persons (80 %) with no accident or experience of illness report stable health versus only 52 percent with such an experience. Surprisingly however, almost equal proportions of the latter indicate worsened (28 %) and improved health (21 %)[14].

As expected, ill-health in 2000 is strongly related to the *1999 health status* (Table 4). Those in poor health in 1999 are almost seven times more likely to also be in poor physical health a year later (col. 3), they are eight times more likely to experience poor mental health (col. 4) and five times more likely to suffer from strong health impediments (col. 5). Negative life events which have occurred during this period also affect health in 2000: independently of prior health status, persons who have experienced a *serious illness or an accident* during the 1999–2000 period are about three times more likely to be in *poor physical health* in 2000 and/or to suffer from *strong health impediments*; the impact on mental health is less strong, but still significant. Other negative life events also present significant and linear effects, in similar proportions for the three health measures.

14 This apparently contradictory reports might be due to inappropriate time references when reporting changes in health in relation to an illness or an accident; while interviewees were asked to take as a reference point the interview one year before, some interviewees may have referred to the period following the health event itself.

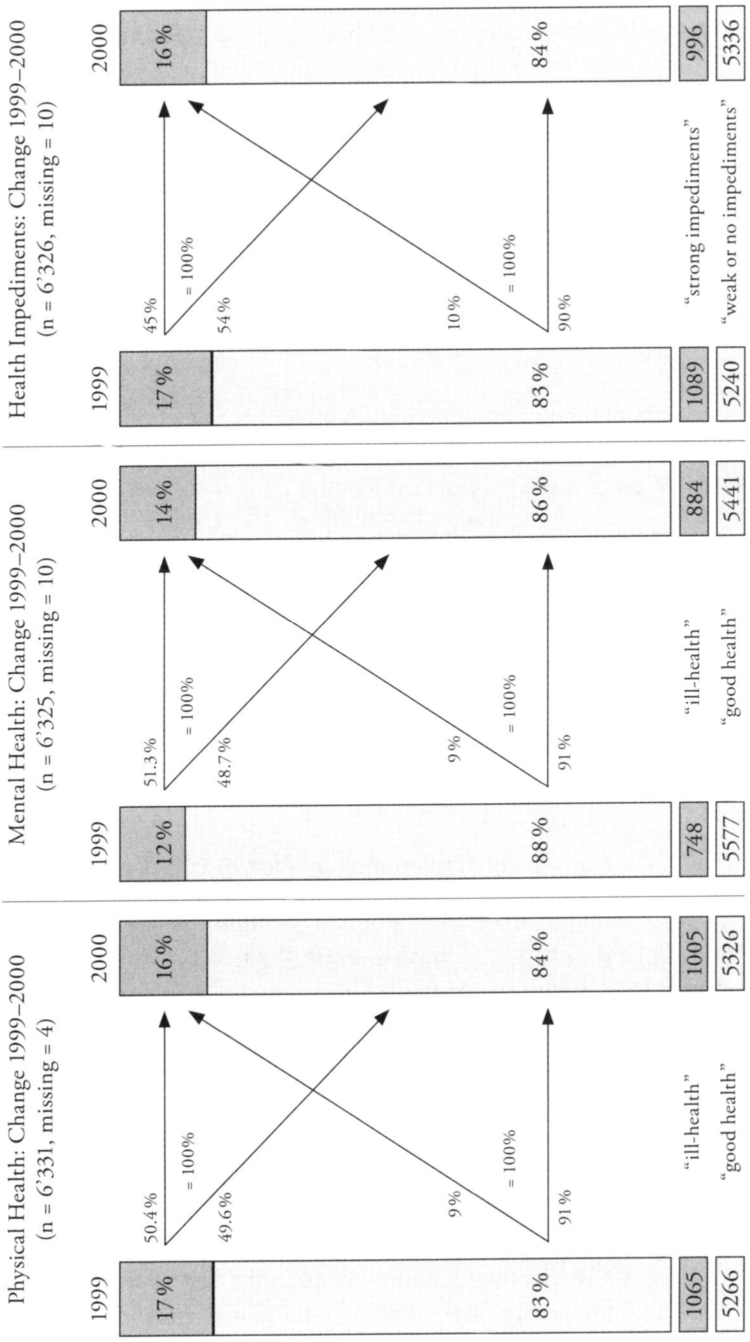

Figure 3: Health Changes 1999–2000

Table 4: Chronic Conditions, Health in 1999 and Life Events as Determinants of Ill-Health in 2000 (Logistic Regression – Adjusted Odds Ratios)

	Dependent variables	Poor Physical Health 2000 (n = 6,325)		Poor Mental Health 2000 (n = 6,319)		Strong Health Impediments 2000 (n=6,319)	
Characteristics	Categories	aOR	(95 % CI)	aOR	(95 % CI)	aOR	(95 % CI)
Chronic Health problems	No	1.0	—	1.0	—	1.0	—
	Yes	2.2	(1.8–2.6)	1.6	(1.4–1.9)	2.2	(1.9–2.6)
Health 1999	Good	1.0	—	1.0	—	1.0	—
	Poor	6.8	(5.7–8.0)	7.8	(6.5–9.3)	5.3	(4.5–6.2)
Life Events 1999–2000							
Serious Illness or accident	No	1.0	—	1.0	—	1.0	—
	Yes	3.2	(2.7–3.9)	1.6	(1.3–2.0)	2.7	(2.3–3.2)
Other negative Life Events	No events	1.0	—	1.0	—	1.0	—
	One event	1.4	(1.1–1.6)	1.2	(1.0–1.5)	1.2	(1.0–1.5)
	2–6 events	1.6	(1.3–2.0)	1.8	(1.5–2.2)	1.6	(1.3–2.0)
Pseudo R^2	(Nagelkerke)	.297	—	.196	—	.240	—

Note: aOR = adjusted odds ratios, bold = significant at the $p \leq .05$ level.

A Combined Model for Understanding Health Changes 1999–2000

Are *social characteristics* such as *gender, age, education* and *nationality of origin* significant predictors of ill-health in 2000 when controlling simultaneously for prior health status and negative life events? The answer is yes!

To predict health changes 1999–2000, combined logistic regression models with *baseline health* (1999), *life events* 1999–2000 and *social characteristics* are estimated with regard to health in 2000 (Table 5). Taking into account *social characteristics* in addition to *life events* for explaining health changes clearly helps to improve the statistical fit of the model, particularly for *mental health* (Pseudo R^2=.278 versus Pseudo R^2=.196 in Table 4).

Social characteristics – *gender, education and ethnicity* – are significantly related to health changes: females, people with low education, those beyond age 44 and foreigners originating from Eastern and Southern Europe are

Table 5: Longitudinal Determinants of Ill-Health in 2000 (Logistic Regression)

	Dependent variables:	Poor Physical Health 2000 (n=6,308)		Poor Mental Health 2000 (n=6,302)		Strong Health Impediments 2000 (n=6,302)	
Characteristics	Categories	aOR	(95% CI)	aOR	(95% CI)	aOR	(95% CI)
Gender	Male	1.0	—	1.0	—	1.0	—
	Female	1.3	(1.1–1.5)	1.6	(1.3–2.0)	1.3	(1.2–1.5)
Age	14–24 years	1.0	—	n. s.		1.0	—
	25–34 years	1.2	(0.8–1.6)			1.6	(1.2–2.3)
	35–44 years	1.3	(0.9–1.8)			1.6	(1.1–2.2)
	45–54 years	2.2	(1.6–3.0)			2.4	(1.7–3.4)
	55–64 years	2.3	(1.6–3.1)			2.7	(2.0–3.7)
	65–74 years	2.4	(1.7–3.4)			2.2	(1.6–3.1)
	75+ years	2.9	(1.9–4.3)			3.1	(2.0–4.7)
Education	Superior	1.0	—	1.0	—	1.0	—
	Professional	1.3	(1.1–1.7)	1.4	(1.1–1.8)	1.3	(1.0–1.6)
	Compulsory	1.6	(1.2–2.0)	1.9	(1.4–2.5)	1.6	(1.2–2.0)
Nationality of Origin	Only Switzerland	1.0	—	1.0	—	1.0	—
	Northern Europe	1.1	(0.7–1.3)	1.2	(0.8–1.8)	1.0	(0.7–1.5)
	Eastern Europe	2.2	(1.3–3.6)	1.3	(0.8–2.3)	2.7	(1.6–4.3)
	Southern Europe	1.4	(1.1–1.7)	1.9	(1.5–2.3)	1.3	(1.1–1.7)
	Other Countries	1.3	(0.7–2.5)	1.0	(0.5–1.8)	0.8	(0.4–1.5)
Linguistic Region	German			1.0	—	1.0	—
	French	n. s.		2.0	(1.6–2.4)	1.9	(1.6–2.2)
	Italian			2.9	(2.2–3.9)	1.9	(1.4–2.5)
Chronic Health problems	no	1.0	—	1.0	—	1.0	—
	yes	2.1	(1.8–2.6)	1.7	(1.5–2.1)	2.2	(1.8–2.6)
Health 1999	good	1.0	—	1.0	—	1.0	—
	poor	6.0	(5.1–7.1)	6.1	(5.1–7.4)	4.4	(3.7–5.2)
Life Events 1999–2000							
Serious Illness or accident	No	1.0	—	1.0	—	1.0	—
	Yes	3.0	(2.5–3.6)	1.8	(1.4–2.2)	2.7	(2.2–3.3)
Other negative Life Events	No events	1.0	—	1.0	—	1.0	—
	One event	1.4	(1.2–1.7)	1.3	(1.1–1.6)	1.3	(1.1–1.6)
	2–6 events	1.7	(1.4–2.2)	2.0	(1.6–2.6)	1.8	(1.5–2.2)
Pseudo R^2	(Nagelkerke)	.322	—	.260	—	.280	—

n. s. = not significant at the $p \leq .05$ level (Initially not significant coefficients are excluded and the remaining coefficients are recomputed).

a OR = adjusted odds ratios.

not only in worse health at any given point in time, but their health is also significantly more likely to deteriorate over a short period such as one year (1999–2000).

Whilst controlling for prior health and life events, *age* maintains a significant, though considerably weakened relationship with *physical health* and *health impediments in 2000*. This is not surprising. A large part of the well-known impact of aging on health, is mediated by the health status in 1999 and by serious illnesses or accidents much more common among the elderly.

A significant *cultural region* effect can be observed: in the French and Italian speaking regions of Switzerland, *unfavourable mental health changes* are respectively two, and three times more likely than in the Swiss German region. With a somewhat weaker effect, this also holds true for *increased health impediments*.

Discussion and Conclusions

Results in Brief

To what degree is inequality in ill-health based on gender and socio-economic status (SES – education, income and occupational position)?

The analyses of the Swiss Household Panel data consistently confirm for Switzerland the internationally well-known findings about the main determinants of ill-health: older people, women, lower socio-economic persons and non-natives are more likely to experience poor health. Ill-health appears to concentrate in vulnerable categories, these being defined by interactions between various factors resulting in a comparatively lower social status in the whole society.

How does self-assessed health status change over a one year period at the individual level?

About 75 percent of the panellised respondents report no change in health over a period of approximately one year between the two interviews and more than 80 % can be considered stable with regard to the three health indicators – *physical health, mental health and health impediments* – measured at both points in time. On the other hand, one person in five experienced a change in his/her health status.

How much of the observed deterioration of individual health over a one-year period can be explained by illness, accident and other negative life events?

Negative life events which have occurred during the two interview waves significantly affect health changes within this same period. The health of persons who have experienced a serious illness or accident has deteriorated considerably between 1999 and 2000; negative life events which have happened in the persons' environment also have a significant though somewhat weaker unfavourable impact on health. This later impact on health may be related to increased stress and/or a potential loss of social support.

To what extent can individual health changes be attributed to gender, ethnicity and socio-economic status (SES) while controlling for age and health at baseline and health relevant life events?

In line with the literature on health inequalities, we have confirmed that the major and most consistent social determinants of health levels are *gender*, *education* and *ethnicity*. What might be more surprising is that these same determinants are also very significantly related to health changes over a period as short as one year, even when obvious factors such as age and the occurrence of an illness and accident are taken into account.

Discussion and Conclusion

Among the social determinants of health, *age* is, unsurprisingly, a strong predictor of *health status*: *physical health* gradually deteriorates with age and health *impediments* become more prevalent. Mental health, however, appears not related to age when gender and education are simultaneously taken into account. Beyond biological processes, age also refers to the position in the life cycle and differing periods of societal structure and organisation, which have competing and complementary impacts on health of individuals over time. Health relevant conditions and behaviours such as very hard physical work or smoking do not have immediate negative impacts on health but may manifest themselves many years later. Besides, age interacts with gender and level of education, as women's roles and average education attainment have been greatly transformed over the course of the last century.

Women are significantly more likely than men to report *physical ill-health and health related* impediments in their everyday lives, particularly *mental health problems*. Various explanations have been offered for this systematic gap (Verbrugge 1985). Some argue that women are more interested, and specifically more aware, of their health by being more sensitive to changes and experienced symptoms. Their perceptions are notably affected by their experience since they often act as caretakers of close ones' health (children, partner, parents in later life). Differential roles and expectations for men and women might also affect their health. Whereas women were first supposed to experience more stress due to role overload, subsequent research has shown that multiple roles (family and work) can induce either conflict or enhancement, with potential compensations between the two spheres (Lennon and Rosenfield 1992, Tiedje et al. 1990).

People with low *socio-economic status*, both in terms of education and household income are almost twice as likely to experience ill-health as those at the highest corresponding levels. There are three complementary theoretical perspectives on the mechanisms relating SES and health (Adler and Ostrove 1999): a) According to the *selection perspective*, health status is influencing social position; individuals in poor health would be more likely to be relegated to lower social status, b) Differences in *health behaviours* may be held responsible for differences in health outcomes: it is well known that individuals from lower social classes are less health conscious and tend to adopt less healthy behaviours in various domains (eating, tobacco and alcohol consumption, …) and to be less involved in maintaining their health (regular physical activity, …), and finally, c) a more *structuralist explanation* suggests that the living conditions of various social groups are affecting health differentially (working conditions, housing, …). The analysis of longer range longitudinal data might provide some evidence on the relative importance of each of these three explanations (Lantz, 2001).

In a wealthy country, like Switzerland, almost everyone – including the economically poor – enjoys a relatively high standard of living and a guaranteed access to local high quality medical care. Consequently, it may be difficult to pinpoint highly plausible hard causes for inequalities in health related to low socio-economic status. But still, the persistent role of SES in generating inequalities in health confirms the presence of quite subtle mechanisms by which social position affects health and supports the idea that various variables are mediating the relationships between social status and health status (Robert and House 2000). These variables include health behaviours, chronic and acute stress, social support, lack of control, and differential vulnerability. Single effects are usually small, but the combination of these factors allows to explain a significant amount of health differences.

Ethnicity and health are also related. Compared to indigenous Swiss nationals, people from Eastern and Southern Europe are twice as likely to report poor *physical health* and *health impediments*. Belonging to one or the other of the three main cultural regions of Switzerland makes no difference in terms of physical health, a slight difference with regards to health impediments and quite a large difference when it comes to *mental health*. Compared to the Swiss German respondents, the Swiss Italians are 2–3 times more likely to report health impediments and poor mental health. The Swiss French occupy an the position in-between. To a certain extent, these health variations may reflect differences in the regional distribution of health-relevant sociodemographic characteristics: the high incidence of self-reported "poor physical health" in the Swiss Italian region of Switzerland appears to be primarily due to the large proportion of low educated immigrants from Southern European countries (results not shown here).

By demonstrating the impact of social characteristics such as *gender*, *education* and *ethnicity*, the current analyses of longitudinal data confirm the already well known connection between a person's position within the social structure and health. However, it goes further then typical health inequalities studies by highlighting how social determinants also affect health evaluations over time. The fact that women and migrant groups, independently of age, are more likely to experience a downgrading of their health status probably reflects the relatively greater instability or changing nature in their living conditions and arrangements (changes in labour force participation, care for others, etc.). It could also reflect their greater interest for health, in the sense that good health is a basic prerequisite to social participation. In their cases, integration through professional activity is weaker or non-existent as compared to adult native men.

Despite strong stability, changing health at the individual level remains notable. At this stage of the panel study it is, however, impossible to evaluate how much of the change is 'real' and how much of it is simply due to random variations in the self-assessment of health from one interview wave to the other. One can also wonder if individuals do not have distinct ways of assessing their health over time: some could have a very consistent assessment, by which they might be trying to stay close to an ideal average for them *(on the whole, I am in good health)*; while others could have much more fluctuating evaluations, reflecting shorter time feelings and transitions in other spheres of their lives. This highlights the need to conduct the analysis over a longer period of time, with more than two points in time. This will be possible when more recent SHP data will be available for analysis.

Research on health inequalities pinpoints the complexity of social mechanisms resulting in recurrent differences among groups of the population. While some of the mediating variables reflect 'individual choices' (health behaviours for example), others stem from structural factors on which single individuals have little or no influence (differential vulnerability associated with working conditions for example). This confirms that health promotion needs to go beyond health education, especially as such efforts primarily reach the well-to-do and the well-educated. The promotion of health goes along the reduction of social inequalities in the long run, or at least the prevention of an again widening gap between the bottom and the top of Swiss society. Short of being able to change the structural aspects of society in the short run, health promotion may primarily concentrate on targeting people in low social positions by means of collective and individual empowerment strategies. These should help restore the personal and social well-being of particularly vulnerable population groups such as lone mothers, new immigrants, … It can be expected that enhancing positive evaluations, attitudes and behaviours towards health among such groups would have a favourable impact on their children's relationship to health in the future.

References

Adler, Nancy E. and Joan M. Ostrove (1999), Socioeconomic Status and Health: What We Know and What We Dont, in: Adler, Nancy E., Michael Marmot, Bruce S. McEwen, eds., Socioedonomic Status and Health in Industrial Nations: Social, Psychological, and Biological Pathways. *Annals of the New York Academy of Sciences 896* (December).

Annandale, Ellen and Kate Hunt, eds. (2000), *Gender inequalities in health*. Buckingham: Open University.

Arber, Sara and Myriam Khlat (2002), Introduction to 'social and economic patterning of women's health in a changing world'. *Social Science & Medicine 54*, 643–647.

Berkman, Lisa F. (1984), Assessing the Physical Health Effects of Social Networks and Social Support. *Annual Review of Public Health* 5, 413–32.

Berkman, Lisa F. and Thomas Glass (2000), Social Integration, Social Networks, Social Support, and Health, in: *Social Epidemiology* edited by Lisa F. Berkman and Ichiro Kawachi. New York: Oxford Press, 137–173.

Blaxter, Mildred (1991), Fifty years on – Inequalities in Health. *Population Studies 45*, 79–94.

Brown, George W. and Tirril O. Harris (1978), *Social Origins of Depression: A Study of Psychiatric Disorder in Women*. New York: Free Press.

Brown, George W. and Tirril O. Harris (1989), *Life Events and Illness*. New York: Guilford Press.

Budowski, Monica, Robin Tillmann, Erwin Zimmermann, Boris Wernli, Annette Scherpenzeel & Alexis Gabadinho (2001), The Swiss Household Panel 1999–2003: Data for Research on Micro-Social Change. *ZUMA-Nachrichten* 49, Jg. 25, November, 1–29.

Calmonte, Roland, Christophe Koller and Walter Weiss (2000), Santé et comportements vis-à-vis de la santé en Suisse 1997. *Statistique de la Suisse – Enquête suisse sur la santé*, Neuchâtel, Switzerland: Office fédéral de la statistique.

Cavelaars, Adriënne (1998), *Cross-national comparisons of socio-economic differences in health indicators*. Rotterdam, Netherlands: Thesis Erasmus University Rotterdam.

Creed, Francis (1985), Life Events and Physical Illness. *Journal of Psychosomatic Research* 29/2, 112–123.

Cornali, Anne and Christian Vonlanthen (2001), Description de la pondération de l'échantillong du panel suisse de ménages. *Working Paper 4_01*. Neuchâtel: Swiss Household Panel (SHP).

Farmer, Melissa M. and Kenneth F. Ferraro (1997), Distress and Perceived Health. *Journal of Health and Social Behaviour 39 (September)*, 298–311.

Gognalons Nicolet, Maryvonne (2000), La santé psychique, in: Roland Calmonte, Christophe Koller, Walter Weiss, eds., *Santé et comportements vis-à-vis de la santé en Suisse 1997*. Neuchâtel, Switzerland: Statistique de la Suisse – Enquête suisse sur la santé, Office fédéral de la statistique.

House, James S. (2001), Understanding Social Factors and Inequalities in Health: 20th Century Progress and 21st Century Prospects. *Journal of Health and Social Behaviour 43 (June)*, 125–142.

House, James S., James M. Lepkowski, Ann M. Kinney, Richard P. Mero, Ronald C. Kessler and A. Regula Herzog (1994), The Social Stratification of Aging and Health. *Journal of Health and Social Behaviour 35 (September)*, 213–234.

Idler El & Yaël Benyamini (1997), Self-rated health and mortality: a review of twenty-seven community studies. *Journal of Health and Social Behaviour 38*, 21–37.

Joye, Dominique, Monica Budowski and Manfred Max Bergman (2002), Documentation technique du Panel suisse de ménages: Recodification des variables de position sociale. *SHP Working Paper* 19, Neuchâtel: SIDOS and Swiss Household Panel.

Lantz Paula M., John W. Lynch, James S. House, James M. Lepkowski, Richard P. Mero, Marc A. Musick and David R. Williams (2001), Socioeconomic disparities in health change in a longitudinal study of US adults: the role of health-risk behaviors. *Social Science & Medicine 53*, 29–40.

Lennon Mary C. & Rosenfield Sarah (1992), Women and Mental Health: The Interaction of Job and Family Conditions. *Journal of Health and Social Behaviour* 33 (December), 316–327.

Lynch, John W. and George A. Kaplan (2000), Socioeconomic Position, in: Lisa S. Berkman and Ichiro Kawachi, eds., *Social epidemiology*. New York: Oxford University Press, 13–35.

Matthews, Sharon and Chris Power (2002), Socio-economic gradients in psychological distress: a focus on women, social roles and work-home characteristics. *Social Science & Medicine 54*, 799–810.

Moss, Nancy E. (2002), Gender equity and socio-economic inequality: a framework for the patterning of women's health. *Social Science & Medicine 54*, 649–661.

Naud, Jean-François and Michel Latouche (2001), Pondération du Panel suisse de ménages. Vague 2. Description détaillée des tâches. *Working Paper 8_01*, Neuchâtel: Swiss Household Panel (SHP).

Ostrove, Joan M. and Pamela Feldman (1999), Education, Income, Wealth, and Health among White and African Americans. *Annals of the New York Academy of Sciences 896*, 335–337.

Rieker, Patricia P. and Chloe E. Bird (2000), Sociological explanations of gender differences in mental physical health, in: Chloe E. Bird, Peter Condrad and Allen M. Fremont, eds., *Handbook of medical sociology*. Upper Saddle River, NJ: Prentice Hall.

Robert, Stephanie A. and James S. House (2000), Socioeconomic Inequalities in Health: Integrating Individual-, Community- , and Societal-level Theory and Research, in: Albrecht Gary L., Ray Fitzpatrick and Susan C. Scrimshaw, *The handbook of Social Studies in Health and Medicine*. London, Sage, 115–135.

Rose, David (1995), Household Panel Studies: and Overview, *Innovation*, 8/1, 7–24.

Ross, Catherine E. (1990), The Impact of the Family on Health: The Decade Review. *Journal of Marriage and the Family*, 52, 1059–1078.

Ross, Catherine E. and Chia-ling Wu. (1995), The Links between Education and Health. *American Sociological Review* 60, 719–745.

Ross, Catherine E. and Chia-ling Wu. (1996), Education, Age, and the Cumulative Advantage in Health. *Journal of Health and Social Behavior* 37 (March), 104–120.

Ross, Catherine E. and Chloe E. Bird (1994), Sex Stratification and Health Lifestyle: Consequences for Men's and Women's Perceived Health. *Journal of Health and Social Behavior* 35 (June), 161–178.

Tenbruck, Friedrich H. (1990), Repräsentative Kultur, in: Haferkamp, Hans (ed.), *Sozialstruktur und Kultur*. Frankfurt am Main: Suhrkamp, 20–54.

Tessler, Richard & David Mechanic (1978), Psychological Distress and Perceived Health Status. *Journal of Health and Social Behaviour*, 19 (September), 254–262.

Therborn, Göran (1995), *European Modernity and Beyond. The Trajectory of European Societies, 1945–2000*. London, Thousand Oaks, New Delhi: Sage Publications.

Thiede, Michael & Stefan Traub (1997), Mutual Influences of Health and Poverty. Evidence from German Panel Data. *Social Science & Medicine 45/6*, 867–877.

Thoits, Peggy A. (1983), Dimensions of Life Events that Influence Psychological Distress: An Evaluation and Synthesis of the Literature, in: Howard B. Kaplan ed., *Psychosocial Stress: Trends in Theory and Research*. New York: Academic Press, 33–102.

Thoits, Peggy A. (1995), Stress, Coping, and Social Support Processes: Where Are We? What Next? *Journal of Health and Social Behaviour* (Extra Issue), 53–79.

Tiedje Linda B., Camille B. Wortman, Geraldine Downey, Carol Emmons, Monica Biernat, Eric Lang (1990), Women with multiple roles: role compatibility perceptions, satisfaction and mental health. *Journal of Marriage and the Family* 52 (February), 63–72.

Verbrugge, Lois M. (1985), Gender and Health: An Update in Hypotheses and Evidence. *Journal of Health and Social Behavior* 26 (september), 156–182.

Waite, Linda J. & Mary Elizabeth Hughes (1999), At Risk on the Cusp of Old Age: Living Arrangements and Functional Status among Black, White, and Hispanic Adults. *Journal of Gerontology: Social Sciences* 54B, 136–44.

Weiss, Walter (ed.) (1993), *Gesundheit in der Schweiz*. Zürich: Seismo.

Williams, David R. (1990), Socioeconomic Differentials in Health: A Review and Redirection. *Social Psychology Quarterly* 53/2, 81–99.

Williams, David R. and Chiquita Collins (1995), US Socioeconomic and Racial Diffferences in Health: Patterns and Explanations, *Anual Review of Sociology 21*, 349–386.

Williams, David R. (1999), Race, Socioeconomic Status, and Health. The Added Effects of Racism and Discrimination. *Annals of the New York Academy of Sciences 898* (December), 173–188.

World Health Organisation (2002), *Highlights on Health in Switzerland*. Copenhagen, Denmark: WHO Regional Office for Europe – Health Information Unit.

World Health Organisation (1994), *Health in Europe – The 1993/1994 health for all monitoring report*. Copenhagen, Denmark: WHO Regional Office for Europe – Health Information Unit.

Zimmermann Erwin, Thomas Spuhler and Stephanie Zobrist (1995), *Die Schweiz im Europäischen Vergleich – Gesundheit für alle im Jahre 2000 – Fortschrittsmessung – Evaluation 1993/1994*. Bern and Lausanne: Bundesamt für Gesundheit (BAG), Bundesamt für Statistik (BFS), Schweizerisches Institut für Gesundheitswesen (IfG).

Zimmermann Erwin and Mary Haour-Knipe (1988), Stress psychosocial, adaptation et santé. *Médecine & Hygiène*, 46, 2640–2651.

Appendix I: Simple Data Distributions for the First Two Waves (1999–2000)

Table 1a: Distributions of Socio-demographic and socio-economic characteristics

Socio-demographic characteristics	a) Un-weighted (percent / n)	b) Weighted (percent / n)	Difference b) – a)
Gender			
Male	43.2	46.6	3.4
Female	56.8	53.4	–3.4
Total	100.0	100.0	0.0
n =	6335	6335	0
Age Groups			
14–24 years	13.3	13.4	0.1
25–34 years	18.5	18.0	–0.5
35–44 years	23.8	19.7	–4.1
45–54 years	19.7	16.8	–2.9
55–64 years	12.6	16.6	4.0
65–74 years	8.6	11.1	2.5
75+ years	3.6	4.4	0.8
Total	100.0	100.0	0.0
n =	6335	6335	0
Highest educational level attained – 3 levels			
Compulsory education	22.7	26.1	3.4
Secondary education	54.7	52.7	–2.0
Higher education	22.6	21.2	–1.4
Total	100.0	100.0	0.0
n =	6318	6314	–4.0

Table 1b: Distributions of Socio-demographic and socio-economic characteristics

Socio-demographic characteristics	a) Un-weighted (percent / n)	b) Weighted (percent / n)	Difference b) – a)
Income equivalised SKOS 1999 – 5 equal groups			
Low–30'000	17.3	19.7	2.4
30'001–52'500	20.2	21.7	1.5
40'501–52'500	21.2	20.9	–0.3
52'500–70'500	21.0	19.5	–1.5
70'501–High	20.2	18.2	–2.0
Total	100.0	100.0	0.0
n =	5186	5102	–84
Main or Last Job in 2000 or 1999			
Management, liberal, academic	15.4	14.8	–0.6
Intermediate professions	23.6	22.5	–1.1
Intermediate self-employed	18.1	18.4	0.3
qualified non-manual professions	25.2	23.8	–1.4
qualified manual professions	6.0	6.7	0.7
unqualified non-manual and manual collar workers	11.7	13.8	2.1
Total	100.0	100.0	0.0
n =	5639	5569	–70.0
Nationality of origin 1999 – 5 Groups			
Switzerland	83.1	75.9	–7.2
Northern Europe	3.7	5.4	1.7
Eastern Europe	1.5	2.2	0.7
Southern Europe	10.3	14.8	4.5
Other Countries	1.4	1.7	0.3
Total	100.0	100.0	0.0
n =	6334	6333	–1
Foreign nationality 1999			
Swiss national	90.2	81.8	–8.4
Foreign national	9.8	18.2	8.4
Total	100.0	100.0	0.0
n =	6335	6335	0
Language of household with reference person			
German	67.2	66.8	–0.4
French	27.9	27.1	–0.8
Italian	4.8	6.2	1.4
Total	100.0	100.0	0.0
n =	6335	6335	0

Appendix II: Les contributeurs / Die Beiträger

Maddalena Alippi (1972), licence en psychologie à l'Université de Lausanne. Chercheuse auprès du Centre de documentation et de recherche de l'Organisation socio-psychiatrique cantonale du Tessin. Travaille depuis 1997 sur plusieurs études financées par le Fonds national suisse de la recherche scientifique, en particulier sur le thème des nouveaux moyens de communication et leurs impacts sur les individus.

A. Doris Baumgartner, 1961, lic. phil., Soziologin, Inhaberin eines Büros für Sozialforschung in Zürich. Forschungsgebiete: Sozialstruktur und Lebenslauf, Erwerbstätigkeit von Frauen, Arbeitsmarkt, Familiensoziologie und Sozialpolitik. Veröffentlichungen: Familienleben in Zürich. Die Mütter- und Väterbefragung der Stadt Zürich 2003, in: *Büro für die Gleichstellung von Frau und Mann der Stadt Zürich: Kunststück Familie*, Zürich 2003; Teilzeitarbeit – Auf dem Weg zu einem neuen Normalarbeitsverhältnis? Unterschiedliche Teilzeiterwerbstypen am Beispiel der Schweiz, *Schweizerische Zeitschrift für Soziologie*, Vol. 29, 1, S. 7–34.

Irene Becci a étudié aux Université de Lausanne et «La Sapienza» de Rome et obtenu la maîtrise ès sciences sociales en 1998. Actuellement elle est doctorante auprès de l'Institut Universitaire Européen situé à Florence. Sa thèse porte sur les discours et pratiques des institutions pénitentiaires face à la pluralité religieuse en Allemagne et en Italie. Parmi ses publications il y a: (2000) Religionskundlicher Unterricht an der öffentlichen Schule: eine soziologische Einleitung zur Debatte. In Kohler – Spiegel H., Loretan, A. (Ed.), Zurich; (2001) Entre pluralisation et régulation: premiers pas vers une approche en termes de médiations pour la Suisse, in *Social Compass* (vol. 48, no. 1); Becci, I., (2004), The Veil Debate: When the Religious Other and the Gendered Other Are One, in Titley, G., *Resituating Culture*, European Council.

Manfred Max Bergman, Ph.D de l'Université de Cambridge, responsable des questions méthodologiques au SIDOS et Professeur assistant à l'Université de Lausanne. Principaux thèmes de recherche: stratification sociale, méthodologie qualitative et quantitative.

Katja Branger (1970), Dr en sociologie, collaboratrice scientifique à l'Office fédéral de la statistique. Thèmes de recherche: inégalités sociales, qualité de vie, égalité hommes-femmes, délinquance juvénile.

Claude Bovay a obtenu une licence en théologie et un diplôme de spécialisation en sociologie de la religion. Il est depuis 1998 professeur à l'Ecole d'études sociales et pédagogiques à Lausanne, dans le cadre de la Haute école spécialisée Santé-Social de Suisse romande. Ses principales publications comme auteur: «Religion et reproduction de l'asymétrie», *Archives de sciences sociales des religions*, CNRS, Paris, 1996, 95/143–161; *L'évolution de l'appartenance religieuse et confessionnelle en Suisse*, Office fédéral de la statistique, Berne, 1997. Il est coauteur de plusieurs ouvrages, parmi lesquels: *Les Nouveaux travailleurs*, Labor et Fides, Genève, 1998, avec Jean-Pierre Tabin; *Croire en Suisse(s)*, L'âge d'homme, 1992, Campiche R. J. et Dubach A. eds.

Monica Budowski (1957), Dr. phil. I (Ethnology), Scientific head at the Swiss Household Panel and Lecturer at the University of Neuchâtel and Fribourg. Research interests: family and gender studies, social politics and poverty, social change, health.

Claudine Burton-Jeangros (1965), Ph.D. in sociology (Université de Genève), is currently lecturer at the Université de Genève. She is specialised in sociology of health and sociology of risk.

Jean-Marc Falter (1970), Dr en économie, maître assistant à l'Observatoire universitaire de l'emploi, Université de Genève. Thèmes de recherche: économie du travail, travail indépendant, pauvreté et inégalités économiques, discrimination salariale.

Yves Flückiger (1955), Dr en économie, Professeur au département d'économie politique de l'Université de Genève. Il est également membre du bureau de direction du Laboratoire d'économie appliquée et de l'Observatoire universitaire de l'emploi. Spécialités: économie du travail, organisation industrielle, analyse de l'intégration économique. Il est l'auteur de nombreux livres et articles publiés dans des revues internationales.

Beat Fux, 1958, PD Dr. phil., Soziologe, Privatdozent für Soziologie an der Universität Zürich. Forschungsgebiete: Lebensverlaufs- und Familienforschung, Soziodemographie, Sozialpolitik, Werte und Einstellungen. Veröffentlichungen: Which models of the family are en- or discouraged by different family policies? In: Franz-Xaver Kaufmann und Hans-Joachim Schulze, eds.: *Family Life and Family Policies in Europe,* Vol. II: Problems and Issues in Comparative Perspective, Clarendon Press. Oxford 2002, S. 363–418; *Entwicklung des Potenzials erhöhter Arbeitsmarkpartizipation von Frauen nach Massgabe von Prognosen über die Haushalts- und Familienstrukturen.* Zürich und Bern 2003.

Alexis Gabadinho (1969), DESS en démographie, collaborateur scientifique au Panel suisse de ménages et au Forum suisse pour l'étude des migrations et de la population. Intérêts de recherche: analyse démographique, mortalité et fécondité.

Jacques Antoine Gauthier est premier assistant au Centre PaVie. Titulaire d'une maîtrise en Sciences sociales, il a travaillé notamment à l'Office fédéral de la statistique, ainsi qu'à l'Institut suisse de prévention de l'alcoolisme et autres toxicomanies (ISPA). Ses publications portent sur les thèmes du parcours de vie familial et du traitement des abus de substances.

Pascale Gazareth (1970), licence ès sc. sociales, collaboratrice scientifique à l'Office fédéral de la statistique ainsi qu'à l'Institut de sociologie de l'Université de Neuchâtel. Thèmes de recherche: monde du travail, inégalités et exclusion sociale, financement de la culture.

Katia Iglesias (geb. 1976), Lic. phil, Studium in Arbeitspsychologie an der Universität Neuenburg, Hochschulassistentin am Institut de Sociologie et de Science Politique an der Université de Neuchâtel. Arbeits- und Forschungsschwerpunkt in den Bereichen Quantitative Methoden, Soziale Indikatoren und Arbeitszufriedenheit.

Dominique Joye (1955), Dr rer. pol., Directeur du SIDOS et Professeur associé à l'Université de Neuchâtel. Intérêts de recherche: inégalités sociales et régionales, sociologie urbaine et régulation politique, méthodologie et définitions statistiques.

Cristina Molo-Bettelini (1947), psychologue et psychothérapeute. Licence à Milan en sciences politiques, avec thèse en psychologie sociale. Spécialisation en psychologie à l'Université de Milan. Formation théorique et clinique de quatre ans en systémique. Dirige depuis 1986 le Centre de documentation et de recherche de l'Organisation socio-psychiatrique cantonale du Tessin. Membre des comités scientifiques de la Société suisse d'épidémiologie psychiatrique, de la Fondation suisse de recherche sur l'alcool, de l'Institut universitaire Ages et générations de l'UKB de Sion, du groupe d'experts du PNR 39 «Migrations» du Fonds national suisse de la recherche scientifique, et du conseil de Fondation Science et Cité. Responsable de cinq recherches financées par le FNSR, dont une, dans le cadre du PPR « Demain la Suisse » sur les nouveaux moyens de communication et leurs impacts au niveau psycho-social.

Thomas Oegerli (geb. 1966), Lic. phil, Studium der Soziologie an der Universität Zürich, wissenschaftlicher Mitarbeiter an der Fachstelle für Statistik, Volkswirtschaftsdepartement des Kantons St. Gallen. Arbeitsschwerpunkte und Veröffentlichungen in den Bereichen Techniksoziologie, Arbeitsmarkt, vergleichende Sozialstrukturanalyse.

René Levy est professeur à l'Université de Lausanne, à l'Institut d'Anthropologie et de Sociologie. Il a revisité, dans ses nombreuses publications, plusieurs dimensions du social dans la perspective du parcours de vie, notamment la stratification, la mobilité sociale, les rapports de genre et les dynamiques familiales. Depuis octobre 2001 il est le directeur du centre Pavie (Université de Lausanne et Genève). Il a notamment publié «Der Lebenslauf als Statusbiographie», Stuttgart: Enke, 1977, «Structure sociale de la Suisse», Zürich: Pro Helvetia, 1983; «Tous égaux ? De la stratification aux représentations», Zürich, Seismo, 1997.

Caterina Modetta (1969), licence ès sc. sociales, collaboratrice scientifique à l'Office fédéral de la statistique et co-responsable du bureau de recherche ReSo. Thèmes de recherche: politique et action sociales, inégalités, participation sociale et culturelle, monde du travail.

Annette Scherpenzeel (1964), Ph.D. (Psychology), researcher at the Swiss Household Panel. Research interests: Structural equation models; Effects of the formulation of questions and response scales on survey data; Quality of life and life satisfaction, in international comparisons.

Christian Suter (geb. 1956), Professor für Soziologie an der Universität Neuenburg. Arbeits- und Forschungsschwerpunkte: Soziale Ungleichheit und Armut, Sozialer Wandel, Soziale Indikatoren, internationale Verschuldung, politische Soziologie Lateinamerikas, Techniksoziologie, Gesundheitssoziologie. Zahlreiche Veröffentlichungen u.a. „Ungleichhheit und Deprivation: Die Schweiz im Drei-Länder-Vergleich" (*Swiss Journal of Sociology* 28: 217–240, 2002), *Sozialbericht 2000* (Zürich: Seismo, 2000), *Gute und schlechte Regimes* (Frankfurt: Vervuert, 1999), *Debt Cycles in the World-Economy* (Boulder: Westview, 1992).

Robin Tillmann (1967), lic. en sociologie et anthropologie, collaborateur scientifique au Panel suisse de ménages et à l'Office fédéral de la statistique. Intérêts de recherche: stratification sociale, intégration professionnelle, pauvreté et privation, conditions de vie.

Philippe Wanner (1964), Dr en démographie, chef de projets au Forum suisse pour l'étude des migrations et de la population. Thèmes de recherche: analyse et modélisation démographiques, méthodologie d'enquête, mortalité, migrations.

Boris Wernli (1968), Dr. en sciences politiques, collaborateur scientifique au Panel suisse de ménages. Intérêts de recherche: comportement politique, systèmes électoraux et de partis, valeurs, nouvelles technologies de la communication.

Eric Widmer est professeur à l'Université de Lausanne, au centre lémanique d'étude des parcours et modes de vie (Centre PaVie). Il travaille sur les problèmes de famille et de parcours de vie, avec un intérêt tout particulier pour les réseaux familiaux, les trajectoires biographiques, et les normes. Ses publications incluent notamment: «Les relations fraternelles des adolescents». Paris, Presses Universitaires de France, 1999, et (avec Jean Kellerhals et René Levy) «Couples contemporains. Cohésion, régulation et conflits. Une enquête sociologique» (Seismo, 2003).

Erwin Zimmermann (1947), Ph.D. in sociology (University of Chicago) is director of the Swiss Household Panel and associate professor at the Université de Neuchâtel. His main research areas are: survey methods, sociology of health, evaluation of public health measures and outcomes, health reporting and health promotion.

Population, Family, and Society
Population, Famille et Société

Edited by / Edité par
Michel Oris

Cette collection a pour ambition d'accueillir et de promouvoir le dialogue entre les démographes et les spécialistes de la famille, dialogue qui renouvelle profondément tant l'histoire sociale que la sociologie contemporaine. Animée par un réseau international qui s'appuie sur le *Laboratoire de Démographie et d'Etudes Familiales* de l'Université de Genève, la collection est largement ouverte et veut refléter les dynamiques de recherche les plus récentes. Elle privilégie les perspectives comparatives, internationales, ainsi que les approches interdisciplinaires, celles qui mêlent les apports de l'histoire, de l'économie, de la statistique, de la sociologie, de la géographie, de la démographie, de l'anthropologie culturelle, etc. L'innovation méthodologique, dans les domaines du qualitatif aussi bien que du quantitatif, qui permet de refonder les problématiques et d'articuler de nouvelles questions, est particulièrement saluée. La collection accueille aussi bien des contributions individuelles que collectives. Dans le premier groupe se rangent les monographies ou travaux de synthèse issus du milieu scientifique suisse et international, en ce compris les meilleures thèses de doctorat. Le second groupe réunit des recueils d'articles organisés autour d'un thème qui émerge dans le débat scientifique, et qui requiert le croisement de regards venus de multiples horizons disciplinaires et/ ou géographiques.

La collection accueille des ouvrages en langue française, anglaise et allemande.

Vol. 1 Frans van Poppel, Michel Oris & James Lee (eds). *The Road to Independence. Leaving Home in Western and Eastern Societies, 16th–20th centuries.* 2004. ISBN 3-906770-61-3 / US-ISBN 0-8204-5949-6

Vol. 2 Guy Brunet, Michel Oris & Alain Bideau (éds). *Les minorités. Une démographie culturelle et politique, XVIIIe-XXe siècles / Minorities. A Cultural and Political Demography, 18th–20th centuries.* 2004. ISBN 3-03910-220-6 / US-ISBN 0-8204-6874-6

Vol. 3 Erwin Zimmermann & Robin Tillmann (éds/Hrsg.). *Vivre en Suisse 1999-2000. Une année dans la vie des ménages et familles en Suisse / Leben in der Schweiz 1999–2000. Ein Jahr im Leben der Schweizer Familien und Haushalte.* 2004. ISBN 3-03910-370-9